Fundamental Development of the Social Sciences

Fundamental Development of the Social Sciences

Rockefeller Philanthropy and the United States Social Science Research Council

Donald Fisher

Ann Arbor

THE UNIVERSITY OF MICHIGAN PRESS

Copyright © by the University of Michigan 1993
All rights reserved
Published in the United States of America by
The University of Michigan Press
Manufactured in the United States of America

1996 1995 1994 1993   4 3 2 1

A CIP catalogue record for this book is available from the British Library.

Library of Congress Cataloging-in-Publication Data

Fisher, Donald, 1944–
    Fundamental development of the social sciences : Rockefeller
philanthropy and the United States Social Science Research Council /
Donald Fisher.
        p.   cm.
    Includes bibliographical references and index.
    ISBN 0-472-10270-2 (alk. paper)
    1. Social Science Research Council (U.S.)—History.   2. Social
sciences—Research—United States—History.   I. Title.
H62.A1F57   1992
300′.72073—dc20   92-36235
                                                             CIP

To Sue, Katie, and Sara

Acknowledgments

I wish to express my gratitude to the people and the institutions that made this book possible. The study would have been impossible without access to manuscript collections at various archives and without the help of skilled archivists. My particular thanks go to J. William Hess and Thomas Rosenbaum at the Rockefeller Archive Center; David L. Sills at the Social Science Research Council; Stephen H. Stackpole at the Carnegie Corporation of New York; Martha M. English at The Commonwealth Fund; Alice Roberts at the Russell Sage Foundation; and Curtis Clow at The Private Archives of the Messrs. Rockefeller. In addition I gratefully acknowledge the assistance of archivists and librarians at Columbia University; Stanford University; the University of British Columbia; the University of Chicago; the University of North Carolina, Chapel Hill; the University of Pennsylvania; the University of Texas, Austin; and Yale University.

Edward T. Silva, Harold Silver, and Stephen P. Turner took time away from their busy schedules to read versions of the whole manuscript and in turn provided both encouragement and sound advice. Bernard Barber, Edward H. Berman, and Theresa R. Richardson read parts of this book in draft form and provided many useful suggestions. While not directly involved in this specific project, my teacher and friend from Berkeley days, Robert Wenkert, has hovered in the background of my thinking and has continued to be a source of intellectual inspiration. Over the years, I have checked points of evidence and aired the ideas with numerous colleagues. The book has without doubt benefited from their input. At a distance, this group includes Mary Douglas, Richard H. Heindel, Pendleton Herring, Barry D. Karl, Stanley N. Katz, Ellen Condliffe Lagemann, and Franz Samelson. Here at the University of British Columbia the list is a long one: Kogila Adam Moodley, Jean Barman, William Bruneau, Frank Echols, Jane Gaskell, Deirdre Kelly, Leslie Roman, Peter Seixas, Nancy Sheehan, Neil Sutherland, Charles Ungerleider, Patricia Vertinsky, Douglas Willms, and J. Donald Wilson. I must give a particular note of thanks to my friend and colleague in the Centre for Policy Studies in Education, Kjell Rubenson. Flora Bovis typed the bibliography and Robin Van Heck added her excellent editing skills. Finally, I appreciate the care and attention given to my manuscript by the University of Michigan Press. Two anonymous readers provided a critical commentary and many useful suggestions. Colin Day, director of the press, always managed to lift my spirits and give me confidence, while Debbie Evans, assistant to the director, worked diligently to get reviews in.

Grants from the Rockefeller Archive Center, the Social Sciences and Humanities Research Council of Canada, and the University of British Columbia Humanities and Social Sciences Grants Committee allowed me to complete the research. My New York family, John and Joan McWilliam, provided a home away from home when I needed it most. I want to thank my friends Frank Botyrius and Ingrid Jensen in the "village" for their understanding and kindness. Peter and Susan Seixas deserve my gratitude for making available their island retreat at a time when I just needed a week of solitude.

A final word must go to my family, to whom this book is dedicated. My wife Sue has read draft after draft of this book. Her sound advice and her emotional support have been invaluable. The whole family has put up with my absences of body and mind over the years and I thank them for their patience.

Preface

Three books more than any others inspired the writing of this book: Robert S. Lynd's *Knowledge for What? The Place of Social Science in America* (1939), C. Wright Mills's *The Sociological Imagination* (1959), and Russell Jacoby's *The Last Intellectuals: American Culture in the Age of Academe* (1987). While these books span more than half a century, they share a critical perspective and ask similar questions. The three authors provide an analysis of the place of the social sciences in society in the United States and explore the question of appropriate roles for social scientists. Each book in its own way is a radical statement that challenges the division between science and policymaking. These authors advocate responsible objectivity. If "social science" is to mean anything, according to this view, social scientists must not abdicate their cultural and political responsibilities. What follows in this monograph is an account of some of the changes that occurred during the interwar years that set the stage for these three critiques. This work begins with the assumption that the creation and growth of the Social Science Research Council are essential to our understanding of developments in the social sciences since the Second World War. The 1920s and 1930s were, it is argued, the most critical decades in the history of the social sciences because the place of social science and social scientists in the United States was fixed in a way that has had substantial subsequent impact. A bargain was struck between social scientists, Rockefeller philanthropy, and the State that has since become an accepted part of the way we organize social life.

Contents

Abbreviations

AAA	American Anthropological Association
ACLS	American Council of Learned Societies
AEA	American Economic Association
AHA	American Historical Association
APA	American Psychological Association
APSA	American Political Science Association
ASS	American Sociological Society
ASSA	American Social Science Association
ASTA	American Statistical Association
CAM	President's Committee on Administrative Management
CC	Carnegie Corporation
CF	Commonwealth Fund
CREC	President's Committee on Recent Economic Changes
CSS	Committee on Social Security, Social Science Research Council
CSSRC	Canadian Social Science Research Council
DSS	Division of Social Sciences, Rockefeller Foundation
GEB	General Education Board
GRA	Government Research Association
HOP	Howard W. Odum Papers
LSE	London School of Economics
LSRM	Laura Spelman Rockefeller Memorial
NBER	National Bureau of Economic Research
NEC	National Emergency Council
NRA	National Recovery Administration
NRC	National Research Council
NRPB	President's National Resources Planning Board
NSF	National Science Foundation
OSRD	Office of Scientific Research and Development
PAC	Public Administration Committee, Social Science Research Council

PACH   Public Administration Clearing House
PPC   Problems and Policy Committee, Social Science
        Research Council
RAC   Rockefeller Archive Center
RF   Rockefeller Foundation
RFA   Rockefeller Family Archive
RST   President's Research Committee on Social Trends
RTC   President's Recent Trends Committee
SAB   Science Advisory Board
SF   Spelman Fund
SRC   Social Research Council
SSB   Social Security Board
SSFC   Social Science Federation of Canada
SSRC   Social Science Research Council
SSRCA   Social Science Research Council Archives
TVA   Tennessee Valley Authority
WCMC   W. C. Mitchell Collection
WFO   William Fielding Ogburn Papers

CHAPTER 1

Introduction

There is a story that current staff members of the United States Social Science Research Council (SSRC) tell about the move in 1928 into permanent office accommodation. The opportunity was created by the enormous infusion of money into the organization by the Laura Spelman Rockefeller Memorial (LSRM). As the story goes, there was some disagreement as to where to locate. On the one side, in true University of Chicago fashion, were a number of SSRC members who thought it appropriate to have offices among their data base and hence wanted to set up in Manhattan's garment district. On the other side was the director of the LSRM, Dr. Beardsley Ruml, who among other things wanted to increase the prestige of the social sciences. His choice was the New York Central Building at 230 Park Avenue. Built in 1927, it was the second tallest building in New York and dominated mid-Manhattan. While some would claim that the story is apocryphal, for this writer it rings true. It illustrates the continuing tension between the political pragmatism of Rockefeller philanthropy and the narrower, discipline-based attachment to objective research of the social scientists. It was typical of Ruml to go for the grand symbolic gesture, and further, it was typical of the relation between Rockefeller philanthropy and the SSRC that the SSRC should follow his advice.

The material covered in this book is part of a continuing study into the history and sociology of the social sciences. Just as this investigation focuses on the boundaries between social disciplines, so the approach taken here cuts across discipline boundaries. The approach brings together historical description and sociological explanation in the tradition described by Philip Abrams in *Historical Sociology* (1982). Abrams claimed that at the heart of history and sociology is a "common project: a sustained, diverse attempt to deal with . . . the problematic of structuring."[1] As part of the move to integrate the social sciences in the United States during the interwar years, the linkages between history and sociology were discussed extensively,[2] and the ideal

---

1. Philip Abrams, *Historical Sociology* (Bath: Open Books, 1982), p. iv.
2. For example, Franz Oppenheimer, "History and Sociology," in William Fielding Ogburn and Alexander Goldenweiser, eds., *The Social Sciences and Their Interrelations* (Boston: Houghton Mifflin Co., 1927), pp. 221–34; Harry Elmer Barnes, ed., *The History and Prospects*

"historical sociology" was promoted.[3] More recently, C. Wright Mills housed the task and the promise of the "sociological imagination" in this tradition. "The sociological imagination," according to Mills, "enables us to grasp history and biography and the relations between the two within society." For Mills, no study was complete until these intersections had been thoroughly explored.[4] In a broader sense, this approach allows the researcher to bring together agency and structure through time and thereby provide a thorough description of what Anthony Giddens called "structuration."[5]

This study incorporates the contextualist spirit that characterizes Thomas S. Kuhn's work and much of the recent research in the history and sociology of the social sciences.[6] One starting point is what has been labeled as the "critical-conflict" approach to the sociology of science.[7] The critical-conflict perspective focuses attention on the decisive elements in the process of knowledge change.[8] Causes are sought in processes extrinsic to the discipline, like societal-level changes in economy, class, ideology, and hegemony. Specifically, I utilize the approach taken by Edward T. Silva and Sheila A. Slaughter in *Serving Power: The Making of the Academic Social Science Expert* (1984),[9] when trying to explain the development of the social science

of the Social Sciences (New York: Knopf, 1925); and Harry Elmer Barnes, *History and Social Intelligence* (New York: Knopf, 1926).

3. J. O. Herteler, "The Sources and Methods of Historical Sociology," in Luther L. Bernard, ed., *The Fields and Methods of Sociology* (New York: Farrar and Rinehart, 1934), pp. 260–73; and Howard Becker, "Historical Sociology," in Harry Elmer Barnes, Howard Becker, and Frances Bennet Becker, eds., *Contemporary Social Theory* (New York: D. Appleton-Century Co., 1940), pp. 491–542.

4. C. Wright Mills, *The Sociological Imagination* (London: Oxford University Press, 1959), p. 6. For a review of the current literature, see P. Burke, "Historical Sociology: A Review Essay," *American Journal of Sociology* 90 (1985): 905–8.

5. Anthony Giddens, "Agency Structure," in *Central Problems in Social Theory: Action, Structure, and Contradiction in Social Analysis* (London: Macmillan, 1979), pp. 49–95; and Ira J. Cohen, *Structuration Theory: Anthony Giddens and the Constitution of Social Life* (New York: St. Martin's Press, 1989).

6. Thomas S. Kuhn, *The Structure of Scientific Revolutions* (1962; enl. ed., Chicago: University of Chicago Press, 1970); and Thomas S. Kuhn, *The Essential Tension* (Chicago: University of Chicago Press, 1977). Also see Barry Barnes, *T. S. Kuhn and Social Science* (New York: Columbia University Press, 1982).

7. Lengermann provides a table description of three major approaches in the sociology of science taken toward our understanding of the nature and source of change. These approaches are labeled "Developmental," "Kuhnian," and "Critical-conflict." Patricia M. Lengermann, "The Founding of the American Sociological Review: The Anatomy of a Rebellion," *American Sociological Review* 44 (1979): 185–98.

8. Examples of work in this genre include George Lukacs, *History and Class Consciousness* (Cambridge: MIT Press, 1971); and Alvin W. Gouldner, *The Coming Crisis in Western Sociology* (New York: Avon Books, 1971).

9. Edward T. Silva and Sheila A. Slaughter, *Serving Power: The Making of the Academic Social Science Expert* (Westport: Greenwood Press, 1984).

movement. Like Silva and Slaughter, I regard an explanation based on the professionalization interpretation as incomplete, even when these processes are housed in the wider structural trends. Needed here is what Silva and Slaughter referred to as "exchange theory." Such a theory focuses attention on the exchange of power and resources between the academy, the economy, and the State. As universities have become more industrial and technical, so academics have become more dependent and, therefore, more vulnerable to role definitions imposed from outside the profession and the academy. The most significant resource holders, argued Silva and Slaughter, were the philanthropic foundations. The officers and trustees of these foundations "explored complimentary terms of trade, exchanging the professors' social science knowledge for the potential power dammed up in the philanthropic foundations."[10]

Bjorn Wittrock and Peter Wagner in conjunction with the Swedish Collegium for Advanced Study in the Social Sciences at the University of Uppsala produced a similar and equally useful approach for studying the development of the social sciences.[11] They set themselves the task of analyzing how the development of the social sciences in the late nineteenth and early twentieth centuries was influenced by the emergence of the modern State. They documented how the relationship between societal institutions and the social sciences has been transformed during critical periods by alliances and coalitions between scholars and policymakers. Research problems are defined and researched within what the authors called "discourse coalitions." The organizational frameworks of both social research and policy-making are altered as part of these social transformations. For Wittrock and Wagner, the exchanges between social scientists and policymakers are contained within larger institutional and intellectual structures. The alliances and coalitions emerge in the process of "discourse structuration."

Another starting point is the question of demarcation, as posed by Karl D. Popper, which has been so central to the social studies of scientific

---

10. Ibid., p. 243.

11. Bjorn Wittrock, *Social Knowledge and Public Policy: Eight Models of Interaction*, P87-1 (Berlin: Wissenschaftszentrium, 1987); Bjorn Wittrock, Peter Wagner, and Heinrich Wollmann, *Social Science and the Modern State: Knowledge, Institutions, and Societal Transformations*, WZB-Papers P87-3 (Berlin: Wissenschaftszentrium, 1987); and Peter Wagner and Bjorn Wittrock, *Social Sciences and Societal Development: The Missing Perspective*, WZB-Papers P87-4 (Berlin: Wissenschaftszentrium, 1987). This research was critically analyzed during the History of Sociology Meetings, International Sociology Association, held in Amsterdam, 1989. Wittrock and Wagner presented a paper, "Social Science and State Developments: The Structuration of Discourse in the Social Sciences." For a discussion of this work and how it relates to Gidden's work on structuration, see Rob Hagendijk, "Structuration Theory, Constructivism, and Scientific Change," in Susan E. Cozzens and Thomas F. Gieryn, eds., *Theories of Science in Society* (Bloomington: Indiana University Press, 1990), pp. 43–66.

knowledge.[12] The focus is on the social construction of a boundary that separates social science knowledge from everyday knowledge. The general approach is nominalist or what Susan E. Cozzens and Thomas F. Gieryn labeled "postrelativist."[13] The assumption is that neither science nor social science is separate or distinctive in and of itself. What is of interest are the efforts made by practitioners and their patrons to convince themselves and others that this is the case. It is instructive therefore to focus on boundary work not because the boundaries are "real" but rather because the people involved put a great deal of effort into the creation and maintenance of the boundary between social science and other knowledge. Taking this approach means that one can no more separate the internal and external aspects of social science than one can separate structure and agency. Throughout the interwar period, social scientists in conjunction with their patrons and sponsors worked hard to make social science distinctive by trying to emulate the perspectives of natural scientists. This was an exercise in structural legitimation.

The immediate subject of this book is the birth and first two decades of life of the SSRC. Yet this story is the point of entry into a number of larger issues. The growth of the social sciences in the United States is very much a twentieth-century phenomenon. The interwar years were an important watershed in the history of the social sciences. Founded in 1923 the SSRC was the first national social science institution anywhere in the world. As the only national social science organization, this body was necessarily a central component of the changes that occurred. The history of the Council illuminates the decisive reorientation and transformation of the role of social scientists and social science disciplines in society that took place in the interwar years. The continuing tension between "pure" and "applied" conceptions of science and between the ideals of "reform" and "scientific advance" lay beneath this transformation. At the heart of our understanding was the clash between "advocacy" and "objectivity."[14] According to Luther L. and Jessie S. Bernard, the SSRC was one indicator among several in the 1920s of "a trend back to the old social science ideal of organic unity and coordination."[15] The SSRC was regarded as the counterpart to the disintegration of the American Social

---

12. Karl R. Popper, *The Logic of Scientific Discovery* (New York: Harper and Row, 1965). For a discussion of the current way this question is posed, see Steve Woolgar, *Science: The Very Idea* (London: Tavistock Publications, 1988).

13. Susan E. Cozzens and Thomas F. Gieryn, "Introduction: Putting Science back in Society," in Cozzens and Gieryn, *Theories of Science*, pp. 1–14.

14. Mary O. Furner, *Advocacy and Objectivity: A Crisis in the Professionalization of American Social Science, 1865–1905* (Lexington: University Press of Kentucky, 1975).

15. Luther L. Bernard and Jessie S. Bernard, *Origins of American Sociology: The Social Science Movement in the United States* (New York: Thomas Y. Crowell, 1943), p. 606.

Science Association (ASSA) and a countervailing force to specialization and isolation.

The creation of the SSRC was the most important indicator of the dramatic shift in the social disciplines toward a more scientific and systematic approach.[16] The founding of the SSRC was seen by many of the original members as a significant step toward fulfilling the dreams of their predecessors, namely, the creation of a science of society. The focus on interdisciplinary work and the social problem orientation harked back to the activities of the ASSA, but there was an important difference. The professional academic associations that emerged from the ashes of the ASSA at the turn of the century were now searching for ways to extend their authority.[17] By the 1920s the members of these associations were for the most part housed in universities. The key was to firmly establish their disciplines as sciences. Whereas the ASSA had been an elite movement, the SSRC was an alliance between professional academic social scientists and representatives of the ruling elite. Neither the ASSA nor the SSRC was a revolutionary movement. The members of both organizations believed that the desired social reforms or the solutions to social problems could be found and achieved within their current social systems. The Council should therefore be seen as an attempt to refurbish the old ideas of interdependence and social reform under the mantle of scientific procedures and as part of a practical, realistic approach. Academic scientists could, it was believed, best fulfill their responsibilities as scholars by focusing their scientific attention on social problems.

The SSRC was the "logical successor" to the coordinating phase of the ASSA's work. The new institution tried to coordinate the now separate disciplines into a supradiscipline—a new science of society. The concept of an integrated social science, which was so central to the earlier social science movement, was revived but in a milder form. The existence of separate

16. Ibid.; and Dorothy Ross, "The Development of the Social Sciences," in Alexandra Oleson and John Voss, eds., *The Organization of Knowledge in Modern America, 1860–1920* (Baltimore: Johns Hopkins University Press, 1976), pp. 107–38.

17. The disciplinary associations that were formed in this period were the AHA (1884), the AEA (1885), the APA (1892), the AAA (1902), the APSA (1903), and the ASS (1905). The ASTA was founded much earlier in 1839. For a detailed account of the ASSA see Thomas L. Haskell, *The Emergence of Professional Social Science: The American Social Science Association and the Nineteenth Century Crisis of Authority* (Urbana: University of Illinois Press, 1977). Also see Bernard and Bernard, *Origins of American Sociology*; Furner, *Advocacy and Objectivity*; Joseph C. Kiger, "Foundation Support of Educational Innovation by Learned Societies, Councils, and Institutes," in Matthew B. Miles, ed., *Innovations in Education* (New York: Teachers College Press, 1964), pp. 533–61; Lewis M. Coser, "American Trends," in Tom Bottomore and Robert A. Nisbet, eds., *A History of Sociological Analysis* (London: Heinemann Educational Books, 1978), pp. 287–320; and Silva and Slaughter, *Serving Power*.

disciplines was accepted and recognized in the structure of the SSRC. The focus was on new forms of integration that centered on interdisciplinary work. The Council set out to increase the coordination, cooperation, and interrelation across disciplinary lines. The SSRC incorporated a definition of science that was problem oriented, realistic, interdisciplinary, and practical. Fundamental scientific application is probably the best way to describe what the SSRC symbolized.

The desire to reintegrate the social science disciplines was linked to a reemphasis on reformism promoted by large-scale philanthropy. In this way, the history of the SSRC provides an entry into understanding the changing role of philanthropic foundations in Western industrialized societies. The Council was promoted and to a great extent controlled by Rockefeller philanthropy. The SSRC and the definition of science it incorporated was based on an alliance between academic social scientists and the LSRM. The broadening and the expansion of this alliance in the 1930s to include the State was in turn facilitated and enhanced by the policies and programs of two other Rockefeller foundations, the Rockefeller Foundation (RF) and the Spelman Fund (SF). The SSRC was in the middle of the changing relation between, on the one hand, academic social scientists and, on the other hand, philanthropy, the State, and society at large. In this sense, the story of the Council provides insight into the emergence of the modern welfare State and the place of social scientific research in this structure.

This study is informed by Marxist theories of the State.[18] The State is defined as a set of administrative, policing, and military organizations coordinated by an executive authority. This structure includes government at all levels, the State apparatuses (military, police, judiciary, and civil service), and a set of ideological and cultural apparatuses, such as education, religion, and the media. Governments, as the executive authority, coordinate the coercive parts (State apparatuses) and the persuasive parts (the ideological and cultural apparatuses). Because Marxist theories of the capitalist State place this structure in a society that is class divided, the focus is on the relation between class power and State power. Following Nicos Poulantzas, the State is seen here in a position of "relative autonomy." Class struggle and the contradictions inher-

---

18. David A. Gold, Clarence Y. H. Lo, and Erik Olin Wright, "Recent Developments in Marxist Theories of the Capitalist State," pt. 1, *Monthly Review*, October 1975, pp. 29–43; David A. Gold, Clarence Y. H. Lo, and Erik Olin Wright, "Recent Developments in Marxist Theories of the Capitalist State," pt. 2, *Monthly Review*, November 1975, pp. 36–51; Martin Carnoy, *The State and Political Theory* (Princeton: Princeton University Press, 1984); and Bob Jessop, *Theories of the State* (New York: New York University Press, 1983). For a review and an application of these theories, see Donald Fisher and Betty Gilgoff, "The Crisis in B. C. Public Education: The State and the Public Interest," in Terry Wotherspoon, ed., *The Political Economy of Canadian Schooling* (Toronto: Methuen, 1987), pp. 69–93.

ent in the social formation are taken into the very center of the structure, so that while the State is definitely not neutral it must appear to be so. This appearance can only be maintained because of the relative autonomy of the structure. The State therefore simultaneously represents the interests of the ruling class and appears to represent the interests of all.[19]

Theorists in this tradition generally agree that capitalist States serve two major functions. Capitalist States simultaneously coerce and persuade in order to ensure the reproduction of class relations in society. In this way, the State serves the contradictory objectives of creating an environment that allows for the continuing accumulation of capital by the ruling class and legitimating the socioeconomic inequalities present in the society. In this context, Antonio Gramsci's work is especially useful because of the contrast he drew between two forms of political control, namely, "domination" (direct physical coercion) and "hegemony" (ideological control and consent). Gramsci divided the superstructure into two realms: political and civil society. For Gramsci, the functions of these two realms overlap so the State is "hegemony armored by coercion." As Joseph V. Femia concluded, "the critical superstructural distinction is not so much civil/political or private/public as hegemony/ domination" and "individual societies can be analyzed in terms of the balance between, and specific manifestations of, these two types of social control."[20] For Gramsci, no modern State could survive for long if the ruling class merely attempted to dominate. When hegemony is effective, a society settles into a relative equilibrium that is characterized by harmony. Yet when hegemony starts to fall apart, the ruling class will resort to coercion. It follows that hegemony is not just about political or class control; it is also about consciousness and the way the majority of people in a society are convinced that some ideas are natural and mere common sense. This means that the majority actively consent to, and participate in, their own domination. The dominant ideology becomes material practice and the rules by which we conduct our daily lives. Changes in the dominant ideology, the form of hegemony and actions by the State, happen simultaneously and are interconnected.[21]

---

19. Nicos Poulantzas, *Classes in Contemporary Capitalism* (London: New Left Books, 1975); and Nicos Poulantzas, "The Political Crisis and the Crisis of the State," in J. W. Freiberg, ed., *Critical Sociology* (New York: Irving, 1979).

20. Joseph V. Femia, *Gramsci's Political Thought: Hegemony, Consciousness, and the Revolutionary Process* (Oxford: Clarendon Press, 1987), pp. 28–29.

21. Antonio Gramsci, *Selections from the Prison Notebooks*, ed. and trans. Q. Hoare and G. Nowell-Smith (London: Lawrence and Wishart, 1971); and Antonio Gramsci, *Selections from Political Writings, 1921–1926*, ed. and trans. Q. Hoare (London: Lawrence and Wishart, 1978). See also Carl Boggs, *Gramsci's Marxism* (London: Pluto Press, 1976); James Joll, *Gramsci* (London: Fontana, 1977); Walter L. Adamson, *Hegemony and Revolution: A Study of Antonio Gramsci's Political and Cultural Theory* (Berkeley and Los Angeles: University of California Press, 1980); Roger Simon, *Gramsci's Political Thought* (London: Lawrence and

This study traces the part that social scientists, through the SSRC, played in these changes during the interwar years. Academic social scientists were involved in a process of mutual legitimation as they were drawn into the public arena. In exchange for their objectivity and scientific disinterestedness, these academics received from the State public recognition of their status as experts working for the social good. The technocratic bargain depended on both sides honoring their commitment.[22] The cooperation of philanthropy and the State in the bargaining process is indicative of the increasing interpenetration of political and civil society during this period.

It is fair to say that the story of the SSRC is just about the whole story of the changing nature of social scientific research in the United States in the interwar period. Yet there is a dearth of published material on the SSRC, and historical research remains sketchy and uncoordinated. The Council through its publication *ITEMS* has kept a partial record of events and in 1974 published an institutional history to celebrate the fiftieth anniversary.[23] The most serious and wide-ranging attempt to record the developments in the interwar years was undertaken by Louis Wirth in 1937. Wirth was commissioned by the SSRC to do an appraisal of the Council's work, but the report he produced has remained unpublished.[24] While other authors have described the Council's activities,[25] there has not been any attempt to critically analyze the institution or assess its impact on the social sciences and American society. This study fills part of this gap.[26]

Wishart, 1982); John Hoffman, *The Gramscian Challenge: Coercion and Consent in Marxist Political Theory* (Oxford: Basil Blackwell, 1984); Robert Bocock, *Hegemony* (London: Tavistock Publications, 1986); and Femia, *Gramsci's Political Thought*.

22. Guy Alchon, *The Invisible Hand of Planning: Capitalism, Social Science, and the State in the 1920s* (Princeton: Princeton University Press, 1985). The more general point about mutual legitimation is central to the argument proposed by Jurgen Habermas, *Legitimation Crisis* (Boston: Beacon Press, 1975).

23. Elbridge Sibley, *Social Science Research Council: The First Fifty Years* (New York: SSRC, 1974).

24. Louis Wirth, "Report on the History, Activities, and Policies of the Social Science Research Council," August 1937 (henceforth "Report"). This unpublished report is part of the records of the SSRCA, New York.

25. Herbert Heaton, *A Scholar in Action: Edwin F. Gay* (Cambridge: Harvard University Press, 1952), pp. 208–11; Kiger, "Foundation Support of Educational Innovation," pp. 533–61; John Higham, "The Schism in American Scholarship," *American Historical Review* 72 (October 1966), pp. 13–15; and Gene Martin Lyons, *The Uneasy Partnership: Social Science and the Federal Government in the Twentieth Century* (New York: Russell Sage Foundation, 1969), chaps. 2, 3, and 4.

26. For a preliminary and critical overview of the Council's history during the interwar years, see Donald Fisher, "Philanthropic Foundations and the Social Sciences: A Response to Martin Bulmer," *Sociology* 18, no. 4 (1984): 580–87. For a detailed analysis of the creation of the Council, see Donald Fisher, "Boundary Work and Science: The Relation between Power and Knowledge," in Cozzens and Gieryn, *Theories of Science*, pp. 98–119.

My interest in the Council grew out of some continuing work that focuses on the role of philanthropic foundations in Western industrialized societies.[27] During the interwar years large-scale philanthropy performed the role that was subsequently taken over by the State after the Second World War. In the United States, and in many other countries, progress in the social sciences depended on the support of large-scale United States philanthropy, in particular by the Rockefeller foundations. Included in this group for the purposes of this study are the LSRM, the RF, and the SF. For Rockefeller philanthropy, the Council was a central cog in its policy of linking integration and scientism. The Council brought together representatives of the seven social science areas: anthropology, sociology, political science, economics, psychology, statistics, and history. The major objective of the Council was scientific advance through cooperative research. The Council created multi-disciplinary, problem-centered research committees and served a coordinating function for the parallel organizations that had been created at the university level by Rockefeller philanthropy. Further, the Council was the most prominent element in the effort by Rockefeller philanthropy to combat the social and economic crises of the period. The Council was central in the shift from what contemporary commentators labeled "pure" and "purposive" research toward "applied" research.

As noted earlier, this study contributes to the developing literature on philanthropy. The new social science of the 1920s was very similar to the new form of scientific philanthropy that the LSRM epitomized. Efforts were no longer scattered and piecemeal. Foundations like the LSRM did not focus on symptoms but rather put forward systematic schemes designed to get to the roots of social problems. Similarly, the proposed "science of society" aimed at producing the scientific knowledge that would solve those same problems. Social science as described by Charles E. Merriam, political scientist at the University of Chicago, and Ruml seemed merely to be the knowledge-producing extension of philanthropy.

Building upon the descriptive work of authors like Emerson F. Andrews (1956), Robert H. Bremner (1960), and Warren Weaver (1967), as well as the analysis by Merle E. Curti (1963), there has in recent years emerged a litera-

---

27. Donald Fisher, "The Impact of American Foundations on the Development of British University Education, 1900–1939" (Ph.D. diss., University of California, Berkeley, 1977); Donald Fisher, "The Rockefeller Foundation and the Development of Scientific Medicine in Great Britain," *Minerva* 16 (1978): 20–41; Donald Fisher, "American Philanthropy and the Social Sciences in Great Britain, 1919–1939: The Reproduction of a Conservative Ideology," *Sociological Review* 28, no. 2 (1980): 277–315; and Donald Fisher, "The Role of Philanthropic Foundations in the Reproduction and Production of Hegemony: Rockefeller Foundations and the Social Sciences," *Sociology* 17, no. 2 (1983): 206–33; Donald Fisher, *The Social Sciences in Canada: Fifty Years of National Activity by the Social Science Federation of Canada* (Waterloo: Wilfrid Laurier University Press, 1991).

ture that takes an analytic and at times critical stance.[28] This genre includes the work of Barry D. Karl and Stanley N. Katz (1981) on the relation between the private and public spheres and the continuing study of the Carnegie foundations undertaken by Ellen Condliffe Lagemann (1983, 1987, and 1989).[29] Five studies stand out as exemplars of the critical trend that is part of this genre: Richard E. Brown's *Rockefeller Medicine Men: Medicine and Capitalism in America* (1979), Robert F. Arnove's edited collection, *Philanthropy and Cultural Imperialism: The Foundations at Home and Abroad* (1982), Edward H. Berman's *The Influence of the Carnegie, Ford, and Rockefeller Foundations in American Foreign Policy: Ideology and Philanthropy* (1984), the study referred to earlier by Silva and Slaughter, *Serving Power: The Making of the Academic Social Science Expert* (1984), and, Theresa R. Richardson's *The Century of the Child: The Mental Hygiene Movement and Social Policy in the United States and Canada* (1989).[30] This study is part of the critical trend.

Most analysts of large-scale philanthropy agree that these institutions have been and continue to be run by an elite segment of society in the United States.[31] Foundations, like society, are run by a carefully selected elite. The

---

28. F. Emerson Andrews, *Philanthropic Foundations* (New York: Russell Sage Foundation, 1956); Robert H. Bremner, *American Philanthropy* (Chicago: University of Chicago Press, 1960); Warren Weaver, ed., *U.S. Philanthropic Foundations: Their History, Structure, Management, and Record* (New York: Harper and Row, 1967); Merle E. Curti, *American Philanthropy Abroad: A History* (New Brunswick: Rutgers University Press, 1963); and Merle E. Curti and Roderick Nash, *Philanthropy in the Shaping of American Higher Education* (New Brunswick: Rutgers University Press, 1965). A more recent work in the general category is Ben Whitaker, *The Philanthropoids: Foundations and Society* (New York: William Morrow and Co., 1974).

29. Barry D. Karl and Stanley N. Katz, "The American Private Philanthropic Foundation and the Public Sphere, 1890–1930," *Minerva* 19 (1981): 236–70; Ellen Condliffe Lagemann, *Private Power for the Public Good: A History of the Carnegie Foundation for the Advancement of Teaching* (Middletown: Wesleyan University Press, 1983); Ellen Condliffe Lagemann, *The Politics of Knowledge: The Carnegie Corporation, Philanthropy, and Public Policy* (Middletown: Wesleyan University Press, 1989). For an overview of foundations activity in the 1920s, see Robert E. Kohler, "Science, Foundations, and American Universities in the 1920s," *OSIRIS* 2d ser., 3 (1987): 135–64.

30. Richard E. Brown, *Rockefeller Medicine Men: Medicine and Capitalism in America* (Berkeley and Los Angeles: University of California Press, 1979); Robert F. Arnove, ed., *Philanthropy and Cultural Imperialism: The Foundations at Home and Abroad* (Bloomington: Indiana University Press, 1982); Edward H. Berman, *The Influence of the Carnegie, Ford, and Rockefeller Foundations on American Foreign Policy: Ideology and Philanthropy* (Albany: State University of New York Press, 1984); Silva and Slaughter, *Serving Power*; and Theresa R. Richardson, *The Century of the Child: The Mental Hygiene Movement and Social Policy in the United States and Canada* (Albany: State University of New York Press, 1989).

31. Edward C. Lindeman, *Wealth and Culture: A Study of 100 Foundations and Community Trusts and Their Operation during the Decade, 1921–1930* (New York: Harcourt, Brace and Co., 1936); Waldemar Nielsen, *The Big Foundations* (New York: Columbia University Press,

corporate and foundation worlds share the same values, so officials have consistently moved between the two freely. The trustees and managers of the large foundations accept the social order and actively work toward solving social problems in order to maintain the status quo. As Berman concluded:

> The Carnegie, Ford, and Rockefeller foundations are, in the final analysis, class institutions that attempt to create a world order supportive of the interests of the class that they represent. . . . The foundations are clearly part of the American ruling class. Their vast wealth enables them to articulate programs, set certain agendas, and shape the world order in a manner consonant with the interests of the few associated with them. Much of their work is carried out by carefully chosen and subsidized intellectuals, who elaborate ideologies supportive of the existing social, economic, and political order, in which the foundations play key, but generally unrecognized, roles.[32]

Just as the Rockefeller trustees were a self-perpetuating elite, so Rockefeller philanthropy set out to create similar organizational forms in the institutions it supported. In the SSRC, a small group of social scientists were encouraged to maintain control over the choice of research problems and the distribution of research funds. These intellectuals took on the role of intermediary between the ruling class and the society at large.

While valuable work has been done on the history of the social sciences in the century prior to the First World War,[33] the interwar period has been relatively ignored.[34] This study has been enhanced and strengthened by the

---

1972); Whitaker, *The Philanthropoids*; Brown, *Rockefeller Medicine Men*; Berman, *Influence of the Carnegie, Ford, and Rockefeller Foundations*; and Silva and Slaughter, *Serving Power*.

32. Berman, *Influence of the Carnegie, Ford, and Rockefeller Foundations*, pp. 162 and 176.

33. See Furner, *Advocacy and Objectivity*; Haskell, *Emergence of Professional Social Science*; Bernard and Bernard, *Origins of American Sociology*; Silva and Slaughter, *Serving Power*; and Ross, "Development of the Social Sciences."

34. The best account by a contemporary is by Louis Wirth, "The Social Sciences," in Merle E. Curti, ed., *American Scholarship in the Twentieth Century* (Cambridge: Harvard University Press, 1953), pp. 33–82. More recently see Peter Manicas, *A History and Philosophy of the Social Sciences* (Oxford: Basil Blackwell, 1987). For accounts of the development of individual disciplines, see Joseph Dorfman, *The Economic Mind in American Civilization*, 5 vols. (New York: Viking, 1949); Robert L. Church, "Economists as Experts: The Rise of an Academic Profession in the United States," in Lawrence Stone, ed., *The University in Society* (Princeton: Princeton University Press, 1974), pp. 571–609; Marvin Harris, *The Rise of Anthropological Theory* (New York: Thomas Y. Crowell, 1968); George W. Stocking, Jr., *The Shaping of American Anthropology, 1883–1911: A Franz Boas Reader* (New York: Basic Books, 1974); Edwin G. Boring, *A History of Experimental Psychology* (1929; New York: Appleton-Century-Crofts, 1950); Franz Samelson, "Organizing for the Kingdom of Behavior: Academic Battles and Organi-

publication of two case studies of social science institutions. First is Guy Alchon's fascinating study of the National Bureau of Economic Research (NBER) in the 1920s. Alchon traced the emergence of a "technocratic bargain" between social science and managerial institutions. Alchon showed how this bargain was facilitated by the State and foundations like the Russell Sage Foundation and the LSRM.[35] Second is Donald T. Critchlow's detailed account of the creation and development of the Brookings Institution from the founding of the Institute for Government Research in 1916, to the subsequent founding of Brookings in 1927, to 1952. Critchlow focused on the relationship between social scientists and the State and argued that Brookings was part of a larger political strategy to limit partisan influence in government by depoliticizing public policy.[36] The SSRC is the third in this trio of the most important nongovernment, nonuniversity social science institutions during the interwar years.

During the 1920s and 1930s "social studies" experienced what with hindsight can only be described as a revolution. An unprecedented amount of resources and the social crises during these years combined to catapult these disciplines toward respectability within the academy and society. Much of the impetus came from the belief common to many social scientists, foundation officers, and government officials that the social sciences could solve social problems. Social control based on scientific research was a dominant theme. By the end of the 1930s, social scientists had struck a new bargain with society. The majority had agreed to become technocrats serving an alliance of class and corporate State interests. Others became more vociferous and more strident in their opposition to applied research and retreated further into their respective disciplines. A grand opportunity was presented to social scientists in the 1920s that related to the ideas upon which the Council was based. By the early 1930s, the possibility of fundamental change receded and was closed off by the beginning of the Second World War. It should be pointed out that such an opportunity has not presented itself again.

This researcher's fascination with the interwar years is increased pre-

zational Policies in the Twenties," *Journal of the History of the Behavioral Sciences* 21 (1985): 33–47; Bernard Crick, *The American Science of Politics: Its Origins and Conditions* (London: Routledge and Kegan Paul, 1959); D. Waldo, "Political Science: Tradition, Discipline, Profession, Science, Enterprise," in F. I. Greenstein and N. Polsby, eds., *The Handbook of Political Science*, vol. 1 (Reading: Addison-Wesley, 1975); Albert Somit and Joseph Tannenhaus, *The Development of American Political Science: From Burgess to Behaviourism* (1967; New York: Irvington, 1982); Coser, "American Trends," pp. 287–320; Martin Bulmer, *The Chicago School of Sociology: Institutionalization, Diversity, and the Rise of Sociological Research* (Chicago: University of Chicago Press, 1985); and Stephen P. Turner and Jonathan H. Turner, *The Impossible Science: An Institutional Analysis of American Sociology* (Newbury Park: Sage, 1990).

35. Alchon, *Invisible Hand*.

36. Donald T. Critchlow, *The Brookings Institution, 1916–1952: Expertise and the Public Interest in a Democratic Society* (Dekalb: Northern Illinois University Press, 1985).

cisely because the threat of social disorder is likely to make the relation between social science disciplines and the rest of society that much more visible than in more stable times.[37] The Council emerged from the optimism of the 1920s and then was a significant source of advice and personnel for government throughout the crises of the 1930s. An analysis of the creation and development of the Council allows for an examination of the changing bargain that social scientists in the United States struck with their society. From this analysis some insight into the possible limits of this bargain might emerge.

While a number of reasons have been offered why one should choose to study the Council, there is another equally important theoretical reason why this case was chosen. The creation and development of the SSRC provide an excellent case study of "boundary work."[38] Given the long-term structural trends toward an increasing division of labor, and the concomitant specialization, the Council presents a rare case where an attempt was made to create a new boundary around a group of disciplines that simultaneously involved the breakdown of the existing boundaries between those disciplines. The case therefore allows us to examine the general problem of "demarcation" as we follow social scientists, foundation officers, and State officials through the process of constructing "scientific networks."[39]

The project represented by this book has utilized a diverse set of ideas. These ideas are tied together by a fascination with the work that people do directly and through institutions to create, maintain, and break down boundaries between knowledge units. The concern here is with the boundary that separates the social sciences from other knowledge and the boundaries that separate social science disciplines from each other. The assumption is that power penetrates knowledge systems in part through boundary work. The perspective that emerges pushes toward trying to understand and explain how power is inscribed into and attached to some ideas rather than others. Boundary work incorporates the process whereby legitimacy and cognitive authority are attached to ideas. The concept directs attention to ways in which "fields"[40]

---

37. For an analysis of the way in which social scientists and the State have responded to a crisis, see G. B. Rush, E. Christenson, and J. Malcolmson, "Lament for a Notion: The Development of the Social Sciences in Canada," *Canadian Review of Sociology and Anthropology* 18, no. 4 (1981): 519–44; and Theda Skocpol, "Political Responses to Capitalist Crisis: Neo-Marxist Theories of the State and the Case of the New Deal," *Politics and Society* 10 (1980): 155–99.

38. The model "boundary work" is developed in Donald Fisher, "Boundary Work: Toward a Model of the Relation Power/Knowledge," *Knowledge* 10, no. 2 (1988): 150–76; and Fisher, "Boundary Work and Science."

39. Bruno Latour, *Science in Action: How to Follow Scientists and Engineers through Society* (Cambridge: Harvard University Press, 1987).

40. Pierre Bourdieu, "Intellectual Field and the Creative Project," *Social Science Information* 8, no. 2 (1969): 89–119; and Pierre Bourdieu, *Homo Academicus*, trans. Peter Collier (Stanford: Stanford University Press, 1988).

create "reputational systems"[41] and a hierarchically stratified knowledge system. The distinction between science and nonscience is a critical element. By the turn of the century, "science" and "scientist" had become the most legitimate knowledge labels in North American society. During this century the primary route for increasing the power and raising the status of knowledge has been to make it scientific.[42]

The intellectual roots of this project are set firmly within the sociology of knowledge tradition. The beginning of this particular journey is with Karl Marx and his desire to demonstrate that ideas are conditioned by the distribution of power in society. For Marx, "individuals" and "society" are one; each term includes the other. "Thus the social character is the general character of the whole movement: just as society itself produces man as man, so is society produced by him. Activity and mind, both in their content and in their mode of existence, are social: social activity and social mind."[43] According to Marx, "[S]ociety does not consist of individuals: it expresses the sum of connections and relationships in which individuals find themselves."[44] Intellectual life is conditioned by the mode of production of material life. For Marx,

> In every epoch the ideas of the ruling class are the ruling ideas, that is, the class that is the ruling material power of society is at the same time its ruling intellectual power. . . . The ruling ideas are nothing more than the ideal expression of the dominant material relationships grasped as ideas, hence of the relationships which make the one class the ruling one and therefore the ideas of domination.[45]

Marx saw society relationally and dialectically.

The relativist theme was developed by Karl Mannheim, who provided a framework for studying ideas that went beyond social class to include status and interest groups. In 1966, P. L. Berger and T. Luckman published their classic book *The Social Construction of Reality*. Their call to regard the form and content of all knowledge as a social construct has had a profound effect on

41. R. Whitley, *The Intellectual and Social Organization of the Sciences* (Oxford: Clarendon Press, 1984).

42. Stanley Aronowitz, *Science as Power: Discourse and Ideology in Modern Society* (Minneapolis: University of Minnesota Press, 1988).

43. Karl Marx, *The Economic and Philosophic Manuscripts of 1844*, ed. Dirk J. Struik, trans. Martin Milligan (New York: International Publishers, 1964), p. 137.

44. Karl Marx, *The Grundrisse*, ed. and trans. David McLellan (New York: Harper and Row, 1971), p. 77.

45. Lloyd D. Easton and Kurt H. Guddat, eds., *Writings of the Young Marx on Philosophy and Society* (New York: Anchor Books, Doubleday and Co., 1967), p. 438.

the discipline of sociology and has become the domain assumption within the sociology of knowledge.[46] Developments in the sociology of education and the sociology of science since the early 1970s are a direct outgrowth from, and a celebration of, Berger and Luckman's call to constructivism. At the same time, some researchers in both subdisciplines have emphasized the importance of macrostructures and social forces. Sociologists have been increasingly concerned about opening up the "black box" of either education or science. The best work has sought explanation through a combination of internal and external factors.

Sociologists of education have turned their attention to processes of knowledge production.[47] Taking insights from the sociology of knowledge, the "new" sociology of education has focused attention on what happens inside educational institutions and turned away from the traditional focus on input and output variables.[48] Drawing on the classical sociological theories of Marx, Max Weber, and Emile Durkheim, as well as the interpretative-interactionist tradition,[49] contemporary sociologists have explored the ways knowledge gets "framed" by the social context of schooling and, more specifically, the ways society selects, classifies, transmits, and evaluates public knowledge. The dominant metaphor used to link the structures is cultural

---

46. Karl Mannheim, *Ideology and Utopia: An Introduction to the Sociology of Knowledge,* trans. Louis Wirth and Edward Shils (New York: Harvest Books, Harcourt, Brace and World, 1936); P. L. Berger and T. Luckman, *The Social Construction of Reality* (New York: Doubleday and Co., 1966); J. E. Curtis and J. W. Petras, eds., *The Sociology of Knowledge: A Reader* (London: Duckworth, 1970); Peter Hamilton, *Knowledge and Social Structure: An Introduction to the Classical Argument in the Sociology of Knowledge* (London: Routledge and Kegan Paul, 1974); Bukart Holzner and John H. Marx, *Knowledge Application: The Knowledge System in Society* (Boston: Allyn and Bacon, 1979); and G. Bohme and N. Stehr, eds., *The Knowledge Society* (Dordrecht: D. Reidel, 1986).

47. P. Wexler, *The Sociology of Education: Beyond Equality* (Indianapolis: Bobbs-Merrill Co., 1976); J. Karabel, "The Sociology of Education: Perils and Possibilities," *American Sociologist* 14 (1979): 85–91; Wilfred B. W. Martin, "Neglected Aspects of the Sociology of Education in Canada," *Canadian Journal of Education* 3, no. 4 (1978): 15–30; Donald A. Hansen and V. A. Johnson, "Educational Services," in M. E. Olsen and M. Micklin, eds., *Handbook of Applied Sociology* (New York: Praeger, 1981); Olive Banks, "The Sociology of Education, 1952–1982," *British Journal of Educational Studies* 30 (1982): 18–31; Michael W. Apple and Lois Weis, "Ideology and Schooling," *Education and Society* 3 (1985): 45–63; and John G. Richardson, ed., *Handbook of Theory and Research for the Sociology of Education* (Westport: Greenwood Press, 1987).

48. J. Karabel and A. H. Halsey, eds., *Power and Ideology in Education* (New York: Oxford University Press, 1977); and Geoff Whitty, *Sociology and School Knowledge: Curriculum Theory, Research, and Politics* (London: Methuen, 1985).

49. Thomas P. Wilson, "Normative and Interpretative Paradigms in Sociology," in Jack Douglas, ed., *Understanding Everyday Life* (Chicago: Aldine Publishing Co., 1970); and Peter Woods, *Inside Schools: Ethnography in Educational Research* (London: Routledge and Kegan Paul, 1986).

reproduction.[50] The general approach has been set within what Wilson labeled the "interpretative paradigm." Social researchers drew on phenomenology and symbolic interactionism and proceeded to become participant observers and ethnographers. The most sophisticated work has tried to bring together the "structuralist" and "constructivist" approaches.[51]

Within the new sociology of education, researchers have looked at what counts as knowledge in the classroom,[52] the stratification of knowledge,[53] and the social construction of knowledge categories.[54] Of particular interest in this study is Basil Bernstein's concept, "integration."[55] Building on the Durkheimian distinction between "mechanical" and "organic" solidarity, Bernstein developed the contrasting "collection" and "integrated" educational codes. In knowledge systems, the "classification" process symbolizes the distribution of power in society. The collection code is characterized by strong classification. Strong boundary maintenance exists between knowledge units so that fields, disciplines, and the people in them stand in a closed relation to each other. In contrast, the integrated code is characterized by weak classification. Boundaries between knowledge units and people stand in a more open relation to each other. An inherent tension exists in the dichotomy because the structural force that changes the social order is the increasing division of labor. For Bernstein, as society becomes more fragmented and specialized, we are likely

---

50. M. F. D. Young, ed., *Knowledge and Control* (London: Collier-Macmillan, 1971); Pierre Bourdieu and J. C. Passeron, *Reproduction in Education and Society* (London: Sage, 1977); Pierre Bourdieu and J. C. Passeron, *The Inheritors: French Students and Their Relation to Culture*, trans. Richard Nice (Chicago: University of Chicago Press, 1979); Pierre Bourdieu, *Distinction: A Social Critique of Taste* (Cambridge: Harvard University Press, 1984); Michael W. Apple, *Ideology and Curriculum* (London: Routledge and Kegan Paul, 1979); Michael W. Apple and Lois Weis, eds., *Ideology and Practice in Schooling* (Philadelphia: Temple University Press, 1983); and Stanley Aronowitz and Henry A. Giroux, *Education under Seige* (South Hadley, Mass.: Bergin and Garvey Publishers, 1985).

51. For example, Paul Willis, *Learning to Labor: How Working Class Kids Get Working Class Jobs* (1977; New York: Columbia University Press, 1981).

52. Apple, *Ideology and Curriculum*; and N. Keddie, "Classroom Knowledge," in Young, *Knowledge and Control*.

53. J. Anyon, "Social Class and School Knowledge," *Curriculum Inquiry* 11 (1981): 3–42.

54. I. F. Goodson, *School Subjects and Curriculum Change* (London: Croom Helm, 1983); and I. F. Goodson, *Social Histories of the Secondary Curriculum* (London: Falmer Press, 1985).

55. Basil Bernstein, *Towards a Theory of Educational Transmissions*, vol. 3 of *Class, Codes, and Control*, rev. ed. (London: Routledge and Kegan Paul, 1977); Basil Bernstein, "Codes, Modalities, and the Process of Cultural Reproduction: A Model," in M. W. Apple, ed., *Cultural and Economic Reproduction in Education* (Boston: Routledge and Kegan Paul, 1982), pp. 304–55; Basil Bernstein, *The Structuring of Pedagogic Discourse*, vol. 4 of *Class, Codes, and Control* (London: Routledge, 1990).

to see in educational systems a movement toward an integrated code, which is characterized by new forms of interdependence and cooperation.

Bernstein pointed out that we are most likely to see indications of these new forms of solidarity among teachers and academics who are in the front ranks of what he, and others, have called the "new middle class."[56] This fraction of the middle class consists of those who are responsible for symbolic control. The "new middle class" has a direct relation to the process of cultural reproduction, yet it is indirectly related to the economic mode of production. Bernstein escaped some of the ambiguity of his earlier formulations by making it clear that the ruling class is the dominant cultural category. Members of the ruling class are those who dominate production by deciding the means, contexts, and possibilities. Bernstein argued that "there is a division between dominating power (production) and dominating control (cultural reproduction) and the former limits the latter."[57] The ruling class's control over cultural production is indirect. In knowledge production, control is exercised through philanthropic foundations, the State, the academy, and research institutes. The limitations change in different historical periods, but they are expressed in the principles of classification and control. There is no necessary progression from collection to integrated codes, but there is value in focusing on classification and control when trying to understand the relation between power and knowledge.

Similarly, Pierre Bourdieu has become increasingly interested in the process of classification within and between "fields."[58] In *Homo Academicus*, Bourdieu's object is to explicate the principles of classification and the continuous transformation between social, economic, academic, and scientific forms of capital. For Bourdieu, "the university field is, like any other field, the locus of struggle to determine the conditions and the criteria of legitimate membership and legitimate hierarchy, that is, to determine which properties are pertinent, effective and liable to function as capital so as to generate the specific profits guaranteed by the field."[59] In this way, Bourdieu directs our attention to the struggle for territory and, in this study, the struggle to create a boundary around the social science field.

---

56. See Bernstein, *Towards a Theory*; Poulantzas, *Classes in Contemporary Capitalism*; Alvin W. Gouldner, *The Future of Intellectuals and the Rise of the New Class* (New York: Seabury Press, 1979); Erik Olin Wright, *Class, Crisis, and the State* (London: New Left Books, 1978); and Erik Olin Wright and J. Singleman, "Proletarianization in the Changing American Class Structure," in M. Burawoy and Theda Skocpol, eds., *Marxist Inquiries: Studies of Labor, Class and States*, supplement to the *American Journal of Sociology* 88 (Chicago: University of Chicago Press, 1982), pp. 5176–5209.

57. Bernstein, *Towards a Theory*, p. 191.

58. See Bourdieu, "Intellectual Field" and Bourdieu, *Homo Academicus*.

59. Bourdieu, *Homo Academicus*, p. 11.

Finally, sociologists of education have in the past two decades tried to utilize and develop Marxist theory.[60] The theoretical approach adopted here emerges from, and is set within, the relation between the modes of economic and cultural production. The book draws extensively on the work of Gramsci. It seems particularly appropriate when studying the interwar period to utilize the analysis of one of the most perceptive contemporary theorists. At the same time, this decision clearly reflects the rediscovery and popularity of Gramsci's ideas among current social scientists.[61] Gramsci's work is particularly appealing because he developed his theories connecting base and superstructure in a relational manner. Ideas are not determined, but rather they are constructed and are part of a dynamic struggle for power. The focus is on the production and reproduction of cultural hegemony. Cultural hegemony is the ideologies that disseminate the consciousness of the ruling class and organize the consensus of the population to the existing social order. It is in this sense that one can talk about the "rule of ideas." The ideas are translated into structures and activities as well as values, attitudes, beliefs, and morality that support the established order and the dominant class interests. So that to the extent that hegemony is internalized, it becomes the common sense of a society.

Hegemony is a process whereby approved views are able to saturate all facets of social life. For Raymond Williams, cultural hegemony is a dynamic process that incorporates the "significant past" but also looks forward. The process includes three aspects of culture, the "emergent," the "dominant," and the "residual."[62] One would expect all three aspects to be present simultaneously as elements of any historic social formation. Hegemony is according to Gramsci a "moving equilibrium." It has to be won, maintained, and sustained. The ruling class manifests its supremacy both as "domination" and as "intellectual and moral leadership." This group persuades subordinate groups to accept as natural and given its political and ideological leadership. As Carl Boggs explained: "Hegemony, in this sense, might be defined as an 'organizing principle' or world-view (or combination of such world views), that is diffused by agencies of ideological control and socialization into every area of daily life."[63] Yet it must be made clear that while Gramsci saw hegemony as

60. For example, Samuel Bowles and Herbert Gintis, *Schooling in Capitalist America: Educational Reform and the Contradictions of Economic Life* (New York: Basic Books, 1976); R. Sharp and A. Green, *Education and Social Control* (London: Routledge and Kegan Paul, 1975); Martin Carnoy and Henry M. Levin, *Schooling and Work in the Democratic State* (Stanford: Stanford University Press, 1985); Aronowitz and Giroux, *Education under Seige*; and Roger Dale, *The State and Educational Policy* (Philadelphia: Open University Press, 1989).

61. Within the sociology of education Gramscian theory has provided the intellectual foundation for much of the "critical theorizing" in North America and the United Kingdom.

62. See Raymond Williams, "Base and Superstructure in Marxist Cultural Theory," *New Left Review* 83 (1973): 3–16; and Raymond Williams, *Marxism and Literature* (Oxford: Oxford University Press, 1977).

63. Boggs, *Gramsci's Marxism*, p. 39.

ethical-political he was adamant that it must also be economic. For Gramsci, hegemony had to "be based on the decisive function exercised by the leading group in the decisive nucleus of economic activity."[64] The equilibrium that is cultural hegemony always accompanies the emergence of a ruling class that is both dominant and directive not only in economic terms but also in intellectual and moral terms. Consent is won and shaped so that the power of the ruling class appears both natural and legitimate.

Ideology incorporates ideas and material practices. For Gramsci ideologies have a psychological significance because "they 'organize' human masses, and create the terrain on which men move, acquire consciousness of their position, struggle, etc."[65] The material existence of ideology provides people with rules of practical conduct and moral behavior. Ideologies bind people together and act as agents of social unification. Ideologies involve both external and internal aspects. The external aspect legitimates the social relations of the social formation. At the same time, the ideology of the ruling class is internalized and made into the common sense of society. As the ideology penetrates, so active consent is created and recreated.

This study utilizes a Marxist definition of social class. The focus is upon whose interests are served by particular acts and structures. Yet as noted earlier, the mode of cultural production does occupy varying degrees of relative autonomy. The limitations on the ruling class and the "new middle class" change in different historical periods so that the balance between direct and indirect control alters. Gramsci placed intellectuals in a separate social category. Organic intellectuals advise and speak for social classes. Conservative organic intellectuals speak on behalf of the ruling class while other organic intellectuals speak for the proletariat. This formulation is particularly useful because it focuses attention on the political nature of intellectual work. It follows that in addition to performing their intermediary role between classes, academic social scientists also have choices about whether to use their voices to support, to ignore, or to oppose the ruling class. The balance is determined in the process of boundary work.

A most important group of boundary workers within the class structure are the "new middle class." Erik Olin Wright and J. Singleman argued that academics occupy a contradictory location within class relations.[66] Academics are located in both the proletariat and the petite bourgeoisie. They occupy wage-dependent status and therefore lack control over the means of academic production, yet at the same time, they retain a high degree of control over the work environment and labor process at the ideological level.

---

64. Gramsci, *Selections from the Prison Notebooks*, p. 61.

65. Ibid., p. 377.

66. Erik Olin Wright, "Intellectuals and the Class Structure of Capitalist Society," in P. Walder, ed., *Between Labour and Capital* (London: Black Rose Press, 1978); and Wright and Singleman, "Proletarianization."

Academics are located between labor and capital. They are held responsible for the elaboration and dissemination of bourgeois ideology while at the same time they are deprived of effective control of either their educational institutions or the products of their labor. Academics have a degree of autonomy that allows them to pursue knowledge for its own sake and to produce ideas that confront and resist the domination of capital. In this study, it is assumed that these contradictions will be most visible for academic social scientists. In part this is because social scientists attempt to analyze and explain social life and are therefore placed in more exposed and more extreme positions than their colleagues. It is also the case, as Bourdieu pointed out, that social scientists have stood between the natural sciences and the arts and occupy a double subordinate position in both the old and the new hierarchies. As part of their efforts to escape from the purity of the traditional arts disciplines and to emulate the methods and practices of the natural sciences, social scientists have been at the forefront of the expansion of applied research. The contradictions between Bourdieu's "social power" and "academic power," or in our terms, between the power associated with a contradictory class position, are made visible as social scientists are charged with the double negative of impurity.[67]

In the sociology of science a segment of recent research has been concerned with the boundaries that separate science from nonscience. This work grows out of the "problems of demarcation," but the questions have been restated in two distinctive ways. One line of inquiry examines the style and content of the professional ideologies of scientists. G. Watson (1984) used an interpretive framework to provide insight into the social construction of boundaries between the schools of social and cultural anthropology. He focused on the content of these two schools and showed how participants have used "rhetoric" and "reification" to create boundaries.[68] Gieryn's research described the boundary work that has separated science from nonscience. He described how professional ideologies of scientists construct a social boundary that cordons off some intellectual activities as nonscience. Gieryn concluded that "the boundaries of science are ambiguous, flexible, historically changing, contextually variable, internally inconsistent, and sometimes disputed."[69] To create an effective theory of science in society, Gieryn and Anne E. Figert concluded that we "must attend first to the interpretative

67. Bourdieu, *Homo Academicus*.

68. G. Watson, "The Social Construction of Boundaries between Social and Cultural Anthropology in Britain and North America," *Journal of Anthropological Research* 40 (Fall 1984): 351–66.

69. Thomas F. Gieryn, "Boundary Work and the Demarcation of Science from Non-Science: Strains and Interests in Professional Ideologies of Scientists," *American Sociological Review* 48 (1983): 792.

flexibility of science, to its roving boundaries, its contextually contingent territory."[70]

A second line of inquiry examines practices and patterns of discourse in laboratory settings that form the scientific process.[71] The initial emphasis on constructivism in the social studies of science has become a series of theoretical and methodological formulas.[72] The most important contribution is by Bruno Latour, *Science in Action: How to Follow Scientists and Engineers through Society* (1987). Latour assumed that scientific knowledge emerges from and is caused by a combination of internal and external factors. No boundary separates science and society. The construction of the sciences is defined as a collective process. The job, according to Latour, is to trace the "empirical and variable limit" between scientists and their society.[73] We have to follow the actors and take their roles as they struggle over the mobilization and exchange of resources. For Latour, scientists engage in trials of strength over the claim to objectivity. This claim to legitimacy is the major resource that scientists use to build "social scientific networks." To describe "science in action" it is necessary, according to Latour, to accept what social scientists do rather than trying to impose an extreme form of relativism on them. The aim is to maintain a relativist stance while at the same time focus on the battles over objectivity. As much as we are able to follow social scientists, Latour instructed us to try to unearth what they and their networks regard as firm and that which is regarded as relative.

The work of Michel Foucault cuts across the boundaries that separate the sociologies of education and science. Foucault provided a schema for tracing the emergence of new domains of knowledge and inquiry. These domains or "discursive formations" emerge as part of the overall process of knowledge differentiation. The trajectory of these emergent forms of discourse moves across a series of "thresholds," which are symbols of the strength and the power of the emerging boundary. The thresholds of "positivity," "scienticity,"

---

70. Thomas F. Gieryn and Anne E. Figert, "Ingredients for a Theory of Science in Society: O-Rings, Ice-Water, C-clamp, Richard Feynman, and the Press," in Cozzens and Gieryn, *Theories of Science*, p. 91.

71. Bruno Latour and Steve Woolgar, *Laboratory Life: The Construction of Scientific Facts*, 2d ed. (1979; Princeton: Princeton University Press, 1986); Karin Knorr-Cetina, *The Manufacture of Knowledge: An Essay on the Constructivist and Contextual Nature of Science* (Oxford: Pergamon, 1981); Karin Knorr-Cetina and Michael Mulkay, eds., *Science Observed: Perspectives on the Social Studies of Science* (London: Sage, 1983).

72. Michael Mulkay, *The Word and the World: Explorations in the Form of Sociological Analysis* (London: George Allen and Unwin, 1985); Michael Callon, John Law, and Arie Rip, eds., *Mapping the Dynamics of Science and Technology* (London: Macmillan, 1986); Latour, *Science in Action*; Woolgar, *Science*; and Steve Woolgar, ed., *Knowledge and Reflexivity: New Frontiers in the Sociology of Knowledge* (London: Sage, 1988).

73. Latour, *Science in Action*, p. 159.

and "formalization" symbolize the progressive inscription of power into the boundary.[74]

The juxtaposition of power and knowledge provides the theoretical context for all of Foucault's work. Power and knowledge are fused together in practices that make up history so that knowledge only becomes an object when power is exercised. Foucault developed the category power/knowledge (pouvoir/savoir) most clearly in *Discipline and Punish* (1979) and *Power/Knowledge: Selected Interviews and Other Writings, 1972–1977* (1980).[75] For Foucault, power is diffused throughout society and is present at all levels. While there is an assumption that power is not merely hierarchical, at the same time Foucault did not deny that some levels of society are more powerful than others. Class relations exist but do so within power/knowledge. In tandem with knowledge, power serves both positive and negative ends simultaneously so that it coerces, prohibits, and represses action at the same time as it releases, permits, and produces action. For our purposes, power/knowledge incorporates the process of boundary work. The concept directs attention to the ways that "social forces" are inscribed into boundaries. The dialectic of power/knowledge is the engine that drives the social formation.

Cultural hegemony is very similar to Foucault's power/knowledge. In this context, the inclusion of this concept locates power/knowledge concretely within a Marxist theoretical frame. Power/knowledge is part of the relation that connects the modes of economic and cultural production. In one sense, the production/reproduction of cultural hegemony is contained within power/knowledge. In another sense, cultural hegemony goes beyond power/knowledge by making concrete the imminent quality of power in Foucault's formulation so that control from within is linked to dominant ideologies that are firmly grounded in the two modes of production.

This book is reflexive in the sense associated with the interpretative tradition.[76] Throughout the process of writing it I was aware of the interaction between my perspective, the literature, the evidence, and the emerging theory. In this sense the focus on boundary work is not something that I brought to the project whole, but rather these ideas emerged out of the above dialogue. These ideas are also grounded in and applicable to my own experience as an academic and the process of writing this book.[77] Yet I have not gone the next

---

74. Michel Foucault, *The Archeology of Knowledge*, trans. A. M. Sheridan Smith (New York: Pantheon, Random House, 1972).

75. Michel Foucault, *Discipline and Punish* (New York: Vintage Books, 1979); and Michel Foucault, *Power/Knowledge: Selected Interviews and Other Writings, 1972–1977*, ed. Colin Gordon (Brighton, Sussex: Harvester Press, 1980).

76. See the discussion of reflexivity in Martyn Hammersley and Paul Atkinson, *Ethnography: Principles in Practice* (London: Tavistock, 1983).

77. See the discussion by Bourdieu on reflexivity in *Homo Academicus*.

step and made reflexivity the subject of this book.[78] The intention is to take Latour's advice to heart and follow the boundary workers as they attempt to close and open boundaries. The desire is to document their absolutism and relativism and to place their strategies in the relevant social contexts. The approach does not allow for any division between internal and external causes. The irony is that while in theory one cannot separate social science from non–social science, in practice, social scientists have done so. Their definitions of the situation are real and have real consequences.

The book combines a diverse set of ideas on demarcation and the relation power/knowledge. Concepts like "field," "discourse coalition," "classification," "threshold," and "boundary work" focus attention on the social construction of the social sciences. The central aim is to document and analyze the social conditions that shaped the production of social scientific knowledge. To do "Social Science in Action" means to move inside the world of social scientists, their patrons, and sponsors in order to explain to the outside what occurred. The book documents the scientific pretensions of social scientists. The attempt here is to represent one episode, albeit a crucial one, in the continuing battle to fix the idea of social science.

The rest of the chapters in this book are grouped into two major sections. Chapters 2 through 5 chronologically describe and analyze the creation and development of the Council, beginning in the early 1920s and ending in 1946 when the social sciences were excluded from the proposed National Science Foundation (NSF). Chapter 2, "Creation and Organization of the Council," traces the beginnings of the Council in the early 1920s through the initial period of organization that ended in 1927. This was a time of rising expectations and the period when the close relationship between Rockefeller philanthropy and some leading social scientists was established. Chapter 3, "Expansion and Growth of the Council: The Gilded Age," documents the rapid and enormous expansion that occurred during the late 1920s and ends with the publication of the federal government's report, *Recent Social Trends in the United States*. From a time in 1928 when fundamental development of the social sciences seemed to be ensured, the Council was by 1930 beginning to embrace an applied definition of research. Chapter 4, "Consolidation and Retrenchment, 1930–36," documents the concentration of work by the Council on specific applied areas of research. This trend culminated in the establishment of a major research committee on social security and one on public administration through which the Council explicitly served the federal government's New Deal initiatives. Chapter 5, "Self-Criticism, Reconstruction, and Planning, 1937–45," documents the process of self-evaluation that was

---

78. Mulkay, *The Word and the World*; and Malcolm Ashmore, *The Reflexive Thesis: Wrighting Sociology of Scientific Knowledge* (Chicago: University of Chicago Press, 1989).

initiated by the Council and the reaction of a significant part of the leadership of the Council against applied research. The sense of disillusionment and disappointment about the lack of progress in the social sciences was compounded when these disciplines were excluded from the proposed NSF.

Chapter 6, "The Impact of the SSRC on the Social Sciences in North America: Changing the Boundaries," provides a detailed analysis and evaluation of the Council. This material is grouped under the following headings: research relations, relations with governments, social research, and boundary work. The question of Rockefeller control is examined critically under the headings of finance, policy, program, and people. Chapter 7, "Conclusion," utilizes and develops the model "boundary work" to approach an explanation of the failure of the Council to achieve the main objective concerning integration and "fundamental" scientific development of the social sciences. The book ends with a discussion of the limits and possibilities of the bargain that social scientists are able to strike with the society in which they live.

Part 1

CHAPTER 2

Creation and Organization of the Council

The early 1920s mark a critical turning point in the history of the social sciences. The creation of the SSRC in 1923 was the most important indicator of the dramatic shift in the social disciplines toward a more scientific and more synthetic approach.[1] The focus on interdisciplinary work and the social problem orientation harkened back to activities of the ASSA, but there was an important difference. The professional academic associations that emerged from the ashes of the ASSA at the turn of the century were now searching for ways to extend their authority.[2] The key was to firmly establish their disciplines as sciences. The SSRC, and the definition of science it incorporated, was based on an alliance between academic social scientists and a new Rockefeller foundation, the LSRM.

Two men, one representing the academy and the other representing Rockefeller philanthropy, were the architects behind the creation of the SSRC. On the academic side, there was Charles E. Merriam, the president of the American Political Science Association (APSA) in 1921 and from 1923 the chair of the Department of Political Science at the University of Chicago. Merriam aimed at transforming the social sciences in the United States into a coordinated group of scientific disciplines. On the philanthropic side, there was Beardsley Ruml, the young director of the LSRM who similarly had developed a grand design for the social sciences in the capitalist world. The overriding intent of this design was the conversion of social studies into academic social sciences. The objective was the spread of cooperative scientific research that would attack "real" social problems. By the middle of 1925 these two men had formed a partnership that was to last throughout the interwar period.[3] Both brought to the task the progressive era's faith in the potential of the social sciences to solve society's problems. Yet both men were clear that this self-defined boundary would separate the new corps of social

---

1. See Bernard and Bernard, *Origins of American Sociology*; and Ross, "Development of the Social Sciences."

2. See Haskell, *Emergence of Professional Social Science*; Furner, *Advocacy and Objectivity*; and Silva and Slaughter, *Serving Power*.

3. For a detailed account of Merriam's career, see Barry D. Karl, *Charles E. Merriam and the Study of Politics* (Chicago: University of Chicago Press, 1974).

scientists from the humanities and from the reformist and amateurish tendencies that had been so central to the ASSA. These disciplines were to be harnessed to solve social problems in a professional and scientific manner. The SSRC represented a convergence of the interests of professional social scientists and, through the foundations, the interests of the ruling class in the United States.

While there had been some dissatisfaction expressed by the American Sociological Society (ASS) and the American Economic Association (AEA) about the lack of research funding and the need for collaboration,[4] it was left to Merriam and the APSA to take the lead. Merriam was the foremost advocate of what he labeled as "the new science" of politics. In his influential essay "The Present State of the Study of Politics" (1921) Merriam called for a "reconstruction of the methods of political study and the attainment of larger results in the theoretical and practical fields."[5] As president of the APSA, Merriam was instrumental in creating a "Committee on Political Research" with himself as chairman. The committee's report lamented the almost total lack of provision for scientific social research in political science in the United States. But then as a reflection of Merriam's broader concerns, the report also drew attention to the trend in the social sciences toward the utilization of scientific methods and the need to counteract the overspecialization that had occurred, with some effective means for coordination and cooperation. The report recommended the establishment of a social research council that would bring together political scientists, economists, sociologists, and historians.[6] Following conversations between members of the APSA, the AEA, and the ASS, a meeting was held on February 24, 1923.

Social Research Council

At this initial meeting only the political scientists and the sociologists were authorized to proceed with setting up a council. The economists sent observers while the historians were as yet uncertain about dividing their attention between two organizations as they were already part of the American Council of Learned Societies (ACLS). Even so, this temporary group recommended the formation of a permanent organization to be called the Social

---

4. Wirth, "Report," p. 9, SSRCA. I have relied primarily on two documents to check historical details on the development of the Council. The report by Wirth and the SSRC, *Decennial Report, 1923–1933* (New York, 1934). See also Augustus Frederick Kuhlman, "Social Science Research Council: Its Origins and Objects," *Social Forces* 6 (June 1928): 583–88.

5. Charles E. Merriam, "The Present State of the Study of Politics," *American Political Science Review* 15 (1921): 174.

6. Wirth, "Report," pp. 8–9, SSRCA. See also the SSRC, *Annual Report*, 1928–29 (New York, 1929).

Research Council (SRC), with two representatives from each of the four associations. In line with Merriam's APSA report, this group noted that the proposed Council would be a powerful force in helping to organize and coordinate social research as well as a means for hastening the development of scientific methods in these disciplines. Significantly, a number of projects were discussed at this meeting that subsequently turned out to be among the Council's leading enterprises. Professor Francis Stuart Chapin, representing the sociologists, brought forward a suggestion from the ASS's Committee on Standardization of Research to abstract social science periodicals. This committee was suggested as a means to increase cooperation between disciplines. Chapin had been trained at Columbia by Franklin H. Giddings and since graduating in 1911 had held a position at the University of Minnesota, Minneapolis.[7] Merriam brought forward two suggestions: first, that the Council might cooperate with the National Research Council (NRC) on their Human Migration Project and second, that the Council should examine the possibility of getting Congress to provide a digest and index of state laws. Finally, the meeting approved the idea of obtaining a report on the teaching of social science in American universities and colleges to get a clearer idea of the possibilities for closer coordination.

The SRC was founded at a meeting between representatives of the three main associations in May 1923. Merriam was chosen as chairman with Professor Horace Secrist, an economist from Northwestern University, as secretary. In addition to the topics outlined earlier Secrist agreed to look into the idea of surveying the scope and methods of existing social research agencies in the United States.[8]

The SSRC and the NRC

The final meeting of 1923 took place in Chicago during November. By this time the name of the Council had been changed to the Social Science Research Council. Further, it was decided that the Council should attempt to become part of the NRC but should not seek membership in the ACLS.[9] With

7. See Albion W. Small, "Fifty Years of Sociology in the United States—1865–1915," *American Journal of Sociology* 21 (May 1916): 721–864; Albion W. Small, *Origins of Sociology* (Chicago: University of Chicago Press, 1924); and Howard Washington Odum, *American Sociology: The Study of Sociology in the United States through 1950* (New York: Longman, 1951).

8. See "Confidential Report to Colonel Woods on Activities of Seven Organizations Assisted by the Laura Spelman Rockefeller Memorial," Folder 678, Social Science—Pamphlet and Report, LSRM, Series 3, 63, RAC, Tarrytown, N.Y. Specific details are contained in Charles E. Merriam to Ruml, June 5, 1923, Folder 682, SSRC, 1923–24, LSRM, Series 3, 64, RAC.

9. Merriam to Ruml, November 16, 1923, Folder 682, SSRC, 1923–24, LSRM, Series 3, 64, RAC. It should be noted that this letter contains the first reference to the new title.

Merriam's heavy emphasis upon the importance of the scientific approach and his belief in the interdependence of the social and natural sciences, it was predictable that the SSRC should opt for the NRC. There was an additional personal factor. Merriam had as a model his brother John C. Merriam, the president of the Carnegie Institution in Washington, chairman of the Executive Board of NRC, and a leading member of the NRC's Committee on Scientific Problems of Human Migration. Following in his brother's footsteps, Charles E. Merriam was expected to lead "a movement to transform the socially purposeful study of society into a scientific program of progressive reformation, a reformation built upon the interdependence of social science and natural science."[10]

In October, Charles E. Merriam had consulted with his brother and the psychologist Robert M. Yerkes, the chairman of the Migration Committee.[11] Following the November decision, it was left to Yerkes to pursue the negotiation for the SSRC's entry. Yerkes, a Harvard Ph.D. in psychology who had taught at Harvard and the University of Minnesota, appeared to be the ideal choice for such a task. He had been instrumental in obtaining a place for psychology under the mandate of the NRC in 1916 and subsequently became chair of the NRC's Committee for Psychology, which was established the following year. As chair of this committee Yerkes ran the army testing program during the First World War, which did so much to raise the prestige and perceived utility of psychology and, by extension, the social sciences generally.[12] Of the social science disciplines, only psychology and anthropology were formally represented in the NRC.

Meanwhile the Council sent out membership invitations to four other groups, namely, the historians, the statisticians, the psychologists, and the anthropologists. By March 1925, all four organizations had accepted.[13] As the organization grew in strength it began to receive some project funds for the migration study and some exploratory work on international communication. In May 1924, Edmund E. Day, the dean of the School of Business Administration, University of Michigan, and a representative of the American

10. Karl, *Merriam and the Study of Politics*, p. 12.

11. See Merriam to Ruml, May 19, 1923, Folder 682, SSRC, 1923–24, LSRM, Series 3, 64, RAC.

12. See Robert M. Yerkes, ed., *The New World of Science: Its Development during the War* (New York: Century Co., 1920); James Reed, "Robert M. Yerkes and the Mental Testing Movement," in Michael M. Sokal, ed., *Psychological Testing and American Society, 1890–1930* (1987; New Brunswick: Rutgers University Press, 1990), pp. 75–94; Edwin G. Boring, ed., *Psychology for the Armed Services* (Washington, D.C.: Infantry Journal, 1945); A. Hunter Dupree, *Science in the Federal Government* (Cambridge: Harvard University Press, Belknap Press, 1959); and Lyons, *Uneasy Partnership*. The standard reference on the history of psychology is Boring, *History of Experimental Psychology*.

13. First to accept was the ASTA in December 1923, followed by the APA in December 1924, then, finally, the AAA and the AHA, respectively, in January and March of 1925.

Statistical Association (ASTA), was elected treasurer.[14] Formal incorporation came in December 1924 following the first major appropriation to the Council from any source for a continuing program. Earlier that month the LSRM had appropriated $425,000 to cover fellowships over the next five years.

In the statement of incorporation the Council outlined its broad purposes. This was a more inclusive statement of purposes than the earlier commitment to coordination and research methods and one that placed the emphasis firmly on science. The aims were as follows:

> The object for which it is formed is to encourage, and, counsel, support, direct, or to carry on or conduct, directly or indirectly, (1) any scientific work of investigation or research in any of the general fields of social sciences, and/or (2) any group, movement, institution, or organization engaged in any scientific work of investigation or research in any of the general fields of social sciences, and/or (3) the development or management of any machinery, methods, devices, means, agendas or instrumentalities that may be useful in any scientific work of investigation or research in any of the general fields of social sciences.[15]

In essence, the Council gave itself a blank check with regard to its future activities as long as they were within the bounds of scientific social studies. Further, it was decided that each association should send three representatives for three years on a staggered basis. The seven member associations were as follows: American Anthropological Association (AAA), AEA, American Historical Association (AHA), APSA, American Psychological Association (APA), ASS, and ASTA. Council membership has remained constant since 1925.

The LSRM's Strategy for the Social Sciences

It is impossible to tell the story of the SSRC without constant references to Rockefeller philanthropy.[16] At the same time that Merriam was assembling the APSA report, Ruml was presenting a major policy document to the trustees of the LSRM.[17] Ruml had obtained his Ph.D. in psychology at the University of Chicago in 1917. He did a thesis on the reliability of

14. See letter, Merriam to Ruml, May 19, 1924, Folder 682, SSRC, 1923–24, LSRM, Series 3, 64, RAC.

15. SSRC, *Annual Report*, 1924–25 (Chicago, 1925). See also SSRC, "History and Purposes of the Social Science Research Council," app. A in *Annual Report*, 1928–29, pp. 39–48.

16. For a detailed description of the Rockefeller policy for the social sciences refer to Fisher, "Role of Philanthropic Foundations."

17. "General Memorandum, October 1922," Folder 677, Social Sciences—Policy, LSRM, Series 3, 63, RAC.

mental tests and was taught by James Rowland Angell, a leading member of the new breed of experimental psychologists.[18] He joined Yerkes in the Office of the Surgeon General to help organize the massive program of intelligence testing in the army. It was Angell, as president of the Carnegie Corporation (CC), who brought Ruml into the world of foundations by appointing him as his assistant in 1920. With the support of Angell and on the advice of Abraham Flexner, John D. Rockefeller, Jr., gave Ruml the task of doing something about the social sciences. Ruml became director of the LSRM in May 1922 and decided that the memorial should concentrate on the social sciences and public administration.[19] Throughout his foundation career Ruml maintained an overwhelming commitment to scientific advance. Yet it must be understood that this twenty-six year old had tremendous ambition. He was conscious of the power that he wielded with Rockefeller money and wanted nothing less than the transformation of the social sciences.[20] Later Ruml was labeled as "the founder of the social sciences in the U.S." by Robert Maynard Hutchins, president of the University of Chicago.[21]

The transformation Ruml envisaged did not encompass a challenge to the current socioeconomic structure. Social science was going to help solve the problems faced by capitalist systems, not contribute to their downfall. As one would expect, Ruml, Merriam, and other leading characters in this story were respectable men of their times. They certainly had a vision for the social sciences, but none of them had arrived at the positions they occupied in 1923 because of their opposition to the status quo. Rather they were sophisticated conservatives who wished to preserve the underlying structure of society by

18. For his own account of the Chicago years, see "Autobiography of James Rowland Angell," in C. Murchison, ed., *A History of Psychology in Autobiography* (New York: Russell and Russell, 1961), pp. 1–38.

19. Ruml was appointed at the substantial salary of $7,500. It should be noted that the decision to appoint Ruml had been made toward the end of 1921. In December 1921, Raymond B. Fosdick, the personal lawyer of JDR, Jr., and trustee of the LSRM, wrote to Ruml to welcome him into "our family." See letter, Fosdick to Ruml, December 23, 1921, Folder 5, Series 1, Box 5, Papers of Beardsley Ruml (henceforth Ruml). These papers are housed in the Department of Special Collections, University of Chicago.

20. For a biographical account of Ruml, see Martin Bulmer and Joan Bulmer, "Philanthropy and Social Science in the 1920s: Beardsley Ruml and the Laura Spelman Rockefeller Memorial, 1922–1929," *Minerva* 19 (1981 [appeared in 1983]): 347–407. Some authors underestimate the extent to which Ruml wanted to exercise power and the degree to which he wished to further the interests of the Rockefeller trustees and the family. For a different interpretation of Ruml's role and the discussion that ensued, see Fisher, "Role of Philanthropic Foundations"; Martin Bulmer, "A Reply to Donald Fisher"; and Fisher, "Philanthropic Foundations and the Social Sciences."

21. Quoted in Alva Johnston, "Beardsley Ruml: The National Ideas Man—III," *New Yorker* 20 (February 24, 1945): 33. Cited by Lagemann, *Politics of Knowledge*, p. 70.

increasing the quantity and quality of social scientific knowledge. Merriam was convinced that scientific advance and the progress of liberal democratic systems went hand in hand.[22] For Merriam, the "new science" of politics, involving cooperation and coordination with other disciplines, would permit a "more intelligent control of government" and facilitate "the conscious control of human evolution toward which intelligence moves in every domain of life."[23] Similarly, Ruml had a deep and abiding faith in the potential of social science knowledge for putting things right.

Ruml believed that the route for advancing human welfare was through scientific social research. As the social sciences became more "scientific" in the natural science mode, so he felt these disciplines would be more efficient in helping to solve the "real," "practical" problems that society faced. In October 1922, Ruml presented a long memorandum to the trustees of the LSRM that outlined his strategy.[24] Ruml had a mandate to spend $20 million in a decade, and he decided to attack in a bold manner. Rather than play safe, by distributing money across a whole range of subjects, Ruml decided that the LSRM should focus on a basic need. In line with the memorial's previous interests, Ruml examined the social welfare field and concluded that the primary need was "the development of the social sciences and the production of a body of substantiated and widely accepted generalizations as to human capacities and motives and as to the behaviour of human beings as individuals and in groups."[25]

The social sciences were defined as sociology, ethnology, anthropology, and psychology, as well as certain aspects of economics, history, political science, and biology. For Ruml, it was clear that social welfare organizations, business, industry, and government required knowledge of social forces if they were to combat the complex social problems of the age. The situation was made more urgent because of the lag between the natural and the social sciences. The increasing control of physical forces was compared with the lack of development in the social field. While Ruml accepted that the social sciences were relatively young subjects and that by definition the subject matter was difficult, he was still critical of this lack of progress. In his view, the universities did not organize programs that were favorable to social research so that production from these institutions was "largely deductive and speculative" and was based on "second hand observations, documentary evi-

---

22. See Karl, *Merriam and the Study of Politics*, p. 41.

23. Charles E. Merriam, *New Aspects of Politics* (Chicago: University of Chicago Press, 1925), p. xvi. Quoted by Somit and Tannenhaus, *Development of American Political Science*, p. 111; and partially by Crick, *American Science of Politics*, p. 143.

24. "General Memorandum, October 1922," Folder 677, Social Sciences—Policy, LSRM, Series 3, 63, RAC.

25. Ibid., p. 2.

dence and anecdotal material."[26] For Ruml, the memorial's mission was to change the direction of this work not for academic reasons but because of the foundation's practical interest in increasing human welfare.

Ruml used the rest of the memorandum to outline a major program for the development of the social sciences. The program had four phases. The first was the definition and isolation of a class of related problems within the social field. The second was the creation of possibilities for advancing "practical" and "scientific" research. For Ruml, the label "practical" as applied to social research had a specific meaning. He was not concerned with immediate utility. Rather Ruml believed that research ought to provide a better knowledge of those social forces that have "concrete" impact on human welfare.[27] The study of these "real problems" implied for Ruml a collaborative approach. It followed therefore that Ruml should encourage cooperative work between the social disciplines. Because of their permanence and traditional status it was felt that existing universities offered the best auspices for research. Within the universities the LSRM intended to improve the organization and facilities so that "a far more intimate contact of the social scientist . . . with concrete social phenomena" would become possible. Under phase two, it was felt that social research should ordinarily be associated with opportunities for undergraduate and graduate teaching and that there ought to be better facilities for scientific publication. The third phase aimed at increasing the number of highly able men working in the social sciences by improving research facilities and through the provision of scholarships. The scholarships would, according to Ruml, "tend to place the social sciences in a more equal relation to the physical sciences and to the arts."[28] The fourth phase of the program focused on the dissemination of new knowledge and ways to increase practical utilization. Ruml concluded the memorandum by stating that results from scientific social research would certainly have a positive influence on public welfare.

In line with the idea put forward by the SRC at its first meeting in February 1923, Ruml commissioned Lawrence K. Frank to prepare a report on the status of the social sciences in the United States.[29] For the purposes of the survey the social sciences were defined as economics, sociology, and political science, although the report did include discussions of psychology,

---

26. Ibid., p. 3.

27. Ibid., pp. 2–3.

28. Ibid., pp. 5 and 7.

29. Frank later became an officer in the LSRM and the SF (another Rockefeller foundation) as well as a leading figure in the Child Study movement. See Stephen C. Schlossman, "Philanthropy and the Gospel of Child Development," *History of Education Quarterly* 21 (Fall 1981): 275–99. For a more general and inclusive account of the relationship between philanthropy and child study, see Richardson, *Century of the Child*.

anthropology, and history. Frank concentrated on the fifteen universities that granted a Ph.D. in the social sciences as well as those outside agencies that had been organized to study scientific problems. Among the universities, the bulk of graduate work was concentrated in five institutions: the University of Chicago, Columbia University, Harvard University, University of Pennsylvania, and University of Wisconsin, Madison. From a content analysis of Ph.D. titles between 1918 and 1922, Frank concluded that "almost all are what may be called works of scholarship, involving library studies and consultations of records and authorities, as contrasted with scientific research involving actual investigation and experiment." Frank concluded that there was hardly any provision for training in scientific methods, the lack of which he attributed to "the dominant tradition of the social sciences and to a lack of adequate funds to support investigations and experiment."[30] Frank recommended that the universities become the instrument for developing the social sciences. He wished to dispel the old scholastic traditions through the instigation of what he called a "new departure." This departure involved two phases: "the training of young men and women who are entering the science, in the habit of mind called scientific method and the accumulation of a body of verified knowledge and of techniques for investigation and experimentation."[31] The growth of science was according to Frank conditioned primarily upon the availability of scientists. In addition to direct support for the universities, Frank also proposed a fellowship system that would provide for scientific training. This type of support Frank believed would produce the opportunity for academics and graduate students to conduct an "experimental study of society."[32]

Ruml's memorandum and Frank's report were the base upon which the LSRM's policy was built. What emerged during 1924 and 1925 was a grand sweeping strategy that was designed to change the direction of the social sciences. The LSRM wished to convert the social sciences into a coordinated set of empirical, realistic, and practical subjects. A central objective of this emerging policy and the program that accompanied it was the creation of a more equal relationship between the social sciences and the natural sciences. While Ruml considered the universities to be the best vehicle for the development of scientific work, it was also clear to him that an organization like the NRC would be necessary in order to coordinate work in the social sciences.[33] Considering this predisposition and the overlap between Merriam and Ruml

---

30. Frank, "The Status of the Social Sciences in the United States," 1923, pp. 4–6, Folder 679, Social Science—Pamphlet and Report, LSRM, Series 3, 63, RAC.

31. Ibid., pp. 17–18.

32. Ibid., p. 26.

33. Memorandum, Ruml to Fosdick, July 16, 1923, Folder 39, Beardsley Ruml, 1922–23, RF, 910, Record Group 3, 3, RAC.

one would have expected the latter to jump at the opportunity to create the SSRC. Instead, the early contacts were cautious and to some extent confusing. The first formal contact concerning the Council came in June 1923 when Merriam outlined the creation of the SRC in a letter to Ruml.[34] It is not clear whether or not the prospect of such a council had been discussed with Ruml,[35] and at this stage, Ruml did not favor Merriam's group. Instead, Ruml saw the ACLS as the best prospect for a parallel organization to the NRC.[36]

By November 1923 the situation had changed. Merriam had obtained a guarantee that the LSRM would support a viable research organization, and Ruml indicated that the migration study would receive support.[37] Before the November meeting Merriam gave Ruml the opportunity to pass on any suggestions he thought fit.[38] This writer infers that it was Ruml who suggested the new "scientific" name for the Council and that he gave his nod of approval to the proposed merger between the SSRC and the NRC. This was in spite of the fact that there were indications that the directors of the NRC were against the merger.[39]

---

34. Merriam to Ruml, June 5, 1923, Folder 682, SSRC, 1923–24, LSRM, Series 3, 64, RAC.

35. There is confusion. In July 1923 Ruml stated that he had "not talked personally with any of the people who propose the formation of this council." See memorandum, Ruml to Fosdick, July 16, 1923, Folder 39, Beardsley Ruml, 1922–33, RF, 910, 3, 3, RAC. Yet Wirth is clear that informal discussions had been going on between representatives of foundations and the original organizers as early as the first meeting in February 1923. Wirth, "Report," p. 11, SSRCA. This is confirmed indirectly by the discussion at this meeting of the inquiry from Mary van Kleeck of the Russell Sage Foundation with regard to cooperation on the study of human migration with the NRC. SSRC, *Decennial Report*, p. 3. Rockefeller philanthropy was involved in this project. Furthermore, it was common practice for foundation personnel to share information. According to Bulmer, Ruml knew Merriam well. See Bulmer, *Chicago School of Sociology*, p. 138. While it is certain that Ruml would have come into contact with Merriam while he was a student at Chicago, I can find no evidence to suggest that they knew each other well during these early years.

36. Memorandum, Ruml to Fosdick, July 16, 1923, Folder 39, Beardsley Ruml, 1922–33, RF, 910, 3, 3, RAC. For an account of the details of the relationship between the foundations and the various councils and societies, see Kiger, "Foundation Support of Educational Innovation"; and Joseph C. Kiger, *American Learned Societies* (Washington, D.C.: Public Affairs Press, 1963).

37. "Work of the National Bureau of Economic Research, Inc., 1922–23: A Statement for Dr. Pritchett, May 13, 1923," p. 6, File, NBER, 1920–24, CC. Also Wirth, "Report," p. 12, SSRCA. The records of the CC are housed in the New York office.

38. Merriam to Ruml, November 1, 1923, Folder 682, SSRC, 1923–24, LSRM, Series 3, 64, RAC. Wesley C. Mitchell is mentioned in this letter. As the director of research for the NBER from 1920 to 1945 he was an important conduit for information. The CC and the LSRM were already funding the bureau's business cycle research. Ruml already knew Mitchell, who was at this stage the leading "scientific" economist of his generation.

39. Merriam to Ruml, November 1, 1923, Folder 682, SSRC, 1923–24, LSRM, Series 3, 64, RAC, 21.

Human Migration Research and the Drive
toward Integration

There was no doubt in Merriam's mind about Ruml's importance. Merriam had already begun to routinely send Ruml copies of minutes plus his own impressions of Council meetings. The November SSRC meeting ended with the agreement that Merriam should consult with Ruml, Wesley C. Mitchell, the director of research of the NBER, and Mary Van Kleeck of the Russell Sage Foundation concerning the creation of a joint NRC/SSRC research committee on human migration.[40] Mitchell was an important figure in any such negotiation because in addition to his membership in the SSRC and his personal relationship with Ruml, he was also running the one NRC research project that dealt with the socioeconomic side of migration.[41] Yerkes had asked the NBER to cooperate in the spring of 1923. Subsequently, the LSRM provided funds to the NBER for a study of the relation between business cycles and immigration.[42]

Similarly, Van Kleeck was a key figure in this negotiation since she had taken some responsibility for broadening the work of the NRC's committee to include the social sciences.[43] Yerkes's initial intention was to establish a major research program on race within the NRC division of anthropology and psychology that would take as its starting point the work done by scientists on eugenics and heredity. The creation of the NRC Committee on Scientific Problems of Human Migration flowed naturally from the conferences in 1920 and 1921 on biological research that had been sponsored by the Carnegie Institution. John C. Merriam, a supporter of eugenics, was responsible for these conferences. In an attempt to anticipate changes in immigration policy in the United States, Yerkes and his committee argued that policymakers

40. Merriam to Ruml, November 16, 1923, p. 2, Folder 682, SSRC, 1923–24, LSRM, Series 3, 64, RAC.

41. For a biographical account of Mitchell's academic life see Arthur F. Burns, *Wesley Mitchell and the National Bureau*, Twenty-ninth Annual Report of the NBER (New York: NBER, 1949), pp. 2–55. Also see Wesley C. Mitchell, *The Backward Art of Spending Money and Other Essays* (New York: Augustus M. Kelley, 1950); and Lucy Sprague Mitchell, *Two Lives: The Story of Wesley Clair Mitchell and Myself* (New York: Simon and Schuster, 1953).

42. See "Work of the National Bureau of Economic Research, Inc., 1922–23: A Statement for Dr. Pritchett, May 13, 1923," File, NBER, 1920–24, CC. It should be noted that on Fosdick's advice JDR, Jr., granted a total of $4,000 to the NBER in 1921 and 1922. Fosdick in turn acted on behalf of JDR, Jr., and sent a note to Ruml saying that the bureau should be on his list of priorities. See memorandum, Fosdick to JDR, Jr., June 29, 1921, File 95, NBER, Box 18, JDR, Jr., Economic Reform Interest, RFA. Also Fosdick to Ruml, note attached to "Memorandum to Mr. Fosdick: National Bureau of Economic Research," October 20, 1922, Ruml to Fosdick, Folder 538, Economic Foundation, 1922–24, LSRM, Series 3, 71, RAC. The RFA was located in the Rockefeller Center, New York. These papers are now housed at the RAC.

43. For an account of Van Kleeck's career, see Alchon, *Invisible Hand*.

needed scientific information on ethnic and racial groups and proposed to focus on immigration into the United States and the movement of southern blacks to northern cities.[44]

In the fall of 1922, Yerkes obtained a grant from the Russell Sage Foundation of $5,000 to bring academics together in order to prepare a larger proposal.[45] While this group consisted primarily of biologists, psychologists, and anthropologists, all of whom shared a eugenicist/hereditarian perspective, Yerkes also invited Van Kleeck and the anthropologist Clark Wissler to participate. Neither Van Kleeck nor Wissler agreed with the eugenicist views expressed by colleagues, and both wanted the committee to go beyond a purely biological research program to include social and economic interests. It was Van Kleeck who suggested that the NRC should cooperate with the social scientists that were attempting to organize their own council. As already noted, Charles E. Merriam raised the issue at the preliminary meeting of the Council in February 1923. Van Kleeck's request for cooperation was discussed and this initiative led the SSRC to appoint its own Committee on Scientific Aspects of Human Migration with Yerkes as a member.[46]

Finally, it was Ruml, as director of the LSRM, who held the most accommodating purse strings. During his time at the CC, Ruml would almost certainly have been in personal contact with all the major figures of the NRC's migration committee. In 1919 the CC provided the NRC with a $5 million endowment and continued, thereafter, to be that institution's major supporter.[47] Further, Ruml had shown good faith and interest in the project when the LSRM agreed to fund the NBER, and he had pretty well assured Merriam that the LSRM would stand behind the Council's efforts in the area of human migration.

Ruml and Merriam were pushed into closer contact during the latter half of 1923. The LSRM provided its first University of Chicago social science

44. See Hamilton C. Cravens, *The Triumph of Evolution: American Scientists and the Hereditary-Environment Controversy, 1900–1940* (Philadelphia: University of Pennsylvania Press, 1978), pp. 181–84; and Robert M. Yerkes, "The Work of [the] Committee on Scientific Problems of Human Migration, National Research Council," *Journal of Personnel Research* 3 (1924–25): 189–96.

45. "Report of NRC—1922–23," p. 8, File, National Academy of Sciences—NRC, 1922–27, CC.

46. Ibid.; Cravens, *Triumph of Evolution*; and the SSRC report, Committee on Scientific Problems of Human Migration, December 18, 1926, Folder 712, SSRC—Human Migration, 1928–30, LSRM, Series 3, 68, RAC.

47. During the interwar years the CC and the various Rockefeller boards were the major sources of support for the NRC. See Kohler, "Science, Foundations, and American Universities." Kohler estimated that the CC and the Rockefeller foundations transferred nearly $12 million to the NRC between 1916 and 1940. P. 143. See also Kiger, "Foundation Support of Educational Innovation."

grant in 1923.[48] While Merriam was the chief negotiator at this stage, the foundation contact was Raymond B. Fosdick. Fosdick had been appointed a trustee of the LSRM in 1921 and was the lawyer and most trusted advisor of John D. Rockefeller, Jr. Throughout the interwar years Fosdick acted as a link between the Rockefeller family and its philanthropies.[49] Only as Ruml and Merriam began to work on the SSRC and Chicago proposals did they cement their academic and personal relationship. In essence, the two councils, that is, the SSRC at the national level and the Local Community Research Committee at the University of Chicago, emerged simultaneously. The creation of the committee at Chicago was the first step for the LSRM in the development of its policy to establish "centers of excellence" in the social sciences within North America and throughout the world.[50] The stamp of Chicago on the national Council remained strong throughout the interwar years. This was achieved because of the influence of men like Merriam, William Fielding Ogburn, the leading quantitative sociologist who moved from Columbia University to the University of Chicago in 1927, and Ruml, who became the dean of social science at Chicago in 1930. The reciprocal impact of the SSRC on Chicago also accounts to some degree for the dominant position in the social sciences that the university held nationally during the interwar years. This dominance was particularly pronounced in the two Chicago schools of sociology and political science.

The principle of breaking down the barriers between the social disciplines had become basic LSRM policy by 1924.[51] This orientation was shared by many leading social scientists in the early 1920s. Merriam was the chief advocate for greater coordination and interrelation among disciplines, which in turn meant greater collaboration and cooperation among research workers. He singled out the disciplines of statistics and psychology as the most fertile ground for interdisciplinary efforts with political science but was, more than any other social scientist of his time, committed to breaking down the boundaries between all the sciences. While Merriam took the lead, other social

---

48. See Donald Slesinger, "Report Development of Social Science Research," March 23, 1934, Folder 355, 216S, University of Chicago—Social Science Report, 1940, RF, 1.1, 200S, 26, RAC. Also Martin Bulmer, "The Early Institutional Establishment of Social Science Research: The Local Community Research Committee at the University of Chicago, 1923–1930," *Minerva* 18 (1980): 51–110; Bulmer, "The Local Community Research Committee, 1923–1930" in *Chicago School of Sociology*; and Dennis Smith, *The Chicago School: A Liberal Critique of Capitalism* (New York: St. Martin's Press, 1988).

49. For Fosdick's own account of his relationship with JDR, Jr., see Raymond B. Fosdick, *Chronicle of a Generation: An Autobiography* (New York: Harper and Bros., 1958), pp. 214–17.

50. For a detailed account of the development of this policy, see Fisher, "Role of Philanthropic Foundations."

51. "Meeting, 26 February 1924," p. 18, Folder 6, Dockets January–February 1924, LSRM, Series 1, 1, RAC.

scientists like Mitchell (economics), Ogburn (economics and sociology), Robert E. Park and Ernest W. Burgess (sociology), and Harry Elmer Barnes (history) did share this perspective. Under the heading "Correlating the Existing Work in the Social Sciences" Ruml noted that the SSRC "may be the opportunity of such a correlating effort" along the lines of the NRC.[52] Specifically, the organization seemed ideally suited for the pursuit of both the larger objectives of the LSRM as well as a means for supporting the interests of the ruling class. Just as the LSRM's funding of eugenic research under the NRC's committee emerged from the desire to have an impact on immigration policy,[53] so there was equal interest in getting data on the broad social impact of these changes. Scientific testing had already been used to support passage of the immigration control acts of 1917 and 1921.

Because of the cooperation that was required between the SSRC and the NRC during the negotiations surrounding the migration project, it turned out that this case was instrumental in defining the scope and limit of the Council's operation. As important, the career of this negotiation served a consolidating function with respect to the relation between the Council and Rockefeller philanthropy. The negotiation set a precedent for the subsequent form and practice of this relation. With Mitchell's help, Ruml orchestrated the preparation of a proposal for which he had already guaranteed funds. This process was facilitated by the decision taken by the SSRC to authorize a responsible officer of the Council to negotiate financial support for activities that the Council had agreed to undertake. In practice, this meant that Ruml and Merriam could "responsibly" work out all the arrangements.

The proposal requested the LSRM to finance a study of the mechanization of industry to be conducted by the NBER under Mitchell's direction. Specifically, Professor Harry Jerome of the University of Wisconsin planned to ascertain the extent to which substitutes might be introduced for immigrant labor. The research was to be supervised by the SSRC's Committee on Scientific Aspects of Human Migration. While Yerkes and Merriam had favored a cooperative joint committee between the NRC and the SSRC, there was opposition to this from within the two councils. After discussions with members of the social science committee, Yerkes came to the conclusion that the cultural and the scientific aspects of migration should be dealt with separately. Park had insisted that immigrants should be regarded as members of subcultures not as biological individuals, while Ogburn wanted nothing less than a

---

52. Docket, "Correlating the Existing Work in the Social Sciences," May 26, 1924. Contained in "Memorial Policy in Social Science: Extracts from Various Memoranda and Dockets," p. 12, Folder 677, Social Sciences—Policy, LSRM, Series 3, 63, RAC.

53. See Russel Marks, "Legitimating Industrial Capitalism," in Arnove, *Philanthropy and Cultural Imperialism*, pp. 87–122.

thorough division of labor between the natural and the social scientists.[54] The proposal outlined how the NRC would henceforth limit itself to the psychological and anthropological aspects of migration while the SSRC took up the political, social, and economic aspects.[55] This division of labor is particularly interesting given the fact that during the next twelve months both the psychologists and the anthropologists would become members of the SSRC. The LSRM duly appropriated $18,000 to the SSRC of which $2,500 was for conference and committee expenses. The SSRC committee was appointed in May 1924 with three representatives from the NRC.[56] The LSRM extended its separate funding of the committee in 1925–26 to continue the mechanization study and for a statistical study of the "great immigrations" between 1820 and 1920. The latter study was conducted under the auspices of the NBER with Professor W. F. Willcox as the investigator. This study was published with the help of an LSRM grant.[57] While the Committee on Scientific Aspects of Human Migration ceased to exist after 1927, interest in this research area continued under the headings "pioneer belts" and "population."[58]

The whole idea of merging the SSRC and the NRC faltered and eventually failed with the migration committee.[59] A final effort by Ruml early in 1925 to get the two councils to cooperate in the selection of strategic research problems and research institutions seems to have come to nothing.[60] The full

54. Merriam to Ruml, November 16, 1923, pp. 4–5, Folder 682, SSRC, 1923–24, LSRM, Series 3, 64, RAC. Detailed accounts of the early projects undertaken are contained in two documents: (1) "National Social Science Research Council—Meeting, November 28, 1924"; and (2) "National Social Science Research Council—Committee on Scientific Aspects of Human Migration," June 1925, Folder 710, SSRC—Human Migration, 1924–25, LSRM, Series 3, 68, RAC. See also, Cravens, *Triumph of Evolution*, p. 181.

55. Letter/proposal, Merriam to Ruml, April 10, 1924, Folder 710, SSRC—Human Migration, 1924–25, LSRM, Series 3, 68, RAC. Also docket, May 1, 1924, Migration Research, p. 8, Dockets, May—June 1924, LSRM, Series 1, 1, RAC.

56. "Minutes of the Meeting of the SSRC, May 17, 1924," p. 2, Folder 682, SSRC, 1923–24, LSRM, Series 3, 63, RAC.

57. The LSRM provided a grant of $10,000 to the NBER to publish this study. See Folder 607, NBER—Publications Fund, 1926, LSRM, Series 3, 56, RAC. Detailed accounts of the projects referred to here are contained in "Confidential Report to Colonel Woods on Activities of Seven Organizations Assisted by the Laura Spelman Rockefeller Memorial," Folder 678, Social Science—Pamphlet and Report, LSRM, Series 3, 63, RAC. See W. F. Willcox, ed., *International Migrations*, Committee on Scientific Aspects of Human Migration (New York: NBER, 1929–31); and Harry Jerome, *Migration and Business Cycles* (New York: NBER, 1926).

58. SSRC, *Decennial Report*, pp. 60–61.

59. It is not clear the extent to which Ruml supported the proposal for the SSRC to join the NRC. The emphasis on science in the LSRM's developing policy would lead one to assume that he would favor the proposal. Yet there is no evidence to confirm that he actively put pressure on the NRC to agree.

60. Ruml to John C. Merriam, January 16, 1925, Folder 618, NRC, 1924–26, LSRM, Series 3, 64, RAC, 37.

NRC committee continued to meet during the fall of 1924 and into the summer of 1925, but the two groups of scientists grew further and further apart. Van Kleeck and Mitchell were angered by what they perceived as the unilateral action of the natural scientists on the committee when plans were drawn up for studies on Negro intelligence and racial blood groups with regard to immigration. In May 1925, Van Kleeck obtained an agreement from the committee that henceforth all the social scientific work would be handed over to the SSRC. This decision marked the separation between the natural and the social sciences. The social scientists, and particularly the sociologists, were searching for their own language of justification, their own domain concepts. As Hamilton C. Cravens concluded, the dual processes of professionalization and specialization set the stage for sociologists to establish their autonomy by breaking from the evolutionary models favored by biologists and some psychologists and anthropologists.[61]

An important part of the boundary work in these early years concerned the relationship between the natural and the social sciences. The negotiation on migration studies served as a means for demarcating more clearly the boundary between these two discipline groups. The line was drawn within the disciplines of anthropology and psychology, where the potential for institutional overlap and integration was greatest. While the Merriam brothers still pushed for integration and saw no theoretical or political problems, others were more concerned about establishing independence. These men and women were convinced the social sciences could not achieve independence if tarred by the eugenicist/hereditarian brush. Like the physical sciences, the route toward cognitive authority and legitimation for the social sciences meant the adoption of objective theory and methods. The social scientists wanted to capture their own "scientific" ground and not be dependent on the natural scientists. This meant that the current definition of science had to be expanded to include the social. Even though these social scientists accepted that their subject matter was different from that of the natural sciences they simply saw that difference as a challenge rather than an obstacle. For men like Charles E. Merriam, Mitchell, and Ogburn, the challenge was to utilize statistics and quantitative methods in order to develop a science of society.[62] The contradiction between wanting to be different from and the same as the natural sciences

61. This is the argument made by Hamilton C. Cravens, "The Abandonment of Evolutionary Social Theory in America: The Impact of Academic Professionalization upon American Sociological Theory, 1890–1920," *American Studies* 12, no. 2 (1971): 5–20.

62. See Merriam, "Present State of the Study of Politics"; Merriam, *New Aspects of Politics;* William Fielding Ogburn, *Social Change with Respect to Culture and Original Nature* (New York: B. W. Heubsch, 1922); and Mitchell, "Quantitative Analysis in Economic Theory," presidential address delivered to the American Economic Association, 1924, reprinted in *Backward Art of Spending Money.*

would later come back to haunt the social scientists as they battled for recognition from the State. Within the larger contradiction there was internal tension within the SSRC as different and competing definitions of science came to the fore. Four divisions were already beginning to emerge: sociology, political science and economics, anthropology and psychology, and history. As quickly as social scientists tried to establish the boundary around the social science field so the conflict between discipline discourses was exacerbated.

The best indicator of the LSRM's decision to utilize the SSRC came just after incorporation with the appropriation of $425,000 over a period of five years for fellowships. As noted earlier, the commitment to scientific training through research fellowships was a major objective of LSRM policy. The LSRM asked the SSRC to draw up plans similar to those developed by the NRC and the RF in the natural sciences.[63] In response to this request, the SSRC appointed a committee to outline a fellowship plan.[64] One member of this committee, Arnold B. Hall, president of the University of Oregon and a Council member representing the APSA, consulted with the NRC and gained that organization's support.[65] Like Merriam, Hall was determined to convert the study of politics into a science. He was spokesman for the series of National Conferences on the Science of Politics (1923–25), whose central purpose was "to investigate the possibility of developing and employing more scientific methods for testing the theories and hypotheses of current political science."[66] Merriam was responsible for getting these conferences off the ground.

The Fellowship Committee recommended a system of postdoctoral fellowships to counteract the almost total lack of financial support available for research in the social sciences and hence the difficulties encountered by young instructors in attempting to carry out research. As the committee noted, "The development of an adequate scientific method and the recruiting and training

---

63. "Minutes of the Meeting of the SSRC, May 17, 1924," Folder 682, SSRC, 1923–24, LSRM, Series 3, 64, RAC, 37. Memorandum, SSRC Fellowships, 1924–25, Folder 706, LSRM, Series 3, 67, RAC. See Stanley Coben, "Foundation Officials and Fellowships: Innovation in the Patronage of Science," *Minerva* 14 (1976): 225–40; and Stanley Coben, "American Foundations as Patrons of Science: The Commitment to Individual Research," in Nathan Reingold, ed., *The Sciences in the American Context: New Perspectives* (Washington, D.C.: Smithsonian Institution Press, 1979), pp. 229–48.

64. "Minutes of the Meeting of the SSRC, May 17, 1924," Folder 682, SSRC, 1923–24, LSRM, Series 3, 64, RAC. Also, letter, Merriam to Ruml, October 24, 1924, SSRC—Fellowships, 1924–25, LSRM, Series 3, 67, RAC, 39.

65. Merriam to Ruml, October 15, 1924, Folder 706, SSRC—Fellowships, 1924–25, LSRM, Series 3, 67, RAC. Also Merriam to Ruml, October 24, 1924, Folder 706, SSRC—Fellowships, 1924–25, LSRM, Series 3, 64, RAC.

66. *American Political Science Review* 17 (1923): 463–64, quoted by Somit and Tannenhaus, *Development of American Political Science*, p. 123.

of an increasing number of competent research men are the two indispensable elements in the progress of social science." To support these fellowships Merriam requested $250,000 over five years.[67] Ruml was pleased with the proposal but took exception to the idea of discipline quotas. Ruml informed Merriam that he wanted merit to be the decision criterion regardless of discipline.[68] This directive and other suggestions concerning the bylaws that were to govern the fellowships were duly followed by the Council.[69] Early in 1925, Mitchell was made chairman of the Fellowship Committee with Chapin as secretary and Merriam as the third member. The provision of postdoctoral fellowships continued as a central activity of the SSRC for the rest of the interwar period (see table 1, app. 2).[70]

Three interdependent factors combined to create the SSRC.[71] First was the lag that existed between the development of the natural sciences and the social sciences. The concern of social scientists and foundation personnel was to narrow the gap that modern science had created between material development on the one hand and agencies of social control on the other. The theoretical basis for this lag had been discussed by Ogburn in his major book, *Social Change with Respect to Culture and Original Nature* (1922).[72] Ogburn attempted to explain the patterns of social change and social control in society by focusing on the imbalance between the technological and economic sectors and the normative and cultural sectors. Second was the desire among social scientists and foundation officers to break down the barriers between social disciplines in order to make them both more scientific and more realistic. The precedents set by the organization of the NRC for the natural sciences and the ACLS for the humanities clearly provided an impetus. Third was the intrusion of Rockefeller philanthropy into the social sciences. Social scientists became aware of Rockefeller interest and realized the potential of pursuing these

---

67. Merriam to Ruml, October 24, 1924, Folder 706, SSRC—Fellowships, 1924–25, LSRM, Series 3, 64, RAC.

68. Ruml to Merriam, October 27, 1924, Folder 706, SSRC—Fellowships, 1924–25, LSRM, Series 3, 64, RAC.

69. "Confidential Report to Colonel Woods on Activities of Seven Organizations Assisted by the Laura Spelman Rockefeller Memorial," Folder 678, Social Science—Pamplet and Report, LSRM, Series 3, 63, RAC. Also letter, Hall to Ruml, December 11, 1924, Folder 682, SSRC, 1923–24, LSRM, Series 3, 64, RAC.

70. All future references to finance can be checked by referring to table 1, app. 2.

71. Merriam, transcript, pp. 3–6, "Report of Joint Conference of the Committee on Problems and Policy of the Social Science Research Council Meeting with Other Representatives of the Social Sciences in Attendance upon the Dartmouth Conference of Social Scientists and Allied Groups," August 31 to September 3, 1925 (henceforth Hanover Report, 1925), Folder 569, Hanover Conference Joint Committee Report, 1925, LSRM, Series 3, 53, RAC. Also Wirth, "Report," p. 15, SSRCA.

72. Ogburn, *Social Change*.

funds. Here again the relationship between the CC and the NRC served as a model. Rockefeller philanthropy wanted to create the SSRC to fulfill some of its own policy objectives as well as have the Council act as a front organization. Behind the general policy objectives of integration and scientization was the desire on the part of foundation officials to separate their organization from the controversy that surrounded the social sciences. The SSRC could serve this function by running programs for the LSRM and by acting as an advisor and arbiter among all the research proposals that were flooding in.

By the time of incorporation the SSRC's policies were indistinguishable from those of the LSRM. Agreement at the levels of general policy reflected and were part of the long-term structural trends of professionalization and scientization. Specialization was suppressed at this stage in favor of integration. At the personal level, Ruml and Merriam developed strong bonds of friendship and trust. The Council leadership and Rockefeller trustees and officials had created a viable social science network.

Public Controversy and Rockefeller Philanthropy: The Need for Control

The new Council entered 1925 with an array of ongoing activities. In addition to the committees on migration, abstracts, indexing state laws, and scientific methods,[73] the Council had approved a "Committee on International News and Communication" with Walter S. Rogers as chairman (see table 2, app. 2).[74] As it turned out, the activities of this latter committee became a critical precipitating factor in the creation of the most significant organizational unit of the Council, namely, the Problems and Policy Committee (PPC). The Council received its first grant for the topic of international news. After some discussion with two sociologists, Professors Jerome Davis of Dartmouth College and H. A. Miller of Oberlin College, Ruml decided that the best procedure was to route the plan through the newly formed SRC.[75] The ASS duly submitted a project entitled "A Survey of Foreign News Sources and Distribution" to the SRC, and the fledgling Council agreed to sponsor the project.[76] The LSRM appropriated $2,500, and a conference on international

---

73. SSRC, *Decennial Report*, p. 67.

74. All future references to SSRC committees can be checked using table 2. For purposes of continuity the history and development of each committee will be completed in that section of the manuscript that covers the time when the committee was created.

75. Memorandum, Ruml (circulated within Rockefeller group), September 17, 1924, attached to letter, Ivy L. Lee (personal adviser to JDR, Jr.) to Ruml, October 1, 1924, Folder 713, SSRC—International News, 1924–28, LSRM, Series 3, 68, RAC.

76. Wirth, "Report," p. 12, SSRCA.

communication was held in Washington to plan the larger study.[77] What began as a promising project quickly became an embarrassing obstacle. The September 6 issue of the *Editor and Publisher* contained an article by Dr. William T. Ellis, which was introduced by a heading on the front page, "Rockefeller Fortune Backs Investigation of Newspapers."[78] While Ruml insisted that the family was in the clear, the damage had been done and this publicity marked the end of this committee's work. Rogers created the independent Institute of Foreign Affairs, while internally the SSRC created the Advisory Committee on International Relations (1926–30) under the rubric of the PPC.

The Rockefeller family was particularly sensitive to public attack since the MacKenzie King affair in 1914. The Rockefeller family had been accused of using RF funds to further its business interests. The accusation centered on the funding by the RF of a research project to study industrial relations with W. L. Mackenzie King as director. The uproar and the subsequent investigation by the United States Commission on Industrial Relations arose because the country had just experienced perhaps the most savage strike in the history of industrial relations. The strike of the Colorado mine workers was against a number of firms but included as one of the largest the Colorado Fuel and Iron Company, in which the Rockefeller family held shares. The strike had ended with the tragedy of the "Ludlow Massacre," where many strikers were either killed or wounded.[79] If controversy was to be avoided, then it was essential that Rockefeller interest in, and utilization of the SSRC, be kept secret. Yet while anonymity was important so was control. In order to achieve these dual objectives a new structure was needed that as Louis Wirth noted would preserve the "forms of democracy without some of its substance."[80] At Ruml's suggestion the PPC was created during the spring of 1925.[81] The projects committee was abandoned. The LSRM had by this stage guaranteed administrative expenses for five years and had provided a grant to bring the PPC together for its first meeting at Dartmouth College that summer. As

---

77. SSRC, *Decennial Report*, pp. 47–48. Also "Confidential Report to Colonel Woods on Activities of Seven Organizations Assisted by the Laura Spelman Rockefeller Memorial," Folder 678, Social Science—Pamphlet and Report, LSRM, Series 3, 63, RAC.

78. Memorandum, Ruml (circulated within Rockefeller group) September 17, 1924, attached to letter, Lee to Ruml, October 1, 1924, Folder 713, SSRC—International News, 1924–28, LSRM, Series 3, 68, RAC.

79. Fisher, "Role of Philanthropic Foundations," pp. 208–9. For more detail refer to Silva and Slaughter, *Serving Power*.

80. Louis Wirth, draft, "Report on the History, Activities, and Policies of the Social Science Research Council" (henceforth Draft Report), p. 44, Folder 1, Box 32, Papers of Louis Wirth (henceforth Wirth), University of Chicago, Chicago.

81. Merriam to Ruml, October 27, 1925, referred to in "Confidential Report to Colonel Woods on Activities of Seven Organizations Assisted by the Laura Spelman Rockefeller Memorial," p. 69, Folder 678, Social Science—Pamphlet and Report, LSRM, Series 3, 63, RAC.

Wirth put it in his 1937 report, the PPC was "in part a response to the dependence of the Council upon support from foundations." Further, it was felt that "the foundations would not be disposed to turn over to a loose body composed of shifting representatives of different societies over the selection of which the foundations had no control, the large sums of money that they were prepared to give."[82] The twenty-one-member Council was effectively bypassed, and the six-member PPC became the "selected, responsible and more continuous nucleus of the Council."[83] In line with its own practices, the LSRM had created a self-perpetuating elite to run the affairs of the SSRC.

The LSRM organized and paid for two overlapping conferences at Hanover, New Hampshire, in the summer of 1925. The first conference brought psychologists together, and the second conference was called specifically to organize the PPC. For Ruml, this was essentially a joint conference that would, as he put it, create "a vision from which new ideas may emerge."[84] That Ruml chose the psychologists to provide a lead reflected his own training in that discipline and his belief that progress in behavioral studies might provide the key for a scientific breakthrough in the social sciences.[85] As noted earlier, Merriam was particularly interested in exploring the potential of psychology for improving scientific methodology.[86] Even though the PPC met separately, it is the case that these men along with other social science colleagues did join the psychologists for general discussions on the future of the social sciences. It was probably still the case that Ruml hoped to use this conference format as a means for building bridges between the NRC and the SSRC.[87]

PPC

While the Hanover Conference was called to organize the PPC, it also provided the first opportunity for a full consideration of the Council's program. Merriam had no doubts about the vital importance of the PPC. He explained

---

82. Wirth, Draft Report, p. 44, Folder 1, Box 32, Wirth, University of Chicago.

83. Ibid.

84. Transcript, report, "Conference of Psychologists Called by the Laura Spelman Rockefeller Memorial," p. 4, Folder 572a, Hanover Conference—Psychologists, 1925, LSRM, Series 3, 53a, RAC.

85. Docket, Psychological Conference, March 11, 1925, Folder 572a, Hanover Conference—Psychologists, 1925, LSRM, Series 3, 53a, RAC.

86. In their history of political science, Somit and Tannenhaus concluded that Merriam was responsible for turning the discipline toward behavioristic studies and toward behaviorism generally. Somit and Tanenhaus, *Development of American Political Science*, p. 113.

87. Ruml to Merriam, January 16, 1925, Folder 618, NRC, 1924–26, LSRM, Series 3, 57, RAC.

to Howard Washington Odum that the summer meeting would not only receive suggestions from the Council but would also "consider broadly the future scope and method of the Council itself."[88] Odum, a leading sociologist, was asked to prepare an agenda and was appointed acting chairman. Odum, who had been a student of Giddings at Columbia University, graduating with a Ph.D. in 1910, was a predictable choice for the job. From Columbia he took a strong commitment to statistically based empirical research. Following his appointment as director of the School of Social Welfare, and then as head of sociology at the University of North Carolina in 1920, Odum proceeded to make that university the social science center for the south. As part of this effort Odum was instrumental in the creation of the journal *Social Forces* in 1922. Odum was one of the most active proponents of cooperative social science research in the country and he had obtained a grant from the LSRM to establish the interdisciplinary Institute for Research in Social Science at North Carolina.[89] For the rest of the interwar period Rockefeller philanthropy regarded the University of North Carolina at Chapel Hill as its social science center of excellence for the Southeast.

The outcome of the conference was summarized in a report of the PPC produced at Merriam's request by Odum, Hall, and Edwin F. Gay.[90] Gay had been involved in one of the earliest attempts by the Rockefeller family to get involved in the social sciences with the prewar plan to create an Institute of Economic Research.[91] He had gone on to help found the NBER in 1919, and after a detour into journalism Gay had returned to his professorship in economic history at Harvard in the fall of 1924. In addition to his university responsibilities Gay had also agreed to codirect with Mitchell the research activities of the NBER.[92] It is significant that neither Odum nor Gay was a Council member at this time. They along with three other non–Council members, namely, John J. Coss, professor of philosophy at Columbia University, Harold G. Moulton, director of the Institute of Economics, Washington, D.C. (first president of the Brookings Institution, 1927),[93] and Edward L. Thorndyke, professor of psychology at Columbia, had been invited by Merriam and Ruml to take part in the PPC deliberations.

88. Merriam to Odum, June 16, 1925, Box 4, April 1925–January 1926, HOP. The Odum Papers are housed in the Southern Historical Collection, University of North Carolina, Chapel Hill.

89. See Guy Benton Johnson and Guion Griffis Johnson, *Research in Service to Society: The First Fifty Years of the Institute for Research in Social Science at the University of North Carolina* (Chapel Hill: University of North Carolina Press, 1980); and Wayne Brazil, "Howard Odum: The Building Years, 1884–1930" (Ph.D. diss., Harvard University, 1975).

90. Hanover Report, 1925, p. 131, Folder 569, Hanover Conference Joint Committee Report, 1925, LSRM, Series 3, 53, RAC.

91. See Fisher, "Philanthropic Foundations and the Social Sciences."

92. See Heaton, *Scholar in Action*.

93. For a detailed account of Moulton's career, see Critchlow, "Harold G. Moulton: Effi-

The report outlined the structure and operating practice of the PPC and in effect set the guidelines for the future operation of the Council. From the first meeting it was apparent that this committee would take up a position of leadership in all the Council's activities.[94] It was decided that the PPC should in addition to considering general Council policy, make decisions in three areas: (1) administration and finance, (2) reports on the specific problems and projects referred to it, and (3) new lines of research. To further these aims the committee recommended the Council first canvas its members and constituent societies on research interests and, second, take as one of its first tasks the securing of funds. Significantly, it was decided that members of the PPC should be chosen by the president of the SSRC (later the Executive Committee) on the basis of research ability and experience and should not be limited to members of the Council.[95] This meant that the constituent associations had been rendered powerless and the Council was that much more open to external manipulation.

At Merriam's urging the Council adopted the policy of favoring research into major social problems that involved more than one discipline.[96] It was agreed that ordinarily the Council would not undertake investigations directly and should serve only as a research clearinghouse in the social science field.[97] It became then a major function of the PPC not just to evaluate projects presented to it but also to devise and recommend research problems. To accomplish this the PPC was given power to appoint special advisory committees "to consider the formulation of a problem, to analyze the problem into parts susceptible of scientific treatment, to study the character and scope of the investigation which seem desirable and to suggest agencies whose cooperation can profitably be enlisted in the work."[98] Specific guidelines for the examination and approval of research projects were posited, including the appropriateness of personnel, research techniques, and the practicality of the problem for scientific investigation. Finally, the PPC recommended that a full-time secretary be appointed who would also serve all the standing committees.

Rockefeller philanthropy had achieved its objective. The membership of

ciency, Economic Expertise, and the Founding of the Brookings Institution," in *Brookings Institution*.

94. Minutes, PPC, August 31, 1925, pt. 1, August 1925–December 1926, SSRCA.

95. Hanover Report, 1925, p. 191, Folder 569, Hanover Conference Joint Committee Report, 1925, LSRM, Series 3, 53, RAC.

96. Minutes, PPC, August 31, 1925, pt. 1, August 1925–December 1926, SSRCA. Merriam's role is best understood by examining his participation in the conference. Hanover Report, 1925, Folder 569, Hanover Conference Joint Committee Report, 1925, LSRM, Series 3, 53, RAC.

97. Hanover Report, 1925, p. 191, Folder 569, Hanover Conference Joint Committee Report, 1925, LSRM, Series 3, 53, RAC.

98. Ibid., pp. 191–92.

the PPC appointed in October was Hall (chairman), Shelby M. Harrison, Wissler, Robert Sessions Woodworth, and two non-Council members, Gay and Moulton.[99] The members were among the leaders in their disciplines in the general movement toward a more scientific approach and were clearly aligned with the LSRM's aims. The credentials of Hall, Gay, and Moulton have already been discussed. Harrison, a Council member representing the ASS, was the director of the Department of Surveys and Exhibits at the Russell Sage Foundation. Wissler, a Council member representing the AAA, was a member of the newly formed Institute of Psychology at Yale. This institute was funded by the LSRM and was seen by Ruml as a step in the direction of interdisciplinary work.[100] Woodworth, a Council member representing the APA, was a professor of psychology at Columbia University. Under the guiding hand of Merriam the committee could be expected to steer the Council in the right direction. The ability to appoint advisory committees provided the ideal mechanism for masking Rockefeller involvement. Not only would the topic and the funding all be under the PPC heading but it could also be made to look as though the idea had come from the social scientists rather than from outside. The first five advisory committees, on the Eighteenth Amendment, the Negro, industrial relations, crime, and agricultural economics, provide excellent illustrations of how the system worked.

Social Problems Research and Social Control

The suggestion that the SSRC should study prohibition came from Colonel Arthur Woods, the ex–police commissioner of New York, who was acting on behalf of John D. Rockefeller, Jr. Woods had close personal and business ties with the Rockefeller family. He was the vice-president of the infamous Colorado Fuel and Iron Company and director of the Bankers Trust Company. Woods was a trustee of the LSRM, the International Education Board (another Rockefeller foundation), and the RF. He became the acting president of the LSRM in 1928 and later the chairman and a trustee of the SF of New York. In this instance, Woods communicated his suggestion to Fosdick, who, in turn, asked Merriam if the SSRC would conduct the study.[101] While Merriam was rather reluctant, he eventually agreed to take the suggestion to the Council.[102]

---

99. Merriam to Ruml, October 21, 1925, Folder 683, SSRC, 1925–26, LSRM, Series 3, 64, RAC.

100. See J. G. Morawski, "Organizing Knowledge and Behaviour at Yale's Institute of Human Relations," *ISIS* 77 (1986): 219–42.

101. Memorandums, Woods to Fosdick, Fosdick to Woods, March 24, 1925, and March 25, 1925, Folder 718, SSRC—Prohibition Survey, 1925–27, LSRM, Series 3, 68, RAC. Also Merriam to Odum, June 9, 1925, Box 4, April 1925–January 1926, HOP, University of North Carolina.

102. Merriam to Odum, June 9, 1925, Box 4, April 1925–January 1926, HOP, University

Indeed, the fact that funds were on the table for this study may well have contributed to the formation of the PPC. Merriam would have had enormous difficulty getting such a controversial request approved by the whole Council, and yet it was essential that the Council show good faith. The LSRM was at this stage providing almost all the Council's money and was the best prospect for future grants.

Merriam brought the proposal to the Hanover meetings and the Special Advisory Committee on Eighteenth Amendment Study (1925–28) was appointed with John L. Gillin as chairman. Gillin was a professor of sociology at the University of Wisconsin, a graduate of Columbia University in 1906, and one of the original SRC members in 1923 representing the ASS. Gillin became the president of the ASS in 1926. John D. Rockefeller, Jr., provided a grant of $16,000 for this work, which resulted in the publication by G. E. G. Catlin of *Sources of Information Concerning the Operation of the Eighteenth Amendment* (1928).[103] Catlin, a political scientist at Cornell University, was a leading proponent of scientism and proclaimed himself a "political experimental scientist." His *Science and Method of Politics* (1927) was the most fully developed argument for the "new science" to appear during the 1920s.[104] Copies of the prohibition publication were made freely available to the public much to the annoyance of some Council members.[105] It was the intention of the family to conduct a much larger study,[106] but this idea was dropped.

Four other advisory committees were approved at Dartmouth College. The intent was to tackle some of the most pressing social problems of the day. As noted earlier, the labels used for these fields of public concern were "Negro," "industrial relations," "crime," and "agricultural economics." Certainly the first three fields can be traced back to the philanthropic interests of the Rockefeller family. The LSRM had incorporated these interests in the social problem policy orientation, which became a program for the promotion of research into four areas of social disturbance: criminology, interracial relations, industrial relations, and international relations.[107]

---

of North Carolina. Also Woods to Whitney H. Shepardson (officer, GEB, another Rockefeller foundation), March 27, 1925, Folder 718, SSRC—Prohibition Survey, 1925–27, LSRM, Series 3, 68, RAC.

103. SSRC, *Decennial Report*, pp. 37–38.

104. G. E. G. Catlin, *The Science and Method of Politics* (New York: Knopf, 1927).

105. See report on SSRC to LSRM, letter, Merriam to Ruml, December 1926, pp. 31–32, Folder 687, Reports, LSRM, Series 3, 64, RAC. For background see letter, Ruml to Woods, September 9, 1926, Folder 718, SSRC—Prohibition Survey, 1925–27, LSRM, Series 3, 68, RAC.

106. Memorandum, Woods to Fosdick, January 26, 1927, Folder 718, SSRC—Prohibition Survey, 1925–27, LSRM, Series 3, 68, RAC.

107. "Appropriations, October 18, 1918, through April 30, 1928: The Laura Spelman Rockefeller Memorial, PRO-5a," Folder 11, 910, Program and Policy—Reports, PRO 5–5a, 1928, RF, 910, 3, 2, RAC. Also "Development of the Social Science Program: Summary

The recommendation that a committee be appointed to study the general problem of crime was presented by Merriam.[108] Merriam was particularly anxious that the decisions concerning alcoholism and crime be given no publicity.[109] The Advisory Committee on Crime (1925–28 and 1929–32) was appointed with Day as chairman. The first three years saw close and continuous contact between the LSRM and the Committee. Lawrence B. Dunham, the LSRM officer (1925–28) with special responsibility for criminology, coordinated the work.[110] He passed on Ruml's research suggestions,[111] attended meetings of the committee, and was to a great extent responsible for organizing the most significant work of the committee on delinquency.[112] This work was conducted by the subcommittee on Personality Traits and Community Factors in Juvenile Delinquency (1926–27) for which the LSRM offered earmarked, conditional funds.[113]

This part of the larger committee's work was very much a Chicago phenomenon. The LSRM was in a particularly powerful position to coordinate the work. They were already providing general funds for the social sciences through the University of Chicago Local Community Research Committee. This fund supported the work of the sociologists Park and Burgess, which later spawned such classic studies as Frederic Thrasher's *The Gang: A Study of 1,313 Gangs in Chicago* and Ernest Mowrer's *Family Disorganization*.[114] It was Burgess, as chairman of the SSRC subcommittee, who was instrumental in the commissioning of the Institute for Juvenile Research to un-

Statement," prepared by Janet M. Paine (RF officer) for Joseph H. Willits (director of DSS, RF), January 30, 1939, Folder 16, 910, Program and Policy—Reports, PRO-25–30, 1938–41, RF, 910, 3, 3, RAC.

108. Hanover Report, 1925, Folder 569, Hanover Conference Joint Committee Report, 1925, LSRM, Series 3, 53, RAC.

109. Merriam to Odum, October 28, 1925, Box 4, April 1925–January 1926, HOP, University of North Carolina.

110. A total of $250,000 was appropriated by the memorial for criminology. The largest appropriation of $117,000 went to the American Law Institute. "Appropriations, October 18, 1918, through April 30, 1928: The Laura Spelman Rockefeller Memorial, PRO-5a," Folder 11, 910, Program and Policy—Reports, PRO-5–5a, 1928, RF, 910, 3, 2, RAC.

111. Dunham to Merriam, December 6, 1926, Folder 705, SSRC—Crime, 1926–28, LSRM, Series 3, 67, RAC.

112. See Dunham to Day, April 19, 1926, Dunham to Gillon (replacement chairperson on committee for Day), December 22, 1926. With regard to the work on delinquency see letter, Dunham to Merriam, March 21, 1927, Folder 705, SSRC—Crime, 1926–28, LSRM, Series 3, 67, RAC.

113. Dunham to Merriam, March 21, 1927, memorandum, Dunham to Ruml, March 28, 1927, Folder 705, SSRC—Crime, 1926–28, LSRM, Series 3, 67, RAC.

114. Frederic Thrasher, *The Gang: A Study of 1,313 Gangs in Chicago* (Chicago: University of Chicago Press, 1927); and Ernest Mowrer, *Family Disorganization* (Chicago: University of Chicago Press, 1927).

dertake some of this work.[115] In order to take up the conditional funds the SSRC decided to contact Dr. Herman Adler, director of the Institute. He controlled the Behavior Research Fund, which was eventually used to match the LSRM funding.[116] In this way the LSRM was able to bring about a closer association between the university and the institute while at the same time putting money on both the sociologists and psychologists in the field of delinquency. Clifford R. Shaw, who as director of the institute from October 1926 was responsible for these studies, had been a research student of Burgess, doing a study of juvenile delinquency in relation to population movements in the city. When the larger advisory committee was reconstituted in 1929 after a gap of a year, E. H. Sutherland, professor of sociology at the University of Minnesota, was made the chairman,[117] and Dunham, now director of the Bureau of Social Hygiene, became a member of the committee. Sutherland had obtained his Ph.D. in sociology from Chicago in 1913 and later joined the department (1930–35). Shaw was responsible for two classic pieces of investigation in the field of delinquency studies, namely, *The Jack-Roller: A Delinquent Boy's Own Story* (1930) and *The Natural History of a Delinquent Career* (1931), as well as the seminal work on the causes of delinquency, *Social Factors in Juvenile Delinquency* (1931), which he coauthored with Henry D. McKay.[118]

The proposal to focus on Negro studies emerged from discussions led by Wissler, Fay Cooper-Cole, and Leonard Outhwaite. Outhwaite was the LSRM officer (1923–28) in charge of anthropology and race relations.[119] Cooper-Cole was a professor of anthropology at the University of Chicago, in the Department of Sociology and Anthropology. He was vice-chairman of the Division of Anthropology and Psychology of the NRC and a Council member representing the AAA. While Gay proposed the motion, it no doubt reflected

---

115. Dunham to Merriam, March 21, 1927, Folder 705, SSRC—Crime, 1926–28, LSRM, Series 3, 67, RAC.

116. See Woodworth (professor of psychology, Columbia University) to Ruml, October 26, 1927, Folder 684, SSRC, 1927, LSRM, Series 3, 64, RAC. Also Day to Woodworth, November 1, 1927, Folder 715, SSRC—Project Budgets, 1926–28, LSRM, Series 3, 68, RAC. For an account of this fund and of Burgess's role as a coordinator of people and resources see Bulmer, *Chicago School of Sociology*, pp. 123–25.

117. Dunham recommended Sutherland. Memorandum, SSRC—Advisory Committee on Criminology, Dunham to Day, November 4, 1927, Folder 705, SSRC—Crime, 1926–28, LSRM, Series 3, 67, RAC.

118. Clifford Shaw, *The Jack-Roller: A Delinquent Boy's Own Story* (Chicago: University of Chicago Press, 1930); Clifford Shaw, *The Natural History of a Delinquent Career* (Chicago: University of Chicago Press, 1931); and Clifford Shaw and Henry D. McKay, *Social Factors in Juvenile Delinquency*, National Commission on Law Observance and Enforcement, Report on the Causes of Crime, vol. 2 (Washington, D.C.: Government Printing Office, 1931).

119. Hanover Report, 1925, Folder 569, Hanover Conference Joint Committee Report, 1925, LSRM, Series 3, 53, RAC.

Odum's own academic and personal interest in this field and fitted into his plans for developing the University of North Carolina at Chapel Hill. The Advisory Committee on Problems Related to the Negro was set up in 1925. A year later the title had been changed to the Advisory Committee on Interracial Relations (1925–30) and W. W. Alexander of Atlanta, Georgia, took over as chairman. Outhwaite fulfilled a coordinating advisory role with respect to the committee on behalf of the LSRM.[120] Among the many research projects funded by this committee were the St. Helena Island studies under Odum's direction, the study of the Negro family conducted by Franklin E. Frazier, and the Survey of Investigation of Problems of the Colored Race in the United States conducted by Charles S. Johnson.[121] The books that emerged from this research like that by Thomas J. Woofter, Jr., *Black Yeomanry: Life on St. Helena Island* (1930) and Frazier's *The Negro Family in Chicago* (1932) and Johnson's *The Negro in American Civilization* (1930) served to define the field of race relations. Another element of the committee's work was the focus on racial differences. This reflected the impact of the psychologists and anthropologists and resulted in the subcommittee on Tests for Race Differences (1928–30) and the Joint Conference on Racial Differences with the Division of Anthropology and Psychology of the NRC in 1928.

The Advisory Committee on Industrial Relations (1926–30) began life as the Committee on Capital and Labor. The focus on the relation between capital and labor was clearly in line with the aims of John D. Rockefeller, Jr., with respect to industrial relations that he had made public at the time of the MacKenzie King affair. Gay wanted to establish some uniform methods for computing international wage statistics and saw the committee as an ideal vehicle. He interested Henry S. Dennison, a Taylorite and leading member of the "business regulation movement," in the committee and Dennison subsequently became chairman and set aside some funds for the work on wage statistics.[122] The new committee undertook two major surveys. The first in 1927 was a survey of industrial research in universities and was conducted under the supervision of Professor J. H. Willits of the Wharton School at the

---

120. Harrison to Ruml, October 7, 1926, with attached minutes of PPC at Hanover in August–September 1926, Folder 690, SSRC—Conference, 1926, LSRM, Series 3, 64, RAC.

121. SSRC, *Decennial Report*, pp. 51–52. Also see Johnson and Johnson, *Research in Service*; and John H. Stanfield, *Philanthropy and Jim Crow in American Social Science* (Westport: Greenwood Press, 1985). The three books cited were Thomas J. Woofter, Jr., *Black Yeomanry: Life on St. Helena Island* (New York: Henry Holt, 1930); Franklin E. Frazier, *The Negro Family in Chicago* (Chicago: University of Chicago Press, 1932); and Charles S. Johnson, *The Negro in American Civilization* (New York: Henry Holt, 1930).

122. See Heaton, *Scholar in Action*, p. 211; and, for an account of Dennison's career, see Alchon, *Invisible Hand*. Dennison along with Mitchell and Day had joined Gay at the Division of Planning and Statistics during the First World War.

University of Pennsylvania. The Wharton School and Willits were predictable choices. John D. Rockefeller, Jr., had been supporting the work of Elton Mayo in the Department of Industrial Research since 1923.[123] The LSRM took over this task in 1925 and then in June 1927 transferred $150,000 to the school for five years.[124] To facilitate the survey the memorial awarded Willits a traveling professorship.

The second survey was a broad study of problems of employer/employee relations most in need of investigation.[125] This fitted in with a suggestion made internally by Day who was now on leave from the University of Michigan and working for the LSRM in charge of social science in the United States.[126] It was envisaged that the LSRM would back a coordinated program of industrial research. The survey conducted by Dr. Herman Feldmen of Dartmouth College was part of this general plan and was completed in 1928. The work of the committee was taken over by the Advisory Committee on Industry and Trade, which was created in 1931 and continued to operate throughout the 1930s.

The Committee on Social and Economic Research in Agriculture was founded in 1925 and continued to operate throughout the interwar period.[127] This committee was suggested by Professor Edwin G. Nourse, director of agricultural economics at the Institute of Economics (later the Brookings Institution). This move reflected the continuing interest by the Department of Agriculture in utilizing social scientific research. The department had in 1921 brought together several research units to create the Bureau of Agricultural Economics.[128] Special reference was made to the Purnell Act

123. The initial contact between Mayo and JDR, Jr., came via Ruml and the LSRM. See letters, Woods to JDR, Jr., January 17, 1923, and letter/report, Willits to Ruml, January 21, 1924 (attached report from Mayo), Folder 790, University of Pennsylvania, 1923–24, LSRM, Series 3, 75, RAC.Also see Loren Baritz, *The Servants of Power: A History of the Use of Social Science in American Industry* (Middleton: Wesleyan University Press, 1960)

124. Memorandum, Ruml to Woods, May 7, 1925, Folder 791, University of Pennsylvania, 1925–29, and letter/resolution, Ruml to J. H. Penniman, June 7, 1927, Folder 792, University of Pennsylvania—Wharton School, 1926–28, LSRM, Series 3, 67, RAC.

125. Herman Feldman to Ruml, April 4, 1928, Folder 685, SSRC, 1928–31, LSRM, Series 3, 64, RAC.

126. Memorandum, Kenneth Chorley (assistant to Ruml, 1923–28) to Day, Industrial Research, February 27, 1928, and Day to Mitchell, March 2, 1928, Folder 685, SSRC, 1928–31, LSRM, Series 3, 64, RAC.

127. While there is no specific mention of agricultural economics in the policy discussions of the LSRM, this subject did fit under Ruml's heading of "real" research. Further, in 1924, the LSRM appropriated $20,000 to the Institute for Research in Land Economics to study tenancy and rural land ownership. See "Appropriations, October 18, 1918, through April 30, 1928: The Laura Spelman Rockefeller Memorial, PRO-5a," Folder 11, 910, Program and Policy—Reports, PRO-5-5a, 1928, RF, 910, 3, 2, RAC, 92.

128. Lyons, *Uneasy Partnership*, pp. 30–33 and 93.

of 1925 under which the department was authorized to make grants to state agricultural experimental stations for research in the economic and sociological aspects of agriculture. The intent of the SSRC committee was to make the research conducted under the Purnell Act more scientific. Under the editorship of John D. Black of Harvard University the committee produced twenty-one Council bulletins between 1930 and 1933.[129] These bulletins provided critical appraisals of the method and scope of research in the field of agricultural economics and made suggestions for improvement. The committee soon added a rural sociologist to its number, and in 1928 Nourse became chairman of a new Committee on Fellowships in Agricultural Economics and Rural Sociology (1928–33). This committee was created to provide advanced training in these two subjects. It was an emergency measure that was prompted by the dearth of competent trained personnel to deal with the socioeconomic crisis that was facing rural America. The LSRM provided a grant of $150,000 to cover these fellowships. Then in 1930 Nourse chaired a subcommittee of the original advisory committee under the title Special Graduate Training in Agricultural Economics and Rural Sociology. This committee completed the circle by organizing a series of advanced courses taught by specialists from the Department of Agriculture and Brookings Institution, attended in the main by government workers. Specifically, the RF provided $40,000 between 1931 and 1937 to support these courses.

It was no accident that Rockefeller philanthropy and socially aware academics wished to focus attention on societal problems. The United States experienced a general economic recession in 1920–21. As part of the recession, farm prices had fallen to the extent that farm income and land prices collapsed. The crisis for farmers, which remained constant for most of the interwar period, revolved around the lack of balance between production and market demand. After 1921 the rest of the economy of the United States moved into what appeared on the surface to be a state of prosperous equilibrium. Real wages and per capita personal income rose, and there was a dramatic increase in production, particularly in those industries that produced the new consumer goods like phonographs, electrical appliances, and automobiles.[130] Yet in the midst of all this prosperity there were dangerous countercurrents.

In many ways society seemed to be falling apart. Racial tensions between whites and blacks remained high throughout the decade. The First World War produced a great increase in black settlement in northern cities.

---

129. SSRC, *Decennial Report*, pp. 28–29. For example, John D. Black, ed., *Scope and Method of Research in Agricultural Economics and Rural Sociology*, Advisory Committee on Social and Economic Research in Agriculture (New York: SSRC, 1930).

130. For details of the economic changes during this period, see Dorfman, *Economic Mind*, vols. 4 and 5, 1918–33.

This migration and the resulting tensions had precipitated in 1919 the disastrous Chicago race riot in which 38 people died and 537 were injured. This riot led to the setting up of the Chicago Commission on Race Relations, which in turn commissioned Johnson to undertake a massive study of the riot and race relations. The study, *The Negro in Chicago*, was published in 1922.[131] The size of the black ghettos continued to expand during the 1920s, and the reality of white supremacist violence against blacks was a continual reminder that something had to be done. As part of the same phenomenon, there was at the end of the war increased interest in the "nationality question" as it was then called. Even though the flow of immigrants had been interrupted in 1920, there occurred in American cities a nativist reaction against ethnic pluralism. The reality of ethnic segregation and the political battles around the issues of assimilation and acculturation drew the attention of social scientists to the problems that the foreign-born experienced as they became incorporated into the social structure of the cities. This concern was exemplified in the work of the Chicago sociologist W. I. Thomas, who in collaboration with Park and Miller produced *Old World Traits Transplanted* (1921) and coauthored with Florian Znaniecki the classic study *The Polish Peasant in Europe and America* (1918–20).[132]

Alongside the above concerns were the problems of criminality and industrial relations. There appeared to be a crime epidemic as the cities tried to adjust to the consequences of war. The number of murders in the United States increased dramatically between 1920 and 1925.[133] Delinquency, urban gangs, and organized crime were all part of the reality of living in urban centers like Chicago. Similarly, while there had been a lull in the battle between capital and labor during the war, it was short-lived. The opposition to trade unions reasserted itself, and there was a return to the violence and coercion that had characterized prewar industrial relations. Union membership grew rapidly during the war, and there was the fear on the part of owners that not only would the numbers continue to increase but that the socialist party, the Industrial Workers of the World (IWW), and the newly formed communist groups would increase their influence.[134] The "Red Scare" of

131. Chicago Commission on Race Relations, *The Negro in Chicago: A Study of Race Relations and a Race Riot in 1919* (Chicago: University of Chicago Press, 1922).

132. W. I. Thomas, with the assistance of Robert E. Park and Herbert A. Miller, *Old World Traits Transplanted* (New York: Harper and Row, 1921); and W. I. Thomas and Florian Znaniecki, *The Polish Peasant in Europe and America*, 2 vols. (New York: Knopf, 1927). The original work had been published in five volumes between 1918 and 1920.

133. Morris Janowitz, *The Last Half-Century: Social Change and Politics in America* (Chicago: University of Chicago Press, 1978), table 10.1, p. 371.

134. The Communist Labor party and the Communist party of America were both established in 1919. For an account of the radicalism of this period, see Dorfman, "Radicalism and Reform," in *Economic Mind*, vol. 4, pp. 86–124.

1919 left a deep impression on the ruling class. Trade union membership reached a peak in 1920, but then surprisingly for the rest of the decade the figure declined yearly.[135] In part this was due to the transformation of management authority during the 1920s and the initiatives taken by managers as they tried at the shop floor level to deal with inefficiency and discontent. Psychologists were at the center of the attempts to "scientifically manage" workers. The Psychological Corporation was founded by James McKeen Cattell in 1921. This holding company provided a respectable structure through which scientists could be hired as private consultants by industrialists. Cattell developed a relationship with Samuel Gompers, the leading trade unionist of the day, while men like Willits and Mayo found that owners and managers were easy to convince when it came to the question of whether or not industrial psychology could help increase profits. As noted earlier, the most important breakthrough in this area was the famous Hawthorn Studies that began in 1924.[136]

What brought the social scientists and the foundations together was the concept of "social control." For sociologists, this concept had become the central theoretical thrust behind their attempts to investigate social problems. Park and Burgess asserted in their most influential text, *Introduction to the Science of Sociology* (1921), that "all social problems turn out to be problems of social control."[137] But as Morris Janowitz made clear, it was not just the sociologists who subscribed to this theory. Institutional economists like Mitchell utilized the concept as a means of linking together their efforts to improve upon the mechanisms of competition and the marketplace. Political scientists like Merriam and Harold R. Gosnell were similarly influenced as they searched for the reasons why people did not participate in the political process.[138] There was general agreement that the city was the research laboratory from which the answers would emerge. This view was particularly prevalent in Chicago and served as the motif for the survey of research edited by Thomas V. Smith and Leonard D. White, *Chicago: An Experiment in Social Science Research* (1929). Chapter 1, by Park, was titled "The City as a Social Laboratory," and the book had a running heading that read "Chicago, a Research Laboratory."[139] The theoretical and the practical merged as these

---

135. Ibid., p. 66.

136. See Baritz, *Servants of Power*.

137. Robert E. Park and Ernest W. Burgess, *Introduction to the Science of Sociology* (Chicago: University of Chicago Press, 1921), p. 785. For a discussion of the concept of "social control" see Janowitz, *Last Half-Century*, pp. 39–44.

138. See Charles E. Merriam and Harold F. Gosnell, *Non-Voting: Causes and Methods of Control* (Chicago: University of Chicago, 1924).

139. See Thomas V. Smith and Leonard D. White, eds., *Chicago: An Experiment in Social Science Research* (Chicago: University of Chicago Press, 1929).

social scientists and foundation officials like Ruml sought to use social scientific research to solve social problems and thereby increase the degree to which society was socially controlled. Rather than an end, social control was regarded as a means of enhancing the inevitable progress toward the ideal of democracy. These men believed that the political and economic system of the United States was on the right track and simply needed to be helped along.

To support the "social disturbance" projects and the ongoing research the LSRM provided three special project grants that totaled $177,500.[140] These grants were provided over the next four to five years between 1925 and 1930. Administrative expenses of the Council had been guaranteed in late 1925 and early 1926 with a grant from the LSRM. The memorial contribution of $25,000 was particularly important because it was spread over the five-year period 1926–31. When this was coupled with the memorial grants for fellowships and research that also ran through to the end of the decade, it was inevitable that 1926 was a year in which the Council displayed increasing confidence and optimism. During the year, the Council succeeded in obtaining the support of two other foundations, the Russell Sage Foundation and the CC. The requests for $5,000 each for five years were granted in full, and both these institutions continued to provide support throughout the interwar period. The Commonwealth Fund (CF) provided only one grant of $5,000 in 1926–27. As Wirth put it, these grants "contributed materially to giving the members a sense that they were building a permanent organization."[141] This feeling was given even more substance with the repetition and extension of the Hanover Conference into three weeks of meetings in 1926.

The Hanover Conferences

For the LSRM the Hanover Conference served the larger purpose of bringing leaders of different disciplines together and thereby accelerating "the tendency toward the breaking down of departmental categories in the social science[s]."[142] The LSRM expected the conference to cement new friendships across discipline lines and to serve the general function of diffusing and disseminating the new approach to social science research. In retrospect, it is difficult to see how these meetings could have failed to go some way toward

---

140. The first grant of $50,000 was provided specifically for the migration project. The major appropriation of $127,500 was divided into two parts. The first $85,000 came without conditions and supported all the ongoing advisory committees. The second part was a conditional $42,500 that was to be claimed on a dollar for dollar basis. It is this latter sum that was matched by the Behavior Research Fund for the delinquency studies referred to earlier.

141. Wirth, "Report," p. 19, SSRCA.

142. "Summer Conference for Social Scientists, March 18, 1926," Folder 19, Dockets, March–April 1926, LSRM, Series 1, 1, RAC.

achieving these objectives. All of the SSRC committees plus other leading social scientists and representatives of the foundations attended.[143] Altogether a total of ninety-six individuals were present. The LSRM was represented by Ruml, Dunham, Frank, Outhwaite, and Frank B. Stubbs; the CC by Frederick P. Keppel, the president; the CF by the president, Max Farrand, and the secretary, Robert S. Lynd; and, finally, the Russell Sage Foundation by Harrison and Van Kleeck. Meetings were scheduled in the mornings and evenings, leaving a substantial amount of time for socializing and relaxation. The Hanover Inn was both an idyllic and luxurious setting. As Robert Redfield was to recall later, these conferences brought together "pedants and potentates." The purpose was, according to Redfield, to set priorities and policies for future social scientific research.[144] Everything was paid for by the LSRM.

For disciplines and individual academics that had up until this time been excluded from any major financial support, this was a new and unprecedented experience. A full record of all the conference speeches and discussions was subsequently typed and distributed.[145] The evening sessions dealt with major topics concerning either the development of the social sciences at both the level of theory and method or research topics. For example, B. Malinowski of the London School of Economics (LSE) was brought in by the memorial to provide a forceful account of functionalism as the new scientific approach, L. L. Thurstone (University of Chicago) talked about "The Measurement of Opinion"; Dr. Sumner H. Slichter (Washington University) gave a paper entitled "Labor Policies and Industrial Output"; F. H. Allport (Syracuse University) read "The Pluralistic Measurement of Human Behaviour and Attitudes as a Basis of Political Science"; Mayo read "The Approach of Psychological Investigation"; and Mitchell talked about the "Scientific Method." The chairman of the PPC, Hall, organized a debate around SSRC policy with Dr. W. V. Bingham of the Personnel Research Federation and Professor Woodworth (Columbia University), a member of the PPC, under the heading "A Constructive Program for the Social Science Research Council." Bingham had been secretary to the NRC Committee for Psychology, which Yerkes chaired, and continued to be a forceful proponent of intelligence testing. In this discussion, the question was raised as to whether the Council was forwarding fundamental developments in social science or merely reacting in a scattergun manner by supporting the most persuasive or the most influential applicants. For Day, who contributed to the debate, there was no contradiction at this stage. He believed that the SSRC should be "interested in making

---

143. A full transcript of the meeting is contained in Folders 694, 695, and 697, SSRC—Conference Report, 1926, LSRM, Series 3, 65 and 66, RAC (henceforth Conference, 1926).
144. "50th Anniversary of the 1930 Hanover Conference: The Letters of Robert Redfield," *ITEMS* 34 (1980): 35–37. Cited by Lagemann, *Politics of Knowledge*, p. 156.
145. Folders 694, 695, and 697, Conference, 1926, LSRM, Series 3, 65 and 66, RAC.

scientific method bear on these [social] problems which are of very general interest because they do involve social welfare."[146] This tension between fundamental long-term objectives and immediate practical utility was to be a continuing theme in SSRC discussions.

The final day saw the first attempt by the memorial to bring together and begin coordinating the university-based research councils. As already noted, a major plank of the LSRM's policy for the social sciences was aimed at the development of regional centers of scientific research. Each center was required to develop a smaller version of the SSRC in which each discipline was represented. These committees or councils applied for and distributed the memorial's funds. The first two centers to be chosen by the LSRM were Chicago and Columbia. As in the case of Chicago, where Merriam was a leading member of the Local Community Research Committee, it was inevitable that those most active at the university level were also the most active members of the national Council. The first meeting included descriptions of the organization and progress at Chicago and Columbia by Fay Cooper-Cole and Woodworth, respectively. In addition, Gay provided information on Harvard, which was at a slightly different stage but did begin receiving funds from the LSRM in 1928. The whole conference was a great success. As Wirth put it: "The feeling was general that in this conference lay an effective device for personal contact, mutual understanding among members of different disciplines and with diverging interests and the creation of a sense of solidarity among the social science disciplines."[147] The conference became an annual event, which did as much as anything else to hold the SSRC together.

Another pattern was established at the second Hanover Conference. As with the 1925 meetings the PPC met extensively.[148] These summer meetings became the major decision-making events of the year. These became the forum for policy discussions and program planning. Mitchell attended the PPC meetings in an ex-officio capacity. Invited guests included Ruml, Farrand, and Lynd. The 1926 sessions approved new advisory committees on international relations, corporate relations, cultural areas, and grants-in-aid.[149] The PPC also endorsed the program of another committee on pioneer belts, which had already been approved.

---

146. Folders 694, 695, and 697, Conference, 1926, p. 455, LSRM, Series 3, 66, RAC. My brackets.

147. Wirth, "Report," p. 19, SSRCA.

148. On this occasion the PPC held thirteen sessions between August 27 and September 2.

149. Harrison to Ruml, October 7, 1926, attached to minutes of PPC Meetings, Folder 690, SSRC—Conference, 1926, LSRM, Series 3, 64, RAC. See Merriam, report of SSRC to LSRM, December 27, 1926, Folder 687, SSRC—Reports, LSRM, Series 3, 64, RAC. Also the memorandum, Woods to Fosdick, January 26, 1927, Folder 718, SSRC—Prohibition Survey, 1925–27, LSRM, Series 3, 68, RAC.

Structural Relations

The Advisory Committee on Pioneer Belts (1926–28) began life as a joint effort with the NRC. As already noted, this project was an extension of the rather grandiose plans to study human migration. The project grew out of a preoccupation on the part of the LSRM and social scientists with the whole issue of immigration, settlement, and, in a subsidiary way, race relations. Isaiah Bowman, the director of the American Geographical Society, was the key figure in the development of this committee. He had taken over from Yerkes as the chairman of the NRC committee on migration in May 1925 and as a consequence was also a member of the SSRC committee. As interest in the issue of migration subsided at the NRC, the discussions at the SSRC summer conference in 1925 were in contrast wide-ranging. There was ambitious talk of the intention to study world statistics on migration, studies of immigrant communities using *The Polish Peasant in Europe and America* research as the model, internal migrations within the United States, legal and administrative policies affecting immigration, as well as the topics that were actually undertaken on the mechanization of industry and the "great immigrations." Significantly, Canada was also mentioned as a country that would be suitable for study because the lateness of immigration ensured a good statistical record and because the patterns of immigration and settlement would provide the basis for comparing immigration policies and colonial administration between the United States, Australia, and Britain.

The initial proposal for the work on pioneer belts was put before the NRC in 1925, then to the SSRC at Hanover in 1926. Park was appointed chair of the new committee, with Bowman as a member. Bowman gradually took over the project and was responsible for the work being transferred to the American Geographical Society in 1928. Bowman argued for a series of interdisciplinary investigations that would focus on questions of immigration, land use, and settlement in all the major uninhabited areas of the developed world. He argued against further settlement of the urban centers and proposed studies that would provide the knowledge necessary for scientific settlement. Bowman wanted to have an impact on State policymakers.[150] The SSRC approved a budget for a study of "pioneer areas" of Canada in 1927 after a group of Canadian academics had conferred with the SSRC at Hanover. This study resulted in the publication of an eight-volume series under the heading *Frontiers of Settlement*.[151]

---

150. See Isaiah Bowman, "The Scientific Study of Settlement," *Geographical Review* 16 (October 1926): 647–53.

151. SSRC, *Decennial Report*, pp. 59–60. For an outline of the research, see W. L. G. Joerg, ed., *Pioneer Settlement: Cooperative Studies by Twenty-six Authors* (New York: American Geographical Society, 1932). For a detailed account of the development of this project, see

The Advisory Committee on International Relations (1926–38), chaired by James T. Shotwell of Columbia University, was appointed to take over from the earlier committee on international news. Shotwell was firmly committed to an empirical approach in international affairs. For Shotwell, the protection of democracy meant the collection of relevant facts. As he put it in 1921, "we must apply scientific methods to the management of society as we have been learning to apply them to the natural world."[152] The creation of this committee reflected the policy orientation of Rockefeller philanthropy. International relations was a long-standing interest of Fosdick, who had worked for the League of Nations before taking the job with John D. Rockefeller, Jr. At the LSRM this field was gradually assuming the position of a focal point even though there was no formal policy of concentration.[153]

Another factor was the pressure exerted by the newly formed Institute of Pacific Relations. On Ruml's advice, both the Institute and the SSRC began to receive substantial funds from the LSRM.[154] The initial interest in international relations was transformed into a major area of concentration in 1931 by the SSRC and this phase of the work is dealt with later. The early achievements inevitably reflected the Pacific focus, including a section on the international, financial, and economic relations in China under the supervision of Carl F. Remer[155] and work on Asian agriculture by Carl L. Alsberg. The other major focus of the committee's work was an attempt to survey research in the field of international relations under the direction of Joseph P. Chamberlain, who was also the chairman of the committee between 1928 and 1931. Two major publications resulted: *Research Activities of the League of Nations* by Herbert Feis and *Research in International Law since the War* by Quincy Wright.[156]

Marlene Shore, "Frontiers of Settlement," in *The Science of Social Redemption: McGill, the Chicago School, and the Origins of Social Research in Canada* (Toronto: University of Toronto Press, 1987), pp. 162–94.

152. James T. Shotwell, *Intelligence and Politics* (New York: Century Co., 1921).

153. See Fosdick, *Chronicle of a Generation*. Also "Memorandum on the Connection of the Foundation with the League of Nations," Fosdick to Syndor M. Walker (officer of the LSRM and the RF), February 3, 1930, Folder 60, Program and Policy—International Relations, 1929–41, RF, 910, 7, RAC. The policy changes are described in Fisher, "Role of Philanthropic Foundations."

154. E. J. Carter ("The Inquiry") to Ruml, June 7, 1926, Folder 582, Institute of Pacific Relations, 1925–26, LSRM, Series 3, 54, RAC. The LSRM began funding the institute in 1926. Other funding for research in international relations went to the Economic Foundation and the Royal Institute of International Affairs.

155. SSRC, *Decennial Report*, pp. 49–50.

156. Quincy Wright, *Research in International Law since the War: A Report to the International Relations Committee of the Social Science Research Council* (Washington, D.C.: Carnegie Endowment for International Peace, 1930); Herbert Feis, *Research/Activities of the League of Nations* (Old Lime, Conn.: Old Lime Press, 1929). See also SSRC, *Decennial Report*, p. 49.

The Advisory Committee on Corporate Relations (1926–30) was created to consider the problem of ownership and control in the modern corporation. Gay molded the proposal and insisted that the research be undertaken by an economist and a lawyer working hand in hand.[157] George O. May, head of Price, Waterhouse and Company, was appointed chairman, and the committee included other businesspeople and lawyers. The major investigation was into trends in recent corporate development under the direction of Adolf A. Berle, Jr., and Gardiner C. Means. Among the publications were *Materials in the Law of Corporate Finance* by Berle and *The Modern Corporation and Private Property* by Berle and Means.[158] In this most influential book, Berle and Means argued that management had taken over control of the corporations from the owners. According to Janowitz, Berle and Means were responsible for launching a research tradition that began from the perspective of "social control." This tradition focused on the degree of concentration in industrial production and sought to explicate the extent to which actual ownership was separated from the ownership of the "means of production."[159]

The Advisory Committee on Cultural Areas (1926–28) was created at the suggestion of the anthropologists Wissler and A. L. Kroeber, University of California at Berkeley.[160] An ethnographic survey of North America was produced which led to a joint conference with the NRC on regional phenomena.[161] The PPC also appointed the Committee on Grants-in-Aid. This committee began as an advisory committee, but in 1928 it was reconstituted as a Council committee. The committee was active throughout the interwar period. It was created to deal with and, in some ways, encourage applications that did not fit into either the project or fellowship categories. Finally, the PPC decided that each of its members should take special responsibility for one or more of the advisory committees, and it duly divided up the ten active committees.

Conclusion

By the beginning of 1927 the SSRC was organized. All the Council committees, except for the Executive Committee, the Committee on Social Science Abstracts, and the Committee on Scientific Method in the Social Sciences,

---

157. Heaton, *Scholar in Action*, p. 211.

158. Adolf A. Berle, Jr., and Gardiner C. Means, *The Modern Corporation and Private Property* (New York: Macmillan, 1933). See also SSRC, *Decennial Report*, p. 33.

159. See Janowitz, *Last Half-Century*, p. 227.

160. For an account of Rockefeller interest in anthropology, see Donald Fisher, "The Scientific Appeal of Functionalism: Rockefeller Philanthropy and the Rise of Social Anthropology," *Anthropology Today* 2, no. 1 (February 1986): 5–8; also see Fisher, "Boundary Work."

161. SSRC, *Decennial Report*, p. 37.

were PPC advisory committees. Policies governing the funding of research and the SSRC's role vis-à-vis the development of the social sciences were in place. The central thrust of the Council's activities was to bring about a major shift in the social sciences toward more realism, more science, and more integration. Through the SSRC, leading social scientists along with foundation trustees and officers had created a social scientific network. The new definition of science was the main discourse element in this coalition. Structurally the network was extended into the universities through the SSRC committees and the regional local university research councils. Yet inscribed in the new boundary around the social sciences was the old tension between advocacy and objectivity. For thirty years or more social scientists had turned their backs on activism as they struggled to establish their separate disciplines within the academy. In the SSRC, academic social scientists and foundation officers and trustees brought social reform back under the banner of scientific investigation. In this way, different and competing definitions of science were built into the basic structure of the Council.

The process of developing a boundary around the social sciences was fraught with contradictions that were based in the class locations of the participants. This particular case involved three major groups: the LSRM trustees, the LSRM officers, and the academic social scientists. The trustees represented the ruling class with their emphasis on "practical social control." The most influential trustees were Colonel Woods and Fosdick. Both the foundation officers and the social scientists displayed behavior that reflected their contradictory class locations. Ruml and Frank were trained social scientists and were committed to "basic" research. They were interested in the advance of the social sciences and committed to the goals of creating a "science of society." Yet as noted earlier, their concern for the autonomy that comes from doing "pure" research was tempered by their pragmatism. Like their bosses they were "sophisticated conservatives" who wished to make the status quo more stable.

As Merriam and his colleagues struggled to establish the dominance of the scientific approach, they displayed their sympathy with the interests of the ruling class. This was apparent in the negotiations on the foreign news and prohibition projects as well as in the creation of the PPC. Yet as one would expect, they also emphasized their academic commitment to pure scientific research. Science as a concept and an ideal was the central aspect of the ideological convergence of the tenets of the new science and the objectives of the LSRM. Science meant objective empirical study that led to practical improvements in social affairs. The science of society promised results that would solve the overwhelming problems that faced society in the United States.

During the early 1920s the form of cultural hegemony in the United

States was changing. The part of the ideology that emphasized social control linked together scientific social science with the major social problems that faced the United States: immigration, delinquency and organized crime, race riots in northern cities, as well as the "Red Scare" about the trade union movement. The contradictory class location of foundation officials and social scientists meant that they simultaneously represented the interests of those that ruled, those who were ruled, and themselves as knowledge producers. The "discourse coalition" formed around the concept of social control, which was seen as the means for enhancing progress toward the ideal of democracy. The ideological convergence of the elements that were an emergent form of cultural hegemony and the ideas and interests of men like Ruml and Merriam formed a boundary around the social science field. The legitimacy and the cognitive authority that were attached to social science increased. In addition to furthering their own careers and social status within the academic world, social scientists also believed that the knowledge they were producing was superior. At the side of the older, speculative and deductive approaches the new science of society offered theoretical, methodological, and practical advance. It should also be noted that these social scientists were progressive. While not wanting to overthrow the status quo they did expect that social science knowledge would genuinely improve their society. The social sciences were offered as an instrument for the conservation of the social order as well as a means for making that order more stable.

For many leading scientists, this was a time of tremendous optimism. The Council had appointed a full-time assistant to the chairman, a role that was later converted into that of permanent secretary. The summer conferences, the research activities, the appointment of fellows, and the funds that philanthropy was providing all combined to create, as Wirth put it, an "atmosphere of buoyancy" among Council members. The future of the SSRC and of the social sciences in the United States looked bright for the first time in the combined history of all these disciplines. This faith was reflected in Chairman Merriam's report in 1926 when he noted that the social sciences were on the verge of providing reliable knowledge that would resolve some of society's pressing problems.[162] This faith and optimism were certainly not misplaced, at least in the short term. The next years marked a period of unprecedented expansion of the social sciences.

---

162. SSRC, *Annual Report*, 1925–26 (Chicago, 1926).

CHAPTER 3

Expansion and Growth of the Council: The Gilded Age

At the 1927 Annual Meeting of the Iowa Association of Economists and Sociologists, Burgess, the eminent sociologist from the University of Chicago, read a paper that drew attention to the availability of funds through the LSRM and the SSRC for the social sciences. He noted that the size of these funds would have seemed staggering even five years earlier.[1] Burgess was at the forefront of the campaign to make the social sciences more scientific in the natural science mode. In 1921 he had coauthored and coedited with Park what turned out to be the most influential and widely read social science text during the 1920s. Their book *Introduction to the Science of Sociology* was a bold attempt to cut across the boundaries that separated the social science disciplines and to use sociology as the discipline that could help make a general science of society. In contrast to history, sociology was defined as a discipline that "seeks to arrive at natural laws and generalizations in regard to human nature and society, irrespective of time and place." Park and Burgess charted how sociology was connected to and should be regarded as fundamental to the other social sciences. Psychology was excluded from the chart and placed at the same level of scientific advance as sociology. Both disciplines, according to Park and Burgess, were primarily concerned with the social control of behavior, at the individual and collective levels, respectively. Sociology was concerned with that class of social problems that focused on social forces and human nature. Burgess's sensitivity to changes in the funding of social research was predictable because the book had outlined what amounted to a massive social problem/social control research agenda.[2]

In retrospect, one might have expected social scientists like Burgess to do more than stagger at the change in their fortunes. The year 1927 was a turning point in the history of the social sciences in the United States. The new era was heralded in by the appropriation of almost $2 million to the

---

1. Ernest W. Burgess, "Statistics and Case Studies as Methods of Sociological Research," paper read at the 1927 Annual Meeting of the Iowa Association of Economists and Sociologists. Contained in Folder 678, Social Science—Pamphlet and Report, LSRM, Series 3, 63, RAC.

2. Park and Burgess, *Introduction to the Science*, pp. 11 and 44–45.

SSRC by the LSRM.[3] Included here were three major appropriations: $750,000 as the General Project Fund (1927 to 1932); $550,000 for administration (January 1928 to December 1939); and $500,000 for the establishment and development of the *Journal of Social Science Abstracts* (1928 to 1938). Further, at Ruml's suggestion, Julius Rosenwald, Jr., granted $50,000 to the SSRC for administration over a five-year period, 1928 to 1933.[4] With administrative expenses guaranteed until 1940, the Council's earlier timidity was replaced with a new confidence. Reflecting the mood of the period social scientists saw this as the time for bold, long-term strategies, a time to put a permanent seal on the place of the social sciences in the academy and the polity.

The most fitting symbol of the new approach to social science was the publication of a collection of essays edited by Ogburn and Alexander Goldenweiser, *The Social Sciences and Their Interrelations* (1927). The commitment was to integration of the social science disciplines as the only means for attacking and solving social problems. As they put it:

> The social sciences, moreover, are not merely theoretical disciplines but also tools to be employed in the solution of the concrete practical problems of an existing and developing society. As tools they must constantly cooperate, with an all but complete disregard for academic and classificatory distinctions. The problems of living society do not range themselves so as to fit the artificial isolation forced upon the social sciences by differences of specific subject and method. These problems are what they are. If they are to be solved, whatever knowledge we possess about society must be called into service, wherever needed.

Ogburn and Goldenweiser summarized their position in three propositions. First, that scientific advance in the social disciplines would depend on how well they adopted statistical methods. Second, that the theoretical unit of the social sciences was "man in society," which meant that sociology was "the natural meeting-ground of the social sciences and the sphere par excellence of their interrelations." Finally, the authors repeated the social problem orientation and noted that however far apart the disciplines may be in their conceptual specialization "they must ever be prepared for the call to pragmatic reunification and cooperation."[5] Important events were to occur between the

---

3. "SSRC Active Appropriations," Folder 713, SSRC—International News, 1924–28, LSRM, Series 3, 68, RAC.

4. Edward Embree (president, Julius Rosenwald Fund) to Ruml, April 30, 1928, Folder 685, SSRC, 1928–1931, LSRM, Series 3, 64, RAC. Day wrote Embree to express his pleasure at the appropriation. It should be noted that Embree was secretary to the RF (1917–23), the director of the Division of Studies, RF (1924–27), and, finally, the vice-president, RF, in 1927.

5. Ogburn and Goldenweiser, *Social Sciences*, pp. 7–8 and 9.

publication of Ogburn and Goldenweiser's book in 1927 and the books on social science that appeared in the early 1930s.

Organizing the Relationship between the LSRM and the SSRC

The infusion of such a large amount of money signaled a change in the relationship between the LSRM and the SSRC. There had been some dissatisfaction expressed within Rockefeller philanthropy about the explicit dependence of the SSRC on the LSRM. A tension existed in the relationship between Rockefeller philanthropy and the social scientists because the Rockefeller side wanted the Council to appear to be an independent institution while, at the same time, the Rockefeller side wanted to maintain control. The Council would have lost value for both the Rockefeller group and the social scientists if it could be charged with being a "Rockefeller baby." The charge of bias would have undermined the development of fundamental science and also decreased the utility of these men and disciplines for the maintenance of a democratic social order. Yet the social scientists were having a difficult time raising funds from alternative sources and in trying to interpret the confusing signals from the Rockefeller people. Nobody wanted to kill the golden goose, and hence the foundation representatives received exaggerated respect.

Outhwaite brought up the subject of perceived and real autonomy with Ruml in 1926. He was concerned about the LSRM method of financing the Council, which had the Council applying for funds that were already guaranteed by the memorial. Outhwaite was sure that this arrangement had to be altered if the Council's position as a national deliberative body in the social science fields was going to be maintained. Outhwaite presented the alternative in the following way:

> if, by our attitude and action, we showed that we respected the Council's judgement and regarded it as perhaps not final but authoritative, if we made it an agency that within the limits of its recommendation could use some discretion in the allocation of monies, we should of course, be increasing its duties, but I believe also be making a consummate addition to its usefulness to ourselves and to social science generally.[6]

One essential service that the SSRC could perform for Rockefeller philanthropy was to sift and choose research projects for support. The memorial did not want to open itself up to the charge of discrimination or censorship against institutions, subjects, topics, or individuals. It was eminently more suitable

---

6. Memorandum, Outhwaite to Ruml, March 6, 1926, Folder 711, SSRC—Human Migration, 1926–27, LSRM, Series 3, 68, RAC, 5.

that the SSRC should be utilized as an "agency for discrimination,"[7] especially as all the decisions were now being made by the PPC.

The sensitivity to the charge of control was heightened by the publication in the *New Republic* of an anonymous article entitled "The Fat Boys."[8] The article provided an amusing but critical account of the behavior of Ruml and Frank at the 1926 Hanover Conference.[9] The writer described how he gradually came to realize how important these men were as he watched the way in which distinguished colleagues paid attention to their every word. It was at this point that the writer remembered that one of the "boys" had sent some of his friends on a year's sabbatical. Exhibiting some of the anger and frustration that many of these distinguished scholars secretly must have harbored, the writer went on to describe the "boys" as "young, confident, busy," who "seemed to know everything, although in reality they only knew about everything." They displayed an "irritating blend of ignorance and omniscience" against which the writer felt compelled to protect himself. These "boys," "backed by the consciousness of millions behind them, flattered by the attendance of those whom they held in their astonished grasp, striving manfully to conceal their astonishment and to reconstruct as invisibly as possible a front that will do justice to the magnificence of their position."[10] In describing what was implied by the presence of foundation executives at the conference, the anonymous author foreshadowed Harold J. Laski's 1928 article "Foundations, Universities, and Research," which appeared in *Harper's* magazine.[11] Laski delivered a slashing attack on the power of foundations to control the development of both universities and research. He attributed to the foundations the drift toward concrete fact in the social sciences rather than the consideration of ultimate principle and the increasing emphasis on methodology as an end in itself. Laski described the relationship between foundation officers and university professors as one involving an "important customer" and a "deferential salesman."

> When you see him [foundation executive] at a college, it is like nothing so much as the vision of an important customer in a department store.

7. Memorandum, "Social Science Research Council Research Projects in Social Science," p. 1., pt. 3, Folder 22, Dockets, November 1926, LSRM, Series 1, 3, RAC.

8. "The Fat Boys," *New Republic*, February 2, 1927, pp. 500–501. Contained in Folder 704, SSRC—Conference, 1929, LSRM, Series 3, 67, RAC.

9. The article and the identity of the two men first came up in Robert Havinghurst, interview with author, Vancouver, British Columbia, July 19, 1979. Havinghurst worked for the GEB (a Rockefeller foundation) under Day's guidance during the 1920s.

10. "Fat Boys," p. 501, Folder 704, SSRC—Conference, 1929, LSRM, Series 3, 67, RAC.

11. This article was republished in Harold J. Laski, *The Dangers of Obedience and Other Essays* (London: Harper and Bros., 1930).

Deferential salesmen surround him on every hand, anticipating his every wish, alive to the importance of his good opinion, fearful lest he be dissatisfied and go to their rival across the way. The effect on him is to make him feel that in fact he is shaping the future of the social sciences.

In commenting on the control exercised by foundations, Laski felt that this control suffered nothing from being implicit rather than direct. "It is merely the fact that a fund is within reach which permeates everything and alters everything. The college develops along the lines the foundation approves. The dependence is merely implicit, but it is in fact quite final." With respect to control, Laski specifically mentioned the power exercised by the foundations through the focus on specific areas of study and the always present fear on the part of recipients that the foundation might withdraw its funds.[12] Both Laski and the anonymous author exposed the power exercised by foundations over the development of research. The relationship between the foundations and social scientists encouraged them to become servants of power and to become salespeople for the ruling class.[13]

Perhaps as a reaction to these early attacks and as a means of resolving the tension between control and independence the LSRM had begun what was to become the continuous process of co-opting leading members of the SSRC. Guy S. Ford, the dean of the graduate studies at the University of Minnesota and Council member representing AHA from 1925, and Coss had been hired by the LSRM in 1924 to conduct fellowship surveys in Europe. Ford joined the memorial full-time for the academic year 1925–26. During 1926, Ruml and Merriam discussed how they might change the social sciences in Europe, and even though Merriam eventually refused the offer to run the newly established Paris office, he was by that time firmly identified with Rockefeller philanthropy.[14] In 1927, Merriam began receiving funds for research assistance, a practice that continued yearly through the interwar period.[15] As important was the appointment of Day, the SSRC treasurer and the dean of the School of Business Administration, University of Michigan, early in 1927 as an officer of the memorial with particular responsibility for the social sciences in the United States. Ruml and Day proceeded to spend part of the academic year 1927–28 traveling through the southern and western parts of the country visiting social science departments. In October 1928, Day became director of

---

12. Ibid., pp. 164 and 170–71. For a discussion of this article and its impact on Ruml, see Fisher, "Impact of American Foundations," pp. 439–41.

13. Thomas R. Bates, "Gramsci and the Theory of Hegemony," *Journal of the History of Ideas* 36 (April—July 1975): 351–66.

14. Karl, *Merriam and the Study of Politics*, pp. 182–83.

15. See Folder 601, Charles E. Merriam, 1925–27, LSRM, Series 3, 56, RAC.

the social sciences in preparation for the merger of the LSRM into the RF. Day played a crucial role in tying together the SSRC and Rockefeller philanthropy. Day actually continued as an official representative of the ASTA on the Council until March 31, 1931.[16] He maintained an indirect but tight control over policy-making in the SSRC.

The movement between the foundations, the SSRC, and the academy served in a structural sense to strengthen the network ties and to more clearly establish a boundary around the preferred definition of social science. Certainly the LSRM was delighted that Merriam and Day were now publicly identified with the aims of Rockefeller philanthropy.[17] These two men contributed to the internal LSRM debates that laid the groundwork for the SSRC to apply for the large appropriations.[18] The memorial attached great significance to the SSRC appropriations because of the "influence of the Council in the promotion of social science in this country and the demonstrated usefulness of the Council in the development of the Memorial's own social science program."[19] The memorial made it clear that the purposes of the SSRC concerning integration and scientization were in line with LSRM policy, which is interesting because a form of double deception was at work. Ruml underplayed the LSRM's influence on the development of the SSRC to preserve at least partially the image of an independent institution to his trustees. While Ruml admitted the importance of the funding he explicitly denied that the memorial had undertaken to shape the plans of the Council.[20] At the same time, it was made clear that the Council was very much the LSRM's creation, in that, without the sustained financial assistance, the Council would not have grown.

The proposals asked Rockefeller philanthropy to provide a full-scale guarantee to the Council over the next decade. Ruml justified these appropriations to his trustees by referring to the memorial's "direct and positive interest in the Council's effectiveness." The Council provided the LSRM with a "competent and representative body of advisors," and allowed the memorial to remain anonymous. As the report put it, the LSRM was through the SSRC "able to promote lines of work in social science which clearly need to be done

---

16. Wirth, "Report," p. 38.

17. "Report of the Executive Committee and Director, 1926–27," November 22, 1927, p. 6, Folder 29, Dockets, November 1927, LSRM, Series 1, 4, RAC.

18. LSRM staff meetings, August 24–27, 1927, Hanover, Separate Book, LSRM, Series 2, 3, RAC. Also see detailed account of projects in letter/proposal, Mitchell to Ruml, October 28, 1927, Folder 715, SSRC—Project Budgets, 1926–28, LSRM, Series 3, 68, RAC.

19. The best summary of the arguments put forward in this debate appears in "Report of the Executive Committee and Director, 1926–27, November 22, 1927," p. 26, Dockets, November 1927–29, LSRM, Series 1, 4, RAC.

20. Ibid, p. 33.

but which could not possibly be undertaken wisely by the Memorial itself."
Ruml particularly welcomed the proposal that the SSRC should take control
of the research funding. This move protected the memorial from the charge of
censorship and, as Ruml put it, rendered "a service which is indispensable in
the Memorial's general programs in social science."[21] While the report regis-
tered the need for the Council to attract other funding,[22] the memorial had
already decided to provide maximum support to the Council.

While the Council applied for $500,000 for administration over ten
years, the LSRM provided $550,000 over twelve years. The grant was used to
expand the secretariat to include a permanent secretary and aides in order "to
bind together more closely, the many interests represented in the Council,
secure a constant cross-fertilization of ideas, keep the Council in touch with
scientific developments and scientific workers in all parts of the country, and
to give fresh momentum to the movement for solving social problems."[23]
Further, it was intended that the permanent secretary would act as a liaison
officer with the foundations. After receiving the endorsement of Frank, the
sociologist Robert S. Lynd (CF) was appointed to the position (1927–31).
Over the next two years Lynd proceeded to forge a strong and binding relationship with Rockefeller officers. Frank had recommended Lynd after hearing a positive report from Wissler about Lynd's research in Muncie, Indiana.
This research, which Lynd conducted jointly with Helen M. Lynd, resulted in
the classic series of community studies on *Middletown*.[24] The following year
Professor John V. Van Sickle, an economist at the University of Michigan,
was appointed to the newly created position of secretary in charge of fellowships and grants-in-aid (1928–29). In 1929, Van Sickle became assistant
director of the newly created Division of the Social Sciences (DSS) at the RF.

In essence, the SSRC became an information center and clearinghouse
for the social sciences. One of Lynd's first acts was to distribute the 1927
Annual Report to every member of all the seven associations and to all the
major libraries in the country. For the first time the social science community
became aware of the volume and breadth of the research support that was

---

21. Ibid., pp. 33 and 36–38.

22. On November 1, 1927, Ruml talked to Keppel about the CC increasing its grant for
administration to the SSRC. "F. P. Keppel and Beardsley Ruml, Social Science Research Council, November 2, 1927," File, SSRC, through 1931, CC.

23. Letter/proposal, Mitchell to Ruml, October 28, 1927, p. 5, Folder 715, SSRC—
Project Budgets, 1926–28, LSRM, Series 3, 68, RAC, 20.

24. Merriam to Frank, April 12, 1927, and Frank to Merriam, April 14, 1927, Folder 684,
SSRC, 1927, LSRM, Series 3, 64, RAC. See Robert S. Lynd and Helen M. Lynd, *Middletown*
(New York: Harcourt Brace, 1929); and Robert S. Lynd and Helen M. Lynd, *Middletown in
Transition* (New York: Harcourt Brace, 1937). For an account of the relationship between Robert
S. Lynd and JDR, Jr., see Charles E. Harvey, "Robert S. Lynd, John D. Rockefeller, Jr., and
Middletown," *Indiana Magazine of History* 79 (December 1983): 330–54.

available. The reputation and status of the Council increased immensely as the community became aware of these resources and implicitly it recognized the power of the organization. The appropriation for administration included provision for permanent offices, and as noted earlier, in 1929 the SSRC moved from the temporary headquarters on Forty-Second Street into the high-rise status of Park Avenue. To consolidate the whole process Professor Edwin B. Wilson was appointed full-time president in 1929. Wilson was the professor of vital statistics in the School of Public Health at Harvard and an ASTA Council member.

General Research Grant

The proposal for the General Research Grant asked for $550,000 over three years.[25] Again the memorial increased the amount, this time to $750,000, and extended the time period to five years.[26] The provision of such a large amount of undesignated funds placed a tremendous responsibility on the PPC. For the first time in the history of the social sciences in the United States, or anywhere else, academics were given charge of a major research fund. A tremendous upsurge of activity occurred over the next two calendar years, 1928 and 1929.

By the beginning of 1930 the SSRC had appropriated or earmarked almost all the $750,000. As a result of these allocations, the Council had increased its total number of active committees to twenty-four (see table 2, appendix 2). In addition to expanding or reconstituting the work of the existing committees,[27] the PPC created sixteen new committees.[28] Included in this number were the Business Research Committee (1928–31), the Family Committee (1928–32), and the Public Administration Committee (1928–45). Social statistics and culture and personality each emerged as areas of interest that resulted in the formation of a series of interrelated committees. Some of these topics symbolized the closer ties that were beginning to emerge between

---

25. Letter/proposal, Mitchell to Ruml, October 28, 1927, Folder 715, SSRC—Project Budgets, 1926–28, LSRM, Series 3, 68, RAC.

26. "SSRC Active Appropriations," Folder 713, SSRC—International News, 1924–28, LSRM, Series 3, 68, RAC.

27. This is the case with the Advisory Committee on Fellowships in Agricultural Economics and Rural Sociology (1928–33) and the reconstituted Advisory Committee on Crime (1929–32). Further, the Advisory Committees on Industrial Relations, International Relations, Interracial Relations, and Population all utilized the new grants to significantly expand their work.

28. This total does not include the Committee on Investments (1928 onward), which was created as a standing committee of the Council. Two of these committees are not included in the 1930–31 total as they had already been discontinued. These committees were the Special Technical Committee on the Measurement of Attitudes and Public Opinion (1928–30) and the Special Advisory Committee on Problems of Philanthropic Funding (1927–29).

social scientists and the State. Finally, as part of a policy shift the PPC created two regional committees: the Pacific Coast Regional Committee (1929–46) and the Southern Regional Committee (1929–47). With their newfound wealth and, at least on the surface, their new autonomy, one might have expected an increase in research proposals emanating either from Council members or other social scientists. Instead, to use an analogy used later by an SSRC officer, the Council simply became a longer tail to the Rockefeller kite.[29]

The Business Research Committee (1928–31) was created after Day had made specific recommendations concerning industrial research to Mitchell, the chairman of the SSRC (1927–29).[30] Day referred to the Committee on Recent Economic Changes (CREC), which had been appointed in 1927 by Hoover under the rubric of the "President's Conference on Unemployment." The conference was chaired by Colonel Woods and had been in operation since 1921 when Hoover was at the department of Commerce. The CREC was a continuation of the work undertaken by the NBER under the guidance of the Committee on Business Cycles and Unemployment.[31] The CREC appointed Gay and Mitchell through the NBER to study the economy since 1921 with a view to help maintain the then current prosperity. Since 1921 the economy had experienced stable expansion with increased mechanization and steadily rising wages and living standards. Yet within this general prosperity there were anomalies. Mitchell and Van Kleeck among other social scientists pointed to rising unemployment and the depression within important productive sectors like agriculture, textiles, and coal. In addition, the economy suffered a mild recession in 1927. The CREC began work in February 1928 with $75,000 from the LSRM and $75,000 from the CC.[32]

Day was conscious of the anomalies and suggested that similar investigations to the ones proposed for the CREC might profitably be started on a

29. "Confidential Memorandum for Personal Use of Dr. Keppel from Robert T. Crane," 1935 (probably July), File, SSRC, 1932–36, CC.

30. Day to Mitchell, March 2, 1928, Folder 685, SSRC, 1928–31, LSRM, Series 3, 64, RAC.

31. Since 1921 the NBER had produced two major reports under the auspices of the President's Conference on Unemployment: *Business Cycles and Unemployment* (New York, 1923) and *Seasonal Operations of the Construction Industries: The Facts and the Remedies* (New York, 1924).

32. See Folders 4578–81 on President's Conference on Unemployment, RF, 1.1, 200S, 387, RAC. Also "Memorandum, Robert M. Lester (secretary, CC) to Keppel, December 12, 1927," File, NBER, 192⁶-29, CC. For accounts of the origins of the CREC, see *The Memoirs of Herbert Hoover: The Cabinet and the Presidency, 1920–1933*, vol. 2 (New York: Macmillan, 1952), p. 176; and Alchon, *Invisible Hand*, pp. 129–45. The CREC presented its report in 1929: *Recent Economic Changes in the United States*, Report of the CREC of the President's Conference on Unemployment (New York: McGraw-Hill, 1929).

continuing basis. The idea was to organize institutes of research on four or five major industries. Each institute would be based at a university with arrangements that ensured the close cooperation of the business organizations operating in each industry. Day contemplated comprehensive studies of all the major problems facing such industries as textiles, coal, iron and steel, automobiles, and meat packing.[33] Gay was appointed chair of the Business Research Committee, and in line with Rockefeller policy the Council appointed a full-time research secretary in industrial relations and related fields.[34] Meredith B. Givens was appointed to this position in 1929. Over the next two years the committee recommended and gained approval for the studies of four industries, but none were financed. In 1931 this committee was incorporated into the newly organized Committee on Industry and Trade (1931–45). The fact that this research was postponed and eventually abandoned is explained primarily by the creation of President Hoover's survey of recent social trends, which included major industrial investigations.[35] As is made clear in a later section, the Research Committee on Social Trends was only independent in theory. In reality this committee was both an expansion and a focus of SSRC activities during the period 1929–33.

The creation of the PAC (1928–45) reflected the joint interests of Merriam and Ruml.[36] White, political scientist and executive secretary of the Local Community Research Committee at Chicago, became the first chairman. In 1926, White had published what was to become the classic text in this field, *Introduction to the Study of Public Administration*.[37] In the early years

---

33. Day asked that the question be raised at the next meeting of the PPC. Mitchell wrote to assure Day that the suggestion would be passed on to the PPC. The Business Research Committee was formally authorized in April by the PPC. Letter, Mitchell to Day, March 6, 1928, Folder 685, SSRC, 1928–31, LSRM, Series 3, 64, RAC. Also SSRC, *Decennial Report*, p. 31.

34. Willits was a member as was Franklin D. Roosevelt during the first year. SSRC, *Decennial Report*, p. 31.

35. *Recent Social Trends in the United States*, Report of the RST, 2 vols. (New York: McGraw-Hill, 1933). Included in this publication are chapters on the general topic of industry, namely, "Trends in Economic Organization," by Gay and Leo Wolman (Columbia University); "Shifting Occupational Patterns," by Ralph G. Hurlin of Russell Sage and Meredith B. Givens (SSRC); "Labour Groups in the Social Structure," by Leo Wolman (Columbia University) and Gustav Peck (College of the City of New York); "The Influence of Invention and Discovery," by William Fielding Ogburn; and "Utilization of National Wealth," a chapter divided into two major sections, "Mineral and Power Resources," by F. G. Tryon and Margaret H. Schoenfeld (Institute of Economics, Brookings Institution), and "Agriculture and Forest Land," by O. E. Baker (Bureau of Agricultural Economics).

36. Rockefeller philanthropy was involved in funding the National Institute of Public Administration and the PACH. For an account of this involvement, see Barry D. Karl, *Executive Reorganization and Reform in the New Deal* (Cambridge: Harvard University Press, 1963).

37. Leonard D. White, *Introduction to the Study of Public Administration* (New York: Macmillan, 1926).

this committee focused on surveying research in the field, work that resulted in the publication by John M. Gaus of a *Survey of Research in Public Administration* (1930).[38] As Council policy changed during the early 1930s, the committee took on a new significance, and public administration became a major area of concentration. White authored the chapter on public administration in the recent social trends report.

The closely allied fields of the "family" and "personality and culture" were both assigned to committees at the suggestion of Frank. He was in charge of the major programs in child study and parent education funded by the memorial.[39] It was therefore somewhat predictable that an exploratory committee was appointed to investigate research possibilities in those areas that pertained to social problems involved in the relationship of the sexes, like sex education, marriage, and the family. This first committee cooperated with the NRC Committee on Research on Sex, which John D. Rockefeller, Jr., had been supporting.[40] The committee organized several conferences on family research,[41] and for a time in 1930 it looked as though this field might become an area of concentration. Frank chaired the Family Committee between 1929 and 1931, and he contributed a chapter to the recent social trends report under the title "Childhood and Youth." The report also included a chapter, "The Family and Its Functions," written by the director of research for the Research Committee on Social Trends, Ogburn. Ogburn had moved from Columbia University in 1927 to become professor of sociology at the University of Chicago. Ogburn was president of the ASS in 1929 and of the ASTA in 1931. In 1928 he coauthored *American Marriage and Family Relationships*.[42] Ogburn was a Council member representing ASS and a member of the PPC. The chapter in the recent social trends report drew heavily on the background research of the SSRC committee.

The two committees on personality and culture originated with Frank, who favored the idea of a systematic study of comparative cultures.[43] The

---

38. SSRC, *Decennial Report*, p. 66. John M. Gaus, *Survey of Research in Public Administration* (New York: SSRC, 1930).

39. The memorial allocated approximately $1 million for the program in child study and parent education. See "Appropriations, October 18, 1918, through April 30, 1928: The Laura Spelman Rockefeller Memorial, PRO-5a," Folder 11, 910, Program and Policy—Reports PRO-5–5a, 1928, RF, 910, 3, 2, RAC. For a detailed account of Frank's work see Steven C. Schlossman, "Philanthropy and the Gospel of Child Development," in Gerald Benjamin, ed., *Private Philanthropy and Public Elementary and Secondary Education*, Proceedings of the RAC Conference, June 8, 1979 (Tarrytown, N.Y.: RAC, 1979), pp. 15–32.

40. Folder 618, NRC, 1924–26, LSRM, Series 3, 64, and 57, RAC.

41. SSRC, *Decennial Report*, p. 39.

42. E. R. Groves and William Fielding Ogburn, *American Marriage and Family Relationships* (New York: Henry Holt and Co., 1928).

43. "Memorandum: Appointment of Fellows in Connection with the Project for the Study

PPC created the Advisory Committee on the Seminar on Culture and Personality (1930–34) with Frank as chair. With the consolidation of the LSRM into the RF, Frank had become an officer in another Rockefeller foundation, the General Education Board (GEB). Stressing the comparative aspect, it was decided that twelve to fifteen foreign fellows would be selected by the RF to come and spend a full year doing research in the seminar. The RF made the arrangement with Yale University, and the seminar was subsequently run by a committee member, the anthropologist Edward Sapir. The more general Advisory Committee on Personality and Culture (1930–40) emerged as a result of the SSRC conference on this topic, which was held at Hanover in 1930. A group of mainly anthropologists and psychologists was called together by Frank as part of a concurrent series of conferences that were designed to explore possible fields of concentration.[44] E. A. Bott, a psychologist at the University of Toronto,[45] became chair, and this area of study was maintained through the 1930s as a field of concentration. According to Robert S. Lynd, this committee never reached its full potential because some of the older and more established disciplines, like history, economics, and political science, paid little attention to this development. In his view, the SSRC missed a major opportunity to cross-fertilize disciplines by failing to recognize personality and culture as the "field of all the social sciences."[46]

In 1929, the PPC established two committees that dealt with the availability of social data. The Advisory Committee on the Utilization of Social Data (1929–31) was created primarily to undertake an analysis of materials in the archives of the Census Bureau and then publicize the holdings. The Advisory Committee on Social Statistics (1929–36) was created because of the need for the standardization of public welfare statistics. Day let Ogburn, Chairman of the PPC for 1928–29, know that there was considerable interest at the RF in the prospect of work in this area.[47] Apart from general interest it is certain that Day was expressing a personal concern. He had been a member of the Central Bureau of Planning and Statistics, created by the federal government under Gay's leadership in 1918. This body operated as an independent agency under the president and served the function of clearinghouse for

---

of the Impacts of Culture and Personality," Day to Van Sickle, December 3, 1930, p. 1, Folder 4828, 200S, SSRCA—Yale Seminar, 1930–31, RF, 1.1, 200, 408, RAC.

44. Letter/proposal, Wilson to N. S. Thompson (secretary, RF), January 8, 1931, Folder 4813, 200S, SSRC, 1931–36, RF, 1.1, 200, 408 RAC.

45. Frank suggested that Bott be invited to an SSRC conference in 1927. See letter, Frank to Hall, April 6, 1927, Folder 684, SSRC, 1927, LSRM, Series 3, 64, RAC.

46. Robert S. Lynd, *Knowledge for What? The Place of Social Science in American Culture* (Princeton: Princeton University Press, 1939), pp. 51–53.

47. Day to Ogburn, April 9, 1929, Folder 714, SSRC—McComb, 1929, LSRM, Series 3, 68, RAC. Day went so far as to say that it might be possible to put through a special grant although he felt it was advantageous to have the project financed through the Council.

all statistical services. Gay, Mitchell, who was also on staff, and Day all saw the bureau as the base for developing a permanent centralized system. Day outlined how useful the bureau would be during demobilization and how essential such a body was in the process of making public policy. As Day observed, "If possible the Clearing House should be strengthened and its permanency assured," either "by alliance with some permanent Government office" or by establishing the bureau "as a permanent extra-departmental Central Statistical Office."[48] Further, while the ASTA and the AEA were somewhat ambivalent about too much involvement in public affairs, both organizations had through their Committees on Federal Statistics tried to promote a central bureau. Despite all these efforts the bureau was allowed to expire in 1919.[49] Finally, Day had been a representative of the ASTA to the SSRC since 1924.

The aim of having a direct impact on the provision of national statistics was not achieved during the early life of the Committee on Social Statistics. While the committee did cooperate with the Research Committee on Social Trends, it was for the most part involved in rather ineffectual attempts to increase the use of social statistics. The committee did serve the general purpose of providing advice on projects that involved statistics. Harrison was chairman (1929–31) and Stuart A. Rice, professor of sociology and statistics, University of Pennsylvania, was the staff member assigned as secretary to the committee (1931–32). These two social data committees were merged under the heading "Committee on Social Statistics" in June 1931.

The third large appropriation of $500,000 reflected that part of the LSRM's policy that emphasized integration and that dealt with dissemination. The Advisory Committee on the Organization of a Journal of Social Science Abstracts (1925–27) presented its final report at Hanover in 1927. A separate corporation was organized in 1928 to produce and maintain the *Journal of Social Science Abstracts*. The initiator Chapin was appointed editor in chief, an office he held until the demise of the journal in 1933. Chapin, a professor of sociology at the University of Minnesota, was an original Council member representing ASS and secretary to the Council (1925–27). By the early 1930s, the output of social science literature proved to be so vast that, after consideration, the Council decided that it could not justify allocating so much of its resources to this activity. This decision also reflected the fact that the RF had effectively dropped integration as a policy objective and that the Council lacked large-scale funding.

48. Quoted by Alchon, *Invisible Hand*, p. 36.

49. For accounts of the creation and operation of the Central Bureau of Planning and Statistics, see Alchon, *Invisible Hand*, pp. 28–38; Heaton, *Scholar in Action*; and Wesley C. Mitchell, "Statistics and Government," presidential address at the Eighteenth Annual Meeting of the ASTA, December 1918, republished in *Backward Art of Spending Money*, pp. 42–57.

Various efforts were made to increase contacts with other disciplines and scientific organizations. In 1928 an informal committee of cooperation with the NRC was organized, and contacts were maintained through joint committees and conferences. A similar liaison, albeit less productive, was established with the ACLS. At the first meeting in February 1928 the joint committee agreed on the division of subject areas and how it would handle problems in historical studies, which was the only area of overlap.[50] At one stage in 1929 there was even the possibility of a merger between the SSRC and the ACLS but the plan came to nothing.[51] Another aspect of these efforts by the SSRC were the plans made in 1928 to add a number of members-at-large to the Council in order to secure the services of scholars in fields like education and law that were not represented by the constituent associations. This change also meant that key network members who were not representing their discipline could either be retained or added as Council members. This was the case with Woodworth, who became one of the first members-at-large in 1929. Others in this category were Mitchell (1933–46), Mark Arthur May (1934–35), Day (1938–39), and Harrison (1938–48). Incredibly, this meant that Harrison, who was the archetype of the social scientist as foundation officer, was a Council member for twenty-four years, from 1924 to 1948.

The Quest for Scientific Methods in the Social Sciences

It is ironic that almost at the same time as the Council was receiving large appropriations from Rockefeller philanthropy another one of the LSRM's treasured objectives was being dealt a negative blow. Rockefeller officers and leading members of the SSRC hoped that the Committee on Scientific Methods in the Social Sciences (1923–29) would provide a road map for the conversion of social studies into scientific disciplines. Professor Secrist of Northwestern University chaired the committee from its inception until 1928 when Professor Robert M. MacIver took over.[52] The committee included among its members Van Kleeck, Thurstone, and Sapir. The tone had been set by Merriam in the 1926 *Annual Report* when he drew attention to the "vital importance of more severely scientific methods" in the social sciences. The committee aimed to formulate the problems and methods of the social sci-

50. Memorandum, conference, ACLS and SSRC, February 2, 1928, Folder 685, SSRC, 1928–31, LSRM, Series 3, 64, RAC.

51. Waldo B. Leland (president, ACLS) to Mitchell, March 22, 1929, and Mitchell to Day, March 25, 1929, Folder 685, SSRC, 1928–31, LSRM, Series 3, 64, RAC.

52. Initially Secrist was appointed as a committee of one to study the aims and methods of research agencies. It was not until 1926 that the committee was renamed and that the members ·vere charged with much larger tasks.

ences, to systematize the conclusions that were in place, and to provide standards of reference for scrutinizing social science research projects. These ambitious objectives stimulated some of the most important discussions about social science that occurred in the Council's deliberations. The Council organized special sessions at the Hanover conferences in 1926 and 1927 to discuss the issues. The need was expressed for a clear statement of the central theme of method in the social sciences and a formulation that in Rice's words "should show what scientific method means to the social scientist, and it should illustrate how the methods are carried out in each of the disciplines" and it "should be a synthesis and integration of methods so far developed." Much doubt was expressed about the possibility of achieving the main objectives and indeed whether or not a social science in the natural science mode was even a possibility.[53] Little headway had been made by 1929. It was therefore decided to discontinue the committee with the provision for the preparation and publication of a casebook on scientific methods in the social sciences that would present examples and partial analyses of the methods employed in a selection across social science literature. Rice, Hubert R. Kemp (University of Toronto), and Harold D. Lasswell were hired to work as coinvestigators with MacIver on this project. The project resulted in the publication of *Methods in Social Science: A Case Book* (1931), edited by Rice.[54]

The progress and work of the Committee on Scientific Methods in the Social Sciences provides insight into the difficulties that the Council faced as it tried to build a science of society that was clearly separate from the natural sciences and that cut across the boundaries that separated the social disciplines. The shape of these difficulties was expressed clearly by Rice in the foreword, introduction, and appendix, "A History and Organization of the Case Book," of the casebook. Rice referred to conflicting attitudes and viewpoints and far-reaching differences when it came to questions of definition and boundary maintenance. The committee was unable to come to an agreement about what was meant by method. As Rice observed: "No problem in the present study has offered greater difficulties than that of attaching to the terms 'method' and 'methods' consistent interpretations acceptable to all persons involved." The committee therefore decided to adopt what Rice referred to as an "inclusive interpretation" of the terms so that when it came to selecting contributions to the book the committee emphasized three broad objectives in

---

53. For details of these discussions refer to the transcripts of the 1926 and 1927 SSRC Hanover Conferences. Folders 694–97, SSRC—Conference Report, 1926, and Folders 699–700, SSRC—Conference Report, 1927, LSRM, Series 3, 65 and 66, RAC. Also see Stuart A. Rice, ed., *Methods in Social Science: A Case Book* (Chicago: University of Chicago Press, 1931), pp. 732–33.

54. Rice, *Methods in Social Science.*

the social sciences: definition, ascertainment of sequence and change, and discovery of relations. After failing to reach agreement on the numerous suggestions made by committee members, it was decided that Rice should proceed with the help of Lasswell to organize the analysis of the methods employed so that the "best" among the "genuine contributions to scientific knowledge" were included. To help the committee select outstanding contributions, the seven societies were asked to appoint advisory committees to select and recommend studies from their disciplines and fields. Even so, as Rice observed, the committee still felt that it should look beyond the "traditional divisions" in the social sciences because the most vital work often overlapped the "habitual boundaries." It turned out to be a losing battle. Echoing what must have been a keen sense of frustration for many participants, Rice concluded that the

> investigators were confronted on every hand with the existing lines of demarcation among the social sciences. Members of the Council, members of the Committee, the special advisory committees by virtue of their appointment, the prospective analysts, and all other participants, including the investigators themselves, were identified with one or another of these existing divisions.

The irony was that these men and women had found it "necessary to work within molds, from which at the same time" they "were trying to escape." What emerged from these struggles was the best compromise, but the contents fell far short of the original promise.[55]

The book contained fifty-two case analyses.[56] Yet as contemporary reviewers and later analysts pointed out, the painstaking detail contained in the cases did not take the reader far along the path from beginnings to ends. As Crick observed: "Nothing approaching a scientific law emerges from any of the Case Studies, although there are plenty of shrewd precepts for aiding greater objectivity in research and for gaining comparability of results."[57] Similarly, Mannheim concluded in his book review for the *American Journal*

---

55. Ibid., pp. v, 3, 5, 731, 734, and 737–38.

56. The cases were divided into nine sections: (1) "The Delimitation of Fields of Inquiry," (2) "The Definition of Objects of Investigation," (3) The Establishment of Units and Scales," (4) "Attempts to Discover Spatial Distributions and Temporal Sequences," (5) "Interpretations of Change as a Developmental Stage," (6) "Interpretations of Temporal Sequences with Consideration of Special Types of 'Causation'," (7) "Interpretations of Relationship among Unmeasured Factors," (8) "Attempts to Determine Relations among Measured but Experimentally Uncontrolled Factors," and (9) "Attempts to Determine Quantitative Relations among Measured and Experimentally Controlled Factors."

57. Crick, *American Science of Politics*, p. 171.

of Sociology that there existed "a very marked and painful disproportion between the vastness of the scientific machinery employed and the value of the ultimate results." The need to specify exact methods was according to Mannheim tied to an unhealthy fascination with the natural sciences, a fascination that leads analysts away from theoretical concerns to the more technical aspects of social research.[58] The book was a symbol and an indicator of the movement within the social sciences during the late 1920s and early 1930s away from fundamental, theoretically grounded research toward more practical and more technical approaches. As social scientists sought the legitimacy of scientific method they retreated within the boundaries of their own disciplines and furthered the trend toward increased professional specialization and the fragmentation of knowledge. This particular episode is a striking illustration of the difficulties these boundary workers faced as they tried to demarcate the social sciences from other knowledge.

Long-Term Objectives

During the period 1927–30 critical discussions took place concerning the long-term objectives of the Council. While these discussions certainly received an impetus with the arrival of major funding, it is the case that in early 1927 questions were already being raised about whether or not the Council was straying from its original purpose. From the beginning, Day took a leading role in these discussions. Dissatisfaction was expressed by Council members about the way in which resources were being spread too thinly over a large number of discrete projects rather than focused upon a few strategic objectives. Questions were also raised about the vetting of projects where it seemed that often the proposers and sponsors of projects were also the most influential members of the PPC, and the Council, who then made the final decision.[59]

In April 1927, Merriam appointed a Committee on Fundamental Policies and also proceeded to ask for advice from his friends at the LSRM. Frank responded to the request by commenting on the purpose and functioning of the SSRC but asked that Merriam keep his views confidential in view of the relation between the memorial and the Council. Frank made two main points. First, on the topic of integration and coordination, Frank hoped that the Council would find ways encourage social scientists from different disciplines to pool their experience and plan research problems with the objective of revealing the implications for other branches of social science. In this way,

58. Karl Mannheim, review of Rice, *Methods in Social Science*, *American Journal of Sociology* 38 (September 1932): 273–82. Quoted in Crick, *American Science of Politics*, p. 172.
59. Wirth "Report," p. 21, SSRCA.

Frank felt the Council could help discharge its obligations to coordinate the separate social science disciplines. Frank was clear that the Council should take coordination as its paramount responsibility. Second, Frank stated that it would be desirable to have the PPC "concern itself not so much with the specific details of the proposals made to it by its advisory committees as to resolve itself into a committee for the critical scrutiny of the fields of research and the implications of the problems presented to them."[60] In other words, Frank wanted the PPC to consider fundamental issues in the development of the social sciences and not get bogged down with details. The committee's report echoed the views expressed by Frank, and at times the conclusions were identically phrased.[61] The committee was convinced that the Council ought to discriminate more and that it should concentrate on finding common aims rather than approving almost everything that was presented. The committee felt that the Council had lost sight of its original objective of improving the methods of social science and seemed content to merely increase the quantity of social science knowledge.

While the level of dissatisfaction was high, there was still tremendous confidence about the Council's ability to achieve these ends. Merriam's report on the Hanover Conference noted that the Council was seeking "new patterns of research" that would bring disciplines together and that advanced the frontiers of scientific knowledge. He hoped the committee would serve in miniature the same purposes as the whole Council. Merriam ended by stating that the Council had "looked toward social invention and in a broader sense toward social intelligence as a factor in social affairs."[62] This was the point made implicitly by Ogburn and Goldenweiser in their edited collection, *The Social Sciences and Their Interrelations* (1927), and the one made explicitly by Mitchell in speeches and essays.[63] As discussed later, the language of "social intelligence" and "planning" became central elements in the internal

---

60. Letter and memorandum, Frank to Robert T. Crane (secretary, SSRC), July 13, 1927, pp. 4–5, Folder 684, SSRC, 1927, LSRM, Series 3, 64, RAC.

61. See, Wirth, "Report," pp. 21–22. This conclusion emerges from a comparison of the wording of the memorandum, Frank to Crane, July 13, 1927, and the report contained in the 1927 Conference Report. Folder 684, SSRC, 1927, and Folders 699–700, SSRC—Conference Report, 1927, LSRM, Series 3, 64–66, RAC.

62. Merriam, conference report, pp. 1–4, Folder 699, SSRC—Conference Report, 1927, LSRM, Series 3, 66, RAC.

63. Ogburn and Goldenweiser, *Social Sciences*, pp. 7–9; and Mitchell, *Backward Art of Spending Money* (first published by McGraw-Hill in 1937). Specifically, see "Quantitative Analysis in Economic Theory," (presidential address, Thirty-seventh Annual Meeting, AEA, December 29, 1924) pp. 20–41; "Statistics and Government" (presidential address, Eighteenth Annual Meeting, ASTA, December 1918), pp. 42–57; and "The Prospects of Economics," pp. 342–85, reprinted from Rexford Guy Tugwell, ed., *The Trend of Economics* (New York: F. S. Crofts and Co., 1924), pp. 3–34.

policy-making process at the RF. In any event, at this stage the Council was, according to Wirth, "looking for sectors of social science where the interest of several disciplines converged, for new frontiers, and for strategic points of contact."[64] The Council needed an explicit policy to guide it.

A major review of Council policy was undertaken at Hanover in 1929. Day exerted pressure both internally and externally and had as an ally the permanent secretary, Robert S. Lynd. The views that Lynd made clear in correspondence with Day[65] were a precursor to his more extensive public exposition, *Knowledge for What? The Place of Social Science in American Culture* (1939).[66] In Lynd's view there were two groups in the SSRC. One group believed that the social sciences would best be furthered by plunging in and doing many specific pieces of research while the other group believed in a more coordinated approach. Lynd was clearly in favor of coordination and against what he labeled as "pick and shovel" research. As he put it: "the Council is so concerned with spending its available money for easily grasped, near at hand projects that it is underplaying its potentialities as the general staff coordinating agency for research in the social sciences." Lynd suggested a larger scheme whereby a senior scholar might be brought into the office to quietly, over a five-year period, coordinate a program that encouraged "certain salient trends in research in the social sciences."[67]

In a confidential memorandum Lynd repeated and expanded the views he had expressed earlier to Day.[68] As he described the situation, there was neither integration nor coordination. The two-discipline requirement usually meant that each of the attacking disciplines simply fired at the problem from its respective angle without any attempt at a new joint strategy. There was in Lynd's view an almost complete lack of coordination among the advisory committees for which he felt the LSRM was partly to blame because it had imposed its own interests on the Council. Lynd made it clear that some of the committees like those on crime and interracial relations were created and had developed because of memorial interest in these fields. Further, he posed the direct question about the extent to which the Council was obligated to care for the "isolated chicken feed research" of which the memorial sought to be relieved. Lynd observed that the PPC was "in the uncomfortable position of not wanting to appoint more committees but of recognizing that the existing

---

64. Wirth, "Report," p. 22, SSRCA.

65. The first piece of correspondence was a letter that Lynd wrote in April 1928 to formalize a telephone conversation between himself and Day. The second document was a confidential memorandum that Lynd sent to members of the PPC and Day in August 1928.

66. Lynd, *Knowledge for What?*

67. Lynd to Day, April 27, 1928, Folder 685, SSRC, 1928–31, LSRM, Series 3, 64, RAC.

68. Confidential memorandum by Lynd, August 15, 1928, minutes, PPC, app. 3, pt. 5, SSRCA.

groups do not cover the field."[69] As he saw it, the existing committees devoted their time to burying the PPC under a mountain of bigger and better research. The imperative was to drive research proposals through so that they could receive approval at Hanover each summer. This criticism of Council operations was supported by Gay, who, while not a member of Council, did sit on the PPC from 1925 to 1928. He described the Hanover conferences as a "fierce drive" through the proposals involving endless sessions each day of the week.[70] Rather than focusing on policy issues of fundamental significance, the PPC, and hence the Council, was in Lynd's view caught in the supervision of a "manufacturing process" that continuously diversified its products. Lynd thought the SSRC ought to be looking carefully at the relation, both actual and potential, between the federal government and social science research.[71] With Hoover in the White House Lynd felt the prospects were bright. Finally, Lynd believed that the SSRC should follow the lead given by the LSRM when it called a conference of economists to Hanover for the first week in September 1928. Lynd saw this action as the sharpest challenge to the Council yet delivered, because the memorial was organizing the type of long-term planning that the PPC was supposed to be doing.

Lynd's views were discussed by the PPC at Hanover,[72] yet little was done. For the record, Day denied that the Council had any obligation to the memorial and encouraged the Council to review its past practice. Day used the Council meetings and the economists' conference that he had convened as the forum for discussions. Day was on the eve of taking up his permanent appointment as director of the social sciences for the RF, which meant that these few weeks provided the last opportunity to speak to colleagues without constraint. During the Council meetings Day presented a paper, "Trends in Social Science," in which he focused on the development of a new relationship between government and the social sciences. He described the way in which the social sciences were being embraced as relevant disciplines as government increased the scope of its activities. He concluded that this was particularly true in the case of economics.[73]

The economists' conference was convened specifically to provide Day with advice on the best policy for developing the subject of economics. At the same time, Day did include a session chaired by Mitchell on the "Interrelation

69. Ibid., pp. 3 and 4.

70. See Heaton, *Scholar in Action*, pp. 209–11.

71. This relates back to the earlier letter where Lynd had asked Day to comment on a proposal to survey research by government committees. Lynd to Day, April 27, 1928, Folder 685, SSRC, 1928–31, LSRM, Series 3, 64, RAC.

72. Minutes, PPC, August 19, 1928, Hanover Conference, pp. 5–8, pt. 4, SSRCA.

73. For an account of this speech refer to the transcript of the economists' conference, pp. 79–80, Folders 702–3, SSRC—Conference Report, 1928, LSRM, Series 3, 67, RAC.

between the Social Sciences."[74] Day organized the session because he was dissatisfied with the debate within the SSRC. While no definitive conclusion was reached either about the scientific nature of the social sciences or the possibilities for integration, the meetings did have a direct influence on SSRC policy. Day made it clear that he believed it was possible for social scientists to separate their functions as scientists and citizens, that is, to separate facts and values. Even in those cases where a researcher was personally interested in the problem, Day still felt that the social scientist could proceed with complete detachment.[75] While Day was in favor of a problem-oriented approach as a means of promoting integrated social scientific research, he also felt that economics would, because of the lead established, be extremely important in such a movement. Included in the conference were some of the leading members of the SSRC: Merriam, Gay, Moulton, Ogburn, and Mitchell.

For all the attempts to promote interdisciplinary work and interrelations between the social science disciplines, it appeared that what Rice would later call the "habitual boundaries" were already too strong. Most social scientists found themselves pulled into doing boundary work that fortified their own discipline or field rather that the general aim of a social science. Ironically these actions were encouraged in a latent and unanticipated way by the institutions and the social scientists that led the fight for more coordination and integration. The bargain that social scientists were striking with the State in order to increase the legitimacy of their disciplines and to further their own careers as public persons was explicitly tilted toward practical, quantitative investigations. Similarly, although in a less obvious way, Rockefeller philanthropy was moving toward a definition of science that implied a more realistic approach to research and toward the relationship between the social sciences and government. Scientists like Merriam, Mitchell, Ogburn, Gay, and Moulton were part of the trend, although they held on to what might be labeled as fundamentally oriented social problem research. In any event, the drive toward statistically based science in the service of government meant, as Lynd and Day pointed out, that fundamental development at the level of theory and basic research was inhibited. Social science ideology was by the end of the 1920s tilting firmly in the direction of the interests of the ruling class and the State. The boundary around the social sciences embodied enough legitimacy and cognitive authority for these disciplines and scientists to be used as tools in the quest for stability and order. The internal dissension between and within the social disciplines was a reflection of the contradictory forces that pressed on institutions and social scientists as they tried to simulta-

---

74. Ibid., pp. 135–227.
75. Ibid., p. 77.

neously serve opposing interests. These tensions became increasingly obvious within the SSRC and the RF.

Consolidation of Rockefeller Philanthropy: The Division of the Social Sciences

In 1929, Rockefeller philanthropy consolidated most of its separate interests into one organization, the RF. The LSRM became the DSS, with Day as director. Some of the most sensitive tasks were taken over by the SF, a new foundation that concentrated on public administration. Ruml was made Director of the SF. As early as 1926 it was envisaged by John D. Rockefeller, Jr., and other RF officers that Rockefeller philanthropy ought to consolidate its separate pieces into a larger whole.[76] To prepare for the incorporation of the LSRM into the RF it was considered desirable to appoint a committee to review the record of the memorial and make recommendations for the future. A committee of three trustees, which included Fosdick (chair), Woods, and Ernest M. Hopkins, president of Dartmouth College, was appointed to the task. The committee undertook an extensive process of consultation with academics, foundation officers, and trustees. These three sources generally agreed that the LSRM was neglecting the practical application of the findings of social science and that there ought to be more activity in the social technology part of the program.[77] The committee endorsed the international nature of the program, the focus on institutional centers, and the development of able personnel. The promotion of scientific social research remained the central underpinning of the committee's recommendations. Yet there was a shift. The report recommended that the program should extend to include applied branches of social science such as business, public administration, law, and social work. The general purposes were described in the following way:

> (a) increase the body of knowledge which in the hands of competent technicians may be expected in time to result in substantial social control; (b) enlarge the general stock of ideas which should be in the common possession of all intelligent members of civilized society; and (c) spread the appreciation of the appropriateness and value of scientific methods in the simplification and solution of modern social problems.[78]

---

76. Letters, JDR, Jr., to JDR, April 9, 1926, and JDR to JDR, Jr., May 4, 1926, Folder 36, John D. Rockefeller, Jr., 1919–28, LSRM, Series 2, 3, RAC.

77. "Digest of Opinions—Committee of Review," p. 1, Folder 531, Committee of Review—Social Sciences, February–December 1928, LSRM, Series 3, 50, RAC.

78. "Tentative Report of the Trustee Review Committee of Three," pp. 1–2, Folder 531, Committee of Review—Social Sciences, February–December 1928, LSRM, Series 3, 50, RAC.

The primary interest of the program was described as "those phases of social science and social technology which bear some direct relation to *contemporary* social problems." Possibilities for social experimentation and opportunities for practical demonstration were to be kept constantly in mind.[79] The general tone reflected the belief that the LSRM should not be so much concerned with knowledge or the development of science but with the production of knowledge that could be utilized directly to increase social control.

In October 1928, Day took over from Ruml as director of the LSRM in preparation for the memorial's incorporation into the RF.[80] Inevitably the report of the review committee guided Day in his new role. Like Ruml, Day believed in the potential of the social sciences to contribute to human welfare. Furthermore, Day, along with other RF officers and trustees, worried that the crash of the stock market in 1929 might be the beginning of a major challenge to the social order. In this context, the need for scientific research that contributed to social control was even more pressing than before.

Day set out his plans for the development of the social sciences in a series of meetings in 1930. While Day accepted that the scientific attitude had spread during the 1920s, he still felt that as young disciplines the social sciences were in an experimental stage. He tried to resist the pressure from the trustees to focus on the immediate and the practical and argued that the DSS should continue the work of the LSRM by emphasizing the fundamental development of the social sciences. Day wanted the DSS to pursue two directions. First, the attempt "to apply scientific methods to the analysis of social phenomena; and second, an experiment in utilizing the results obtained from scientific analysis to effect substantial and significant methods of social control." Science was an attitude rather than simply a method. Just as methods like laboratory experiments were inappropriate for the social sciences, so Day felt that broad generalizations that characterized the natural sciences were inaccessible. Yet great advances could be made if the DSS hastened "the general adoption of the scientific attitude" by fixing firmly in the social sciences "the scientific tradition and habit of mind."[81] The program must in Day's words "activate a scientific approach in the sense of an objective, dispassionate treatment and interpretation of dependable observations of social phenomena."[82] In this way Day hoped that scientific social inquiry would eliminate controversy and therefore be valuable as a mechanism of

---

79. Ibid., pp. 2–3.

80. Day was appointed at the enormous annual salary of $20,000.

81. "Staff Meeting, January 14, 1930," p. 1, Folder 2, Program and Policy, 1929–32, RF, 910, 1, RAC.

82. "A Brief Summary of the Conference of Trustees and Officers, October 1930," pp. 14–15, Folder 166, Program and Policy—Reports, PRO-15, PRO-22, 1926–30, RF, 900, 22, RAC.

social control. The "science" of these investigations and the validity of the knowledge produced would become clear as the knowledge was utilized and social control attained.

The justification for this policy repeated the concern expressed earlier within the LSRM and by other social scientists about the gap that modern science had created between material development and agencies of social control. The need to narrow this gap had become that much more urgent as society plunged into the worst economic crisis of the twentieth century. Without substantial control Day felt that "the prospect of civilization assumes a different color, and there cannot but be grave doubts about the possibility of overcoming some of the difficulties which are developing increasingly in our social relations."[83] Similarly, Fosdick observed that the natural sciences had revolutionized methods of living. He was convinced that in no other field was there such an urgent need as the development of a scientific approach to social problems. In economics the world had become a single organization where countries were mutually dependent. Yet international relations had not kept pace. As Fosdick put it: "One of the real dangers which the world faces today lies in the fact that economic internationalism has far outstripped political internationalism. We have been trying to run a 20th century civilized world with the social apparatus devised for an 18th century agricultural civilization."[84] Fosdick posed the question of how the RF could "harness social intelligence" to the tasks that faced the international order.

For Day, the SSRC was an essential part of the promotion of fundamental social science. The SSRC contributed services to the RF that could not be obtained from universities or research institutes, and it had an impact on the social sciences as a whole through the provision of advisory and planning services and the administration of grants-in-aid, fellowships, and small projects.[85] Even so, the move within the RF to concentrate resources and effort did have an effect upon the DSS. While the LSRM had not formally concentrated attention on specific areas, certain programs had gradually assumed the character of focal points. This was certainly the case for economic planning and international relations and to a lesser extent held for cultural anthropology, criminology, legal research, and personality and behavior.[86] By

---

83. "Staff Meeting, January 14, 1930," p. 1, Folder 2, Program and Policy, 1929–32, RF, 910, 1, RAC.

84. "Memorandum on the Connection of the Foundation with the League of Nations," Fosdick to Walker (officer of the LSRM and DSS), March 20, 1930, p. 2, Folder 60, Program and Policy—International Relations, 1929–41, RF, 910, 7, RAC.

85. "Staff Meeting, January 14, 1930," Folder 2, Program and Policy, 1929–32, RF, 910, 1, RAC.

86. "The Rockefeller Foundation Agenda for Special Meeting, April 11, 1933," pp. 42–43, Folder 168, 900, Program and Policy—Reports, PRO-23, PRO-24, 1933, RF, 900, 22, RAC.

the end of 1930, the principle of increased specialization, with regard to fields of interest, had been adopted by the DSS. At a staff conference in January, Day outlined three fields of social disturbance as the ones most appropriate for concentrated support. These fields were international relations, interracial relations, and industrial relations. This movement toward specialization and the focus on real, practical concerns were again responses to the review committee's report and the developing economic crisis. Day emphasized the practical theme when he referred to the program in social technology. Day observed that if practical effect was to be given to the social sciences then "they need to work out thorough social technology—work over into govern-ment administration, modify business practice, etc."[87]

In late October 1930, the trustees and officers of the RF met at Princeton University to formulate policy. This group came to a formal agreement that concentration and specialization were desirable objectives for all the divisions of the RF. Even though the DSS was in part released from the policy, "fields of interest" did take on a new significance. Day suggested that the division might focus on six fields, which included the three already mentioned as well as personality development, public administration, and community organiza-tion and planning. Public administration was to be pursued in conjunction with the SF.[88]

A Redefinition of SSRC Policy:
The Seven Roman Numerals

Soon after taking over at the RF Day intervened directly in the affairs of the SSRC. He suggested a separate appropriations committee with complete re-sponsibility for funds in order to force the PPC to "devote itself to developing issues, policies and contacts."[89] Day felt that the Council's work showed little evidence of planning a general campaign for the social sciences. Day urged the PPC to study the patterns of work of the Council's committees and to ask itself if there were not other ways of promoting research apart from simply funding projects. A week of the 1929 Hanover Conference was eventually set aside for major policy discussions.

Day and Ruml dominated these summer talks. There was no pretense about separation between Rockefeller philanthropy and the Council. In the first meeting when Ogburn raised the question whether the Council should be

---

87. "Staff Meeting, January 14, 1930," pp. 3–4, Folder 2, Program and Policy, 1929–32, RF, 910, 1, RAC.

88. "A Brief Summary of the Conference of Trustees and Officers, October 1930," DR 428, pp. 15–16, Folder 166, 900, Program and Policy—Reports, PRO-15, PRO-22, 1926–30, RF, 900, 22, RAC.

89. Minutes, PPC, November 24, 1928, p. 268, pt. 3, SSRCA.

concerned with social engineering or social science, Day came down emphatically on the side of science. As recorded in the minutes, "Mr. Day insisted that the Council's concern is with fundamental societal problems in dealing with which it is possible to develop certain scientific techniques, recognizing certain patterns that would tend to preserve the highest possible standards of procedure. He stressed the importance of the scientific solution."[90] Moulton and Day were appointed as a committee of two to prepare a list of topics for discussion.[91] The committee came back with a list of seven topics that significantly included as the first five suggestions the ones that Day had made in the previous meeting. This list was to become the celebrated Roman Numerals that guided Council activity through the 1930s. Committees were appointed to prepare a statement on each problem.[92] Ruml who chaired the first and most important policy committee on research organization felt the primary planning ought to be done in the six category committees while his committee remained at the general level. As he put it: "There should be definite recasting of projects, the pursuit of an active policy rather than an inactive policy."[93] Day along with Moulton and Arthur M. Schlesinger were appointed as a committee to codify the objectives. Schlesinger was a Council member representing AHA, and in 1929 vice-chairman of the SSRC.

The seven Roman Numerals became the principal objectives of the Council. They were as follows: (I) improvement of research organization; (II) development of research personnel; (III) enlargement, improvement, and preservation of research materials; (IV) improvement of research methods; (V) dissemination of methods and results of investigation; (VI) facilitation of research work; (VII) enhancement of the public appreciation of the significance of the social sciences.[94] Each objective was made specific through detailed rules and procedures. The original commitments to scientization, to coordination, and to integration were specified. This was particularly the case in three of the most important objectives, namely, I, II, and VI.[95] Yet there was less emphasis on integration than one might have expected. The tentative commitment to integration was given form in the 1928–29 *Annual Report*

---

90. Minutes, PPC, August 19, 1929, p. 119, pt. 8, SSRCA.

91. Minutes, PPC, August 20, 1929, pt. 8, SSRCA.

92. The problems and the membership of each committee were as follows: (1) organization of social science research (Ruml, Merriam, and Harrison), (2) competent personnel (Van Sickle and Woodworth), (3) basic materials (Arthur M. Schlesinger, professor of history at Harvard, Wilson, and Givens, an RF officer), (4) improvement of method (Mitchell and Ogburn), (5) publication and dissemination (Lynd and Frank), (6) enhancement of the public appreciation of the significance of the social sciences (Hall and Day), and (7) facilitating research projects (Moulton and John Lewis Beyl). Minutes, PPC, August 21, 1929, pt. 3, SSRCA.

93. Ibid., p. 131.

94. Review of council policy, SSRC, pp. 1–12, SSRCA.

95. Ibid.

when the Council drew attention to a possible misunderstanding that it was only interested in "merged research." The report observed that the Council did not mean to exclude single discipline–based investigations. In any event, the numerals represented no less than a charter for the SSRC that covered both policy and program.

The new president of the SSRC, Wilson, downplayed the significance of the numerals by describing them as a definition of policy rather than a reorganization or a reordering of priorities. At the same meeting, Day made it very clear that there had not only been an ordering of objectives but also that some new interests had been included. Day emphasized the need for action. As the minutes recorded: "Mr. Day thought it would be unfortunate if the plan were simply accepted and made the basis for study during the next year without specifically undertaking some of the functions which are here recognized for the first time as dominant Council interests."[96] And, as already noted, the process was underway. At the same time as the PPC was discussing policy, it also approved the Committees on Social Statistics, on the Utilization of Social Data, on Materials for Research, and on Scientific Publications. Further, Day pushed for the appointment of a committee to take up the general issue of personnel (numeral II). The Advisory Committee on Social Science Personnel (1930 onward) had Day as the first chairman. This committee oversaw the development of research personnel in the social sciences, paying particular attention to recruitment and training. The Committee on Research Fellowships in Social Science was merged into this general committee in 1933.

Significant efforts were underway to improve research organization (numeral I). Following the policy discussions the local university research councils were invited to hold a conference at Hanover.[97] This was the group's first official meeting, and the SSRC hoped that means might be found for cooperation and interaction between the councils. The Council wanted to help the local councils find better means for integrating disciplines. The SSRC saw itself as the coordinator and clearinghouse for all these efforts. Representatives came from all the Rockefeller regional social science research centers: Chicago, Columbia, Harvard, North Carolina at Chapel Hill, Stanford, Texas at Austin, Virginia, and Yale. Schlesinger, the representative from Harvard and a member of the PPC, opened with a statement about the objectives of the SSRC concerning coordination and integration. In the final resolution the councils congratulated themselves about the ways in which they had contributed to integration and the development of problem-oriented research. Yet

---

96. Minutes, PPC, August 21, 1929, p. 139, pt. 8, SSRCA.

97. The meeting was held between August 26 and 28. "Report to the SSRC of a Committee of Representatives of University Research Councils," Hanover Conference, August 26–28, 1929, minutes, PPC, app. 4, pt. 9, November 16, 1929–April 3, 1930, SSRCA.

the resolution was really window dressing. Even with the presence of forceful advocates like Ruml, little progress was achieved. It was agreed that the SSRC ought to be a clearinghouse and that the conferences should be repeated. The representatives could not agree on anything that at the local level might further integration. They could find no best organizational structure and saw no need for any defined relation between the councils. The agreement to back the development of a strategic, long-term program was countered by the clause that allowed individual research interests that lay outside the general program to be included within the regional research programs.[98]

Integration as an objective receded into the background, but the attempts at coordination continued through the 1930s. The local councils met again in 1934 and 1935, and the Advisory Committee on University Social Science Research Organizations (1935–46) was created. This committee proceeded to sponsor annual conferences. Finally, the SSRC appointed a Committee for the Chicago World Fair (1930–33), and Odum was persuaded to organize a social science exhibit on behalf of the Council.[99]

Regionalism: The Pacific and Southern Committees

Other moves to improve research organization involved the Council in a policy shift that embraced regionalism as an organizing concept. The PPC approved the creation of two regional committees: the Southern Regional (1929–47) and the Pacific Coast Regional (1929–46). Several factors combined to produce this striking development. Within the Council it was clear that the organization had from its inception been dominated and heavily biased toward Chicago and the northeastern section of the country. This background coupled with the long distances that separated the regions made it difficult for the Council to effectively coordinate research. The continuous strand of Rockefeller policy that emphasized regional development was also important in encouraging both the regional institutions and the Council to consider this option. Finally, individual figures like Odum and Hall were terribly important, for it was they who acted as advocates for their specific regions and pointed to some of the problems that could only be tackled on a regional basis. It was therefore decided that these committees should carry through the policies of the Council, should organize at least one regional conference a year, and should prepare research recommendations on regional problems.[100]

---

98. Ibid.

99. See Howard Washington Odum, "Notes on Recent Trends in the Application of the Social Sciences," *Social Forces* 11 (May 1933): 477–88.

100. SSRC, *Decennial Report*, p. 57.

Appropriately, Odum became the first chair of the Southern Regional Committee. From the beginning of Odum's relationship with Ruml and the memorial he aimed at making the institute at the University of North Carolina at Chapel Hill the social science research center for the South.[101] To this end he founded the journal *Social Forces*, obtained substantial research funding for the University of North Carolina from the LSRM, and organized a number of southern social science teacher conferences. As already noted, Odum was supervising research projects on southern topics through various SSRC committees, the St. Helena work being the most prominent example. Odum certainly had high hopes that the new committee would change social research in the South and proceeded to push men like Wilson Gee of Virginia and other southerners to get involved.[102]

The Southern Regional Committee was appointed in 1929 to represent thirteen southern states, including Texas.[103] Odum organized the first meeting in 1930. Annual conferences began, and Odum proceeded during the next five years to organize and supervise the research funded by the SSRC, which resulted in the epoch-making *Southern Regions of the United States* (1936).[104] For this work Odum obtained a separate grant of $45,000 over four years, 1931 to 1935, from the GEB.[105] This enormous undertaking provided a composite picture of the region and suggested a framework and a series of strategies for regional planning. The team adopted a regional-national viewpoint and saw the South as the testing ground for American regionalism. The SSRC committee hoped that the wealth of graphs, statistics, and cultural description would provide the basis for "stable practical planning." As Odum observed in his introduction: "The emphasis has . . . been pre-eminently upon practical design and planning so geared to regional reality and national administration as to insure results commensurate with the demands of crisis and change and in harmony with the living principles of American institutions."[106] The book was a testament to the continuing faith displayed by men like Odum in the capacity of social scientific knowledge to both inform and effect public policy.

---

101. Odum's ambition for the University of North Carolina and his perseverance from Rockefeller philanthropy is well documented. See Box 1, 1910, 1919–22, Box 2, 1923–September 1924, and Box 3, October 1924–March 1925. HOP, University of North Carolina.

102. Odum to Ogburn (chairman of PPC, SSRC), November 4, 1929, Box 9, July 1928–December 1929, HOP, University of North Carolina.

103. Minutes, PPC, November 16, 1929, pt. 9, November 16, 1929–April 3, 1930, SSRCA.

104. Howard Washington Odum, *Southern Regions of the United States* (Chapel Hill: University of North Carolina Press, 1936; New York: Agathon Press, 1969).

105. Docket, June 16, 1933, Folder 4816, 200S, SSRC–TVA, 1933, RF, 1.1, 200, 407, RAC.

106. Odum, *Southern Regions*, p. ix.

In conjunction with the newly formed Southern Regional Committee the PPC had in 1929 appointed a Committee on Southern Fellowships in the Social Sciences (1929–33), with Professor Alexander of Atlanta University as chairman. These fellowships were funded by a grant of $50,000 from the Julius Rosenwald Fund and were aimed at stimulating social science personnel and activities in the South. This scheme was introduced as a result of the pressure by Odum and the fact that by the year 1929–30 only one graduate of a southern university had received a SSRC fellowship.[107] The new fellowships, which were only open to graduates of southern colleges, were intended to fill this gap. A total of sixty-three awards were made over the next four years, including four reappointments. The grant from the Rosenwald Fund was not renewed.

The Pacific Coast Regional Committee held its first meeting in March 1930 and selected Hall as the chair. The committee aimed to represent the three western states as well as British Columbia in Canada. The primary activity during the 1930s was the annual conference of the Pacific Institute of Social Scientists, which began in 1931. At the third annual conference in 1933, Kroeber, L. M. Terman, and Ogburn all presented papers under the conference title "How Far are Social Forces Controllable?"[108] No major studies were undertaken and western social scientists continued to compete for the SSRC fellowships. This is not so surprising in that graduates of Stanford University and the Universities of California at Berkeley and Oregon had achieved limited success in this competition.[109]

Recent Social Trends

The most significant action pursued under numeral VII, "enhancement of the general appreciation of the significance of the social sciences," occurred during the period 1929 to 1933 with the organization and work of the Presidential Recent Trends Committee (RTC). While social scientists had been involved in giving advice to, and conducting research for, government departments increasingly since the beginning of the First World War,[110] it was still the case that the appointment of the RTC marked a major turning point in the relation between government and the social sciences. This was an exercise in mutual legitimation. There were three key players: President Hoover, Rocke-

---

107. Walter R. Sharp, "Report on the Results of the Research Fellowship Programs for the Period, 1925–1931," minutes, PPC, app. 10, p. 24, table 4A, pt. 14, June 21–July 1, 1931, SSRCA.

108. A. L. Kroeber et al., *How Far Are Social Forces Controllable?* (San Francisco: Social Science Research Conference of the Pacific Coast, 1933).

109. Ibid.

110. Lyons, *Uneasy Partnership*, ch. 11.

feller philanthropy, and the SSRC. Throughout his career as a federal politician Hoover was constantly trying to encourage philanthropy, industry, and the academy to work together at producing scientific knowledge about social problems.[111] As secretary of commerce he had been instrumental in the creation of the President's Conference on Unemployment in 1921. This action was prompted by the depression and subsequent collapse of business in 1920–21. Under Hoover's leadership, business, labor, government, philanthropy, and the academy were brought together to attack a major social ill. Mitchell and the NBER were commissioned to undertake three national economic surveys by the conference. The last such study was *Recent Economic Changes in the United States* (1929),[112] which set out to describe and analyze the economic changes that had occurred in the seven years since 1922. This two-volume report was the embodiment of what Alchon referred to as the "technocratic bargain" between government, social scientists, and the foundations.[113]

As noted earlier, Gay and Mitchell were in charge of the project. The report is optimistic about the future and inevitably incorporates the confidence that these economists placed in the potential of social scientific knowledge for solving social problems. They began by noting that "acceleration rather than structural change is the key to our understanding of our recent economic developments." In the section on "economic balance" the authors noted that the period under study was one in which the people of the United States had been welded "into a new solidarity of thought and action." The last seven years had been characterized by a "more marked balance of production-consumption" and "a balance between economic forces . . . which has enabled the intricate machine to produce and serve our people." The authors made a special plea for the increased support of social research as a means of maintaining the balance and establishing control over the economy. As the authors observed:

> To maintain the dynamic equilibrium of recent years is, indeed, a problem of leadership which more and more demands deliberate public attention and control. Research and study, the orderly classification of knowledge, joined to increasing skill, well may make complete control of the economic system a possibility. The problems are many and difficult, but the degree of progress in recent years inspires us with high hopes.

---

111. *Memoirs of Hoover*, vols. 2 and 3.

112. *Recent Economic Changes*. The RF subsequently provided $50,000 in 1930 toward the continuation of this work. See Docket, President's Conference on Unemployment, May 8, 1930. Folder 4578, 200S, President's Conference on Unemployment, 1930–31, RF, 1.1, 200, 387, RAC.

113. Alchon, *Invisible Hand*.

The report ends with the recommendation that society must develop "a technique of balance," that is, those practical processes by which the wide swings in the business cycle might be avoided, thereby ensuring more continuous growth and prosperity. The CREC believed that the skillful work of economists, engineers, and statisticians was an essential component in this development process. As the authors observed: "Informed leadership is vital to the maintenance of equilibrium. It depends upon a general knowledge of the relations of the parts each to the whole. Only through incessant observation and adjustment of our economy, can we learn to maintain the economic balance."[114]

Through the 1920s, Rockefeller philanthropy was intimately involved in the work that brought the State and social science together. The continuing interest of the family and the memorial in the work of the NBER and the close personal ties with Mitchell provided for both formal and informal input into these studies. Social control was the object and aim of these studies. As noted earlier, Day was in 1928 discussing industry as a research area that might benefit from the approach that was adopted in the study of recent economic changes. Further, during 1928–29 there were constant references to increased possibilities for government-sponsored research within Rockefeller philanthropy and among social scientists. Day made the relation between social science and government the centerpiece of his speech to the 1927 Hanover Conference, and then at the 1928 economists' conference, he organized a session on the same topic.[115]

Leading members of the SSRC were in no doubt about the positive benefits to be obtained through government research, both for society and for their disciplines. Merriam, Mitchell, Moulton, Hall, Gay, Ogburn, Odum, and Wilson were fully aware of the importance of such contacts. Part of the PPC's policy meetings in 1929 were taken up with discussions about the need for social scientists to be more actively involved in government research. As Merriam put it, the ideal situation would be one where the Council attained "such a position of leadership that governments would automatically consult the Council or local councils before starting on a problem such as city planning, housing planning, etc., where social science was involved."[116] Hall was convinced that the time was coming when governments were going to make use of social scientific advice wherever possible. Wilson drew on his experience with the NRC and recommended the SSRC firmly take the initiative in its relations with government. During these meetings the leaders of the SSRC

114. *Recent Economic Changes*, pp. ix and xix–xxii.

115. Transcript of economists' conference, Folders 702–3, SSRC–Conference Report, 1928, LSRM, Series 3, 67, RAC.

116. Minutes, PPC, August 20, 1929, Hanover Conference, p. 123, pt. 8, August 19–30, 1929, SSRCA.

held their first discussions of the RTC idea.[117] It followed that Ogburn and Odum made an offer to President Hoover to collaborate on a preliminary survey.[118]

Soon after entry into the White House in 1929, President Hoover began casting around for means by which the government could sponsor a major scientific study of the social problems facing American society.[119] Hoover, the "great believer" in science, was clear that before action could be taken to solve some of the major social policy issues like employment insurance, better housing, and old-age pensions it was necessary to produce "a competent survey of the facts in the social field."[120] Building on the success of the President's Conference on Unemployment and the contacts with social scientists Hoover quickly established that a study would be undertaken. The earliest contact occurred in April 1929 when Fred Strother, Hoover's administrative assistant, asked Odum for some input in identifying the most important social problems and about the most expedient ways in which the president might solve these problems.[121] Odum responded positively and was invited to lunch at the White House to discuss what Strother labeled the "Big Idea."[122] Over the next few months Odum acted as the organizer and coordinator of the project on behalf of the White House. Odum drew Strother's attention to the existence of the SSRC and the possibility that this organization would be the best vehicle for undertaking the study.[123]

During the fall there was an almost continuous pilgrimage of social scientists and RF officers to the White House. Hoover was determined to get the project underway. From the beginning, the RF was the most likely candidate for funding, and consequently Day decided to maintain a low profile so as not to compromise the funding recommendation.[124] Yet inevitably Day was

117. Ogburn traced the first discussion within the SSRC of the RTC idea to the 1929 Hanover meetings. "Council Relationship to Report—Social Trends," minutes, PPC, February 25, 1933, pt. 17, January 22, 1933–June 17, 1933, SSRCA.

118. Letter, Fred Strother (assistant to President Hoover) to Odum, August 22, 1929, Box 9, July 1928–December 1929, HOP, University of North Carolina.

119. See the account by Harold Orlans, "Academic Social Scientists and the Presidency: From Wilson to Nixon," *Minerva* 24 (1986): 172–204. See also David Burner, *Herbert Hoover: A Public Life* (New York: Knopf, 1979); and Eugene Lyons, *Herbert Hoover: A Biography* (Garden City: Doubleday and Co., 1964).

120. *Memoirs of Hoover*, vol. 2, p. 312.

121. Strother to Odum, April 10, 1929, Box 9, July 1928–December 1929, HOP, University of North Carolina.

122. Odum was invited to lunch on April 26, 1929. Strother to Odum, June 11, 1929, Box 9, July 1928–December 1929, HOP, University of North Carolina.

123. Strother to Odum, July 17, 1929, Box 9, July 1928–December 1929, HOP, University of North Carolina.

124. See Strother to Odum, September 15, 1929, Box 9, July 1928–December 1929, HOP, University of North Carolina.

consulted at every point along the way,[125] and in the middle of September gave formal notice to Ogburn of RF interest in the project.[126] The discussions led to a White House dinner in late September with the group that formed the nucleus of the RTC. The five social scientists who formed the reconnaissance committee were Mitchell (chair), Merriam, Ogburn, Odum, and Harrison. These men were in the forefront of the scientific social science movement, and with the exception of Odum, they were leaders of the SSRC. Mitchell and Merriam were both ex-chairs of the SSRC, and Ogburn had just finished his year as chair of the PPC. These three men and Harrison attended PPC meetings either as full or ex-officio members as follows: Harrison (1925–32), Ogburn (1927–35), Mitchell (1925–31), and Merriam (1925 onward). While Odum was clearly an important figure within the SSRC and was in 1929–30 the president of the ASS, he never represented the sociologists on the Council nor for that matter did he become a member of the PPC after his initial organizing efforts in 1925. All five men had close ties with Rockefeller philanthropy and were the key actors in the social science network represented by the SSRC.[127]

The reconnaissance committee proceeded to produce a report that also served as a proposal.[128] The report outlined a mammoth program of twenty-four investigations, each conducted by a committee over a two- to three-year period. The committee sketched the general area of investigation, made suggestions as to the composition of the research committees, and put a tag of approximately $1,550,000 on the enterprise. The committee made clear its view that the plan represented a unique opportunity for utilizing social research to improve social relations. As the RTC put it to President Hoover: "We believe that a precedent set by yourself may prove in future to be a factor of the first importance in bringing scientific method to bear upon the solution of social problems."[129] In its statement of instruction, the committee noted that the intent was to provide a review that "might supply a basis for the formulation of large national policies looking to the next phase of the national

---

125. For example Ogburn met with Day on his way to the White House meeting, September 4, 1929. See letter, Strother to Odum, September 5, 1929, Box 9, July 1928–December 1929, HOP, University of North Carolina. Mitchell had lunch with Day and Ruml on September 30, 1929. See letter, Ogburn to Odum, October 1, 1929, Box 9, July 1928–December 1929, HOP, University of North Carolina. Background information about the scientists is contained in letter, Ogburn to Day, September 5, 1929 (marked personal and confidential), Folder D, Edmund E. Day, Box 11, WFO, University of Chicago, Chicago.

126. Ogburn to Day, September 5, 1929, Folder D, Edmund E. Day, Box 1, WFO, University of Chicago.

127. Ibid. Ogburn really wanted Day to attend the meeting, but the latter insisted that he be left off the list.

128. Report of the President's Committee on Social Research, October 21, 1929, Folder 3873, 200S, Committee on Social Changes, 1929, RF, 1.1, 200, 326, RAC.

129. Ibid., p. 16.

development." The authors also noted that "the summons was unique in our history."[130]

The negotiation around the funding of this work was well in hand. Day and Ruml met with Mitchell in September to sort out the financial details as well as to discuss the project.[131] Hoover did his part by inviting George E. Vincent, the retiring President (1919–29) of the RF, and the incoming president, Max Mason (1929–36), to separate dinners at the White House during October.[132] These contacts were followed by a letter/proposal from Strother to Vincent attached to a copy of the report of the reconnaissance committee.[133] As Strother observed, the plan promised to "produce a rounded and explicit picture of the whole American social scene, with such a wealth of facts and statistics and conclusions as to form a new and unique basis of thought and action for social scientists, social workers, and those officers of government who, like himself, have a special responsibility in relation to such problems." Strother stated that President Hoover wished to assume responsibility for the project which he regarded as fundamentally important and "certain to be of the highest public as well as scientific value."[134] In his reply, Vincent nodded his hat to the office of president before assuring that the proposal would receive the most careful and sympathetic examination.[135]

At this stage there was some disagreement concerning the role of the SSRC in this project. Robert S. Lynd was against the Council assuming control. As he saw it, the RTC would take too much of the Council's energy on what he expected to be essentially a popularizing work. He was convinced that Hoover would stifle the research emphasis and would use up funds that might otherwise be used to advance the cause of scientific research. In reference to the proposal Lynd noted that

> Despite all the window-trimming regarding research embodied in the statement, I think there is every likelihood that this study will work out about as our Council surveys have worked out: a great deal of time,

130. Quoted in *Memoirs of Hoover*, vol. 2, p. 312.

131. Odum to Day, September 23, 1929, Box 9, July 1928–December 1929, HOP, University of North Carolina.

132. See Max Mason's diary, October 2, 1929. Visit at White House on President Hoover's invitation in George E. Vincent's diary, October 14, 1929. Mr. Charley (RF staff). Both in Folder 3873, 200S, Committee on Social Changes, 1929, RF, 1.1, 200S, 326, RAC. Max Mason, while still the president of the University of Chicago, had been a member of the CREC. For an account of Vincent's career, see the obituary by Ernest W. Burgess, "George Edgar Vincent 1864–1941," *American Journal of Sociology* 46 (1941): 887.

133. Report of the President's Committee on Social Research, October 21, 1929, Folder 3873, 200S, Committee on Social Changes, 1929, RF, 1.1, 200, 326, RAC.

134. Ibid.

135. Vincent to Strother, October 23, 1929, Folder 3873, 200S, Committee on Social Changes, 1929, RF, 1.1, 200, 326, RAC.

energy, and money will be put into making explicit a situation which we already can trace in its rough general proportions, and we are left at the end about where we were at the beginning as regards critical next steps on the research level.[136]

For these reasons and because the close ties between the membership of the committee and the SSRC guaranteed influence, Lynd recommended that the study come under a separately organized committee.

While there is no evidence to suggest that there was ever any doubt about Rockefeller funding, the RTC still had to present the case so that it would pass muster with both Hoover and the RF.[137] After careful negotiations with Strother,[138] Day was able to prepare a docket to present to the trustees. The DSS saw the proposal as a way of furthering scientific research, of developing the image of the social sciences as a group of disciplines, and of influencing public policy. As the docket put it: "Research of the sort proposed, given the full backing of the present administration at Washington, promises far-reaching results."[139] It was clear that the president hoped to make the report the basis of subsequent administrative action. The original reconnaissance committee was named the "President's Research Committee on Social Trends" (RST), and it chose Mitchell as chairman, Ogburn as director of research, Odum as assistant director of research, and Harrison as secretary. Edward E. Hunt of the Department of Commerce was added to the RST as a representative of the federal government and became the executive secretary.[140] Hunt had served as Hoover's representative and in similar roles in the work of the unemployment conferences and the CREC.

The RF appropriated $560,000 to the RST and made the SSRC the fiscal agent for these funds. In retrospect, it seems appropriate that the federal government was bringing social scientists into its service. The ripples of unease from the recent stock market crash were signaling the beginning of the worst economic crisis of this century. Yet by the end of 1929 the signals were not clear. Hoover defined the crash as a setback and was optimistic that an investment and wage alliance between industry and labor, and the commit-

---

136. "Memorandum to Mr. Day from Mr. Lynd," October 23, 1929, Folder 3873, 200S, Committee on Social Changes, 1929, RF, 1.1, 200, 326, RAC.

137. Ogburn (chair, PPC) to Odum, October 22, 1929, Box 9, July 1928–December 1929, HOP, University of North Carolina.

138. See latter part of files in box 9, July 1928–December 1929, HOP, University of North Carolina.

139. Docket, President's Committee on Recent Social Changes, November 13, 1929, Folder 3873, 200S, Committee on Social Changes, 1929, RF, 1.1, 200, 326, RAC.

140. Mitchell to Day, December 9, 1929, Folder 3873, 200S, Committee on Social Changes, 1929, RF, 1.1, 200, 326, RAC.

ment to increase government spending on public works, could restore the necessary balance.[141] It was against this background that the RST began its work. At least one observer was skeptical about the appointment of these men, seeing it as an indication that President Hoover was getting shorthanded. As Will Rogers saw it, the RST had no practical men. These men were all college professors, and as Rogers put it, "knowing college professors he [Hoover] gave them three years to agree on an answer."[142]

Throughout the life of the RST, Day was intimately involved in its activities. He was constantly asked to attend meetings, give advice, and use his influence.[143] Sydnor M. Walker, an officer in the DSS carried over from the LSRM, was given leave from the RF to investigate philanthropy and privately supported welfare activities.[144] Frank was released by the RF to join the committee full-time for just over a year in 1930–31 before resigning to take up an appointment with the GEB.[145] Further, there was a great deal of overlap between the activities of the RST and the SSRC. Lynd predicted correctly when he assumed that this study would be a drain on the resources of the SSRC. Many leading members of the Council and several advisory committees devoted all their energies to the RST. Yet Lynd had underestimated the commitment of Rockefeller philanthropy and the concerned social scientists to the production of a scientific rather than a popular document.

Ogburn took the first step when he organized a conference to discuss ideas and suggestions about the organization of the study.[146] Over the next two years the committee worked diligently. The main burden of the work fell to Ogburn, Odum, and Harrison. The final result was published in 1933 under

---

141. See Ellis W. Hawley, *The Great War and the Search for a Modern Order, 1917–1933* (New York: St. Martin's Press, 1979).

142. Letter, "Will Rogers Lists Reasons for Our Social Changes," December 20, 1929, *New York Times*, December 21, 1929.

143. When Hoover suggested that a woman be added to the committee, Mitchell asked for Day's approval and suggestions. Dr. Alice Hamilton of Harvard Medical School, who was on Day's list, was subsequently chosen. See letters, Hoover to Mitchell, January 8, 1930, and Mitchell to Day, January 8, 1930, Folder 3874, 200S, Committee on Social Changes, 1930, RF, 1.1, 200, 326, RAC.

144. Walker was worried about taking the job on two counts. First, she did not feel adequate to the task. Second, she expected that there might be adverse criticism when, and if, the public became aware of her role with the RF. Walker to Odum, April 17, 1930, Box 10, January–April, 1930, HOP, University of North Carolina.

145. See Ogburn to Ruml, March 22, 1930, Ogburn to Frank, April 9, 1930, and Frank to Ogburn, April 17, 1931, Folder, Lawrence K. Frank, Box 12, WFO, University of Chicago.

146. "Memorandum on the Princeton Conference, March 8–9, 1930," Mitchell to Day, Folder 3874, 200S, Committee on Social Changes, 1930, and Folder 4812, RF, 1.1, 200, 326, and 407, RAC. In addition to Ogburn, Odum, and Hunt, the following people attended this conference: Schlesinger, Rice, George Soule, Paul Kellogg, E. A. Ross, F. H. Giddings, Hornell Hart, Louis L. Lorwin, and Alvin S. Johnson.

the title *Recent Social Trends in the United States* and represented an enormous achievement.[147] In addition to the two main volumes the RST published thirteen volumes of special studies and supporting data. Over one thousand of the nation's leading specialists had been involved in the work of the RST committees. As Odum and Charles A. Beard commented, in a special issue of *Social Forces*, the RST was a unique event in the history of the United States. What had occurred was a "comprehensive, well integrated, and coordinated campaign in which the social sciences jointly attacked the emerging social problems of the nation."[148] Never before had the academy in the United States tried to capture the whole picture in such an inclusive manner. Never before had social scientists had such status bestowed upon them or been given such an opportunity to influence and formulate national policy. Contained here was a sweeping, penetrating analysis of almost every aspect of American society.

Some aspects of economic change were not covered, but this was probably because the NBER had already done much of the background analysis in the work on *Recent Economic Changes in the United States* and because the CREC was still operating. A subsidiary study on the "Planning and Control of Public Works" began in the summer of 1929, and in 1931 the committee obtained RF funding for a series of projects that were explicitly aimed at discovering "a technique of balance."[149] Alongside these efforts Gay and William Beveridge (LSE) had been successful with the support of the SSRC in obtaining $250,000 from the RF for a five-year international study of prices. The study began in January 1930 and was run by the Economic Foundation of New York.[150] In addition, Mitchell was away for most of the academic year 1931–32 on leave at Oxford University, England, and according to Odum he had refused to submit his part of the manuscript on economic backgrounds.[151] It was also likely that the members of the RST were reluctant

---

147. *Recent Social Trends*. Ogburn sent advance copies to Mason, Fosdick, Woods, Vincent, Day, and Ruml.

148. Odum, "Notes on Recent Trends," pp. 480–81; and Charles A. Beard, "Limitations to the Application of Social Sciences Implied in Recent Social Trends," *Social Forces* 11 (May 1933): 505–10.

149. The list of studies is reproduced in Alchon, *Invisible Hand*, p. 158. The CREC ceased to function in the spring of 1932. Three books were published under the auspices of the NBER as a result of the "technique of balance" studies: Frederick C. Mills, *Economic Tendencies in the United States: Aspects of Pre-War and Post-War Changes* (New York: NBER, 1932); John Maurice Clark, *Strategic Factors in Business Cycles* (New York: NBER, 1934); and Ralph Epstein, *Industrial Profits in the United States* (New York: NBER, 1934).

150. Fisher, "Impact of American Foundations," pp. 538–39; also Heaton, *Scholar in Action*.

151. Odum was incensed when Mitchell was given some credit for the final product. Letter, Odum to Walker, January 12, 1933, Folder 3877, 200S, Committee on Social Changes, 1933, RF, 1.1, 200, 326, RAC.

to draw any conclusions that might later prove to be premature when they were in the midst of so much economic confusion. The report *Recent Economic Changes in the United States* had come under intense criticism because it had not been able to predict the crisis and had presented such a positive outlook with respect to the possibilities for controlling the economy.[152] For no obvious reason the report did not include a section on either international relations or foreign policy.

Despite some shortcomings the report was still an amazing achievement. The report provided an exhaustive "scientific" survey of social problems and social organization in the United States. Data was catalogued on population, communication, family, labor, consumption, leisure, crime, health, education, racial and ethnic groups, women, public welfare, economic organization, public administration, and government. While the authors varied in the extent to which they analyzed events and made recommendations, in general they did agree about the importance of collecting social scientific knowledge in order to increase social control. The authors also displayed a fair amount of optimism about the possibilities for social engineering. Frank in his chapter "Childhood and Youth" focused on the nature/nurture debate and observed that the "belief in plasticity of human nature" and the "faith in the possibility of molding human nature and conduct" were powerful factors in child welfare work. He concluded that the "outstanding development" in the field of childhood was "the growing belief in the possibility of directing and controlling social life through the care and nurture of children." Similarly, Sutherland and C. E. Gehlke, Western Reserve University, in their chapter "Crime and Punishment" were conscious of the difficulties that a society faces when trying to achieve social control, but at the same time they were confident that the "ability to prevent crime apparently must rest on a knowledge of the processes by which crime originates and is developed." Finally, Walker in her chapter "Privately Supported Social Work" discussed how some general public policy considerations might bear on future social welfare activities. She believed that a well-conceived system of public education would go a long way to increasing economic and social self-sufficiency. Walker concluded that "public health, mental hygiene, eugenics and birth control activities have potentialities for reducing dependency due to physical and mental disorder."[153]

Even though the chapters did not include a sustained analysis of the depression, the authors did recognize the enormity of the crisis and endorsed the emerging consensus around the necessity for increased government intervention. Gay and Leo Wolman, Columbia University, in one of the two chapters to deal directly with economics noted that the recession of 1929 had

152. Alchon, *Invisible Hand*, pp. 150–66.
153. *Recent Social Trends*, vol. 2, pp. 752, 798, 1167, and 1223.

become a "depression of exceptional magnitude." They concluded that the public appeared to accept that government would play a larger part in ensuring "individual stability and financial security," and they thought that it was likely that government would take more control of the banking system and of public utilities. Walker observed that as never before the depression had "brought out clearly the economic origin of much maladjustment." Similarly, in their discussion of the "problems of consumption," Lynd and his associate Alice E. Hanson observed that consumption conditioned other social factors like health and child welfare and that, therefore, this area ought to receive attention from government and private agencies.[154]

Four authors dealt explicitly with the changing role of the State and the place of social science knowledge in these new structures. First, in his survey of the field of public administration, White pointed to the utility of "scientific management" as governments and social scientists tried to meet the demand for greater efficiency. White called for some consideration of the shift in the balance of power between federal, state, and city governments. Odum, in his wide-ranging piece on public welfare, traced the development of this field as society in the United States tried to deal with the radical social and economic changes of the nineteenth and early twentieth centuries. For Odum public welfare now occupied a new place in the social forces making the nation and was fast becoming a regular, full-fledged standard function of government as social welfare was placed alongside the other major commitments of the State to education, health, transportation, and finance. Odum outlined what were in his view the three most important emerging needs:

(1) a more adequate public relief, adapted in principle and methods to meet the demands of social change and emergency and economic cycles and depression; (2) the development of a plan for social insurance which will guarantee security and eliminate more and more the strain of social hazards and fear; and (3) social planning which will bring to bear the fullest utilization of social science and social research and their application through social work and public administration.

Carroll H. Woody, University of Chicago, in his chapter on the growth of government functions was less forthright as he looked toward the future. In his review of the period 1915 to 1930 Woody could find no striking new philosophy guiding government activity and implied that the main purpose of government was likely to remain service rather than control. Even so Woody did take into account that policies that had been appropriate during a period characterized by "rising prices, business expansion and public optimism"

---

154. Ibid., vol. 1, pp. 218 and 266–67; vol. 2, pp. 911 and 1221.

were unlikely to be the ones adopted in a period of "falling prices, economic stagnation and uncertainty." He observed that these conditions had resulted in more demands for government action and concluded that the State would face major problems as attempts were made to balance budgets and to make administration more efficient.[155]

The fourth author was Merriam, who contributed the last chapter of the report, "Government and Society." In summary form, Merriam brought together the themes of social control, planning, and strong intelligent government. Merriam made clear that an understanding of the political order depends entirely upon some deeper knowledge of the social and economic context that condition it. In his view, "only a strong government" could "either act intelligently in economic and social crises or refrain from action." Yet the problem facing society was in Merriam's view tremendously complicated. The complications arose in part because of the interpenetration of the social, economic, and political systems and in part because government needed to learn how the new scientific knowledge could be harnessed to produce social control. The danger was that government might damage the political cohesion and the basic values of liberty, justice, and progress that bound the society together. As Merriam put it:

> the developing science of human behaviour is multiplying many fold the possibilities and problems of governmental and social control. . . . The physician, the psychiatrist, the biologist, the social scientist are discovering fundamental facts regarding types and characteristics of human behaviour. They are approaching feasible forms both of social control and of emancipation through education, preventive medicine, mental hygiene, medical treatment, social work, guidance of leisure time, eugenics, semi-custodial care, that are far reaching in their implications for the social and political order. A modern government must be prepared to deal intelligently and judiciously with these new controls and releases as they are perfected and understand how to utilize them for the enrichment of the lives of its citizens in the commonwealth to come.[156]

Merriam's faith in the potential of science to solve social problems was as firm as ever. For the next decade he did all he could to make sure that the federal government used social scientific knowledge and social intelligence in its planning.

The RST report represents the best "science" that the SSRC and, by extension, that social scientists had to offer.[157] Furthermore, the report con-

---

155. Ibid., vol. 2, pp. 1271 and 1427.
156. Ibid., pp. 1489, 1536, and 1540.
157. In addition to the members of the RST it is the case that many of the authors had been

tains in summary form the language of the emerging "discourse coalition" and by extension the ideological foundations for the emerging form of cultural hegemony. The "Review of Findings" divides the analysis into four broad themes: problems of physical heritage, problems of biological heritage, problems of social heritage, and policy and problems. The focus is on the interrelation between institutions and the identified trends. "The outstanding problem" according to the review is "that of bringing about a realization of the interdependence of the factors of our complicated social structure, and of interrelating the advancing sections of our forward movement so that agriculture, labor, industry, government, education, religion and science may develop a higher degree of coordination in the next phase of national growth." The review has the stamp of sociological analysis. Reminiscent of Ogburn's earlier work on "cultural lag," the review places at the center of the document the analysis of rates of social change within the four "great social organizations": economy, government, church, and family. Unequal rates of change in these institutions and the uneven progress of scientific development, according to this analysis, produced "zones of danger and points of tension." In the section on social heritage particular attention is given to the problems arising out of three broad relations: inventions and economic organization, social organizations and social habits, and ameliorative institutions and government. The part on the economy uses the language of the CREC and recommends economic planning to deal with the central problem of "balance."[158]

The Review goes further than Hoover or probably most members of the SSRC would have expected in recommending direct government intervention to solve social problems. The review recommends the utilization of scientific knowledge to increase social control. "The objective of any conscious control over the process (of social change)" is "to secure a better adjustment between inherited nature and culture." The means for achieving "social control" is according to the review "social discovery and the wider adoption of new knowledge." The review lists three prerequisites for long-term success in the

---

or were active in the SSRC. This was the case with Thompson (Population, 1927–30), O. E. Baker (Pioneer Belts, 1926–28, and Social Statistics), Leo Wolman (Industrial Relations, 1926–30, and Industry and Trade), Ralph G. Hurlin (Social Statistics), Charles H. Judd (Personality and Culture), Hornell Hart (Crime, 1925–28), S. H. Kolb (Social and Economic Research in Agriculture, 1929–33, and Fellowships in Agricultural Economics and Rural Sociology, 1928–33), Edmund de S. Brunner (Social and Economic Research in Agriculture, 1929–32), T. J. Woofter, Jr. (Interracial, 1929–30, and Social and Economic Research in Agriculture), Edgar Sydenstriker (Eighteenth Amendment, 1925–28, Population, 1929–30 and 1931–32), Frank (Family, 1928–31, and Seminar on Culture and Personality, 1930–31), C. Luther Fry (Social Statistics), Sutherland (Crime, 1929–32), and White (Public Administration, 1928–32, Grants-in-Aid, 1926–29). Gay was one of the original members of the PPC and sat on numerous committees. Rice, Givens, and Lynd were or had been on the SSRC's staff.

158. *Recent Social Trends*, vol. 2, pp. xii, xxxi, and lix–lx.

"constructive integration of social effort": first, the political will and determination to adapt to changes by reorganizing social life; second, recognition of the "role which science must play" in such a reorganization; and, third, recognition of the intimate interrelations between "changing scientific techniques, varying social interests and institutions, modes of social education and action and broad social purposes."[159]

Echoing the words of Merriam, Fosdick, and Day the review recommends an increase in planning and the use of social intelligence.[160] To implement its recommendations the RST was clear that if social intelligence was to be integrated into the policy-making process then social scientists needed to go beyond mere fact-finding and place more emphasis on the synthesis and interpretation of data. The review is forthright about the need for more planning at all levels of government, planning that had to be based on social intelligence. The committee expected that the SSRC would prove to be "an instrumentality of great value in the broader view of the complex social problems, in the integration of social knowledge," and "in the initiative toward social planning on a high level." Specifically, the RST hoped that the Council might take the initiative and set up machinery for the consideration of ad hoc problems as well as for the "continuous generalized consideration of broader aspects of social integration and planning." Further, the review suggests that the Council organize sponsoring groups of those in authority in government, industry, and society to gather facts on social problems and interpret the data from a broader perspective. It was hoped that this type of action might help dismantle the barriers between government and the economy.[161]

The review recommends planning based on a new synthesis of science, education, economy, and government. The RST felt that it was impossible to make any progress unless these elements were drawn together. The RST hoped that a national advisory council would emerge to give form to this synthesis. The RST suggested that such a council would consider "the basic social problems of the nation" as well as "some fundamental questions of the social order, economic, governmental, educational, technical, cultural, always in their interrelation, and in the light of the trends and possibilities of modern science."[162] The review ends with a warning about the alternatives of

---

159. Ibid., pp. lxx–lxxi.

160. See Day, "Social Intelligence," commencement address, University of Vermont, June 15, 1931, Folder 21, 910, Program and Policy—Reports, PRO-45, 1931, and Day, "Proposed Foundation Program in Economic Stabilization," September 14, 1931, Folder 12, 910, Program and Policy—Reports, PRO-6–12a, 1929–33, RF, 910, 1 and 3, RAC.

161. Ibid., pp. lxxii–lxxiii.

162. Ibid., p. lxxiii.

political dictatorship and the collapse of capitalist democracy. "Unless there can be a more impressive integration of social skills and fusing of social purposes than is revealed by social trends," the Review warns, "there can be no assurance that these alternatives with their accompaniments of violent revolution, dark periods of serious repression of libertarian and democratic forms, the proscription and loss of many useful elements in the present productive systems, can be averted."[163]

On the surface the report is an exemplar of what Day referred to as "purposive science."[164] The committee and the social science community had accumulated a vast array of facts and figures on the major social problems of the day. Yet major disagreements existed within the committee and necessarily in the SSRC about the appropriate relationship between social scientists and policymakers. According to one source, a "deep cleavage" emerged between Ogburn and his colleagues Mitchell and Merriam.[165] This rift emerged because Ogburn was defined as a government man who not only downplayed politically sensitive issues but who also allowed President Hoover to read a draft of the review. Both Mitchell and Merriam were against what amounted to a political review and were critical of the draft because they thought it was too optimistic, too parochial, and ahistorical. That Ogburn had crossed the science/policy divide was not in doubt. As Beard observed, the report went beyond the "barricade of neutrality" to assert values, defend them, and then call for planning at the individual and collective levels.[166] While some commentators like Beard applauded this move, others within the SSRC were much less certain that this was the best route toward respectability for the social sciences. At one end of the continuum, Lynd maintained a skeptical attitude about any direct involvement with government. In the middle were people like Merriam and Mitchell who wanted to cooperate and be part of the policy-making process but also insisted on maintaining their independent status as "scientists." At the other end of the continuum, Ogburn saw no conflict between the roles of social scientist and policymaker. In this view, to fulfill their public role, social scientists had to be prepared to go beyond the collection and presentation of data to interpret, to advise, and to plan. The tension between these positions was exacerbated during the rest of the decade as the alliance between the State and philanthropy drew social scientists more and more into applied, service roles.

The RST report was presented to President Hoover in the fall of 1932 on

163. Ibid., p.lxxiv.
164. See Odum, "Notes on Recent Trends," p. 486.
165. See Orlans, "Academic Social Scientists," pp. 175–76. Orlans relied on the work of Karl, *Merriam and the Study of Politics*, pp. 203–19.
166. Beard, "Limitations to the Application," p. 510.

the eve of Franklin D. Roosevelt's first administration. Initially, it was feared that the change in administration might render the report and the recommendations useless.[167] As it turned out, the report was destined to have a major impact on the SSRC, the government, and the relation between government and the social sciences.

Conclusion

The last five years of the 1920s was truly a gilded age for the social sciences in the United States. There could have been no better reward for the optimism and rising expectations within the social science community than the massive appropriation of funds from Rockefeller philanthropy to the SSRC. Not only did the size of the grants inspire confidence but the length of the commitment effectively guaranteed the future of the Council through the 1930s. The continuation of research on social problems already identified and the expansion of these efforts to include work on business research, the family, public administration, and social statistics were reflections of the general mood. In 1929 the appointment of the RST seemed to place a permanent seal of approval on this group of disciplines.

The Council maintained a strong commitment to scientific advance and to integration through the adoption of the seven Roman Numerals, the creation of the regional committees, and the work of the RST. These efforts were a representation of the ideas expressed by Ogburn and Goldenweiser in their book *The Social Sciences and Their Interrelations* (1927). Yet there were already warning signals that "science" would not serve as the catalyst to break down boundaries between the disciplines. "Science" as an ideal set of practices to be attained did as much to divide and demarcate the social disciplines as bring them together. The divisions were apparent in the discussions at Hanover and specifically came to light in the work of the Committee on Scientific Methods in the Social Sciences. The tensions and contradictions were played out through the actions of men like Day, Lynd, Merriam, Mitchell, and Ogburn. All social scientists in this period, whether they were working for Rockefeller philanthropy or not, were caught between their commitments to discipline, profession, and academic social science, as well as the need to carry out the responsibilities that philanthropy and the State placed on their shoulders.

As noted in chapter 2, the contradictory class positions of foundation officials and social scientists meant that they did try to serve what were often contradictory interests simultaneously. The solution for Day was to favor

---

167. Day to Mitchell, January 3, 1933, Folder 3877, 200S, Committee on Social Changes, 1933, RF, 1.1, 200, 326, RAC.

"purposive scientific work," which allowed for disinterestedness and objectivity but clearly underplayed the push for fundamental theoretical development. For the trustees of the RF the path forward was clear. The social disciplines had advanced far enough as sciences, and now it was time to create a practical "social technology." The pressure from these men was for more concentrated research on the specific danger zones that threatened the foundation of society. The overlap of personnel between Rockefeller philanthropy and the SSRC as well as the strong participation in the affairs of the Council by Ruml, Day, Frank, and Lynd meant that by 1930 the RF had an even firmer grip on the Council than before.

By the end of the decade, the social and economic anomalies of the 1920s were beginning to coalesce into a structural collapse. The bargain struck between the foundations and the social scientists increasingly involved the State and shifted the balance toward the practical, technocratic side of the efforts to increase social control. The social control ideology was in the process of being refined to include the concepts "intelligence" and "planning." The refinement assumed that scientific knowledge about social problems would increase the social intelligence of policymakers and provide them with the bases for rational and effective planning. Rockefeller philanthropy facilitated and pushed the social control ideology in this direction. In this way, philanthropy exercised a fair amount of control over the bridging that occurred between social scientists and government and facilitated the emergence of a new form of cultural hegemony. The social science network now incorporated State interests through the actions of the Hoover administration.

In the process of mutual legitimation social scientists were much more willing than before to put aside fundamental, theoretical development in favor of practical, applied, purposive science. This trend was underway in the late 1920s but achieved heightened expression in the work of the Committee on Scientific Methods in the Social Sciences and the RST. *Methods in Social Science: A Case Book* and the RST report were indicative of the rise of empiricism and how much social scientists relied on technique to make their scientific claims. As a central element in the emerging form of cultural hegemony, Day and his trustees at the RF were moving toward concentrating resources to serve the reorganization of the political and social orders. The programs in public administration and economic/social security that dominated the work of the SSRC in the 1930s were designed as means for preventing the collapse of liberal, democratic capitalism in the United States.

Yet it would be a mistake to think that social scientists began the 1930s any less idealistic or less optimistic about the future of their disciplines than they had been five years earlier. The work of the SSRC and the appointment of the RST marked the strength of the boundary that now separated the social from the natural sciences. Social scientists were recognized in a unique way as legitimate researchers who were best able to produce the knowledge that would solve national social problems. The RST was the strongest possible statement about the utility of the social sciences for helping to maintain the democratic social order. Ogburn as director of research and the rest of the RST were still committed to the search for a science of society and made "interrelation" a key theoretical concept as well as a most important guide for the research. In adopting the seven Roman Numerals the leaders of the SSRC were affirming their faith in the ability of the social sciences to help solve social problems and increase social control. The divisions between science and policy and between empiricism and fundamental development were as yet merely symptoms of what did become an open and damaging rift in the social science field.

CHAPTER 4

Consolidation and Retrenchment, 1930–36

By 1930, research had become the most important function of the social science disciplines. Scientism, empiricism, and integration were the dominant trends. The institutional exemplar of these trends was the University of Chicago. In December 1929, the university dedicated the new Social Science Research Building, which was built with Rockefeller money to house the activities of the Local Community Research Committee. The achievements of the committee had already been recorded in the book *Chicago: An Experiment in Social Science Research* (1929), edited by Smith and White. To celebrate the new building, the committee invited distinguished scholars in the United States and Europe to a symposium. The papers presented at this symposium were subsequently published under the title *The New Social Science* (1930).[1]

The contents of this volume were a symbol of the optimism that imbued the social sciences and reflected the agenda set out by Merriam and Ruml during the 1920s. In his speech "Research in the Social Sciences," Mitchell observed that the social science disciplines were now more aware of their "common interests and their need for active cooperation."[2] As evidence for this trend, Mitchell referred to the numerous publications on interrelationships between the disciplines and used Ogburn and Goldenweiser as his example. He also referred to the soon to be published first volume of the *Encyclopedia of the Social Sciences* (1930), edited by Edwin R. A. Seligman and Alvin S. Johnson.[3] He saw the active work in the borderlands between disciplines and the activities of research agencies and institutes like Brookings, Yale, and North Carolina at Chapel Hill as further evidence for the trend. Mitchell gave pride of place to the organization of the SSRC and the local university councils, which he saw as the best contribution toward the goal of "understanding

1. Smith and White, *Chicago*; and Leonard D. White, ed., *The New Social Science* (Chicago: University of Chicago Press, 1930).

2. Wesley C. Mitchell, "Research in the Social Sciences," in White, *New Social Science,* p. 12.

3. Edwin R. A. Seligman and Alvin S. Johnson, eds., *Encyclopedia of the Social Sciences*, 15 vols. (New York: Macmillan, 1930–35). The first of the fifteen-volume encyclopedia appeared in 1930 and the last in 1935. The project was first suggested by the ASS but was eventually sponsored by ten learned societies. Gay was one of the driving forces behind the project. See

social problems" and the creation of a "common program for all the social sciences."[4]

The theme of integration was also taken up by Moulton and Ruml. In his speech "Cooperation in Social Science Research" Moulton made clear that cooperation on specific problems was the constructive way to contribute to "the solution of significant social problems and to new theoretical generalizations of importance."[5] Moulton stressed that investigations that promised significant advance frequently transcended the "bounds" of particular disciplines and therefore required cooperation. Ruml, in his speech "Recent Trends in Social Science," observed that "the new impetus for research based on an immediate and realistic experience of social phenomena" meant that the traditional social science categories were "crumbling" or were being "pushed aside." While Ruml was not naive enough to believe that a coherent conception of the social sciences had been achieved, he did think that the professional societies were "aware of their inadequacy individually to meet the demands arising from the new orientation in social science" and that steps had been taken "by the societies individually and collectively to facilitate the development of social science as a whole."[6] Even so, both Ruml and Moulton, as two of the principal architects of the movement to create a science of society, were skeptical about the long-term gains. Moulton observed that it was extremely difficult to bring disciplinarians together because each wanted to expand his or her own territory. Ruml recognized that the forces for "separation and isolation" within the associations were probably stronger than those that would lead to integration.[7]

Changing Research Strategies: Fields of Concentration

As one observer noted after reviewing the SSRC's *Decennial Report*, the most noteworthy changes in policy were the decisions to concentrate on a few research fields and to give recognition to the immediacy of important public and social problems.[8] The three years 1930–33 were dominated by efforts to

Heaton, *Scholar in Action*, pp. 207–8; and Alvin S. Johnson, *Pioneers' Progress: An Autobiography* (New York: Viking, 1952). The project was funded by the LSRM. Folder 540, Encyclopedia of the Social Sciences, 1926–28, LSRM, Series 3, 51, RAC.

4. Mitchell, "Research in the Social Sciences," pp. 13–14.

5. Harold G. Moulton, "Co-operation in Social Science Research," in White, *New Social Science*, p. 59.

6. Beardsley Ruml, "Recent Trends in Social Science," in White, *New Social Science*, p. 104.

7. Ibid.; and Moulton, "Co-operation in Social Science Research," pp. 62–63.

8. N. Peffer (reader for CC), memorandum, "Social Science Research Council—Decennial Report," File, SSRC, 1932–36, CC.

consolidate activities and integrate them into what were labeled internally as "fields of concentration." That changes were required was made clear in 1930 when the RF warned that free research funds would no longer be available.[9] This announcement, coupled with the general awareness concerning the need to cultivate the relationship between the SSRC and foundations, prompted Robert S. Lynd to propose a different format for the conferences in the summer of 1930. In a proposal to the RF, Lynd recommended that four conferences should be conducted and posited two major considerations as justification: first, the need to coordinate foundation funding in order to prevent overlap and competition and second, the need to decide on some fundamental lines of program research.[10] The suggested themes for these conferences were: (1) foundations and the social sciences, (2) business and economic research, (3) research in international relations, and (4) social psychology.

The SSRC had already decided that PPC members resident in New York should meet with Day to discuss the Hanover Conferences. This move reflected a significant change in the organization of the SSRC. Beginning in 1930 control of the PPC, and therefore of the Council, was increasingly concentrated in the New York office. Wilson, as full-time president, had also assumed the chair of the PPC.[11] This move led in 1932 to the creation of a new role, the executive director, in which the authority and functions of the president and permanent secretary were combined. Robert T. Crane, a political scientist at the University of Michigan, was appointed to the position in 1932. Crane had been a member of Council since 1923 and had taken over from Lynd as permanent secretary in 1931. The justification for these changes all centered around the goal of efficiency. In addition, these changes were probably markers in the process whereby power in the social sciences gradually shifted from Chicago and evened out to include New York and Boston.[12] If nothing else, the centralization of administrative decision making in New York and in the office of executive director, made contact between the Council and Rockefeller philanthropy that much easier. It was a short cab ride between Broadway and Park Avenue.

Day took a leading part in the PPC's discussion of projects and suggested that over the next few years the Council ought to concentrate on two or three

---

9. Wirth, "Report," p. 25, SSRCA.

10. Letter/proposal, Lynd to Walker, March 18, 1930, Folder 4812, 200S, SSRC— Summer Conference, 1930, RF, 1.1, 200, 407, RAC.

11. "Report on Existing Organization and Procedure," minutes, PPC, April 3, 1930, app. 1, pt. 9, November 16, 1929–April 3, 1930, SSRCA.

12. For accounts of this trend in sociology see Henrika Kuklick, "A 'Scientific Revolution': Sociological Theory in the United States, 1930–1945," *Sociological Inquiry* 43 (1973): 3–22; and Lengermann, "Founding of the American Sociological Review."

lines of approach.[13] Inevitably, the Council followed Day's suggestion and decided to give advice to foundations, either at their initiative or the Council's, on general research strategy in the social sciences, on individuals, and on projects. The Council agreed to seek "financing of projects only when they could be fitted into a scheme of strategy and be seen as important against that whole scheme."[14] It was agreed that Day, the PPC, and the general staff should work together to produce a strategy for the best placement of available resources.[15]

Predictably, the summer conference turned into a forum for discussing the proposed fields of concentration. The PPC meetings occupied the first four days and the mornings for the rest of the week. The afternoons contained five separate but parallel meetings on foundation directors, legal research, economic research, international relations with particular emphasis on nationalism, and personality and culture. The evenings were devoted to speeches by visiting dignitaries. Keppel began with a talk entitled "The Social Science of Spending Foundation Money" while Ruml ended the proceedings with a presentation on "The Training of Research Investigators."[16] The whole conference was an unlimited success from the RF's point of view. Day and Ruml had taken the opportunity to have meetings with the representatives of other foundations.[17] Further, they and Frank had laid out the SSRC's future program. The list of possible research areas that emerged from the conference included "production, prices, and employment," "international relations," "personality and culture," "metropolitan organization and urban life," and "public administration."

Day brought these ideas to an RF staff conference where he explained that a significant feature was that they cut "athwart recognized disciplines" and represented "areas of possible interest in scientific research having to do with certain striking developments in our social system and emergence of fairly definite problems." Day brought up the idea of utilizing the SSRC by supplying funds for an assistant within the Council. When he was questioned about whether or not this action might interfere with the freedom of the SSRC, Day replied that it was "important to broaden the viewpoint of the

13. Minutes, PPC, April 5–6 and June 6–7, 1930, and minutes, PPC, August 27, 1930, p. 26, pts. 10 and 11, June 6–7, 1930, and August 25–September 5, 1930, SSRCA.

14. Minutes, PPC, August 27, 1930, p. 6.

15. Minutes, PPC, August 27, 1930, p. 26.

16. Letter/proposal, Lynd to Walker, March 18, 1930, Folder 4812, 200S, SSRC—Summer Conference, 1930, RF, 1.1, 200, 407, RAC.

17. Other foundations represented were the CC; Julius Rosenwald Fund; Guggenheim Foundation; J. Macy, Jr., Fund; Maurice and Laura Falk Foundation; Twentieth Century Fund; and Canadian National Committee for Mental Hygiene.

Council."[18] It followed that during 1930 and 1931 the SSRC posited six fields of concentration: (1) personality and culture, (2) international relations, (3) industry and trade, (4) public administration, (5) consumption and leisure, and (6) pressure groups and propaganda. The emergence of and early programs in the area of personality and culture have already been discussed. Yet it is worth mentioning that through the decade the Committee on Personality and Culture provided a concerted attack on the then current tendency to posit "social" types of personality. The committee's efforts underlay Melville J. Herskovitz's work on acculturation and Johan Thorsten Sellin's research on culture, conflict, and crime.[19] Thomas joined the staff of this committee in 1932–33. Thomas's appointment links back to earlier work on juvenile delinquency that was arranged by Frank and funded by the LSRM. This study took place between 1925 and 1927 and resulted in the publication of *The Child in America* (1928).[20]

The last two areas, numbers (5) consumption and leisure and (6) pressure groups and propaganda, did not achieve "field" status. The Advisory Committee on Consumption and Leisure (1931–32) was approved at Hanover in 1930 and was subsequently mapped out as a unified field of research interest by Mitchell. The committee survived less than a year. The Advisory Committee on Pressure Groups and Propaganda (1931–34) was considered as a possible area at the 1930 Hanover Conference. It is likely that this committee emerged because of Merriam's influence. After a conference in 1931, the committee was appointed with Merriam's protégé, Harold D. Lasswell, as chair. Lasswell had already published a study of propaganda techniques used in the First World War in his influential book *Psychopathology and Politics* (1930).[21] The committee produced an extensive annotated bibliography on the subject that was published in 1935.[22] The three years of SSRC support served as a launching pad for both Lasswell's career and the movement led by him to

18. "Staff Conference," October 3, 1930, pp. 2–3, Folder 2, 910, Program and Policy, 1929–32, RF, 3, 910, 1, RAC.

19. Johan Thorsten Sellin, *Culture, Conflict, and Crime*, Subcommittee on Delinquency of the Committee on Personality and Culture, bulletin 41 (New York: SSRC, 1938); and Melville J. Herskovitz, *Acculturation: The Study of Culture Contact* (New York: J. J. Augustin, 1938). A subcommittee on competitive-cooperative habits produced a report, Mark Arthur May and Leonard W. Doob, *Competition and Cooperation*, bulletin 25 (New York: SSRC, 1937).

20. W. I. Thomas, *The Child in America* (New York: Knopf, 1928). See Folders 734 and 735, W. I. Thomas, 1925–26 and 1923–29, LSRM, Series 3, 69, RAC.

21. Harold D Lasswell, *Propaganda Techniques in the World War* (New York: Knopf, 1927); and Harold D. Lasswell, *Psychopathology and Politics* (1930; New York: Viking, 1960).

22. Harold D. Lasswell, Ralph D. Casey, and Bruce Lannes Smith, *Propaganda and Promotional Activities: An Annotated Bibliography* (Minneapolis: University of Minnesota Press, 1935).

adopt behavioral psychology as a tool of political science and, more generally, the policy sciences. Lasswell occupies a special place in the history of the social sciences because with his behavioral approach he more than anyone else carried the torch of interdisciplinary integration based strictly on quantitative, objective procedures.[23]

The PPC decided in 1930 that the Council should adopt three fields of concentration: international relations, business finance and industry, and public administration.[24] The SSRC sent in a proposal to the RF that requested $31,250 toward the maintenance for two and a half years of a program of research planning in international relations.[25] The intent was to provide a coordinating body and an advisory service. The proposal noted that the services of Professor Shotwell had already been secured as full-time director. In arguing for a specific grant, Day pointed out that the money would provide a contingent centralized service for the common efforts of various foundations.[26] As Day saw it, the SSRC's program was of "manifest importance to the Rockefeller Foundation." The SSRC would serve both planning and appraisal functions that were essential if the RF was going to properly develop its interest in international relations. As Day put it: "From certain points of view, there are distinct advantages in having the planning operations provided for outside, rather than inside the Foundation, and hence generally available."[27] The grant was provided and a new committee of nonacademics was appointed. Owen D. Young of the General Electric Company chaired the committee, and both Fosdick and Jerome D. Green became members. The participation of Fosdick was in line with his long-standing interest in international affairs, described in an earlier chapter. Green, an RF trustee, had a long association with Rockefeller interests.[28]

Shotwell devoted his energies full-time over the next two years to this field. He was careful to keep Day informed of his plans and at one point was given direct instructions to coordinate his European plans with the RF's gen-

---

23. For an account of Lasswell's intellectual development, see Crick, "The Conceptual Behaviour of Harold Lasswell," in *American Science of Politics*, pp. 176–209; and David Easton, "Harold Lasswell: Policy Scientist," *Journal of Politics* 12 (August 1950): 450–77.

24. Minutes, PPC, October 5–6, 1930, p. 4, pt. 12, October 5, 1930–December 15, 1930, SSRCA.

25. Docket, International Relations, April 15, 1931, Folder 4766, 200S, SSRC—International Relations, 1930–31, RF, 1.1, 200, 403, RAC.

26. Staff conference, March 27, 1931, Folder 4766, 200S, SSRC—International Relations, 1930–31, RF, 1.1, 200, 403, RAC.

27. Docket, International Relations, April 15, 1931, Folder 4766, 200S, SSRC—International Relations, 1930–31, RF, 1.1, 200, 403, RAC.

28. Green was the manager of the Rockefeller Institute of Medical Research (1910–12) and an assistant to JDR (1912–14). In addition to being the secretary of the RF (1917–23) he was a trustee of the institute (1912–32), the GEB (1912–39), and the RF (1917–23, 1928–39).

eral policy.[29] The most important result of this program was the publication in 1934 of a survey of the subject edited by E. E. Ware, *The Study of International Relations in the United States*.[30] Two other studies in this field were funded by the Carnegie Endowment and the CC. The first focused on Canadian-American relations.[31] The second grant came in 1932 from the CC to support and publish the work of Beard on the subject of the national interest.[32] Beard was an interesting choice because among the political scientists he was a vociferous opponent of scientism and the search by people like Merriam for a "science of politics."[33]

The Advisory Committee on Industry and Trade (1931–45) was created as the result of the decision to make "business finance and industry" a field of concentration. In 1930, the PPC had taken a step toward consolidation when it decided that the Business Research Committee and the Committees on Corporate Relations and Industrial Relations should be merged into one central committee. Givens had already been appointed as research secretary in charge of coordinating the work, a post he held from 1929 to 1936. Willits, professor of industrial relations at the University of Pennsylvania, was appointed chair. Willits had close ties to Rockefeller philanthropy. In 1927 he was appointed an LSRM traveling professor and was head of the Department of Industrial Research at Pennsylvania, which was established with LSRM funds.[34] Through the 1930s this section of the SSRC developed and sponsored a general program on the problem of how to control industrial and economic instability. A number of special subcommittees were established. The most

29. Interview, Day with James T. Shotwell, October 28, 1931, Folder 4766, 200S, SSRC—International Relations, 1930–31, RF, 1.1, 200, 403, RAC.

30. See sections on international relations in "New Program in the Social Sciences, Trustees Meeting, April 10, 1935," Folder 13, 910, Program and Policy—Reports, PRO-13–18, 1933–35, RF, 3, 910, 2, RAC. See E. E. Ware, *The Study of International Relations in the United States* (New York: SSRC, 1934).

31. See SSRC, *Survey of the Economic, Social, and Political Relations of Canada and the United States: Outline of Plan* (New York, 1934).

32. Item 1932 concerning funding through SSRC, File, SSRC, 1937–45, CC. Charles A. Beard, *America Faces the Future* (1932; Freeport: Books for Libraries, 1969); and Charles A. Beard, *The Open Door at Home: A Trial Philosophy of National Interest* (New York: Macmillan, 1934).

33. See Somit and Tannenhaus, *Development of American Political Science*, pp. 117–22. In 1933, as part of the general shift in the Council toward government service, the PPC created a Commission on National Policy and International Economic Relations. Docket, Commissions of Inquiry, Folder 4694, 200S, SSRC—Commission of Inquiry, September 1933–April 1934, RF, 1.1, 200, 396, RAC. Also see "New Program in the Social Sciences, Trustees Meeting, April 10, 1935," p. 21, Folder 13, 910, Program and Policy—Reports, PRO-13–18, 1933–35, RF, 3, 910, 2, RAC.

34. Folders 791–94, University of Pennsylvania—Wharton School, LSRM, Series 3, 75, RAC.

important, on unemployment, was chaired by Woods with Willits as vice-chairman. Woods coordinated this committee's efforts into the service of the President's Committee on Unemployment Relief, which he also chaired. This committee focused on the problems of industrial instability and the labor market.[35] Other subcommittees were created during these early years to study statistics, credit banking, special industries, public employment, public utilities, and savings and capital formation. As much as any other part of the SSRC this section of the program set the stage for active involvement in the economic emergency and for practical government service. From 1933 much of this committee's work was subsumed under the heading "social security."

The decision by the SSRC to make public administration a field of concentration was encouraged by government and Rockefeller philanthropy. Early in 1930, Hunt, the executive secretary of the reconnaissance committee RST from the Department of Commerce, contacted Wilson, president of the SSRC, to draw attention to the weak character of research in the service of government. He took the opportunity to encourage the study of public administration, for as Hunt described it, the government was the nation's "greatest business organization."[36] As early as 1927, Hunt had been convinced that the time had arrived for "genuine scientific planning" at the national level. He described the CREC as an "effort to carry over into the field of National policy making the knowledge of experts" and "a conspicuous example of private initiative with government collaboration." He proposed a private or semipublic national planning board composed of senior public men with a permanent research staff.[37]

Wilson provided details of the plans to extend the work of the PAC to Ruml and quoted at length from a memorandum by Robert S. Lynd, "Research in Government."[38] Lynd drew attention to the fact that "government activities underlie certain phases of every aspect of the Council's work in the entire social science field."[39] Wilson listed the research problems and called for the development of a continuing, more intensive, and specialized program in the area of public administration. Merriam and Ruml had themselves pro-

35. The president's committee received a grant of $25,000 in 1931 from the SF. See Folder 389, Special Projects—Unemployment Relief, 1931–47, SF, 4, 21, RAC. Also see *Memoirs of Hoover*, vol. 3, p. 53. Woods resigned as chair in August 1931 due to ill health and overwork.

36. Hunt to Wilson, January 6, 1930, minutes, PPC, p. 133, pt. 9, November 16, 1929–April 3, 1930, SSRCA.

37. Quoted by Alchon, *Invisible Hand*, pp. 132 and 135.

38. Letter, Wilson to Ruml, October 15, 1930, Folder 790, SSRC, 1929–32, SF, 5, 4, RAC.

39. Ibid. The suggestion that research on government agencies might become a central component of the SSRC's work had been made as early as April 1928. See letter, Lynd to Day, April 27, 1928, Folder 685, SSRC, 1928–31, LSRM, Series 3, 64, RAC.

duced an extensive survey of the field of public administration for the RF in 1930.[40]

Public administration became an area of concentration in 1930,[41] and the PAC was invited by the PPC to consider two aspects of the field: direct research in government and the problem of focusing more effective data gathering by government agencies on social problems.[42] Over the next three years this committee duly surveyed the field and brought together an extensive list of possible investigations. This background work served the Council in good stead when in 1934 the RF asked that this area become one of two central foci of the Council's work.

A New Relationship with the State:
The Council's Response to Rockefeller Philanthropy
and to the RST Report

Much of the support for the research areas international relations, industry and trade, and public administration came from a new RF grant. In 1931, President Woodworth (SSRC) wrote to Day to say that the SSRC had decided to estimate its needs under three general headings: "conference and planning," "research in the social sciences," and "grants-in-aid."[43] Woodworth, a psychologist at Columbia University, had been a Council member since 1926 and treasurer between 1927 and 1930. It is a measure of the RF's confidence in the Council that in the following year, 1932–33, the RF appropriated a total of $575,000 to the Council. This sum was divided so that $225,000 was provided over six years for general research projects, $225,000 over six years for conference and planning, and $100,000 over four years for grants-in-aid. In addition, the RF continued to provide money for postdoctoral fellowships through the 1930s. In 1932–33, the RF appropriated $180,000 over two years for these fellowships.

The early 1930s were the cockpit years from which emerged the extensive changes that occurred in relations between the private and public sectors. The crushing impact of the depression forced a drastic reevaluation of the role of the free market in economic organization and of the State in individual

---

40. Merriam and Ruml, "Observations on Trends and Opportunities in Public Administration," October 1930, Folder 94, 910, Program and Policy—Public Administration Reports, 1928–36, RF, 3, 910, 10, RAC.

41. Referred to in letter, Crane to Mason (president, RF), May 28, 1935, Folder, SSRC—Public Administration, January–August 1935, RF, 1.1, 200, 404, RAC.

42. SSRC, *Decennial Report*, p. 65.

43. Letter/proposal, Woodworth (president, SSRC) to Day, November 18, 1931, Folder 4731, 200S, SSRC—General Program, 1931–34, RF, 1.1, 200, 401, RAC.

affairs. Stock market and agricultural commodity prices fell dramatically, the Gross National Product (GNP) and industrial output fell by more than half, and by 1933 one-quarter of the labor force, approximately thirteen million workers, were unemployed, and many millions of families were experiencing real hardship.[44] As never before the two sectors were made aware that they were interdependent. Service to government became a respectable motive for private action. In turn, government intervention and control became acceptable, and "social control" took on a new meaning. The national interest required the State to confront the threat to the economic and political structure of society. The interpenetration of political and civil society became that much more explicit as the State responded to the crisis.

As noted in the last chapter, the preparation for battle had involved the commitment to a bargain between the public and private sectors that placed social scientists and their philanthropic mentors at center stage. The emerging form of cultural hegemony replaced laissez-faire economics with State intervention and State capitalism as the best means for ameliorating the worst evils of the market system. The key word was "planning." Together the State, foundations, the private sector, and social scientists were planning to protect everyone against the collapse of liberal, democratic capitalism. Planning became the central component in the ideology of social control. Social scientists were harnessed to the planning task and were expected to attach the cognitive authority of science to the enterprise. Through the SSRC social scientists sought to strengthen the boundary around their disciplines by entering public life as experts and by adapting themselves to the strictures of contract research. As leaders of the third sector, philanthropic foundations were ideally suited to occupy the role of mediator and become the catalyst for further action. True to their creators' altruistic desires, the Rockefeller foundations could help preserve and expand services that would benefit the whole society. Further, these services would help preserve the social structure that guaranteed the power and privilege of not only the Rockefeller family and foundation trustees but also the ruling class.

Within Rockefeller philanthropy, the key elements of the new definition of social control were the concepts "social intelligence" and "social planning." Day defined social intelligence as the "understanding and control of social institutions and social processes in the solution of pressing problems." Social intelligence was for Day an extension of the concept "intelligence" from problems facing individuals to problems facing society. At both levels intelligence meant understanding and mastery of problems. It was in Day's

---

44. Arthur M. Schlesinger, Jr., *The Crisis of the Old Order* (Boston: Houghton Mifflin Co., 1957); and Arthur M. Schlesinger, Jr., *The Coming of the New Deal* (Boston: Houghton Mifflin Co., 1959).

view absolutely essential that social intelligence be positively and vigorously developed in American society. By the fall of 1931 Day was convinced that the crisis facing American society and world capitalism was of a different order from previous breakdowns. The contrasts were startling. "In the midst of unexampled plenty," Day observed that "individual and family want and deterioration assume frightening proportions." Overproduction, high unemployment, falling price levels, and periodic recessions all pointed to the conclusion that "the afflictions of modern competitive society appear to be essentially organic in character." The depression convinced him that "many of the prescriptions of capitalistic individualism [would] no longer serve." The danger to capitalism and democracy was heightened in Day's view because of the alternative model that communist Russia offered with the five-year plan.[45]

The external and internal challenges to the social order had to be met with objective social planning that utilized social intelligence. As Day observed, "Social planning without adequate objectives will never save the present social order, no more humanity, in its onward march." Effective social planning had to be based on objective, realistic, and farsighted studies of social phenomena. In Day's view, the ideas of planning and control would become more acceptable to the general public as social scientific knowledge was translated into clear social objectives. "Effective social planning and control must for the present be regarded as an ultimately attainable, not as an immediately attainable, objective. Social intelligence, in brief, is to be sought by evolution, not revolution." Against this background and with the support of key Rockefeller insiders like Fosdick, Woods, and Ruml, Day proceeded to develop plans for concentrating research and for a realignment of the relationship between philanthropy and the State.[46]

The SSRC and Government Research

Rockefeller philanthropy had become during the 1920s a major supporter of the service conception to society through government with the surveys of

45. Day, "Social Intelligence," commencement address, University of Vermont, June 15, 1931, pp. 2 and 5, Folder 21, 910, Program and Policy—Reports, PRO-45, 1931, RF, 910, 3, RAC. Also Day, "Proposed Foundation Program in Economic Stabilization," September 14, 1931. pp. 2–4, Folder 12, 910, Program and Policy—Reports, PRO-6, 12a, 1929–33, RF, 910, 2, RAC.

46. Day, "Social Intelligence," commencement address, University of Vermont, June 15, 1931, p. 9, Folder 21, 910, Program and Policy—Reports, PRO-45, 1931, RF, 910, 3, RAC; and Day, "Proposed Foundation Program in Economic Stabilization," September 14, 1931. pp. 2–4, Folder 12, 910, Program and Policy—Reports, PRO-6, 12a, 1929–33, RF, 910, 2, RAC. Also Ruml, "Memorandum to Whom It May Concern. Re: Things That Might Be Done (in the Social Sciences)," September 21, 1931, Folder 2, 910, Program and Policy, 1929–32, RF, 910, 1, RAC.

unemployment and the work of the RST. Woods, Ruml, and Day placed the power of the LSRM, the RF, and then the SF behind these efforts.[47] As the depression worsened, so Rockefeller philanthropy and necessarily the Council searched for ways to combat the crisis. In 1931, Ruml set the stage for the Council to take on an important role in the emergency. In an internal memorandum entitled "Things That Might be Done (in the Social Sciences)," Ruml described how the SSRC had "abundantly proved its usefulness." He recommended that the current budget be stabilized and that "additional funds should be provided from time to time for special committees and special projects."[48] The stimulus for direct action came in 1933 as the economy sank to its lowest depth.

As the year began, the RST report provided guidelines for action, and the new occupants of the White House appeared even more willing than Hoover might have been to take positive, radical action.[49] The combination of these factors underlay the shift within both Rockefeller philanthropy and the Council to a concentration on economic security. This shift was coupled with the rapid movement toward both service and collaboration with government on immediate, practical social problems. It was a shift from the concern with basic research and fundamental development of the social sciences to the practical social welfare type activities that were later to characterize postwar federal contract research. The move was toward the trustees' view of the world. Social control ideology moved from means to ends—from an emphasis on pure science to an emphasis on applied policy. Council involvement occurred in four overlapping ways: the RF/SF emergency program, the Commissions of Inquiry, the programs in public administration and economic security (later social security), and President Roosevelt's National Resources Planning Board (NRPB).[50]

And Ruml, memorandum, December 1933, Folder 33, 910, Program and Policy—Reports, PRO-13–18, 1931–35, RF, 910, 2, RAC.

47. The close ties between Rockefeller philanthropy and government were strengthened in 1932 when Day accepted the position of U.S. representative on the Preparatory Commission of Experts for the World Monetary and Economic Conference. Similarly, Guy Moffet, the executive director of the SF was appointed by the president of the United States to be the country's delegate at the Fifth International Congress of Local Authorities in 1932. See Folder 389, Special Projects—Unemployment Relief, 1931–47, SF, 4, 3, RAC.

48. Ruml, "Memorandum to Whom It May Concern. Re: Things That Might Be Done (in the Social Sciences)," pp. 2–3, Folder 2, 910, Program and Policy, 1929–32, RF, 3, 910, 1, RAC.

49. In the same year the Brookings Institution published four books that looked at ways the economy might be invigorated. See *America's Capacity to Produce*; *America's Capacity to Consume*; *The Formation of Capital*; and *Income and Economic Progress*. These volumes are discussed by Marion Clawson, *New Deal Planning: The National Resources Planning Board* (Baltimore: Johns Hopkins University Press, 1981), pp. 33–34.

50. These undertakings were described by Peffer at the CC as unprecedented departures from the usual relation between the Council and the government. See File, SSRC, 1932–36, CC.

The ground for this diverse involvement was prepared by Ruml and Day during the first few months of 1933. Council debate focused upon the ways the SSRC ought to respond specifically to the RST report and more generally to the present crisis. Crane outlined the work of the Council. As he saw it, the RST report and the interest of President Roosevelt in direct action presented both a great opportunity and a great responsibility. The question was whether the Council should lead or react—whether the Council should serve the cause of scientific research or serve society. In essence, how far was the Council prepared to go in providing service to government? Ruml, a member of the PPC (1931–35), provided an unequivocal answer. He wanted the SSRC to make some decisive gesture in response to the report. It was Ruml's opinion that the Council should provide a road map that would lead society out of the current crisis.[51] Ogburn picked up on this point at a later meeting and proceeded to summarize the activities of the RST. In Ogburn's view, the RST had arrived at two general conclusions. First, that the whole society was interrelated and, second, that the whole social organization of the country was in a process of change with different parts changing at varying speeds. The recommendation was for systematic planning to tackle pressing social problems. While the PPC recognized that the Council was the most likely organization to tackle such planning, it was not clear about the way to achieve this objective.[52]

For Ruml, it was a matter of devising a procedure to pinpoint which issues required the intelligent study of social science. Similarly, Day posed the problem of how the SSRC was going "to single out some specific area of controversy and see how a program in that direction can be implemented." While Day thought the Council had adequate machinery to tackle this, he did question whether the Council was "contributing its utmost toward the right type of thinking" or was "exerting the influence it might in promoting the idea of a detached approach to social problems." Once again Ruml was clear that the Council should take action. He suggested that the PPC be asked or an advisory committee be created to define, clarify, and systematically formulate the important social problems over the next few years. Further, he suggested that the Council might set up Commissions of Inquiry to hold public hearings, stimulate research, and set forth opinions. These commissions would get support from external sources and in Ruml's words: "could be closely associated with the Government though not allied with it." Crane was concerned that this would mean a radical shift in the activities of the Council. For Crane, the Council had to make clear that its function was "to show the relationship between any specific conclusions reached and public policy, rather than attempt to determine what ought to be done or to advise the government on a

---

51. Minutes, PPC, January 22, 1933, pt. 17, January 22, 1933–June 17, 1933, SSRCA.
52. Minutes, PPC, February 25, 1933, pt. 17, January 22, 1933–June 17, 1933, SSRCA.

course of action." Ruml felt that the Council was well suited to such work because of the nonpartisan position of its members. The meeting ended with Ogburn giving the Rockefeller input his stamp of approval. As he observed, the RST had expected the SSRC to carry on its work by "attacking the problems of the political, social and economic organization of the Country as a whole after the manner suggested by Mr. Day and Mr. Ruml with very valuable results."[53] The PPC appointed Ruml and Ogburn as a committee of two to formulate plans for possible lines of action in light of the RST report.

Emergency Work in Face of the Crisis

The SSRC proceeded to formulate a program of emergency work designed to be of utility to the government.[54] The only direct funding from the RF under the emergency heading was a grant of $100,000 to create the Advisory Committee on Government Statistics and Information Services (1933–37). This was a joint committee with the American Statistical Association (ASTA) and reflected Day's long-standing personal interest in the efficient provision of government statistics.[55] Day chaired the advisory committee and supervised its work. Along with other leading social scientists like Ogburn, Mitchell, and Merriam, Day was convinced that social scientific analysis and national planning were only possible if there existed an expanded and centralized system of government statistics. This was part of the more general movement toward the use of statistics in social research. The committee was responsible for the establishment of the Central Statistical Board in Washington, D.C.,[56] with Rice as the first principal officer. In addition to being the editor of the famous *Methods in Social Science: A Case Book,* Rice had also published the first practical manual to guide the use of statistical techniques in political research, *Quantitative Methods in Politics* (1928). In this most influential text, Rice drew a strict distinction between means and ends and between facts and

---

53. Ibid., pp. 12, 13, 14, and 15.

54. In his draft report Wirth is clear that the SSRC's emergency program occurred as a result of Rockefeller influence. Wirth, Draft Report, p. 28, Folder 1, Box 32, Wirth, University of Chicago.

55. Day used this objective as the justification for the provision of grants to the ASTA between 1935 and 1937. This was the only discipline association to receive funds directly from the RF. See Day's remarks, "Staff Conference, November 8, 1934," Folder 3649, 200S, ASTA—Budget, 1934–36, RF, 1.1, 200, 307, RAC.

56. Dean Edgar Furniss, Graduate School of Yale, came to this conclusion in a report on the SSRC that he was commissioned to do by the 1934 RF Trustees Committee on Appraisal and Plan. The report is lost, but extracts are contained in a document, "Excerpts from National Councils, DR502," trustees meeting, December 11, 1935. The reference to the Central Statistical Board is on p. 20 of the document. Folder 27, 910, Program and Policy—Appraisal Committee (SSRC) Reports, 1935–38, RF, 3, 910, 3, RAC.

values. Science was a separate activity that could be clearly demarcated from everyday experience.[57]

The SSRC committee's work culminated in the publication of the report *Government Statistics* in 1937.[58] The report was designed to both improve government statistical and reporting services as well as make social scientists more aware of research possibilities in government source materials. This committee and the general SSRC Advisory Committee on Social Statistics set a precedent by functioning as an advisory service to the Central Statistical Board and was a symbol of the new relationship between the SSRC and the government.

The Rockefeller Foundation Emergency Fund

The rest of the emergency work was funded through a second RF fund. In 1933, the RF Board of Trustees set aside $1 million[59] to combat some of the worst effects of the depression.[60] Specifically, the committee was charged with responsibility for devising both means and measures for the prompt study of pressing social problems. The Special Trustees Committee, consisting of John D. Rockefeller, Jr., Fosdick, and the economist Walter W. Stewart, was appointed to administer the fund. Stewart combined academic respectability with wide governmental experience. In addition to holding academic posts at Amherst College he had been the director of research and statistics for the Federal Reserve Board (1922–25), an economic advisor to the Bank of England (1928–30), and in 1931 he had been appointed American member of the Special Advisory Committee to the Bank of International Settlements. Woods and Ruml at the SF were also active participants. The largest grants from this source went to the Brookings Institution to study the administration of the Agricultural Relief Act, the National Industrial Recovery Act, and a concurrent study of government financial policy.[61]

The largest grant to the SSRC from this source of $78,000 was used to study the redistribution of population as people tried to deal with the impact

57. Stuart A. Rice, *Quantitative Methods in Politics* (New York: Knopf, 1928). Also see Crick, *American Science of Politics*, pp. 164–75.

58. SSRC, *Government Statistics: A Report of the Committee on Government Statistics and Information Services*, bulletin 26 (New York: SSRC, 1937).

59. A sum extended to $1.5 million by the end of the year. See report, Special Trustees Committee, April 11, 1934," Folder 4731, 200S, Social Science—General Program, 1931–34, RF, 1.1, 200, 401, RAC.

60. Docket, Special Trustees Committee, December 13, 1933, Folder 4657, 200S, Social Problems—Special Trustees Committee—RF Minutes of Program and Appropriations under Program, 1933–35, RF, 1.1, 200, 393, RAC.

61. See "The RF and LSRM Grants," Folder 3701, 200S, Brookings Institution, 1939–41, RF, 1.1, 200, 310, RAC. Also Critchlow, *Brookings Institution*.

of the depression. The Advisory Committee on Population Redistribution (1934–37) was created in part as a response to a recommendation from the SSRC's Commission of Inquiry on Geographic Mobility. The federal government recognized the necessity to move people, and a number of agencies had programs. Yet no research had been done and no central plan had been formulated to coordinate the work of the agencies. Donald Ramsey Young, a sociologist at the University of Pennsylvania and the SSRC fellowship and grants-in-aid secretary (1932–35), visited Washington to discuss the objectives of the research project with government officials.[62] He gained support for the idea, and the RF made the grant in 1934.[63] Willits was appointed chairman of the committee, and the Wharton School of the University of Pennsylvania was given charge of the project. Carter Goodrich directed the research, which resulted in a series of publications, among them a volume on migration and economic opportunity.[64] Finally, the related Committee on Migration (differentials) (1936–38) was created to bring some order to the field of population studies and specifically to plan research on the qualitative differences between migrants and nonmigrants. The sociologist Dorothy Swaine Thomas chaired this committee. The committee's 1938 report influenced the collection and analysis of data on internal migrations in the United States.[65] The work of these two committees ran parallel to, and in some ways was a precursor to, the work on population undertaken by the NRPB's Science Committee.

The Trustees Emergency Committee made grants to the SSRC for work in two areas. In each case, the preliminary work served as an introduction to the larger efforts undertaken by the SSRC in public administration and social security. First, a grant of $10,000 was made to study the Tennessee Valley Authority (TVA).[66] Odum was the moving force behind this proposal, the intent being to hold together the group of researchers who had worked on the Southern Regional Study.[67] The government's decision to create the TVA to control and coordinate plans for regional development provided Odum with

62. Letter/report, Young to Day, November 18, 1933, Folder 4784, 200S, SSRC—Population Study, 1933–38, RF, 1.1, 200, 404, RAC.

63. Dockets, January 19, 1934, Folder 4731, 200S, SSRC—Population Study, 1933–38, RF, 1.1, 200, 404, RAC.

64. Carter Goodrich, et al., *Migrative and Economic Opportunity: The Report of the Study of Population Redistribution* (Philadelphia: University of Pennsylvania Press, 1936); and Rupert Bayless Vance, *Research Memorandum on Population Redistribution within the United States*, bulletin 42 (New York: SSRC, 1938).

65. Dorothy Swaine Thomas, *Research Memorandum on Migration Differentials*, Committee on Migration Differentials (New York: SSRC, 1938).

66. Docket, June 16, 1933, Folder 4816, 200S, SSRC—TVA, 1933, RF, 1.1, 200, 407, RAC.

67. See "Interview, Day and Walker with Odum, Thomas J. Woofter, and Mr. McLaughlin," May 14–15, 1933, Folder 4816, 200S, Social Science—TVA, 1933, RF, 1.1, 200, 407, RAC.

the ideal opportunity. The extensive engineering projects involved major changes in agriculture and industry and necessarily required social adjustment. The need to coordinate and rationalize these developments plus the guaranteed cooperation of government officials provided an exceptional opportunity for social scientists to be of direct service. Odum directed the study and expected the SSRC Southern Regional Committee to facilitate coordination among southern universities as well as provide the linkages necessary for practical utilization. The study produced a socioeconomic picture of the authority's region and provided the basis for later work on the TVA conducted under the auspices of the PAC.

A second area was the study of unemployment reserves and relief. The Special Trustees Committee granted $5,000 to the SSRC to plan more extensive research on unemployment.[68] The proposal was sponsored jointly by the SSRC's PAC and Committee on Industry and Trade. Specifically, the work was linked to Woods's subcommittee on unemployment. The justification for the proposal was the rapid trend toward centralization that followed the creation of the Federal Emergency Relief Administration and the passage of the National Industrial Recovery Act. This trend provided an opportunity for a unified study of the theories and practices that were the underpinning of the nation's attempts to combat the crisis. The project included an appraisal of the current federal efforts, the initiation of research on basic problems in the system, and, finally, the organization and integration of previous work and thinking in this field. Government cooperation was ensured.[69] This preliminary study led to the publication of an extensive report in 1934 by two members of the SSRC's Committee on Government Statistics and Information Services: Bryce M. Stewart (Industrial Relations Counsellors) and Givens (executive secretary, SSRC) *Unemployment Reserves and Relief*.[70] This work was incorporated into the larger efforts under the headings "public administration" and "social security." The only other appropriation made directly by the trustees to the SSRC was for the Commission of Inquiry on Nationalism and Internationalism.

Commissions of Inquiry

The task of setting up the Commissions of Inquiry that had begun with Ruml and Ogburn was handed over to Crane.[71] The PPC agreed to create a Committee on Commissions of Inquiry on Public Problems (1933–37), and Ruml

---

68. Docket, October 20, 1933, Folder 4824, 200S, SSRC—Unemployment Reserves and Relief, 1933–35, RF, 1.1, 200, 408, RAC.

69. Letter/proposal, Crane to Day, September 26, 1933, p. 21, Folder 4731, 200S, SSRC—Unemployment Reserves and Relief, 1933–35, RF, 1.1, 200, 407, RAC.

70. Bryce M. Stewart and Meredith B. Givens, *Unemployment Reserves and Relief* (New York: SSRC, 1934).

71. Minutes, PPC, March 15, 1933, pt. 17, January 22–June 17, 1933, SSRCA.

suggested that the SSRC ask President Roosevelt to either appoint or request the SSRC to establish these commissions.[72] Crane sent in a proposal to Day requesting a grant of $172,000 to support commissions on three urgent public problems.[73] These three problems were (1) the place of a controlled national economy in an international system, (2) population and distribution, and (3) public service personnel. The proposal and the subsequent docket both pointed out how these commissions would contribute to the present emergency by collecting facts and helping to clarify public opinion on these questions of broad social policy.[74] It was noted that the present proposals grew directly out of the recommendations of the RST. The commissions were to be modeled on the British Royal Commissions. Public hearings were seen as a means to both collect evidence and draw national attention to these activities. Yet even though the proposals had clearly come from Rockefeller staff, the trustees did not favor the plans. Only the first commission was approved, and this only after Day had persuaded them that limited experimentation with the technique was worthwhile.[75] This lack of enthusiasm for the idea was probably grounded in the old suspicion about any activities that brought Rockefeller philanthropy under public scrutiny.

The trustees appropriated $60,000 to the SSRC to support the Commission of Inquiry on Nationalism and Internationalism.[76] This body was subsequently renamed the Commission of Inquiry on National Policy and International Economic Relations and received approval from President Roosevelt.[77] Hutchins, president of the University of Chicago, was appointed chairman of the commission, and the membership included Ruml and Ford.[78] The commission completed its hearings between March and May of 1934 and produced a confidential report entitled "A National Policy in International Economic Relations."[79] The document concludes that international economic

---

72. Minutes, PPC, September 14, 1933, p. 11, pt. 18, September 7–14, 1933, SSRCA.

73. Proposal, Crane to Day, September 26, 1933, Folder 4694, 200S, SSRC—Commission of Inquiry, September 1933–April 1934, RF, 1.1, 200, 396, RAC.

74. Docket, Commission of Inquiry, Folder 4694, 200S, SSRC—Commission of Inquiry, September 1933–April 1934, RF, 1.1, 200, 396, RAC.

75. Day to Wilson (Harvard), October 30, 1933, Folder 4694, 200S, SSRC—Commission of Inquiry, September 1933–April 1934, RF, 1.1, 200, 396, RAC.

76. Docket, October 20, 1933, Folder 4657, 200S, Social Problems—Special Trustees Committee—RF Minutes of Program and Appropriations under Program, 1933–35, RF, 1.1, 200, 393, RAC.

77. Roosevelt to Crane, November 17, 1933. Referred to in Minutes, PPC, November 1933, pt. 19, October 22, 1933–November 7, 1936, SSRCA.

78. Memorandum, Hutchins and Alvin H. Hansen to members of commission, January 16, 1934, Folder 4694, 200S, SSRC—Commission of Inquiry, September 1933–April 1934, RF, 1.1, 200, 396, RAC.

79. The report is contained in Folder 4696, 200S, SSRC—Commission of Inquiry, 1934, RF, 1.1, 200S, 396, RAC.

planning was an essential foundation of any attempt to combat the inherent tension between economic nationalism and internationalism. Specifically, the commission recommended the Division on Foreign Loans and Investments to oversee such transactions and direct the traffic in appropriate ways. The commission was in favor of lowering tariffs and wanted multilateral trade agreements. In line with President Roosevelt's wishes, the commission recommended that the president should be granted independent power in these areas. The commission did not believe that the United States should rush to reestablish the gold standard. For the Commission:

> Reform, such a liberalization of commercial policy, removal of exchange restrictions, adequate central bank co-operation, removal of the intergovernmental debt problems, and international agreements to sacrifice exchange rigidity in an orderly manner when necessary for the maintenance of international equilibrium, should first be adopted in order to safeguard the workability of the reconstructed international monetary system.[80]

The report ended with a plea for increased coordination and integration within government where the issue of international economic relations was involved. To provide popular education on the issues covered by the commission and as a supplement to its activities, the RF Trustees Committee granted $15,000 to the Foreign Policy Association and the World Peace Foundation.[81]

The proposal to set up a Commission of Inquiry on Public Service Personnel was taken over by the SF. In 1929 the fund took over a commitment begun by the family in 1922 by agreeing to support the Bureau of Public Personnel Administration.[82] The SF granted a total of $67,500 to the SSRC for work on public personnel under the direction of L. O. Coffman.[83] Public personnel were perceived as a problem because of the rapid expansion of governmental activity that had occurred since the First World War, but particularly since 1929. According to the SSRC there was a need to organize and improve at all three levels of government as well as the need to reorient societal attitudes toward public service.[84] Over the next year, the commission canvassed the existing situation with regard to public personnel at the federal,

---

80. Ibid., p. 67.

81. See dockets, February 16, 1934, and January 19, 1934, and report, April 11, 1934, Folder 4657, Social Problems—Special Trustees Committee—RF Minutes of Program and Appropriations under Program, 1933–35, RF, 1.1, 200, 393, RAC.

82. Folder 198, Bureau of Public Personnel Administration, 1928–29, SF, 4, 2, RAC.

83. Folder 382, SSRC—Commission of Inquiry, SF, 4, 21, RAC.

84. Folder 4694, 200S, SSRC—Commission of Inquiry, September 1933–April 1934, RF, 1.1, 200, 396, RAC.

state, and local levels. The commission's report was widely circulated and helped to extend and improve the merit system within the civil service.

Retrenchment at the RF and the SSRC

The movement within the SSRC toward retrenchment necessarily emerged from and was dependent upon changes inside the RF. The Committee of Appraisal and Plan was nominated in December 1933 with Fosdick (chairman), Walter W. Stewart, and Angell as members. Between 1930 and 1937 Stewart was the president of Case and Pomeray Investment Company. He became a trustee of the RF (1931–50) and the GEB (1933–50) and chaired both these boards, from 1940 to 1950 and 1942 to 1950, respectively. Professor Angell, a psychologist, was the president of Yale University (1921–39). In addition to being an RF trustee he had been the acting president of the University of Chicago and president of the CC.

The committee reported that the scientific attitude was established in the social sciences. It recommended the general program be liquidated and the DSS try to apply the accumulated knowledge to solve contemporary problems of social, political, and industrial life. The committee sought "a frank shift of emphasis from the promotion of research as an objective to concrete fields of research."[85] Despite Day's strong opposition the report was accepted, and by the middle of 1935 the DSS was committed almost exclusively to three fields of interest, namely, international relations, economic security, and public administration.[86] The field of international relations had as its overall objective the improvement of relations between nations and was a continuing effort. On the other hand, the new program on economic security went beyond earlier attempts at economic stabilization. The accurate description of business cycles was no longer considered adequate. Rockefeller philanthropy wanted to respond to the social situation with a program that attempted to explain economic change and suggested ways to protect individuals against the negative effects of these changes.[87] The emphasis on public administration was a departure from past practice and rested on the belief that "social progress [is] vitally dependent upon the efficiency of performance of the functions

85. "Report of the Committee on Appraisal and Plan—Trustees Meeting, December 11, 1934," Folder 170, 900, Program and Policy—Reports, PRO-27, 27a, 1934, RF, 900, 1, RAC.

86. "Directors' Report on Program," December 11, 1935, p. 45, Folder 171, 900, Program and Policy—Reports, PRO-30, 1935–36, RF, 900, 23, RAC. To prepare for this meeting the DSS organized a conference to discuss economic security and social insurance. In addition, Day was able to utilize a survey report on research into housing problems. The RF had commissioned Ernest M. Fisher (University of Michigan) to prepare this report in November 1931. Fisher had since become the director of research for the federal administration.

87. Ibid., p. 49.

of government."[88] To achieve social progress the RF and the SF began a series of major collaborative efforts. The objectives of the new program were "(1) a program of research and service projects closely related to important questions of contemporary government policy, (2) the training of personnel for the public service." Research projects had to be "realistic." The aim was to build the infrastructure of the new interventionist State. To guarantee realism it was decided that the RF should enlist those parts of government administration that were aided by the SF "defining studies in a way most likely to make them useful to those responsible for shaping and administering public policy."[89] Underlying these programs was the trustees' belief that social scientific research would lead to practical social control.

One final element in the RF's new program was the decision to give special consideration to the SSRC. As Day observed, the SSRC, like the Brookings Institution, had "a general significance and an underlying bearing upon the specific program."[90] The RF decided that substantial support should continue. The background to this decision included a report on the SSRC that was prepared for the Committee of Appraisal and Plan by Edgar S. Furniss, the dean of the Graduate School, Yale. For the most part, Furniss was complimentary about the development and achievements of the Council. Yet he drew attention to the miscellaneous character of the research funded under the General Project Fund and commented that the Council itself did not consider the activities under this heading as "typical of its essential purpose and policy." The general fund had in Furniss's words "created troublesome problems without contributing substantially towards the furtherance of the Council's essential functions."[91] It was against this background and with Day's continuing strong support that the RF as part of its special programs commissioned the SSRC to focus on two major areas of service to the federal government, namely, social security and public administration. This was the logical extension of the program of emergency work that the Council had begun in 1933 on behalf of the RF. The SSRC was involved in order to coordinate the activities of the RF and the SF and to protect Rockefeller philanthropy from any controversy that might result from public identification with work in sensitive areas.[92] It is clear that the RF regarded the activities of the Council as supple-

88. "New Program in the Social Sciences, Trustees Meeting, April 10, 1935," DR 492, p. 25, Folder 13, 910, Program and Policy—Reports, PRO-13–18, 1933–35, RF, 910, 2, RAC.

89. "Directors' Report on Program," December 11, 1935, p. 54, Folder 171, 900, Program and Policy—Reports, PRO-28, PRO-30, 1935–36, RF, 900, 23, RAC.

90. Ibid.

91. Furniss report, extracts in "Excerpts from National Councils, DR502," trustees meeting, December 11, 1935, p. 20, Folder 27, 910, Program and Policy—Appraisal Committee (SSRC) Reports, 1935–38, RF, 910, 3, RAC.

92. "The Rockefeller Foundation Statement of Program, December 1936," discussed at

mentary to its own in both the general areas of research and training as well as in these special programs.[93]

The acceptance of their role by social scientists marked a substantial shift in the balance of power from the academic social science disciplines toward the State and the ruling class. Through the SSRC and other institutions like the Brookings Institution and the NBER, social scientists provided their skills and expertise directly to the State and indirectly to the ruling class. Social scientists were used to build the infrastructure of the State. The power of the ruling class was extended into the daily routines of managing society. The expertise of social scientists was an essential and necessary component of this intervention as the State increasingly became the tool for maintaining social control. In the process of mutual legitimation social scientists were used to bolster the emergent form of cultural hegemony. There was no pretense about doing fundamental or basic research, rather it was clear that the overriding objective was the search for practical, realistic solutions to problems that only the State could solve. Social scientists became "servants of power."[94] They were harnessed to the State enterprise to provide both scientific legitimacy as well as the practical skills necessary to achieve the overall objective. The alliance between the ruling class and the State was mediated by philanthropy and social scientists.

State Intervention: Administration and Security

The programs in public administration and social security were inevitably framed by, and contributed to, Roosevelt's "New Deal." The election campaign of 1932 and Roosevelt's twelve-year reign as president marked a new relationship between academic social scientists and the State. Columbia University housed the three professors, Rexford Guy Tugwell, Raymond Moley, and Berle, who became known as Roosevelt's "Brains Trust." These men advised Roosevelt during the first presidential campaign and then stayed on as advisors and political appointees after the inauguration.[95] In addition to the

---

Special Trustees Conference, December 15, 1936, pp. 12–13, Folder 171, 900, Programs and Policy—Reports PRO-28, PRO-30, 1935–36, RF, 3, 900, 23, RAC.

93. "Resolution—Institutional Support, April 10, 1935," section under heading "Advisory and Planning Bodies," RF, 910, 1, RAC.

94. This is the label used by Baritz, *Servants of Power*.

95. For accounts of this relationship, see Rexford Guy Tugwell, *The Brains Trust* (New York: Viking, 1968); Rexford Guy Tugwell, *Roosevelt's Revolution: The First Year—A Personal Perspective* (New York: Macmillan, 1977); Rexford Guy Tugwell, *The Democratic Roosevelt: A Biography of Franklin D. Roosevelt*, 1st ed. (Garden City: Doubleday and Co., 1957); and Raymond Moley, *The First New Deal* (New York: Harcourt, Brace, and World, 1966). Moley became an assistant secretary of state before returning to Columbia University and finally breaking contact with Roosevelt in 1936. Tugwell became under secretary of agriculture and later

Brains Trust, Roosevelt attracted many other academic social scientists to Washington, including Ogburn, Merriam, and Mitchell. Ogburn did a short stint as executive director of the Consumers' Advisory Board while Merriam and Mitchell were appointed to the NRPB.[96] Through this structure Merriam and Mitchell were brought to the very center of State decision making as Roosevelt attempted to deal with the crisis.

Roosevelt faced nothing less than the collapse of capitalism and democracy. On the morning of his inauguration the banks closed their doors. In a society faced with mass unemployment, there was no federal program of unemployment compensation or of public welfare. His administration's response was one hundred days of swift, dramatic action. During this period, new agencies were created and important pieces of legislation were passed. The list included the Emergency Banking Act, the National Recovery Administration (NRA), the TVA, the Securities and Exchange Commission, unemployment relief measures, the Public Works Administration, the Agricultural Adjustment Administration, the home owners' loan program, the Civilian Conservation Corps, and the National Industrial Recovery Act.[97] The job for social scientists was to make these structures work.

Public Administration

In 1935, the RF appropriated $165,000 to the SSRC for the new program in public administration.[98] After negotiating with Day and Stacy May, the RF officer in charge of public administration,[99] Crane requested $150,000 over five years for the work of the PAC and the staff as well as $15,000 for

governor of Puerto Rico. It should be noted that since 1925 the LSRM had been supporting the Council for Research in the Social Sciences at Columbia. An account of this support, which was continued by the RF, is contained in "Columbia University—Council for Research in the Social Sciences, 1925–1938," Folder 3858, 200S, Columbia University—Social Science Reports, 1932–38, RF, 1.1, 200, 324, RAC.

96. Following the lead of Marion Clawson NRPB is used to stand for the board and all its predecessors unless the contrary is specifically noted. The organizations under this general heading are National Planning Board (July 20, 1933, to June 30, 1934), National Resources Board (July 1, 1934, to June 7, 1935), National Resources Committee (June 8, 1935, to June 30, 1939), and NRPB (July 1, 1939, to August 31, 1943). See Clawson, *New Deal Planning*, p. xv n. 1. The reference to Ogburn appears in Schlesinger, *Coming of the New Deal*, p. 130.

97. Schlesinger, "The Hundred Days," prologue in *Coming of the New Deal*, pp. 1–26; and Clawson, "The Situation from Which the Board Arose," in *New Deal Planning*, pp. 21–29.

98. Docket, June 21, 1935, Folder 4786, 200S, SSRC—Public Administration, 1934, RF, 1.1, 200, 404, RAC.

99. Crane to Day, November 28, 1934, Folder 4786, 200S, SSRC—Public Administration, 1934, RF, 1.1, 200, 404, RAC. The draft program was prepared by John M. Gaus and Charles S. Ascher. It had been finalized at a meeting in Chicago in the fall of 1934. Stacy May, the RF officer in charge of public administration, attended this meeting. Referred to in let-

exploratory studies.[100] Crane pointed out that public administration had been an area of concentration for the Council since 1930 but made it clear that the proposed program was of a different order. Louis Brownlow, chair of the PAC, provided an outline of the research program. Brownlow was the head of the Chicago-based Public Administration Clearing House (PACH), a nonprofit research and consultation organization. Brownlow was a journalist and former city manager who was brought to Chicago by his friend Merriam to run the PACH.[101]

The research program was a comprehensive outline of the whole field of public administration. General objectives were listed under the following headings: "Institutional," "Functional," "Regional," and "Local." In the words of the proposal, the program was designed "for capturing, recording and laying the basis for the appraisal of measures instituted in the United States for grappling with consequences of the world wide social and technological changes that have been coming to a climax in the post-war period." The ultimate objective of the work was "to get fixed points of guidance—to add to the store of principles of administration so that, as government faces new problems and expands still further its activities, its regulatory functions, and its economic enterprises, those who must make the administrative decisions may profit by recent and current experience."[102]

The PAC's work was intended to serve two major functions: liaison between scholars and administrators and integration of the field of knowledge. In addition, the PAC was expected to choose special projects for the RF to fund, and to undertake urgent and exploratory projects. The goals of efficiency and realism were explicit. The ideological imperative was social control.[103] To make the program effective and to ensure the liaison function, the PAC decided that part of the general grant should pay for the appointment of a director of research and an administrative staff. The PAC appointed Dr. Joseph P. Harris, University of Washington, as director of research, and Charles S. Ascher, PACH, as secretary. Initially the PAC set up headquarters in the PACH building at the University of Chicago, but in 1936 the committee moved into permanent offices in New York. Over the five-year-period 1935–

ter/report, Ascher (secretary) to May, June 25, 1936, Folder 4789, 200S, SSRC—Public Administration, 1936, RF, 1.1, 200, 405, RAC.

100. In May 1935, Crane sent in a detailed proposal to the RF. Letter/proposal, Crane to Mason, May 28, 1935, Folder 4786, 200S, SSRC—Public Administration, January–August 1935, RF, 1.1, 200, 404, RAC.

101. Karl, "Louis Brownlow: The Professionalization of Service and the Practice of Administration," in *Executive Reorganization and Reform*, pp. 82–126; Karl, *Merriam and the Study of Politics*, pp. 226–28; and Orlans, "Academic Social Scientists," pp. 179–81.

102. Orlans, "Academic Social Scientists," p. 1.

103. See docket, June 21, 1935, Folder 4786, 200S, SSRC—Public Administration, 1934, RF, 1.1, 200, 404, RAC.

40 the RF appropriated a total of $386,000 to the PAC.[104] In line with the RF's objective the PAC proceeded to coordinate the whole field of public administration on behalf of Rockefeller philanthropy.[105]

The attention of the staff between 1935 and 1937 was largely centered on administrative studies of the federal government's new Social Security Program in collaboration with the SSRC's Committee on Social Security (CSS). The Social Security Board (SSB) was established almost simultaneously with the PAC's program. The board faced what can only be described as a gigantic problem. An elaborate organization had to be built from ground level to administer the provisions for unemployment, old age insurance, and noncontributory old age pensions. The board faced the problem of providing social insurance to between twenty and thirty million people. The budget for insurance contributions and old age assistance expenditures was expected to total $4 billion, an amount that was larger than the normal federal budget. With prompting from the SSRC the board requested the PAC to undertake research on the administrative problems and planning needs of the new organization. These studies were financed by a special RF appropriation of $80,000 in 1936 and a grant of $30,000 allocated by the CSS from funds also supplied by the RF. Three major studies were undertaken with these funds: the administration of public employment offices;[106] unemployment compensation administration in selected states, Great Britain, and Germany;[107] and admin-

---

104. This total includes the initial appropriation of $165,000; six grants for special projects; three fluid grants of $15,000 each, appropriated in 1936–37, 1938–39, and 1939–40; $10,000 of the $60,000 two-year (1940–42) appropriation for research planning.

105. Walker, Van Sickle, and Stacy May, "Reports on Program," prepared for meeting of Trustees Advisory Committee, March 1938, section on public administration, pp. 1–3, Folder 14, 910, Program and Policy—Reports, PRO-19–24, 1935–38, RF, 3, 910, 2, RAC. The following survey and description of the PAC's activities draw on four key documents: (1) letter/report, Ascher (secretary) to May, June 25, 1926, Folder 4789, 200S, SSRC—Public Administration, 1936; (2) "Appraisal of Public Administration Committee," Folder 4796, 200S, SSRC—Public Administration, 1940, RF, 1.1, 200, 405, RAC; (3) "Committee on Public Administration, Social Science Research Council—Summary of Activities, July 1935–May 1940," Folder 485, 200S, SSRC—Public Administration Reports, 1939; (4) "Committee on Public Administration, Social Science Research Council—Report," October 21, 1939, Folder 4806, 200S, SSRC—Public Administration, 1939, RF, 1.1, 200, 406, RAC.

106. Raymond Cumings Atkinson, L. Odencrantz, and B. Deming, *The Administration of Public Employment Offices in the United States*, Studies in Administration, vol. 5 (Chicago: Public Administration Service, 1939).

107. Walter Matscheck, *The Administration of Unemployment Compensation in Wisconsin and New Hampshire*, mimeograph 52 (Chicago: Public Administration Service, 1936); and Walter Matscheck, *The Administration of Unemployment Compensation Benefits in Wisconsin* (Chicago: Public Administration Service, 1937). Walter Matscheck, *Administration of Unemployment Insurance and Public Employment Service in Great Britain*, CSS (New York: SSRC, 1938); and R. Frase, *Administration of Unemployment Insurance and Public Employment Service in Germany*, CSS (New York: SSRC, 1938). See also V. O. Key, Jr., *The Administration of Federal Grants to*

istration of old age assistance.[108] The study of unemployment compensation had three purposes: to record the history of unemployment as it developed in the United States, to be of immediate practical use to federal and state officials in developing sound administrative machinery for carrying out the unemployment compensation program, and to train a small group of experienced students to advise federal and state administrative officers. The division of control provided by the act, which gave wide discretionary powers to the states, was perceived as a serious handicap to efficient administration. In 1937, the PAC allocated $30,000 to the CSS and transferred most of its studies on administration to this latter committee for completion.

Another early activity of the PAC was to continue the study of the Emergency Relief Program.[109] This was the first example of a methodological technique that the PAC labeled as "capture and record." The approach brought together the historian's respect for documents with an emphasis on participant observation and interviewing. The researcher worked within the agency maintaining field notes on administrative developments. The intent was to tell the inside story of the career of an institution.

During 1937–38 the staff of the PAC was directly engaged in studies of the following topics: British government grants-in-aid to localities, city-manager government,[110] bureaus of governmental research,[111] and training

---

States Studies in Administration, vol. 1 (Chicago: Public Administration Service, 1937); Luella C. Gettys, *The Administration of Canadian Conditional Grants*, Studies in Administration, vol. 3 (Chicago: Public Administration Service, 1938). D. Norman, University of Manchester, England, undertook a parallel study in England under a special grant-in-aid of $3,000 from the RF.

108. Robert T. Lansdale, *The Administration of Old Age Assistance*, Studies in Administration, vol. 6 (Chicago: Public Administration Service, 1939).

109. See John D. Millet, *The Works Progress Administration in New York City*, Studies in Administration, vol. 2 (Chicago: Public Administration Service, 1938); and Robert C. Connery, *The Men's Clothing Code under N.R.A.*, Studies in Administration, vol. 4 (Chicago: Public Administration Service, 1938).

110. Harold A. Stone, Don K. Price, and Katharine Stone published three volumes in 1940: *City Manager Government in Nine Cities* (New York: SSRC, 1940); *City Manager Government in the United States* (New York: SSRC, 1940); and *City Manager Government in Seven Cities* (New York: SSRC, 1940). Additional information on this project is contained in "Appraisal: Social Science Research Council—Study of the Council Manager Form of Local Government," Folder 4696, 200S, SSRC—Council Manager Study, 1937–40, RF, 1.1, 200, 396, RAC. In 1939, the staff arranged for a series of collaborative research studies on county-manager schemes. These studies were begun in counties in Virginia, California, New York, and North Carolina.

111. The bureaus had emerged as a protest against the domination of cities by political machines. The growth of this movement led in 1914 to the foundation of the GRA as their national association. Additional information is contained in "Appraisal: SSRC—Agencies Engaged in Municipal and Governmental Research," Folder 4760, 200S, SSRC—Governmental Research Organizations, 1937–40, RF, 1.1, 200, 402, RAC.

for public service.[112] One of the most interesting studies concerned the administrative development of the TVA. In 1936, the RF provided $20,000 to the PAC to study the administrative development of the TVA.[113] This decision coincided with the publication of Odum's classic study *Southern Regions of the United States*. The book labeled the South as the testing ground of American regionalism and made explicit an attachment to the ideology of planning. To achieve "social control" through "a planned and orderly transitional democracy" it was, according to Odum, essential that the key problem of "regional balance" be attacked.[114] The TVA was a central component in the attempt to achieve this goal. The TVA was also an exemplar of a new type of public corporation and thus provided an excellent case study of administrative development. There had been little technical exploration of the public corporation as an administrative device. Dr. Herman Finer, political scientist at the LSE and a recipient of fellowships and grants from Rockefeller philanthropy,[115] was hired. Finer and an assistant spent approximately a year in 1937 and 1938 doing fieldwork in Knoxville. Finer followed a participant-as-observer methodology more closely than any of the "capture and record" researchers.[116] He had access to every meeting and every document. His enormous manuscript documented all the controversies and was deemed too sensitive for public consumption. Yet from the RF's point of view the project had achieved its objective. The PAC was instructed to release certain information to government officials concerned with undertakings comparable with the TVA.[117]

The PAC initiated a two-year study of the administration of the Department of Agriculture. In 1938 the RF provided $35,000 to the PAC to finance the study, which focused on the functions and activities of the United States Department of Agriculture, including its local and regional impact and its

112. George A. Graham, *Education for Public Administration* (New York: SSRC, 1941). The PAC also retained J. E. Devine to canvass problems of production and distribution of training films as aids in the training of public employees. The report, *Films as an Aid in Training Public Employees* (New York: SSRC, 1937), was widely distributed.

113. Additional information is contained in "Appraisal: SSRC—Study of Administrative Development of TVA." Folder 4815, 200S, SSRC—TVA, Administrative Development, 1938–40, RF, 1.1, 200, 407, RAC.

114. Odum, *Southern Regions*, pp. 578–79.

115. The research support that Finer received came through the research grants that the LSRM and the RF supplied to the LSE beginning in 1923. See Fisher, "American Philanthropy."

116. I am utilizing Raymond Gold's typology of research roles (first suggested by Buford Junker), quoted by Aaron V. Cicourel in *Method and Measurement in Sociology* (New York: Free Press, 1964), pp. 43–44.

117. The PAC Subcommittee on Research Materials developed a case study methodology that brought administrators and researchers together. Between 1937 and 1939, case studies were developed in connection with the SSB and the Management Council of the TVA.

relationship to other agencies of government.[118] The study grew out of a suggestion by Stacy May at the RF. It was expected that this study would not only help the Department of Agriculture to adjust its administrative structure and policies to important changes in its functions but also would be of service to other departments struggling with similar problems. The PAC managed to secure the temporary appointment of Professor John M. Gaus, University of Wisconsin at Madison, to undertake the work. He spent fifteen months in Washington and in the field with his assistant Leon Wolcott. In 1940 Gaus and Wolcott published their classic study of the administration of the Department of Agriculture.[119] The authors noted that by 1939 the Department had established a clear identity for itself. The Department had used the Bureau of Agricultural Economics as a sort of a general staff in order to create some integration of the parts.

The PAC also devoted a considerable portion of its energies to charting areas of needed research and then encouraging scholars to undertake it. The most conspicuous and significant activity in this context was the presentation of a memorandum to the president of the United States that became the basis of work finally undertaken by the Committee on Administrative Management (CAM), which the president appointed in 1936. In PAC meetings during 1935, proposals were formulated for studies of federal fiscal controls and the staffing of the president's secretariat, which were then transferred into the memorandum. Originally Merriam had sought to have the CAM study undertaken by the PAC, but Roosevelt objected on two grounds. First, he wanted to maintain control of the process to make sure that the recommendations fit in with his vision. Second, he was concerned about the political danger if such a high-profile study was associated with the Rockefeller name.[120] Brownlow was appointed chair with Merriam and Luther Gulick as the other two members of CAM. Gulick, a political scientist who was an expert on budget and fiscal management, had been the director of the Institute of Public Administration in New York since 1921. Harris was loaned to the president's committee as di-

---

118. In addition to the four key documents, this subsection also draws on "Appraisal: SSRC—Public Administration, Department of Agriculture Study," Folder 4685, 200S, SSRC—U.S. Department of Agriculture, 1937–41, RF, 1.1, 200, 395, RAC.

119. John M. Gaus and Leon Wolcott, *Public Administration and the United States Department of Agriculture* (Chicago: PACH, 1940). Some smaller studies were undertaken: a special regional study of the Pacific Northwest was completed during the summer of 1938 by Charles McKinley, a study of the fiscal administration of the department was made by La Verne Lewis, and a study of the Chicago regional officers by David Trueman.

120. Richard Polenberg, *Reorganizing Roosevelt's Government, 1936–1939: The Controversy over Executive Reorganization* (Cambridge: Harvard University Press, 1966), pp. 13–14; Karl, *Executive Reorganization and Reform*; and Orlans, "Academic Social Scientists," pp. 180–81.

rector of research. The committee's 1937 report became "a bible setting forth the gospel of executive management." The committee's recommendations eventually guided the Reorganization Program that Roosevelt undertook in 1939.[121]

In 1938–39 the PAC turned from research conducted under its own auspices to an emphasis on planning and stimulating research by other agencies and individuals. This change reflected policy shifts within Rockefeller philanthropy and the SSRC. Studies were completed and the activities in relation to social security were finally concluded with a report on the administration of old age assistance and on the public employment services in the United States. In line with the new emphasis on planning, the PAC initiated the preparation of outlines and guides for research on public personnel administration, administrative organization, public relations, and employee relations. As before, the staff were continuously engaged in bringing the research planning of the PAC to the attention of researchers throughout the country. By the end of 1939 the activities of the PAC and the CSS were overtaken by the needs of the war effort.

The PAC was responsible for stimulating a large number of conferences, studies, and other miscellaneous activities. Yet, as noted earlier, by far the most important activity in this respect was the emergence of CAM. As Gene Martin Lyons put it, this committee served more clearly than any other "as an instrument of presidential, and thus political policy."[122] The committee was clearly an extension of the SSRC's work and carried the interests of social scientists and Rockefeller philanthropy to the center of State power. Planning based on social intelligence was the underpinning to the recommendations that emerged. The committee was convinced that the only way to combat the threat posed by communism and fascism was to strengthen the office of the president. The key functions of fiscal management, personnel, and planning were to be assigned to the Bureau of the Budget, the Civil Service Administration, and the National Resources Committee, respectively, which in turn would be part of the executive office.[123] The recommendations had the enthusiastic support of Roosevelt, who had taken a direct hand in shaping the final document.[124] As Polenberg observed, "Having fashioned the legislation of

---

121. Orlans, "Academic Social Scientists," p. 180. For a detailed account of the committee's work and the subsequent attempts to pass legislation, refer to Polenberg, *Reorganizing Roosevelt's Government*. Karl, *Executive Reorganization and Reform*, devotes chapters to Brownlow and Gulick.

122. Lyons, *Uneasy Partnership*, p. 74.

123. See Orlans, "Academic Social Scientists," p. 180, quoting from Frederick C. Mosher, *Democracy and the Public Service* (New York: Oxford University Press, 1968). For a detailed account, see Polenberg, *Reorganizing Roosevelt's Government*, p. 21.

124. Polenberg, *Reorganizing Roosevelt's Government*, pp. 11–27; and Orlans, "Academic Social Scientists," pp. 180–81.

the welfare state, Roosevelt now attempted to give order to the structure of the state."[125]

As members of the CAM, Brownlow, Merriam, and Gulick stepped across the boundary between science and policy. They did not feel compromised. Yet this feeling was only due to the fact that their science and Roosevelt's politics had reached an ideological convergence. Merriam's scruples about allowing the intervention of an earlier president in the RST investigation were set aside as he allowed himself to be incorporated into the policy-making process through the NRPB. At the same time, Merriam tried to preserve the distinction between policy and administration by maintaining a separation of the social research, fact-gathering part of the study from the process of making recommendations. In line with these beliefs, he avoided discussions with the president during the research phase of CAM's work and strictly avoided any contact with the Congress during his service on the NRPB.[126]

The PAC, through its multifarious activities, served Rockefeller philanthropy admirably. It was predictable therefore that as war overtook the nation, Willits, the new director of DSS, asked the PAC to prepare a wide-ranging memorandum on what he regarded as a major research planning area. Building on Gaus's earlier work, the RF labeled this area as "The Relation of Federal, State, and Local Government."[127]

Social Security

In 1935 the RF appropriated $225,000 over three years to the SSRC for the new program in economic security.[128] Van Sickle, the associate director of the DSS in charge of the economic stabilization policy, suggested to Willits a study that looked toward a wisely planned and effectively coordinated social security program for the United States.[129] This suggestion came as a result of the shift in policy that had occurred within the RF when the trustees accepted the report of the Committee on Appraisal and Plan.[130] Willits discussed the suggestion with colleagues and businesspeople without making Rockefeller interest explicit. He came to the conclusion that it "would be an immense

---

125. Orlans, "Academic Social Scientists," p. 191.

126. Ibid., p. 10; and Polenberg, *Reorganizing Roosevelt's Government*, p. 15.

127. "Memorandum, Willits to Walker to Fosdick, August 19, 1940, Progress Report," Folder 5, 910, Program and Policy, 1940–41, RF, 3, 910, 1, RAC.

128. Docket, June 21, 1935, Folder 4713, 200S, SSRC—Economic Security, 1934–35, RF, 1.1, 200, 397, RAC.

129. Referred to in letter, Willits to Van Sickle, December 21, 1934, Folder 4713, 200S, SSRC—Economic Security, 1934–35, RF, 1.1, 200, 397, RAC.

130. "Report of the Committee on Appraisal and Plan—Trustees Meeting, December 11, 1934," Folder 179, 900, Program and Policy—Reports, PRO-27a, 1934, RF, 900, 22, RAC.

service for any agency to develop the essentials of a coordinated system of social security for the United States."[131] The greatest danger in his view was that the proposed measures would not mesh with each other. Willits wanted a coordinated plan that would tie Washington and the states together and would bring order and efficiency to the system. Unemployment benefit schemes had to be closely coordinated with poor relief. Further, he believed unemployment and health insurance should not just be regarded as systems protecting against loss but should also be linked to prevention. To illustrate, Willits raised the examples of the impact of an intelligent public health program on health risks, the possible effects of public works, the use of investment policy to control business, and the impact of improved labor placement on the problem of unemployment. For Willits, the agency that undertook such a task ought to be independent of government so that it could set its own timetable and bring to the job the prestige of science and objectivity.

To guarantee that programs were practically related to prospective governmental undertakings, the RF sought the advice of a group of experts. This group was assembled at a conference to make plans for the RF's program in economic security.[132] The group included practitioners who were attempting to provide relief as well as academics and administrators who were closely involved with the several forms of social insurance.[133] The conference was unanimous in recommending that the most important contribution the RF could make in the field of economic security would be "the setting up of a central planning board and service agency comparable to the [SSRC] Committee on Government Statistics and Information Services." The conference agreed that the social insurance and relief provisions, namely, those for old age, health, accident, and unemployment, ought to be handled by this board "in a unified program with a view to adequate provision of inclusive minimum security."[134] The SSRC was mentioned as the organization that might appoint such a board. The conference recommended that this board should act as a

---

131. Willits to Van Sickle, December 21, 1934, p. 2, Folder 4713, 200S, SSRC—Economic Security 1934–35, RF, 1.1, 200, 397, RAC.

132. "New Program in the Social Sciences, Trustees Meeting, April 10, 1935," DR 392, pp. 22–24, Folder 13, 910, Program and Policy—Reports, PRO-13–18, 1933–35, RF, 3, 910, 2, RAC.

133. Included were Willits, Guy Moffet (SF), Goodrich (professor of economics at Columbia University and director of the SSRC's Population Distribution Study), Eveline M. Burns (professor of economics at the Institute for Advanced Study and formerly chair of the U.S. Central Statistical Board and economic advisor to the National Emergency Council), W. H. Smith (director of Johns Hopkins Hospital), Stanley Dacies (secretary and general director, Charity Organization Society of New York City), Frank Bane (director of the American Public Welfare Association), Marion R. Trabue (director of the Occupational Research Program, U. S. Employment Service), and Jacob Baker (assistant administrator of the Federal Emergency Relief Administration).

134. "New Program in the Social Sciences, Trustees Meeting, April 10, 1935," DR 392,

bridge between government and researchers. The board was to be charged with doing, promoting, and stimulating research that would contribute to solving the problems faced in the security program. Over the next five years this agenda was followed to the letter.

Following the RF decision to adopt economic security as an area of specialization in April 1935,[135] Van Sickle met with Crane and Donald Ramsey Young of the SSRC.[136] He obtained an agreement from Crane to cooperate by setting up an organization to handle economic security. Crane expressed some concern about whether the organization would play the role of advocate and educator rather than confining itself to the strictly scientific aspects of the program. Van Sickle reassured Crane that the RF did not anticipate that the SSRC would be involved in making value judgments. "The attitude," according to Van Sickle, "was that a government policy had been enunciated and that an organization such as the one here proposed would play a useful role in advising the government how best to accomplish the announced policy."[137] After much discussion about the inherent dangers to the SSRC of agreeing to this plan,[138] the PPC finally agreed to set up the Committee on Economic Security (1935–43), with Willits as chair. Willits was a member of the PPC from 1935 through 1939. While a nod was given both to the business world and to public administrators with the inclusion of Chester I. Barnard (president of New Jersey Telephone and Telegraph) and Brownlow, the committee was overwhelmingly academic. The other members were Harrison, Mitchell, Winfield Riefler, and Slichter.[139]

Crane sent in a detailed proposal to the RF containing a summary of the RF's program.[140] As Crane put it:

> There is need of a bridge between governmental officials whose function is to make decisions and the research men working upon problems underlying social insurance and relief. This bridge should serve in the one direction as a means of furnishing officials with existing knowledge and with potential sources of new knowledge, whether related to long-range

p. 23, Folder 13, 910, Program and Policy—Reports, PRO-13–18, 1933–35, RF, 3, 910, 2, RAC.

135. Ibid.

136. "Interview, Van Sickle with Crane and Young, SSRC," April 22, 1935, Folder 4713, 200S, SSRC—Economic Security, 1934–35, RF, 1.1, 200, 397, RAC.

137. Ibid., p. 21.

138. Crane brought the proposal to the next meeting of the PPC in early May. Minutes, PPC, May 5, 1935, pp. 162–63, pt. 19, October 22, 1933–November 7, 1936, SSRCA.

139. "Final Report by Paul Webbink, August 1943," app. A, p. 25, Folder 4725, 200S, SSRC—Economic Security Reports, 1942–43, RF, 1.1, 200, 398, RAC.

140. Proposal, Crane to Mason, May 28, 1935, Folder 4713, 200S, SSRC—Economic Security, 1934–35, RF, 1.1, 200, 397, RAC.

basic problems or to more immediately pressing short-range questions; and should serve in the other direction as a means of focussing research steadily upon one of the continuing problems of modern society. It should serve at once to give research a socially useful direction and give the results of research socially useful circulation.

Crane outlined three main functions for the committee. The first was to maintain close contact with officials operating governmental and private agencies in order to be aware of the problems they faced and to bring to them the results of research. The second was to maintain close contact with researchers in order to communicate to them "the realistic sense of problems acquired through contact with officials charged with determination of policy or with administration, orienting their work into useful channels, coordinating their work where possible, assembling the results of the work, and stating these results in terms of their relationship to specific problems." The third was to integrate the whole field of economic security by doing and encouraging research. For Crane it was essential that the committee take on the role of central planning. As he concluded: "There is need of coordination of all research in the social security field and of its direction wherever possible into useful channels."[141]

Frederic Dewhurst (economist in residence at the Twentieth Century Fund) agreed to become the director of research.[142] Following RF policy, the PPC changed the name of its committee from "economic security" to "social security" (CSS). The stated reason for the Council's change was to avoid confusion between its committee and the former government committee on economic security.[143] Meanwhile Dewhurst had sent in a long memorandum to Willits in order to clarify the functions of the committee and to outline a possible research program. "A primary purpose of the undertaking," according to Dewhurst, was "to clarify the relationships between the various segments of the field, between administrative policies and practices and economic factors and effects and to bring about a comprehension of the field of social security as an integrated whole."[144] Dewhurst also wanted some clarification about the relationship between the two committees, the PAC and the CSS, an organizational problem that was to plague the SSRC. Initially,

141. Proposal, Crane to Mason, May 28, 1935, p. 2.

142. Letter, Crane to Stacy May, June 14, 1935, Folder 4786, 200S, SSRC—Public Administration, January–August 1935, RF, 1.1, 200, 404, RAC.

143. Minutes, PPC, October 26, 1935, pt. 19, October 22, 1933–November 7, 1936, SSRCA. Also "Excerpted for Van Sickle," Folder 4713, 200S, SSRC—Economic Security, 1934–35, RF, 1.1, 200, 397, RAC.

144. Memorandum, Dewhurst to Willits, October 15, 1935, p. 1, Folder 4788, 200S, SSRC—Economic Security, 1934–35, RF, 1.1, 200, 397, RAC.

there seemed to be every prospect of successful cooperation. In an interview conducted by Van Sickle, Crane and Willits made clear there was no logical division between the committees as they were both concerned with a single problem. They noted the good personal relations that existed between Dewhurst and Harris, which provided for optimism about a successful joint attack.[145] This optimism was given concrete form with the joint study of the SSB.

While the RF always protested its innocence when confronted with the problem of control, there was no doubt in the mind of the SSRC who was in charge of the operations. In 1935, on behalf of the CSS, Young asked permission from the RF to farm out a problem to another research organization. This was something that the committee believed was important but felt could be embarrassing. Van Sickle made it clear that the CSS had this power and that the RF officers would prefer the CSS to reserve for the RF's attention only those projects that exceeded the committee's financing.[146] A similar interaction took place in 1939 between Paul Webbink, the new director of research for the CSS, and Stacy May of the RF.[147] With reference to the need for a proposal for continuing support over a specified period, Webbink stated that this was "in accord with what he understood to be the Foundation's expectations and that it also conformed to SSRC policy since this Committee and the Committee on Public Administration had been taken on by the Council as somewhat irregular activities under general Council policy at the specific suggestion of the Foundation as an accommodation to it."[148] Stacy May turned this back to the CSS stating that the CSS should sort out the best possible program without regard to the RF's preconceptions.

At the same time, the RF was exerting direct control over appointments to the committee. Van Sickle discussed enlarging the committee to include a broader range of nonacademic interests with Willits in early December. A negative evaluation was provided of Leo Wolman, but there was general agreement that George Harrison (Brotherhood of Railway and Steamship Clerks) would provide the necessary standing with labor.[149] Later that month Crane accepted the RF's suggestion that Fred C. Hoeler of the American Public Welfare Association would be a good addition.[150] Both Harrison and

---

145. Interview, Van Sickle with Willits and Crane, December 17, 1935, Folder 4788, 200S, SSRC—Public Administration, October–December 1935, RF, 1.1, 200, 405, RAC.

146. Interview, Van Sickle with Young, December 3, 1935, Folder 4713, 200S, SSRC—Economic Security, 1934–35, RF, 1.1, 200, 397, RAC.

147. Webbink took over from Dewhurst in 1937.

148. Memorandum, May to Willits, April 11, 1939, Folder 4718, 200S, SSRC—Economic Security, 1934–35, RF, 1.1, 200, 398, RAC.

149. Interview, Van Sickle with Willits, December 7, 1935, Folder 4713, 200S, SSRC—Economic Security, 1934–35, RF, 1.1, 200, 397, RAC.

150. Interview, Van Sickle with Willits and Crane, December 17, 1935, Folder 4788, 200S, SSRC—Public Administration, October–December 1935, RF, 1.1, 200, 405, RAC.

Hoeler were duly appointed as were Dorothy C. Kahn (president of the American Association of Social Workers) and A. Linton (president of the Provincial Mutual Life Insurance Company).

Only once did it appear that RF involvement might be exposed. In 1936 it appeared as though the RF might be drawn into what became known as the Landon-Winant controversy. Dewhurst in his dual role with the CSS and the Twentieth Century Fund was at the ceńter of this controversy, and he subsequently resigned from the committee because of the affair. Late in 1935 Governor John G. Winant asked Dewhurst as director of the CSS if he would prepare a financial analysis of the Townsend Plan for amending the method of financing of old age insurance. Dewhurst did not think the CSS ought to be involved and in consequence arranged for the Twentieth Century Fund to execute the study. In March 1936 the fund published its report, *The Townsend Crusade*. Meanwhile Governor Alfred M. Landon's adviser on social legislation, Charles B. Taft, had obtained a draft report from Dewhurst and leaked a version of the work to the *New York Times*. Winant and Landon were competing for the presidential nomination of the Republican party. Winant, who had resigned from the SSB in order to defend the existing Social Security Act, reacted strongly to the claims made by Landon on the basis of the leaked document. The fact that both men were using data produced by Dewhurst and that Dewhurst had positions at both the CSS and the fund could have been awkward.[151] The RF was concerned that relations between the board and the CSS might have been damaged.[152] In fact, Frank Bane, the executive director of the SSB, was able to assure Van Sickle that there had been no unfavorable reaction.[153]

Between 1935 and 1940 the CSS received a total of $430,000 from the RF.[154] As with the field of public administration it was the RF's intent that the CSS should coordinate the whole field of social security on behalf of Rocke-

151. Memorandum, Van Sickle to Fosdick and members of DSS, early October 1936, "The Committee on Social Security of the Social Science Research Council and the Landon-Winant Controversy Re Social Security," Folder 4715, 200S, SSRC—Economic Security, May–December 1936, RF, 1.1, 200, 398, RAC.

152. Van Sickle, memorandum, October 9, 1936, "Landon-Winant Controversy Re Social Security," Folder 4715, 200S, SSRC—Economic Security, May–December 1936, RF, 1.1, 200, 398, RAC.

153. Interview, Van Sickle with Bane (executive director, SSB), October 15, 1936, Folder 4715, 200S, SSRC—Economic Security, May–December 1936, RF, 1.1, 200, 398, RAC.

154. This total included the initial appropriation of $225,000, six grants for special projects, two fluid grants of $15,000 each appropriated in 1938–39 and 1939–40, a grant of $60,000 for research planning between 1938 and 1940, and $10,000 of the $60,000 that the RF appropriated for the two-year period 1940 to 1942. Over the life of the CSS (1935 to 1942) approximately $450,000 was spent. Letter, Webbink to Willits, July 3, 1942, enclosure on finances, 1935–42, Folder 4715, 200S, SSRC—Economic Security, May–December 1936, RF, 1.1, 200, 398, RAC.

feller philanthropy. The CSS was created as an adjunct to the federal social security legislation and fulfilled the role of research planner and organizer for the SSB.[155]

Most of the CSS's efforts in 1935 and 1936 and much of its resources thereafter were absorbed in service activities to the SSB. The committee began its activities slightly in advance of the establishment of government agencies to administer the Social Security Act. During the first year or so the CSS was the only available source of technical assistance and the principal channel for drawing upon the aid of nongovernmental experts and technicians. Government officials were literally overwhelmed by a multitude of organizational, personnel, and procedural problems. There was a sense of extreme urgency about the need to implement the new statutory provisions. There followed a series of pressing calls for help to which, as the RF intended, the CSS was ready and able to respond. The committee assisted in the selection of personnel, brought together officials and nongovernmental experts, advised on research plans generally, and, on the details of specific studies, called attention to sources of pertinent data or accumulated experience, participated in innumerable technical conferences and discussions, and facilitated interagency coordination. The aim was the development of research and administrative programs, the establishment of agencies, and the development of procedures for the administration of the new laws. Because of the newness of the field the work was experimental and exploratory. Development of the program was therefore opportunistic in that it was adapted to rapidly changing official policies and to the shifting nature of the problems.

Inevitably, a major focus for the CSS was the operation of the two major efforts by the State to provide social insurance: unemployment compensation and old age security. As noted earlier in the section on the PAC, the State unemployment project was originally a joint undertaking by the two committees. The arrangement proved unsatisfactory, and in 1939 the program was transferred to the CSS.[156] From 1936 until its termination in 1940 this special project was viewed primarily as a means of accumulating and disseminating among federal and state officials technical experience and advice regarding administrative practices and policies. Walter Matscheck and Raymond Cumings Atkinson visited more that half the forty-eight states, some of them repeatedly. These two men served as unofficial counselors to officials at all

155. The following survey and description of the CSS's activities are drawn from three key documents: (1) "Appraisal, August 1940," Folder 4719, 1940, (2) letter, Webbink to Willits, July 3, 1942, Folder 4721, 200S, SSRC—Economic Security, 1942, (3) "Final Report by Paul Webbink, August 1943," Folder 4725, 200S, SSRC—Economic Security Reports, 1942–43, RF, 1.1, 200, 398, RAC.

156. In addition to the $110,000 that both the PAC and the CSS had allocated from their general budgets, the RF provided a total of $62,500 in three special grants.

levels. Matscheck and Atkinson studied the total process of paying benefits and monitored the federal/state relationship.[157] Numerous memorandums on specific problems, such as "Simplified Benefit Procedure for Unemployment Compensation" (1938), were prepared for operating officials. Similarly, Atkinson prepared a memorandum on the possibility of simplifying the statistical system of the United States Employment Service, which provided the basis for cutting the operating costs of the SSB in half. As noted in the RF's appraisal: "The project was of such scope and the activities of the special staff so various that the enterprise had something of the character of an operating consultative service to the government."[158]

During the first two or three years the CSS concentrated attention on the problems of old age security. The heated controversies over methods of long-range financing of old age insurance and the apparent strength in 1935 and 1936 of the Townsend and similar movements made it seem essential that this problem be given priority. Margaret Grant produced the committee's first publication, *Preliminary Report on the Status of Industrial Pension Plans* (as affected by old age insurance legislation).[159] As noted earlier, staff members participated actively in the studies by the Twentieth Century Fund, which resulted in the Fund's publication *The Townsend Crusade* (1936) and the report *More Security for Old Age* (1937). Grant also conducted a close analysis of European experience in the provision of old age insurance.[160]

While there was material describing individual social insurance in particular European countries, there was little that described an entire program, and no attempt had been made to provide a systematic analysis of the problems encountered in trying to coordinate interinsurance relationships. Clarence Arthur Kulp undertook an extensive study of British and German experience, and his report *Social Insurance Coordination: An Analysis of German and British Organization* (1938) has to be regarded as one of the committee's major achievements.[161] Similarly, Eveline M. Burns was employed early in

157. Walter Matscheck and Raymond Cumings Atkinson, *Problems and Procedures of Unemployment Compensation in the States* (Chicago: Public Administration Service, 1939); and Raymond Cumings Atkinson, *The Federal Role in Unemployment Compensation Administration*, CSS (Washington, D.C.: SSRC, 1941).

158. "Appraisal, August 1940," Folder 4820, 200S, SSRC—Unemployment Compensation, 1937–44, RF, 1.1, 200, 407, RAC.

159. Margaret Grant, *Preliminary Report on the Status of Industrial Pension Plans*, CSS (Washington, D.C.: SSRC, 1936).

160. Margaret Grant, *Old-Age Security: Social and Financial Trends*, CSS (Washington, D.C.: SSRC, 1939). Grant's investigation was supplemented by a field study in Australia and New Zealand on old age pensions conducted by Robert Murray Haig. This study was funded by the CSS.

161. Clarence Arthur Kulp, *Social Insurance Coordination: An Analysis of German and British Organization*, CSS (Washington, D.C.: SSRC, 1938). The CSS also supported the work

1937 to do an intensive study of the British experience of coordinating insurance and relief programs during a period of mass unemployment. The report, *British Unemployment Programs, 1920–1938* (1941) provided a coherent and complete account of the problems faced in the development of British unemployment and assistance policy during the interwar years.[162] Finally, Franz Huber studied the effects of the social security program on the employment practices of employers and on trade unions.[163]

The CSS also concentrated on two other aspects of the developing State infrastructure: relief programs and labor market data. A comprehensive study of federal relief policies during the 1930s was initiated by the CSS in 1936. The intent was to describe and evaluate the shift from exclusively local provision of relief to the establishment of state and federal measures. Particular emphasis was placed on the work relief experiments undertaken by the federal government since 1933,[164] studies of relief experience in individual states and in regions. To make sure such opportunities would not be entirely lost, the CSS in 1936 undertook an intensive study of the development of relief policies in New Jersey. The report (1938) constituted the only comprehensive account of relief policies and their effects during the depression in an entire state.[165] As observed in the RF's appraisal: "The findings were important not only for New Jersey but for other states" and had "significance for future Federal and State systems of relief."[166] Finally, the CSS cooperated with the SSRC's Advisory Committee on Social Aspects of the Depression (1936–38) in the preparation of the *Research Memorandum on the Social Aspects of Relief Policies in the Depression* (1937).[167]

The labor market was one of the first areas of work where the government asked for assistance. Available employment and census statistics were in many respects not adequate for the analysis of questions arising under the 1935 unemployment compensation and old age insurance plans. Problems

---

of Otto Neuburger, which resulted in the publication *Administration of Short-Term Benefits in Germany*, CSS (Washington, D.C.: SSRC, 1938).

162. Eveline M. Burns, *British Unemployment Programs, 1920–1938*, CSS (Washington, D.C.: SSRC, 1941).

163. Franz Huber, *Changes in Employment Practices Resulting from the Operation of the Social Security Program*, CSS (Washington, D.C.: SSRC, 1940).

164. Some of the material from this study was made available in John Chamov, *Work Relief Experience in the United States*, CSS (Washington, D.C.: SSRC, 1943).

165. Douglas Harrison MacNeill, *Seven Years of Unemployment Relief in New Jersey, 1930–36*, CSS (Washington, D.C.: SSRC, 1938).

166. "Appraisal, August 1940," Folder 4780, 200S, SSRC—New Jersey Unemployment Study, 1936–40, RF, 1.1, 200, 404, RAC.

167. Clyde R. White and Mary K. White, *Research Memorandum on the Social Aspects of Relief Policies in the Depression*, Committee on Social Aspects of the Depression, bulletin 38 (New York: SSRC, 1937).

relating to socioeconomic classifications, groupings by size of establishments, shifts between types of employment, and special questions concerning employment and unemployment could not be analyzed without extensively recasting data collected for quite different purposes. Experience in the early months concerning the contribution that an independent research agency might make in the quantitative analysis of social security questions led the CSS to undertake two major enterprises. One was a series of regional labor market studies.[168] The second enterprise was on national labor market trends. Wladimir S. Woytinsky was engaged to reclassify and retabulate the 1930 census occupational statistics and other data into categories that could be used for the study and administration of social security. His general findings were published in *Labor in the United States: Basic Statistics for Social Security* (1938).[169] The book provides an extensive analysis of the types of workers included in and excluded from coverage under the old age and unemployment compensation programs and explores the extent of prospective shifts between employment categories that were included in and excluded from coverage by the act.

The data and methodological investigations developed by Woytinsky were of such value to the SSB and other federal agencies that the board in 1937 asked that means be found to support a collaborative arrangement whereby Woytinsky's time could be shared between the CSS and the SSB. The RF acceded to this request, and during 1938 and 1939 Woytinsky conducted an intensive study of all the available data relating to unemployment and the mobility of labor.[170] A considerable mass of labor turnover, employment, and unemployment statistics were examined and evaluated. A final report, *Three Aspects of Labor Dynamics* (1942), covers the analysis of existing data relating to labor turnover among the unemployed and forced entries into the labor market during depressions. In 1940 and 1941 Woytinsky examined for the CSS the relations between prospective national income and social security trends. His findings dealt largely with the proportion of the national income reported by wages and wage trends in relation to social security and were published in *Earnings and Social Security in the United States* (1943). This work was closely related to the RF-funded research on national income that was being done by the NBER.[171]

168. For a detailed account refer to "Appraisal, March 1938," Folder 4771, 200S, SSRC—Labor Market Studies, 1936–38, RF, 1.1, 200, 403, RAC.

169. Wladimir S. Woytinsky, *The Labor Supply in the United States*, CSS (Washington, D.C.: SSRC, 1936); and Wladimir S. Woytinsky, *Labor in the United States: Basic Statistics for Social Security*, CSS (Washington, D.C.,: SSRC, 1938).

170. "Appraisal—Mobility of Labour and Unemployment, August 1940," Folder 4773, 200S, SSRC—Mobility of Labour and Unemployment, 1937–40, RF, 1.1, 200, 403, RAC.

171. See "Docket, October 20, 1939," Folder 4777, 200S, SSRC—National Income

The service function continued to be a major activity of the CSS throughout its existence and used up much of the resources. From the beginning, the CSS staff developed close and continuing ties with federal and state officials. Advice and consultation were regarded as major responsibilities. Staff services were used by all the major government agencies concerned with social security and many other government agencies.[172] Matscheck was released in 1939 to allow him to take charge of the Railway Retirement Board's administrative research division. Atkinson's services were loaned to the Bureau of the Budget for a time in the summer of the same year to assist in analyzing the problems arising in the consolidation of the United States Employment Service and the SSB's Bureau of Unemployment Compensation. Finally, beginning in September 1941, the services of Webbink, the staff director, were loaned on a halftime basis to the Labor Division of the Office of Production Management in connection with its labor supply operations. Subsequently, Webbink worked in the National Roster of Scientific and Professional Personnel and was part of the Planning Division of the War Manpower Commission.

As already noted, research was intended to be of service to government. The research was expected to provide results of both immediate and lasting value. There were many instances in which studies were undertaken either at the initiative of government officials or because they were of value in illuminating problems that the CSS believed were facing government officials. Problems were chosen because the research could not be done by a government agency. Several projects undertaken by the CSS were too sensitive for government agencies to conduct.[173] On other occasions, the CSS was able to

Study, 1939–41, RF, 1.1, 200, 404, RAC. Wladimir S. Woytinsky, *Three Aspects of Labor Dynamics*, CSS (Washington, D.C.: SSRC, 1942); and Wladimir S. Woytinsky, *Earnings and Social Security in the United States*, CSS (Washington, D.C.: SSRC, 1943).

172. In addition, staff members participated extensively in the work of the Conference Group on Social Insurance Policy, the Old Age Security Committee of the Twentieth Century Fund, the Advisory Committee to the Census, and the National Policy Committee Conferences. The CSS made liberal contributions to several research memorandums of the Division of Social Research of the Works Progress Administration, to studies by the Brookings Institution, to the work of a special Senate committee on unemployment and relief, and to the work of the NRPB. Finally, help was provided to Richard M. E. Sterner's study that constituted part of the CC's project "The Negro in America." Richard M. E. Sterner, *The Negro's Share: A Study of Income, Consumption, Housing, and Public Assistance* (New York: Harper and Bros., 1943). The larger study resulted in the publication Gunnar Myrdal, with the assistance of Richard Sterner and Arnold Rose, *An American Dilemma: The Negro Problem and Modern Democracy* (New York: Harper and Bros., 1944).

173. This was the case with the controversial Townsend studies, the work on "Methods of Clearance between Unemployment Compensation and Relief Agencies," and the 1936 study of the "Status of Industrial Pension Plans as Affected by Old-Age Benefit Sections of the Social Security Act." The study dealt with the highly controversial question of the attitudes of industrialists, organized labor, and insurance companies toward proposed modifications of the act.

arrange for the employment of people whom the government was unable to hire because of the inflexibility of federal personnel recruitment or because of the restrictions against the employment of noncitizens.[174] These latter restrictions were a major factor in the decision to jointly employ Woytinsky between 1937 and 1941. Woytinsky's location in the SSB's offices and his special relation to the staff proved an effective arrangement for close cooperation.[175] He participated directly in the negotiations and discussions, which brought major improvements in the schedules for the 1940 census. Woytinsky's statistical analysis and Clarence Arthur Kulp's work on relief problems, as well as other committee materials, laid the basis for the 1939 amendments to the Social Security Act.

The establishment and financing of the CSS made social security a legitimate field of interest. Over the seven years of its existence the CSS consistently worked toward transforming this field into an integrated research area both within the universities and in government. Through correspondence, publications, conferences, and field visits, the CSS was able to perform the role of a research center. It acted as a clearinghouse "among educational officials, research agencies, students, industrial and trade union executives and all interested persons" who needed information on sources of data, research in progress, and research personnel. The SSB published several documents produced by the committee and acted as a distributor of some of the committee's publications by placing copies in the libraries of each of the state unemployment compensation offices and in public assistance agencies. The aim was to hasten the process of integration of research programs and results in order to contribute materially to making the social security system work.[176]

From 1939 to the committee's demise in 1942, attention was directed toward research planning and the integration and coordination of efforts in the field. Research planning was a major function. The CSS included representatives from business and industry as well as professionals. In this way the interests of both the private and public sectors were brought together. As the final CSS report concludes: "The committee, in its meetings and through the thinking of its members between meetings, actively and conscientiously exercised a responsibility for continuous inquiry into both immediate and long

---

174. The CSS made staff available to the SSB for analysis of the details of newly enacted State unemployment compensation statutes, for a study of seasonal workers under foreign unemployment insurance laws, and for an analysis of the administrative costs of British unemployment insurance.

175. "Appraisal, August 1940," p. 2, Folder 4773, 200S, SSRC—Mobility of Labor and Unemployment, 1937–41, RF, 1.1, 200, 403, RAC.

176. "Final Report by Paul Webbink, August 1943," p. 20, Folder 4725, 200S, SSRC—Economic Security Reports, 1942–43, RF, 1.1, 200, 398, RAC.

range fundamental problems within the broad field of economic security."[177] The entry of the United States into the war in December 1941 meant that all technical efforts were applied to the war effort.[178]

The record of the CSS was impressive. The RF had achieved its objective of helping to make the system work in the most efficient and most scientific manner. The field of social security studies had been established. As the RF's own appraisal put it in August 1940: "Events during the past five years have emphasized the importance of an understanding of the complexities of formulating and administering social insurance legislation, and the implications of a program of social security are seen to extend into the broad area of all social relationships."[179] Through this committee and the SSRC, the RF had played a critical role in helping to develop the necessary infrastructure of the new welfare State.

The NRPB

President Roosevelt in July 1933 followed the recommendations of the RST report and established under the authority of the National Industrial Recovery Act the National Planning Board.[180] While the name of this body changed over the next decade, the personnel remained remarkably constant ("NRPB" is used for the board and all its predecessors unless the contrary is specifically noted).[181] Frederic A. Delano, President Roosevelt's uncle, was a member throughout and chair during its first and final forms. Charles W. Elliott II was the executive officer, and Merriam was a member throughout the board's history. Without doubt it was Merriam who dominated the activities of the board. He brought social science to the very center of power in the State. Even so, for Merriam the board was first and foremost a planning and advisory body.[182] For the first two years, 1933 to 1935, Mitchell was the third

177. Ibid., p. 22.

178. Anticipating postwar problems of population readjustment, the CSS tried to stimulate studies of the extent and nature of migration to war production communities. Two studies resulted from this effort, Clark Kerr, *Migration to the Seattle Labor Market Area*, CSS (Washington, D.C.: SSRC, 1942); and Paul H. Landis, *Loss of Rural Manpower to War Industry through Migration*, CSS (Washington, D.C.: SSRC, 1943).

179. "Appraisal, August 1940," p. 1, Folder 4719, 200S, SSRC—Economic Security, 1940, RF, 1.1, 200, 398, RAC.

180. Karl concluded that the NRPB was an outgrowth of the RST report. See Karl, *Merriam and the Study of Politics*, p. 248.

181. This account of the NRPB is based primarily on the work of Clawson, *New Deal Planning*. Other important sources include Schlesinger, *Coming of the New Deal*; Polenberg, *Reorganizing Roosevelt's Government*; Karl, *Executive Reorganization*; Karl, *Merriam and the Study of Politics*; Lyons, *Uneasy Partnership*; and Orlans, "Academic Social Scientists."

182. For his own account, see Charles E. Merriam, "The National Resources Planning

member. Ruml and Dennison were appointed as advisers and functioned in Mitchell's place.[183] Later George F. Yantis, a lawyer and businessman, was appointed to fill the third place.[184]

Throughout its existence the planning body was dominated by the thinking of social scientists, in particular the view of the social sciences that had been propagated by the SSRC. The board provided the SSRC and Rockefeller philanthropy with the means of bringing social science and therefore, in the board's terms, "social intelligence" to bear on the operation of government. Social facts could be harnessed and become the underpinning of policymaking. Planning was the central organizing concept of the board's activities. Between 1934 and 1943, the NRPB produced an enormous number of reports on natural resources, social problems like housing and public welfare, economic concerns to do with interest rates, income and expenditure, and planning at all levels. Through Delano and Merriam, who was called "Uncle Charley" by Roosevelt,[185] the board had direct, personal access to the president. The NRPB was always defined by its members as an adviser to the president.[186] Merriam, Mitchell, and Ruml linked into this process the resources of social scientists through the SSRC, the NBER, the Brookings Institution, and the PACH and the resources and power of Rockefeller philanthropy.

In 1934 the NRPB called upon the SSRC and the National Academy of Sciences to submit memorandums in support of the call for more effective planning. The SSRC created the Advisory Committee on National Planning and Social Science (1934), whose submission was incorporated into the board's final report, which subsequently become known as "A Plan for Planning."[187] This report provided the intellectual basis for planning and made the case for science in this process. Following the RST report and the SSRC's submission, the board came out strongly in favor of increased cooperation between natural and social scientists. Effective planning, it was argued, had to be based on knowledge that brought together explanation of technical and social change. The report proposed that the planning group be made a perma-

Board," *Public Administration Review*, Winter 1941, pp. 116–21; and Charles E. Merriam, "The National Resources Planning Board: A Chapter in American Planning Experience," *American Political Science Review* 38 (1944): 1075–88.

183. President Roosevelt to Ruml, December 18, 1935, Folder 4, Series 1, Box 4, Ruml, University of Chicago.

184. See Clawson, *New Deal Planning*, pp. 6, 49–50, and 52–71; Lyons, *Uneasy Partnership*, p. 64; and Schlesinger, *Coming of the New Deal*, pp. 351–52.

185. Polenberg, *Reorganizing Roosevelt's Government*, p. 16.

186. Clawson, *New Deal Planning*, p. 4.

187. National Planning Board, *Final Report, 1933–1934* (Washington, D.C.: Government Printing Office, 1934). Section 2 of this report had the title "A Plan for Planning."

nent agency directly responsible to the president. At that stage the NRPB was part of the major New Deal program in the Public Works Administration under Secretary of the Interior Harold L. Ickes. Ickes was a close personal friend of Merriam's and had been his campaign manager when he ran for mayor of Chicago in 1912. The permanent body was intended to serve three main functions: information and education, coordination and advice, and initiation. The initiation function allowed the group to identify and face those social trends and social problems that most needed the attention of central government.

In 1934, Roosevelt reestablished the NRPB under a new name and asked the board to place greater emphasis on planning and the regulation of the numerous government programs in resource development. For Roosevelt, planning was always a matter of practical government and politics. Yet Secretary Ickes insisted that the board become an interdepartmental committee under his direction rather than an executive body. On the surface Roosevelt gave in to this demand, but in practice the former board was simply reconstituted as an advisory committee. This subadvisory committee, with its own staff, continued to have direct access to the president and for all intents and purposes ran the show. Late in 1934, the SSRC created the Advisory Committee on Government Research in Social Science (1934–35) and produced a memorandum on the financing of social science research by the national government.[188] The committee was disbanded with the submission of the memorandum to the NRPB. While the NRPB did reach out to the whole country, the objective of centralized planning was never really achieved. Part of the problem was the lack of cooperation between the natural science and social science communities and the lack of agreement among social scientists about what constituted an appropriate definition of science.

In line with the objective of the Merriam brothers, the SSRC, and Rockefeller philanthropy, the NRPB in 1935 created the Science Committee, with representatives from the National Academy of Sciences, the SSRC, and the American Council of Education.[189] Ogburn and Ford were the SSRC designees to this committee. The Science Committee replaced the previous efforts by the natural scientists to have more influence on the federal government through the Science Advisory Board (SAB).[190] Wilson became the first chair

---

188. See minutes, PPC, December 1, 1934, pt. 19, October 22, 1933–November 7, 1936, SSRCA. The committee members were Cole, Coffman, Gay, Moulton, Ogburn, Rogers, and Ruml.

189. This discussion relies heavily on Lyons, "The New Deal," in *Uneasy Partnership*, pp. 50–79. Also see A. Hunter Dupree, *Science in the Federal Government: A History of Policies and Activities to 1940* (New York: Harper, 1964); and Lewis E. Auerbach, "Scientists in the New Deal," *Minerva* 111 (1965): 457–82.

190. This movement was led by Bowman, chairman of the NRC, and by Karl Compton,

of the Science Committee. Wilson was an ex-president of the SSRC, a Council member representing the ASTA, and throughout the 1930s an ex officio member of the PPC. While the Science Committee was intended as a bridge between the natural and social science communities, it soon was identified as a social science undertaking. The natural scientists withdrew into what were their stronger positions of influence with bureaus and departments and through the National Academy of Sciences.

The SSRC and its representatives were still trying to sort out how science and policy ought to be linked. While Merriam was comfortable with his role as an adjunct to government, for others like Crane this prospect raised fundamental issues. The memorandum submitted to the NRPB in 1934 had drawn "a sharp distinction . . . between scientific fact finding on the one hand and the determination and execution of policies on the other."[191] The fear that through participation social scientists would lose their claim to scientific status made some researchers reluctant to become members of the Science Committee. The tension between the different definitions of science and the different conceptions of the role that social scientists should play in the policy-making process underlay the reports produced by the Science Committee on population changes, on technological trends and national policy, and on research in the federal government. The first two topics had been suggested by the RST. The SSRC appointed the Committees on Population Redistribution (1934–37) and on Migration (1936–38), which provided help on the first topic. The Science Committee produced a major report, "The Problems of a Changing Population," which was published by the NRPB in 1938.[192] Ogburn directed the technology trends study, and in the report he pushed for the active involvement of social scientists in the formulation of policy. Crane was particularly angry that it was not made clear in the report who supported the recommendations. Furthermore, the report goes beyond its mandate to recommend a stronger and more permanent national planning unit. While the Science Committee attempted to resolve the issue internally by declaring that it was not its duty to determine policy, it never escaped the dilemma.[193]

What might have been the Science Committee's most important report, *Research—A National Resource*, bogged down in the ethical difficulties of doing government research.[194] The first part of this report was published by

president of the Massachusetts Institute of Technology and chairman of the SAB. See Robert Kargon and Elizabeth Hodes, "Karl Compton, Isaiah Bowman, and the Politics of Science in the Great Depression," *ISIS* 76 (1985): 301–18.

191. Quoted by Lyons, *Uneasy Partnership*, p. 72.

192. For an account of this committee's work and a summary of the report, see Clawson, *New Deal Planning*, pp. 125–31.

193. Lyons, *Uneasy Partnership*, pp. 73–79.

194. This study of research in the United States was published by the National Resources

the National Resources Committee in 1938 under the title *Relation of the Federal Government to Research*. The lack of understanding between the SSRC and the National Resources Committee was evident during the preparation of the report. Charles H. Judd, who had been a member-at-large of the SSRC since 1931, chaired the subcommittee on research and was in charge of writing this report. It came to the attention of the PPC during the fall of 1937 that Judd was under the impression that the SSRC was both concerned about and to some extent hostile to cooperation with government in matters involving research.[195] The PPC considered this a misrepresentation growing out of the Council's earlier insistence on the distinction between advice on the choice of alternate government policies dependent upon the social objectives and the basic research and advisory services by social scientists not involving a subjective choice of goals. The PPC made it clear that the Council desired to be of great service to government to the fullest extent within its sphere of competence. The Judd report (part one of *Research—A National Resource*) surveys and analyzes the total research capacity of the government and relates government needs to the intellectual resources available, yet it avoids saying what should be done.[196] As discussed later, this dilemma remained at the center of SSRC debates and ultimately resulted in the exclusion of social scientists from the NSF.

Necessarily an important figure in the debate about the appropriate role for social scientists was Crane, the executive director of the SSRC. His overriding concern was to both protect and nurture the definition of social researchers as impartial scientists. For Crane, the SSRC had to be seen to be independent of government and foundations. Some attempt was made to clarify the situation in the report "Relations of Foundations to the Social Science Research Council" in October 1934. This report emerged in reaction to a Lake George meeting of the university-based social science research councils.[197] Crane made his fears about Rockefeller control absolutely clear in his contacts with the president of the CC, Keppel, during July and August of 1935.[198] As Crane observed: "The Council will never realize its poten-

Committee in three parts: *Relation of the Federal Government to Research*, vol. 1 (Washington, D.C., 1938); *Industrial Research*, vol. 2 (Washington, D.C., 1940); *Business Research*, vol. 3 (Washington, D.C., 1941).

195. Judd, "Relations of Government to Scientific Research," report of the National Resources Committee. Contained in minutes, PPC, pt. 20, January 16, 1937–September 14, 1928, SSRCA.

196. See Clawson, *New Deal Planning*, p. 134.

197. Report, "Relations of Foundations to the Social Science Research Council," October 30, 1934, File, SSRC, 1932–36, CC. Also, "Preliminary Meeting of the Conference of University Social Science Research Organization, September 5, 1934," Folder 4813, 200S, SSRC—Summer Conferences, 1931–36, RF, 1.1, 200, 407, RAC.

198. See two documents, "Memorandum of Interview, SSRC, July 16, 1935: Keppel with

tialities as long as it receives funds so predominantly from one source. The Council has been so dependent on this one source that the Council has sometimes been supposed to be one of its agencies." Crane felt that the SSRC had been diverted from its original purpose by Rockefeller philanthropy because of the money that was available for "wholesale work," that is, work that had immediate social effects. Crane was convinced that it was time to "get down to basic, less spectacular work out of which real advance comes."[199] Crane wanted the Council to stay clear of nonscientific work and, instead of vying for research funds, use its expertise to plan and provide direction and leadership. These contacts were indicative of the close relationship that was developing between Keppel and Crane. In response, the CC increased its grant for administration to $15,000 for the year 1935–36.[200]

The internal doubts paralleled the more public debate between the SSRC and the Science Committee. This tension was behind the major discussion of policy at the annual meeting of the Council in September 1936. Crane reviewed the last three years of Council activity and quite naturally highlighted the movement toward practical service rather than fundamental development.[201] Ford as chair of the Council (1936–39) appointed a Committee of Review of Council Policy (1937–38), chaired by Mark Arthur May.[202] This committee was responsible for the production of the 1937 Wirth report.

Other Committees

In 1935, the SSRC began providing predoctoral fellowships. This action came in response to a report in 1932 by the Advisory Committee on Research Personnel. This committee recommended the establishment of predoctoral fellowships to be available (1) on entrance to graduate schools in order to stimulate recruitment of desirable personnel and (2) after course requirements were complete in order to provide a year of experimental or field training. To support these new ventures the GEB provided an initial grant of $100,000, which was repeated both in 1936 and 1937. The Graduate Study Fellowships

Dr. R. T. Crane," and "Confidential Memorandum for Personal Use of Dr. Keppel from Robert T. Crane," 1935 (probably July), File, SSRC, 1932–36, CC.

199. "Confidential Memorandum for Personal Use of Dr. Keppel from Robert T. Crane," 1935 (probably July), File, SSRC, 1932–36, CC.

200. Grant, November 21, 1935. Details of grant and developing relation in File, SSRC, 1932–36, CC.

201. Annual meeting of the Board of Directors of the SSRC, Swampscott, Mass., September 4–6, 1936, File, Foundations and Organizations, SSRC, Board of Directors, Minutes, 1934–40 (Federal-National), DSS, University of Chicago.

202. Crane to Mitchell, October 5, 1936, Correspondence: Robert T. Crane, WCMC, Columbia University, New York. The committee included Schlesinger, Ogburn, Mitchell, and Redfield. Interestingly, Furniss and Rogers refused to sit on the committee.

only lasted two years, from 1935 to 1937, during which time twenty-two college seniors were recipients. The predoctoral fellowships began in 1935 and continued as a separate category until 1946 when all SSRC fellowships were grouped under the heading "research training." Further, it should be noted that in 1935 the postdoctoral fellowships began to focus more on training rather than research projects. The SSRC adopted the objective of selecting students with doctorates in one field who wished to study in an adjacent field. The objective was to broaden the training of young scholars to include a knowledge of other disciplines.

As part of its move toward retrenchment in the mid-1930s, the SSRC was desperately trying to sort out its role and, by implication, that of all social scientists vis-à-vis the major institutions of business, government, and the foundations. A number of committees created during this period reflect this concern. The Advisory Committee on Freedom of Inquiry (1935–38) was stimulated by the passage of regressive legislation that affected the freedoms associated with research, teaching, and publication. The Committee on Public Relations (1933–35) and the Committee on the National Academy of Social Science (1934–35) were both concerned with the relation between the social sciences and society. Finally, the Committee on the Improvement of Research Organization (1934–35) was created to establish guidelines for research in the social sciences.[203] The three members, Ruml, Ogburn, and a young sociologist from Chicago, Everett C. Hughes, drew up a list of criteria for assessing the qualifications of institutions capable of carrying on effective research in the social sciences. The committee recommended that research be conducted in those established research centers that had a tradition of freedom of inquiry and expression, that were organized internally to facilitate collaboration across discipline lines, and that focused attention on trying to solve social problems. The report clearly bore the stamp of the science of society perspective that was so dear to both Ruml and Ogburn.

By the end of 1936 the SSRC had resigned itself to do research planning rather than remain as an agency executing research. As a means of providing background information and research plans on key issues, the SSRC created the Committee on Social Aspects of the Depression (1936–38). As Roosevelt attempted to consolidate the infrastructure that had been established in his first administration, this committee produced a series of memorandums on the impact of the depression on segments of the population, on institutional sectors, and on some of the perennial social problems. Included in this list were memorandums on minority peoples, education, social work, health, religion, family, rural life, crime, internal migration, consumption, and read-

---

203. "Report of the Committee on the Improvement of Research Organization," minutes, PPC, March 17, 1934, app. 1, pt. 19, October 22, 1933 to November 7, 1936, SSRCA.

ing.[204] Through these memorandums the Council provided an academic perspective on many of the same issues that were taken up in the surveys and reports of the NRPB.

Conclusion

The most conspicuous trend in the SSRC during the 1930s was the increasing emphasis on a small number of research fields. These fields of concentration were deemed to be the most important, immediate social problems. The lead was taken by the RF, and the SSRC followed. Day was the most significant figure in this development as he straddled his responsibilities to Rockefeller philanthropy and to the social disciplines. Building on the work of Ruml and Merriam, he pressed for the utilization of "social intelligence" and the inclusive adoption of "planning" in the policy-making process. Social scientists were to be involved at every turn in the production and provision of social intelligence. All this was set against the background of the depression and the perceived challenge to the very bases of the economic and social orders in the United States. The alliance that emerged between the State, Rockefeller philanthropy, and social scientists involved a dramatic shift within the SSRC from fundamental development to an almost exclusive emphasis on practical service.

The crisis of the State was met with a new relationship between the public and private sectors. The form of cultural hegemony that became dominant in this period made State intervention and State capitalism the means for solving social problems. Planning became the central component in the ideology of social control. The State, foundations, the private sector, and social scientists worked together against the collapse of liberal democratic capital-

---

204. What follows is the list of memorandums in alphabetical order by author: Francis Stuart Chapin and Stuart A. Queen, *Research Memorandum on Social Work in the Depression*, bulletin 39 (New York: SSRC, 1937); Selwyn De Witt Collins and Clark Tibbits, *Research Memorandum on Social Aspects of Health in the Depression*, bulletin 36 (New York: SSRC, 1937); Education Policies Commission, *Research Memorandum on Education in the Depression*, bulletin 28 (New York: SSRC, 1937); Samuel Clarence Kincheloe, *Research Memorandum on Religion in the Depression*, bulletin 33 (New York: SSRC, 1937); Ezra Dwight Sanderson, *Research Memorandum on Rural Life in the Depression*, bulletin 34 (New York: SSRC, 1937); Johan Thorsten Sellin, *Research Memorandum on Crime in the Depression*, bulletin 27 (New York: SSRC, 1937); Samuel Andrew Stouffer and Paul L. Lazarsfeld, *Research Memorandum on the Family in the Depression*, bulletin 29 (New York: SSRC, 1937); Warren Simpson Thompson, *Research Memorandum on Internal Migration in the Depression*, bulletin 30 (New York: SSRC, 1937); Roland Snow Vaile, *Research Memorandum on Social Aspects of Consumption in the Depression*, bulletin 35 (New York: SSRC, 1937); Douglas Waples, *Research Memorandum on Social Aspects of Reading in the Depression*, bulletin 37 (New York: SSRC, 1937); and Donald Ramsey Young, *Research Memorandum on Minority Peoples in the Depression*, bulletin 31 (New York: SSRC, 1937).

ism. Through the SSRC, social scientists sought to strengthen the boundary around their disciplines by entering public life as experts and adapting themselves to the strictures of contract research. The political and economic challenges had to be met with objective social planning that utilized social intelligence. Social scientific knowledge was promoted because of its ability to legitimate planning and control. The State and social scientists were tied together in a process of mutual legitimation. As it involved the SSRC, this process was funded, guided, and to some extent controlled by Rockefeller philanthropy. Through the committees on public administration and social security the ruling class was able to exert its influence on the development of State structures.

A number of factors combined in 1933 to change the direction of the SSRC and the social sciences in a dramatic way. The RST report, a new administration in the White House, the shift in policy within Rockefeller philanthropy, and the overwhelming fact that the economy was at its lowest ebb all set the stage for active involvement in the national emergency and for practical government service. A significant move in this direction occurred with the establishment of the SSRC Committee on Industry and Trade, chaired by Willits. This committee aimed at increasing control over industrial and economic instability. These aims were reemphasized in the work of the Committees on Population Redistribution and on Economic Security (later the CSS), which were in turn chaired by Willits. Council involvement in the general process increased over the decade and occurred in four overlapping ways: the RF/SF emergency program, the Commissions of Inquiry, the programs in public administration and economic security (later social security), and President Roosevelt's NRPB.

The centerpiece of the Council's efforts became the painstaking work in public administration and social security. The SSRC was commissioned by the RF to focus on these two areas. The move was a logical extension of the RF and SF emergency work and provided the necessary distance for Rockefeller philanthropy from the danger of public controversy. From 1935 up to the end of 1941 when the United States entered the war, the SSRC was almost exclusively tied to work in these two areas. Technical social scientists flocked to Washington to do detailed studies of the New Deal programs. An enormous amount of data was collected, which resulted in a mountain of reports, memorandums, and pamphlets. Some of the most important work was done by Matscheck and Atkinson on unemployment compensation, by Gaus and Wolcott on the Department of Agriculture, and by Woytinsky on labor markets. These efforts were increasingly tied to State policy-making as Merriam, Mitchell, Ruml, Brownlow, and Gulick were brought in to run the NRPB and staff the CAM. Behind the scenes, Day and Willits were consolidating the form of the alliance between the RF and SSRC.

Through their work on public administration and social security and their participation in the NRPB and the CAM, social scientists became adjuncts to the State. This level of involvement in public affairs by social scientists was unprecedented. The acceptance by social scientists of their new role marked a substantial shift in the balance of power from academic social science disciplines toward the State and the ruling class. Through the SSRC, and other institutions, social scientists were used to build the infrastructure of the State. As the State became the major tool for maintaining social control, social scientists shifted their attention away from fundamental development of their disciplines. Social scientists shifted toward service and collaboration with government on immediate, practical social problems. Social control ideology moved from means to ends; from an emphasis on pure science to an emphasis on applied policy. The SSRC led the movement away from fundamental science to concrete studies of practical concern. The alliance between the ruling class and the State was mediated by philanthropy and social scientists.

Yet the changes were by no means linear or without contradictory tendencies. While scientism and empiricism remained dominant, the definition of science employed by social scientists changed. The push for purposive investigation on problems prescribed by Rockefeller philanthropy and the State meant that the theoretical and critical components of the science of society perspective were now underplayed. Integration increasingly occurred under the prescribed policy fields of concentration. As Ruml and others feared in 1929, the disciplines and the respective associations became increasingly concerned with their own development rather than some larger commitment to the social sciences. Nowhere was this breakdown more clear than in sociology, which had since the late nineteenth century been the discipline to consistently reach for an integrated social science. In the 1930s, social scientists were turning away from the Chicago cooperative model and were moving toward models based in New York and Boston that emphasized "operationalism" and "functionalism."[205]

Some disciplines benefited more than others from the new alliance. The establishment of the Central Statistical Board in 1933 placed a permanent seal of approval on statistics and quantitative social research. The State recognized that national planning was impossible without good statistics. Political scientists rode the wagons of public administration and social security as they molded the boundary of their discipline using behavioral psychology. The psychologists were used extensively to select and classify people as part of the more general testing movement. The economists and sociologists were brought into service, most prominently through the work on economic/social security. The disciplines that benefited least were history and anthropology.

---

205. For a discussion of this trend, see Kuklick, "Scientific Revolution."

Social scientists who did quantitative work were brought into State service in unprecedented numbers by the SSRC and the NRPB. While many leading social scientists like Merriam, Mitchell, Ogburn, and Wilson welcomed this development, others were skeptical. Robert S. Lynd and Crane were outspoken in their opposition to what they variously described as "pick and shovel" or "wholesale" research. For these men, the trend was regressive precisely because it inhibited the development of the social sciences in a fundamental way.

CHAPTER 5

Self-Criticism, Reconstruction, and Planning, 1937–45

Two books published at the end of the decade provide key insights into the ways in which the social science community perceived itself during this period. The first book *Knowledge for What? The Place of Social Science in American Culture* (1939) by Robert S. Lynd is a rousing critique of social scientific research.[1] In this controversial text, Lynd laid bare the internal battle that had been raging within the SSRC about the appropriate role in society for the social science disciplines. The second book, *Eleven Twenty-Six: A Decade of Social Science Research* (1940), edited by Louis Wirth, celebrates the first decade of work in the University of Chicago Social Science Research Building.[2] While Wirth had qualms about the development of the SSRC, he was still optimistic about the future. In *Eleven Twenty-Six* Wirth wrote confidently about the achievements at Chicago, and the book was in Wirth's view a testament to what could be built more generally in the social sciences. As editor and organizer of the conferences upon which the volume was based, Wirth was consistent with his belief that the path toward fundamental development was an integrated one. Ruml echoed Wirth's optimism about the future of the social sciences in his address "Social Science in Retrospect and Prospect."[3] Both Lynd and Wirth agreed that the way forward for their disciplines was to rekindle the original aim of coordination and integration that had been the impulse for the creation of the SSRC.

Lynd's book is particularly interesting precisely because he took the dangerous step of setting himself up as critic. He divided social scientists into two groups: the scholars and the technicians. Throughout the book Lynd described Mitchell and his colleagues at the NBER as exemplars of his technician category. Mitchell and Frederick C. Mills are labeled as the arch-

---

"Self-Criticism, Reconstruction, and Planning, 1937–45" was a subtitle in Wirth's original draft manuscript. Crane had him remove "self-criticism."

1. Lynd, *Knowledge for What?*

2. Louis Wirth, ed., *Eleven Twenty-Six: A Decade of Social Science Research* (Chicago: University of Chicago Press, 1940; reprint ed., New York: Arno Press, 1970).

3. Beardsley Ruml, "Social Science in Retrospect and Prospect," in Wirth, *Eleven Twenty-Six*, pp. 23–27.

empiricists whose only concern was quantification and refined measurement. They are accused of being content to collect data and facts without any commitment to more fundamental questions or to theory building.[4] Such knowledge, according to Lynd, tended to be abstract, separated from its context, and contributed to an ameliorative attitude. Lynd espoused the old goal of integration through research on significant social problems.

To be scientific, social science had to be both innovative and critical. The social sciences, in Lynd's view, had been drawn away from their original purpose and coopted by academic culture. As a result, according to Lynd, the social sciences had "tended to emphasize data gathered rather than data needing to be gathered, normative theory rather than the full range of refractory phenomena, and to stress Knowledge and Order rather than the vast areas of the Unknown and Chaotic." Lynd contrasted his orientation with that of Mitchell by quoting from an address, "Science and the State of Mind," which the latter gave as president of the American Association for the Advancement of Science to the American Science Teachers Association in 1939. For Mitchell, science was concerned only with truth and falsity and could not pronounce judgments. This was not good enough for Lynd. As he observed: "If, however, 'science' does not pronounce such judgments, scientists can: and if they fail to do so, in this world in which the gap between sophisticated knowledge and folk-thinking is so wide, they but aggravate the limitations on the utility of science to man." Lynd came out firmly in favor of the full utilization of social scientists to do both research and planning. For, as Lynd observed, "there is no way in which our culture can grow in continual serviceability to its people without a clear and pervasive extension of planning and control." Later in the book Lynd referred to the work of the NRPB's Science Committee as a step in the right direction. Even so, Lynd still wanted to preserve some elements of positivism. In his discussion of values, Lynd stated that the researcher inevitably must use his values when selecting a problem but should thereafter bracket those same values during the analysis and interpretation of data. Lynd ended by endorsing the responsibility of social scientists to do research and to plan so that they might "yet make real the claims of freedom and opportunity in America."[5]

Included in *Eleven Twenty-Six* is the record of five roundtable discussions: "The Social Sciences, One or Many"; "Quantification: The Quest for Precision"; "Training for Social Science Research"; "Generalization in the Social Sciences"; and "Social Science and Social Action." These discussions provide clear insight into the divisions within the social science community.

4. Mitchell is used as the straw man representing abstract empiricism throughout the book. There are however explicit references to Mitchell, Mills, and the NBER; see Lynd, *Knowledge for What?* pp. 32–33, 119, 144, and 242.

5. Ibid., pp. 118, 150, 209, and 242.

The first roundtable, which had initially been titled "Integration of the Social Sciences," was chaired by Mitchell and included many of the leading members of the SSRC. Lynd's book was referred to, and he played a prominent role in the discussion. Lynd was particularly critical of the contributions from Crane and Mitchell. He accused Crane of favoring a "relapse back to the traditional disciplines" and argued that instead social scientists needed "to attempt to replace the present disciplines . . . by broad problem-areas, such as industrial production, consumption, family living, urbanism, and so on."[6] He felt that "projective" problems were the best means for producing integration. Lynd inevitably differed from Mitchell, who according to Lynd believed that integration was going to happen by "spontaneous combustion." Lynd defended the utility of administrative structures like the SSRC, which Mitchell had labeled as external, quasi-mechanical devices. As one might expect, given the discussion in *Knowledge for What?* Lynd attacked Mitchell's view that social scientists should get all the data and "then" integrate them. In his "pick and shovel" theme, Lynd decried the notion that once "good data" had been gathered, it would "automatically fit as bricks . . . into some constructive building." For Lynd, social scientists had to "stress the gathering of data in relation to a definitely stated problem" if they were "to have any hope of really constructive integration" after they had finished.[7]

In a similar vein, Ogburn was critical of Mitchell for "cultivating specialties" and for expecting that as the volume of sound, accurate knowledge increased so it would become integrated into a structure.[8] Finally, Ruml endorsed the general idea that integration was likely to occur through the study of definite social problems. He was particularly critical of Crane for making the distinction between the possibilities for integration at the levels of practice and theory. Crane felt that integration was most fruitful at the level of practice. For Ruml, this was ominous because it implied that the single discipline approach was best suited to theoretical investigations, which raised a question mark about "the real advantage of the existing disciplines in the study of the social order as it exists in the real world."[9] All did agree that integration was a worthwhile goal, and despite the differences there was a general air of optimism.

In the roundtable discussions on "quantification" and "generalization," it is significant that Talcott Parsons was a prominent contributor. Parsons had recently published his epoch-making *The Structure of Social Action* (1937).[10] This key text in the history of sociology and the social sciences in the United

---

6. Wirth, *Eleven Twenty-Six*, pp. 125 and 126.
7. Ibid., pp. 129 and 129–30.
8. Ibid., p. 136.
9. Ibid., p. 139.
10. Talcott Parsons, *The Structure of Social Action* (New York: McGraw-Hill, 1937).

States turned attention away from the social problem orientation, which asked questions about disorder, to questions concerning the persistence of social order. This book was an important element in the changing nature of the ideology of social control and was the start of the rapid movement toward a new model of integration under the banner of structural functionalism.[11]

Lynd and Wirth had as much as anyone a clear view of developments within the SSRC. Both praised the SSRC either explicitly or implicitly for the attempt to break down boundaries between the social disciplines and cut against the trend toward increased specialization. Yet in these two publications readers are provided with two rather different images of the social science community. On the one hand, *Eleven Twenty-Six* celebrates the attempts to integrate and is optimistic about the future. On the other hand, Lynd in *Knowledge for What?* and in the discussions at Chicago lamented the failure to integrate and charged the technical empiricists and an academic culture that prized disciplined study with the responsibility. Neither man was critical of the foundations, for as each was well aware the key to solving the problems faced by the SSRC then and earlier was the Council's relationship with the RF.

Within the SSRC, the movement toward planning had been in progress since 1933 and was part of the broader shift in this direction in the policies adopted by Rockefeller philanthropy and in society as a whole. Furniss had mentioned planning as an appropriate role for the SSRC in his 1934 report.[12] It was also the case that the fluid funds available to the Council were almost exhausted. This meant that it was impossible to make long-term research plans until the relations with funding agencies were sorted out. At the same time concern was expressed by some members of the SSRC about the ties that were being established with the State through the programs in public administration and social security and the extent to which all other work was pushed aside. These three factors, the structural trend that emphasized planning, the financial stringencies, and the concerns about autonomy, as much as anything else, ushered in the next phase of the Council's history. This phase was dependent on two major appraisals: the first by Louis Wirth in 1937 and the second as part of an RF review of the DSS in 1938.

The financial uncertainty was a major impetus for embarking upon a full evaluation. While Crane had obtained extra support from the CC and expected the Russell Sage Foundation to continue its small grant, the SSRC was still

---

11. See the discussion by Janowitz, *Last Half-Century*, pp. 47 n. 46, 57–59, 61, 64, and 69.

12. Extracts for this report are contained in "Excerpts from National Councils, DR502," trustees meeting, December 11, 1935, Folder 27, 910, Program and Policy—Appraisal Committee (SSRC) Reports, 1935–38, RF, 1.1, 200, 307, RAC.

almost totally dependent on Rockefeller funds.[13] As it stood in late 1936, all the separate Rockefeller grants covering administration, fellowships, conferences, grants-in-aid, and research were due to expire in 1940. Fluid money was already desperately short. The grants-in-aid fund had been extended for just one year, 1936–37. Almost all the research funds were consumed by the designated areas, public administration and social security. While Crane was concerned about the relation between the SSRC and Rockefeller philanthropy, others were critical of him. Certainly key figures like Merriam, Ogburn, and to some extent Mitchell were annoyed at Crane's reluctance to commit the SSRC, and therefore social scientists, to the task of social engineering. They were afraid that what was a golden opportunity to participate in government policy-making was likely to be missed because of the dissension among social scientists. Similarly, Day and Ruml, representing Rockefeller philanthropy, expressed concern about the divisions within the SSRC. They were particularly sensitive to charges that the Council was controlled by Rockefeller money and wanted to change this perception.[14] In addition, internal criticism of Crane was growing because of his leadership style. He tended to be secretive and act autonomously. He apparently found it difficult to delegate responsibility.[15] There was continuing criticism of the power vested in the role of the executive director and the power of the PPC. For some this meant that the Council itself became a rubber stamp. No doubt in the minds of some, Crane often appeared to be simply an agent of the RF.[16]

The executive director was the chief staff officer and the active manager of the business of the Council. Crane represented the Council before outside organizations and the public, made decisions on current problems of policy, and in conjunction with the PPC developed both policy and program. As Wirth put it, Crane was "expected to lead without appearing to dominate." Inevitably, Crane was the major point of contact between Rockefeller philanthropy and the Council. He was expected to both represent the interests of the Council to the RF while at the same time act as its confidential adviser. Because of the almost total dependence on Rockefeller philanthropy and the

---

13. The CC provided $75,000 over three years, 1937–40.

14. It should be noted that Keppel sent the RF an edited version of the Crane memorandum in which he divided up activities of the Council into categories using the degree of external control as the criterion. Letter/enclosure, Keppel to Fosdick (president, RF), October 15, 1936, File, SSRC, 1932–36, CC.

15. Interview, Keppel with Donald Ramsey Young, September 11–12, 1934, File, SSRC, 1932–36, CC.

16. See Beard (APSA council member, 1933–35) to Crane, September 25, 1934. Among Wirth's handwritten notes, Folder 1, Box 32, Wirth, University of Chicago. Also Wirth, "Report," pp. 41 and 44, SSRCA.

continuing shift within these institutions toward concentration, it became the practice for Crane to discuss proposed undertakings that required finance with Day to get prior assurance of funds. Because Crane alone was authorized to seek funds on behalf of the Council, it was essential that a mutual understanding develop between the executive director and the director of the DSS.[17] The key to the relationship was that Crane was willing to go along with what Rockefeller philanthropy wanted. The Council's lack of control was compounded by the fact that very often members selected by the societies did not display much interest in the affairs of the Council, did not contribute to the work, and, sometimes, failed to attend meetings. In an effort to obtain a better type of constituent member the Council, in 1936, decided to move to a panel system. Instead of standard election procedures, the societies were now required to elect members from panels nominated by the Council. Yet the Council decided to include the names of the retiring members in the panel of three, an action that contradicted the new policy. While the official justification for the new policy was to improve the quality of the membership, the ruling seemed designed to make the Council less representative and even more of a self-perpetuating body than it was already.

Internal Review of the Council's Operations: The Wirth Report

The Committee on Review of Council Policy was appointed by Ford, chair of the SSRC, in 1936. Mark Arthur May chaired the committee with Ogburn, Mitchell, Redfield, and Schlesinger as members. The committee was created "in light of the developments" that had occurred "both within the Council and in social science in general since 1929 when the seven Roman numerals were set up and adopted."[18] Crane did not expect the committee to do a major review. He thought that the review was intended to express an opinion on some of the more recent activities of the Council, particularly with regard to the relation between the SSRC and the government.[19] The more inclusive review was probably the result of an intervention by Day. In addition to Ogburn and Mitchell, who were clearly Rockefeller insiders and were publicly lined up against Crane, it should be noted that May, Redfield, and Schlesinger had all been receiving substantial support through their institutions from the RF. On the recommendation of the committee, the SSRC hired the Chicago sociologist Wirth to conduct the "Study of Council Policy."[20] The

17. Wirth, "Report," p. 41, SSRCA.

18. Ibid., Statement by the committee after the table of contents.

19. See Crane's statement to the SSRC council meeting, September 4–6, 1936, Review of Council Policy, SSRCA.

20. SSRC executive meeting, May 3, 1937. Review of Council Policy, SSRCA.

terms of reference stated that Wirth was to make a survey of the Council's history, activities, and policy so that the committee would have the necessary data for its own report. Wirth spent three months in New York consulting records and interviewing people. His draft report was ready by late July 1937.[21]

As one might expect from the background to this study, the report was bound to be controversial. The draft report was quite critical of both the Council and Crane for their lack of independence and reliance on Rockefeller funding. Wirth characterized the Council as a self-perpetuating agency that was by implication out of touch with contemporary developments in the social sciences. Not surprisingly Crane was reluctant to pass on the report without some alterations. Crane reported to Mitchell that he had sent Wirth "pages of comment concerning matters of fact, and references to the Foundation, which seem to me unwise in view of the fact that these documents are never fully confidential."[22] Wirth made some corrections and Crane did some editing that effectively took out all the references to foundations by name and revised the most negative statements about the relationship between Rockefeller philanthropy and the Council. Comments on Crane were either removed or softened. The revised version was 162 pages long and was submitted in August 1937. Appendixes covering a special study of the grants-in-aid program and the financing of the Council were attached.[23] The appendix on grants-in-aid was the report of the separate Committee on Review of Grants-in-Aid (1936–37), which had been appointed at the same time as the general review committee.

The whole report was distributed to council members. While this was clearly a document of substantial interest to the social science community, it was never published. Crane effectively blocked its publication. Even after Crane had made further revisions, in his opinion the report "still contained appreciable duplications, questionable interpretations and statements of fact which seemed practically impossible of correction."[24] Crane did not want either his position or his performance attacked. While Crane wanted to cut into the control exercised by Rockefeller philanthropy, he was realistic enough to know that the Council's future would be endangered if the Rockefellers were publicly attacked. To protect the Council from criticism in the future, Chairman Ford asked Council members when filing the Wirth report to

---

21. Wirth, Draft Report, Folder 1, Box 32, Wirth, University of Chicago.

22. Crane to Mitchell, July 26, 1937, Correspondence: Robert T. Crane, WCMC, Columbia University.

23. Wirth, "Report," SSRCA. Also "Objectives and Administration of Grants-in-Aid of Research," 1938, Folder 47–48, 200S, SSRC—Reports, 1937–38, RF, 1.1, 200, 401, RAC.

24. Minutes, PPC, July 30–31, 1938, pt. 20, January 16, 1937–September 14, 1938, SSRCA.

attach a note saying that it omitted many things and was not considered a wholly accurate picture of the Council's history or interpretation of the Council's work.[25]

Wirth divided his report into six sections: history, formal organization, finance, activities, relations with external institutions, and conclusions and recommendations. The majority of this material has either already been covered in this monograph or appears in a later section that assesses the Council's impact on the social sciences. At this stage it is important to concentrate on the suggestions and recommendations. Wirth was absolutely clear that the SSRC ought to make "the improvement of the social sciences in the United States" the prime objective. This meant that the Council ought to restore and accentuate the primacy of its intellectual function and undertake activities which, as Wirth put it, were "sufficiently fundamental, strategic, and widespread in scope to be worthy of the central national body in the social sciences."[26] He felt that the original objectives of the Council concerning cooperation and integration between disciplines still held good and that the Council ought to carry forward those interests that the social sciences had in common. The Council ought to keep abreast of the development of social science knowledge in order to encourage and direct attention to those issues and fundamental problems to which the social sciences might contribute. While the Council ought to provide the greatest possible contribution to the solution of practical social problems, this had to be done within the bounds of science. Finally, Wirth believed that the SSRC ought to protect the social sciences in those situations where objectivity or freedom were under attack.

With respect to organization, Wirth suggested that the Council ought to watch very carefully the panel system and be prepared to modify it in order to maximize both representation and efficiency. He was in favor of obtaining more input from marginal but related disciplines. Most important, he recommended that the PPC only be selected from Council members. Further he suggested that the PPC should either be reorganized into a policy-forming body or be abolished. If this former course was adopted, then Wirth recommended the creation of five major committees representing the major divisions of the Council's work: research planning, review and criticism, research training and research facilitation, advisory and service functions, and coordination, liaison, and promotion. Each department would have a full-time staff member. In these ways the control of both the executive director and the PPC over the Council would be lessened. Council members were to be encouraged to regard their responsibilities as year-round. Meetings could be

---

25. Council meeting minutes, September 13–15, 1938, Review of Council Policy, SSRCA.

26. Wirth, "Report," p. 152, SSRCA.

divided into two types: first, those discussion meetings that focused on major scientific issues or problems of policy but did not vote on motions, and, second, meetings where motions were formally considered for ratification.

To make the Council more independent Wirth recommended that it either seek endowment or a commitment from the foundations to provide funding for a decade. He was clear that the SSRC "should not accept grants under conditions which would compromise its own scientific standing or which would affect the character of the results of research." Independence from all external institutions had to be scrupulously maintained. In a clear reference to Rockefeller philanthropy, Wirth commented that the Council should not "allow itself to be used as either a blind for them or become subject to pressure from them." He continued: "Only by maintaining its complete independence of judgement can it render its most valuable service to them, to science and to society."[27] Wirth came down firmly on the side of the Council not doing research. The SSRC's proper province was to encourage, stimulate, guide, and plan research. As research planning became more central so the SSRC would have to be more explicitly concerned with coordination and integration. Also, Wirth was convinced that the SSRC ought to serve a critical function. This meant that the Council should fulfill its proper scientific function as a critic both of research and of society. Controversy was to be confronted with science. Facts rather than values would provide the best service to society and for the improvement of the social sciences.

The Committee on Review of Council Policy's own report accepted the majority of Wirth's suggestions. The dominant and controlling purpose of the Council was to be "intellectual leadership in the facilitation and coordination of research in the social sciences." The Council was advised to move away from doing "human engineering" research to concentrate on putting the social sciences on a sounder scientific basis. The committee gave three reasons for this recommendation. First, social science in America had enjoyed a measure of freedom of inquiry and expression rarely matched in the history of science. Not to consolidate the position of the social sciences in those circumstances meant the loss of what was probably only a temporary opportunity. Second, the SSRC was the only organization in the United States capable of exercising intellectual leadership. Finally, the committee believed that the Council could "render its greatest service to society by exploring the fundamentals of social science."[28] The committee was in favor of providing service to all external agencies so long as it remained within scientific guidelines.

The committee outlined four major functions that the SSRC ought to

---

27. Ibid., pp. 158–59.

28. Council meeting minutes, September 14–16, 1937, Report, app. 15, pp. 1 and 2, Review of Council Policy, SSRCA.

fulfill. The first and most important function was "research promotion, appraisal, and planning." Following Wirth, the committee emphasized the need to encourage both scientific development and cooperation among disciplines. The need was for fundamental planning of social research. Second, under the heading "research agencies and institutions" the committee regarded the proper function of the Council as one of liaison, coordination, and the promotion of projects. The committee believed that the SSRC should take the incentive concerning which enterprises were most important and feasible. The third function was "research personnel." In addition to the recruitment and training of social scientists the committee added maintenance. Specifically, the committee recommended that the grants-in-aid program ought to be articulated with the fellowship program. Fourth, under the heading "research materials" the committee included collection, preservation, and dissemination. The committee had therefore taken a further step in the process of rationalizing and defining the Council's activities. Whereas Wirth had replaced the Roman Numerals with five committees, the review committee had moved to the idea of four standing committees. It recommended that the chairs and vice-chairs of the Council should be ex-officio members of the PPC. The committee ended the report with an endorsement of Wirth's recommendation that the SSRC move away from too close a tie to any particular foundation.

The Wirth report and the review committee report were discussed extensively at the annual PPC and Council meetings held in 1937 at Skytop Lodge, Pennsylvania.[29] Those attending agreed that the essential function of the Council was intellectual leadership and that the seven Roman numerals should be revised into the four objectives listed by the review committee. It was recognized that the first heading "research promotion, appraisal, and planning" was of a different order in that it dealt with the development and evaluation of research, while the other three were concerned with implementation. The Council came to the rather bland conclusion that it would maintain a watchful attitude toward the service that the Council provided to governments. Even though there was general acceptance of the report, little action was taken. The only effort to operationalize the recommendations was the appointment of a new standing Committee on Appraisal of Research (1937–46). This action was taken at the insistence of the recently appointed president of Cornell University, Day.

According to Stacy May, Day, who was attending the PPC meetings as an invited guest, led a concerted drive for a survey of the field of social research.[30] Certainly Nourse, the chair of the PPC (1932–39), later recorded

29. Minutes, PPC, September 13, 1937, pt. 20, January 16, 1937–September 14, 1938, SSRCA.

30. Stacy May to Fosdick, October 22, 1937, Folder 4, 910, Program and Policy, 1937–39, RF, 910, 3, 1, RAC.

that Day had "sharply challenged the Council as to whether it had any clearly formulated idea as to what social science really is or whether it was doing anything serious and systematic in the direction of finding out." Nourse pointed to the implicit threat contained in this challenge coming as it did from someone so closely associated with the RF. The conclusion reached by Nourse was that the Council was "hardly justified in seeking substantial funds [from the RF] to be expended in a type of activities about whose standard of performance and the value of whose product, we were so much in a fog."[31] Nourse was the leading agricultural economist in the country. Nourse had been a key member of the Institute of Economics since it was founded by Moulton in 1922. In 1927, Nourse became the director of the institute as it was incorporated into, and became, a division of the Brookings Institution. Nourse was a strong supporter of free trade and believed in the power of the marketplace to solve economic problems. He was at the center of the academic opposition to the New Deal, which was housed at Brookings. In 1933, Nourse was the senior author of one of the "capacity" studies that Brookings undertook for Congress and that was subsequently published as *America's Capacity to Produce* (1934).[32]

In response to the challenge from Day, the PPC set up the Committee on Appraisal of Research, with Day as chair. The other members were Redfield and Schlesinger.[33] The committee had the power to co-opt members, and there was at this stage an implicit agreement that each constituent society ought to be represented. The committee was subsequently enlarged, and over the next three years it embarked upon a program of appraisal that it labeled "Critiques of Research in the Social Sciences." The intent was to publish critical appraisals of what was regarded as some of the best research in the social sciences. What followed was a concerted effort at boundary work. Day and his colleagues were attempting to make clear the line that separated social science from social studies. The first appraisal, by the Chicago sociologist

31. Nourse, Council meeting minutes, September 12–14, 1939, report, p. 3, Review of Council Policy, SSRCA. My insert.

32. Edwin G. Nourse et al., *America's Capacity to Produce* (Washington, D.C.: Brookings Institution, 1934). The other three "capacity" studies were as follows: Harold G. Moulton, Maurice Leven, and Clark Warburton, *America's Capacity to Consume* (Washington, D.C.: Brookings Institution, 1934); Harold G. Moulton, *Income and Economic Progress* (Washington, D.C.: Brookings Institution, 1935); and Harold G. Moulton, *The Formation of Capital* (Washington, D.C.: Brookings Institution, 1936). Nourse had established his reputation with his early text *Agricultural Economics* (Chicago: University of Chicago Press, 1916). For an account of Nourse's career, see Critchlow, *Brookings Institution*; and Nourse's autobiography, *Economics in the Public Service* (New York: Harcourt Brace, 1953).

33. Nourse, Council meeting minutres, September 12–14, 1939, p. 3. Also Annual report, Committee on Appraisal, 1939–40, minutes, PPC, July 27–28, 1940, app. 2, pt. 21, October 22–23, 1938 to July 27–28, 1940, SSRCA.

Herbert Blumer, examined the research methods used in the classic work by W. I. Thomas and Znaniecki, *The Polish Peasant in Europe and America*. This study was followed by appraisals of Frederick C. Mills's *The Behaviour of Prices*, by Raymond T. Bye, and Walter Prescott Webb's *The Great Plains: A Study in Institutions and Environment*, by Fred Albert Shannon.[34] During the war years, this committee undertook critical studies of the use of personal documents in psychological, historical, anthropological, and sociological research.[35]

Rockefeller Philanthropy and Human Control

As the Council was setting up the Committee on Appraisal of Research, Fosdick, the president of the RF, was pursuing his resolve to have the foundation ask itself the key question, namely: "In a chaotic world like this, have the social sciences a contribution to make to the problem of human control? If so, what is it, and how do the social sciences propose to go about it?"[36] His concern had almost certainly been aroused by an editorial in the September 17, 1937, issue of *Nature* that suggested the government should endow a new scientific organization to maintain continuous surveillance of social problems and then proceed to study the problems of immediate and practical concern. To maintain the "effectiveness and stability of present and future social organization" it was, according to this editorial, necessary to find solutions to the general problems that faced society. The editorial called for a "new, centrally constituted scientific body" that would "survey the field of social research" and "set on foot considered programmes of actual investigation on higher biological lines."[37] The DSS, Fosdick, and Wilson, chairman of the Federal Science Committee, supported the idea of a survey and believed that in the United States the SSRC was the appropriate organization to undertake such a survey.[38] The appointment of the Committee on Appraisal of Research was

---

34. Herbert Blumer, *An Appraisal of Thomas and Znaniecki's "The Polish Peasant in Europe and America,"* bulletin 44 (New York: SSRC, 1939); Raymond T. Bye, *An Appraisal of Frederick C. Mills' "The Behaviour of Prices,"* bulletin 45 (New York: SSRC, 1940); Fred Albert Shannon, *An Appraisal of Walter Prescott Webb's "The Great Plains: A Study in Institutions and Environment,"* bulletin 46 (New York: SSRC, 1940).

35. See Gordon Willard Allport, *The Use of Personal Documents in Psychological Science*, bulletin 49 (New York: SSRC, 1942); and Louis Reichental Gottschalk, Clyde Kluckhohm, and Robert Angell, *The Use of Personal Documents in History, Anthropology, and Sociology*, bulletin 53 (New York: SSRC, 1945).

36. Fosdick to Walker, November 9, 1937, Folder 4, 910, Program and Policy, 1937–39, RF, 910, 3, 1, RAC.

37. "The Organization of Social Research," *Nature* 140 (1937): 521–23.

38. Stacy May to Fosdick, October 22, 1937, Fosdick to Walker, November 9, 1937, Walker to Fosdick, November 10, 1937, Folder 4, 910, Program and Policy, 1937–39, RF, 910, 3, 1, RAC.

certainly in line with the editorial, and with Day's involvement, the RF could keep close watch on developments within the SSRC. There was also some satisfaction within the RF because the Council had expressed its willingness to continue being of service while at the same time had renewed the commitment to its initial scientific objectives. Walker observed that at the 1937 Skytop meetings there appeared to be a genuine desire to find the way back to the main road.[39] Wilson informed Fosdick that the Council was a "good organization" that had been "useful" to the RF in the past and could be even more useful in the future.[40] Because the SSRC was the only national social science organization, and because of the close, almost incestuous relationship between the RF and the Council, it was predictable that the Council was placed at the center of Fosdick's review of the DSS.

In 1937, a joint meeting of the trustees of the RF and the GEB decided that a committee of three trustees should be appointed to sit with the president of the RF and officers of the DSS to review their work. The justification provided was the chaotic condition of the world and the judgment that the RF's work in the social sciences was unsatisfactory.[41] Fosdick appointed Harold W. Dodds, president of Princeton University, Walter W. Stewart, and J. Foster Dulles, a lawyer, to the Trustee Committee of Review. What followed was an attempt to clear up misunderstandings between leading members of the social science network. The form and content of the discourse had to be reevaluated so that resources could be exchanged more efficiently. Subsequently, the committee decided to meet with representatives of the SSRC, and at Fosdick's invitation, Crane and Nourse attended a luncheon meeting at Rockefeller Center.[42] Fosdick invited them to evaluate the Council's programs, past and present, and to state what they would like to see the Council become. Fosdick made it clear that the trustees were also interested in discussing the relation between the RF and the SSRC, for as he put it, the "question of satisfactory relationship between the Council and the Foundation is naturally of strong mutual interest."[43]

Crane made it plain that the SSRC must serve only scientific ends. He stated that support for the social sciences could be justified because of the

---

39. Walker to Fosdick, November 10, 1937, Folder 4, 910, Program and Policy, 1937–39, RF, 910, 3, 1, RAC.

40. Wilson to Fosdick, November 20, 1937, Folder 4, 910, Program and Policy, 1937–39, RF, 910, 3, 1, RAC.

41. "Joint Meeting of the Trustees, Rockefeller Foundation, and the General Education Board, Executive Session, November 30, 1937," Folder 4, 910, Program and Policy, 1937–39, RF, 910, 3, 1, RAC.

42. Meeting of Special Trustee Committee for Social Sciences, May 10, 1938, Folder 105, 910, Program and Policy—Trustee Committee of Review, 1938–39, RF, 910, 3, 2, RAC.

43. Fosdick to Crane, May 18, 1938, Folder 105, 910, Program and Policy—Trustee Committee of Review, 1938–39, RF, 910, 3, 2, RAC. An impression of the discussion is contained in three memorandums that Crane submitted to Fosdick in June and October 1938.

contribution that these subjects could make to human welfare by helping to solve social problems. While the current capacity for providing such help was low, Crane was convinced that the time was ripe for the "development of work that is genuinely scientific"—though, he made it clear, not scientific in the natural science mode. To achieve this objective, Crane recommended the encouragement of work on specific problems that would lead to compact, usable reports. Throughout this work, facts and values had to be separated. As Crane observed: "It is necessary to encourage ways of working toward more rigorous induction from data; more rigorous verification of hypotheses, greater coherence and continuity of knowledge." The best contribution that the SSRC could make toward the solution of social problems was to make sure that "research undertakings be chosen for their scientific value and not for their promise of immediate contribution to practical affairs." The primary function of the SSRC and the one of greatest value to society was that of "planning and promoting in the social fields the advance of science itself."[44]

Crane submitted two important memorandums to Fosdick in October 1938.[45] Both documents emerged from the discussions that Crane and Nourse had with the Trustee Committee of Review and from the internal SSRC debate during the summer of 1938. Urgency was injected into the issue of relations with the foundations and particularly the RF at the annual meetings of the Council and the PPC in the summer of 1938. Day came to the PPC meetings to urge that special consideration be given to problems concerning the relations of the Council to foundations. He expressed fears that the relationship might be less than satisfactory in the future unless special consideration was given to these relationships and therefore the more general problem of how to maintain support for the social sciences.[46] While one has to assume that Day was still privy to RF discussions and was therefore voicing a real problem, it is the case that Crane held a contrary view. According to another account of these meetings, Crane described relations with foundations as "uniformly close, cordial, and mutually beneficial."[47] At the next meeting of the PPC, they discussed the memorandum prepared by Crane under the heading "Relations with Foundations."[48] In the discussion the Council confirmed its accep-

---

44. Letter/memorandum, Crane to Fosdick, June 10, 1938, pp. 2 and 3, Folder 105, 910, Program and Policy—Trustee Committee of Review, 1938–39, RF, 910, 3, 2, RAC. This memorandum explicitly excluded any reference to relations between the RF and the Council.

45. Letter/memorandums (2), Crane to Fosdick, October 27, 1938, Folder 105, 910, Program and Policy—Trustee Committee of Review, 1938–39, RF, 910, 3, 2, RAC.

46. Minutes, PPC, September 14, 1938, p. 505, pt. 20, January 16, 1937–September 14, 1938, SSRCA.

47. "Charles Dollard and Annual Meeting of Social Science Research Council, Buck Hill Falls, Pa.," September 13–15, 1938, p. 2, File, SSRC, 1937–45, CC. Charles Dollard was the assistant to the president of the CC. Dollard was in charge of grants-in-aid and overseas visits.

48. Minutes, PPC, October 22–23, 1938, pt. 21, October 22–23, 1938 to July 27–28,

tance of the responsibility for advising foundations on matters concerned with improving the social sciences. Although members expressed some reluctance about involvement in matters of social engineering, it was finally accepted that the Council could not avoid the obligation to give advice on the utilization of the social sciences for purposes of social welfare.

The second of the October memorandums dealt specifically with the Council's reactions to, and recommendation for, the RF's social science program. Crane stated that a foundation program, designed to aid in the solution of social problems through the extension of knowledge and understanding should focus on two distinct lines of activity: first, the improvement of the social sciences as instrumentalities for the attainment and diffusion of knowledge and, second, the utilization of these instrumentalities for attack on questions of public importance. As one might expect, Crane's description of the best program for the RF followed to a great extent the outline of activities that the Council saw as its preserve. Under the heading "improvement," Crane described four phases of work, namely, research, organization, personnel, and dissemination of results and methods. The Council regarded itself as the essential agency for research organization in the social sciences. Planning, coordination, stimulation, and leadership were described as the major phases of the Council's work. Under "research organization" Crane recommended that the universities should continue to be the important seats for the conduct of research. In addition to the support of individual researchers, Crane wanted the RF to continue providing opportunities for cooperative research as part of an integrated plan that coordinated the universities with other agencies. Crane believed the emphasis on research personnel both through the Council and independently ought to be maintained. Apart from the obvious connection between the expansion of scientific research and the availability of trained personnel, Crane also pointed to the direct interest of the RF in having a reservoir of well-trained people who could be utilized to attack larger questions of public concern. The improvement of research methodology was described as the most fundamental endeavor and "the key to real advance in all sciences."[49] Dissemination of results was an area recommended for exploration. Crane noted that the Council by virtue of its composition, facilities, and interests regarded itself as the most competent agency for doing this work. Essentially, the Council stood ready to continue its work for the RF in these four major phases.

Before dealing with the utilization of research results, Crane continued

---

1940, SSRCA. The memorandum was subsequently submitted to Fosdick, October 27, 1938 (see n. 45, this chapter).

49. Letter/second memorandum, Crane to Fosdick, October 27, 1938, p. 3, Folder 105, 910, Program and Policy—Trustee Committee of Review, 1938–39, RF, 910, 3, 2, RAC.

by singing the praises of the RF in its efforts to change the social sciences. The impact of Rockefeller money was described as a "great stimulus" and of "incalculable importance." Social research had been provided with status and position within the academy and in other agencies as well as in society at large. The movement toward a more empirical approach had been hastened. "The character of work" had, according to Crane, "been fundamentally turned from literary and philosophical production based on library sources to direct investigation of the raw materials of the actual social world and oriented to its concrete problems." Cooperation in research had become common and accepted as a desirable goal. The RF had in effect decreased the isolation of disciplines "by securing a realization that the problems of the different social sciences are interdependent problems of society."[50]

Crane used the rest of the memorandum to list the ways in which the Council had acted as a direct agency for the utilization of research results. He gave as examples the social security studies, the work on population redistribution, and the studies of government statistics. The Council recommended the continuation of the programs in social security and public administration but thought that the work in international relations ought to be evaluated. It asked that the RF consider two new fields that the SSRC might develop, namely, public finance and social adjustment. Throughout this section Crane nodded to the major criticism of the RF surrounding its concentration on particular fields by accepting that selection was "an essential and unavoidable function of the Foundation." Yet at the same time the Council wanted the RF to be more flexible. The Council recommended that the RF's program be "reasonably flexible with respect both to fields and to work within them" and that if the RF avoided rules for inclusion or exclusion then consideration could be given to work outside the fields of concentration.[51]

In the first October memorandum Crane dealt exclusively with the relations between the RF and the SSRC. While Crane assured Fosdick that he had the complete support of the Council, there is little in the PPC minutes on the issue of independence. In any event, Crane made it clear that the Council desired to serve a planning and advisory function rather than come as a petitioner for funds. On those occasions where the RF wanted the Council either to administer funds or to act as an intermediary, it was stated that the Council must make a formal request. To avoid the problems associated with requests emerging at the Council's initiative Crane suggested a number of "understandings." First, another agency had to be named to do the research. Second, without a suitable agency, the proposal must be presented as advice and only treated as an application if the RF wholly agreed that the project

---

50. Ibid., p. 4.
51. Ibid., pp. 6 and 8.

should go ahead. Third, that the RF should remember that the Council's essential function was to develop and offer broad research plans. "Sound planning, rigorous criticism, clarification of objectives, determination of practicability, consideration of scientific and social significance" were, according to Crane, "as essential to progress as to economy of effort and expense."[52] Finally, Crane stated that requests from the Council to the RF should be made as infrequently as possible.

While Crane at one stage had been opposed to seeking a permanent endowment for the Council, he had by September 1938 changed his mind.[53] It followed that on the day after he submitted the two memorandums to Fosdick he also sent a proposal for an endowment of $3 million to Walker, the associate director in the DSS. Crane enclosed a copy of the "Relations with Foundations" memorandum referred to earlier. The justification provided for the endowment was that it would place the Council in an unequivocal position in the eyes of everybody "as essentially a planning, advisory, coordinating and stimulating agency."[54] Further, such an endowment would allow the Council to continue its search for technical improvements in ways of working that were the key to real advance in the social sciences. While Crane presented this proposal as a Council decision, it had according to Walker only received approval from the PPC and had not been discussed by the Council, within which there were considerable differences of opinion.[55] No action was taken, and there is no way of knowing whether the trustees committee took any of the SSRC communications into account. Yet it is certain that the newly appointed director of the DSS, Willits, had been part of all the major discussions. Willits resigned from his membership in the PPC, effectively January 1, 1939, and took up his new position officially on February 1, 1939. The trustees committee gave this appointment as its reason for not making a full report. The committee decided that it should continue to function as an informal advisory body while Willits formulated his own plans. The only substantive conclusion to emerge was that the program had been too narrowly stated and too rigidly interpreted. Very much along the lines suggested in the SSRC program memorandum, the trustees recommended more flexibility.

Prior to the United States entering the Second World War, the RF pro-

52. Letter/first memorandum, Crane to Fosdick, October 27, 1938, Folder 105, 910, Program and Policy—Trustee Committee of Review, 1938–39, RF, 910, 3, 2, RAC.

53. "Charles Dollard and Annual Meeting of Social Science Research Council, Buck Hill Falls, Pa.," September 13–15, 1938, File, SSRC, 1937–45, CC.

54. Letter/memorandum, Crane to Walker, October 28, 1938, p. 2, Folder 105, 910, Program and Policy—Trustee Committee of Review, 1938–39, RF, 910, 3, 2, RAC.

55. Memorandum, "SHW (Walker) to RBF (Fosdick) November 20, 1938: Endowment Possibilities in the Social Sciences," Folder 4, 910, Program and Policy, 1937–39, RF, 910, 3, 1, RAC.

gram in the social sciences was to a great extent put on hold while Willits conducted a massive exercise in consultation to discover what social scientists regarded as the major problems. All sections of the DSS's work were continued, but without any long-term commitments. The programs in public administration and social security received grants through to 1943 when they ceased to exist because of the war effort. Similarly, the RF provided short-term grants for administration, fellowships, conferences, and planning. Toward the end of 1939, the RF approved the principle of supporting the three national research councils. The SSRC was still regarded as the "most important organization in America for the stimulation of the research spirit and for the development of personnel for work in the social sciences."[56] Certainly there was no other organization that could serve to both supplement and strengthen the RF's own program in the same way as the SSRC. The CC obviously agreed because it renewed its grant for administration early in 1940 when it appropriated $75,000 for three years.[57]

Rockefeller philanthropy continued as the dominant source of funds throughout the 1940s. Not until 1950–51 was this group of foundations overtaken by the CC. The only new program activities to occur prior to American entry into the war were a series of conferences organized by the Committee of University Social Science Research Organizations. In the fall of 1938, and very much along the lines of Willits's activities inside the RF, the committee asked the fifteen member councils to survey research and recommend topics for conferences.[58] Subsequently, the committee sponsored three conferences, on cultural islands, industrial relations, and urbanism.[59] Then in conjunction with the decennial celebrations at the University of Chicago Department of Social Sciences, the committee under Wirth's chairmanship organized a special conference to discuss the relations between university research councils and other research bodies. Specifically, the committee focused on research in government, industry and business, commercial research organizations, and the research appointments made during the crises of the 1930s.

Action by the SSRC

In 1939 the SSRC responded to a request from the NRC to conduct a survey of social science research under the auspices of industrial concerns. The Com-

---

56. Docket, December 5–6, 1939, Folder 4676, 200S, SSRC—Administrative Budget, 1927–32, RF, 1.1, 200, 395, RAC.

57. Details contained in File, SSRC, 1937–45, CC.

58. It should be noted that the fifteen Councils represented some institutions that had not been part of the Rockefeller centers of excellence plan, namely, the Universities of Michigan, Wisconsin, and Minnesota and Northwestern University.

59. Committee on University Social Science Research Organizations, annual report, 1938–

mittee on a Survey of Research by Business (1939–40) was appointed with first Nourse and then Wilson as the chair.[60] They hired Dr. John H. Cover to prepare a report. This report became the third part of the NRPB's *Research—A National Resource* (1941). The Science Committee endorsed the document without adding anything, and the NRPB merely forwarded it to the president.[61] The RF provided one new major grant. In 1940, $300,000 was appropriated over five years for planning research in the economic history of the United States. The SSRC created an economic history committee (1940–50), which in turn received another large grant in 1945.[62] Finally, the Council in 1940 created the Committee on Social Adjustment (1940–47). This committee was very much the brainchild of Fred Osborn, who was receiving backing from the CC. This committee took up the issue of nature versus nurture and produced a series of reports on heredity and environment, the prediction of personal adjustment, and psychoanalytic concepts.[63]

Through 1939 and 1940 the Council debated internally on what action it ought to take in response to the reviews. In 1939, the PPC discussed an extensive report that Nourse prepared concerning the recommendations of the review committee. The PPC supported the idea of four standing committees.[64] Yet the discussion among the whole Council in September at the annual meeting did little to make the idea a reality.[65] The lack of progress with regard to research planning was highlighted by the discussion of nuclear studies where the Council could not even agree on a definition let alone make plans to proceed. Discussants pointed with obvious envy to the work on prices that had begun in 1935 when Mills organized a conference on that topic. The

---

39, minutes, PPC, July 29–30, 1939, app. 9, pt. 21, October 22–23, 1938 to July 27–28, 1940, SSRCA.

60. Council meeting minutes, September 12–14, 1939, p. 18, Review of Council Policy, SSRCA.

61. National Resources Committee, *Business Research*. See Clawson, *New Deal Planning*, p. 136.

62. The second appropriation was for $207,000. Folder 4700, 200S, SSRC—Economic History, RF, 1.1, 200, 396, RAC.

63. See Charles Dollard's notes on meeting of SSRC, September 9–12, 1940, File, SSRC, 1937–45, CC. See Robert Sessions Woodworth, *Heredity and Environment: A Critical Survey of Recently Published Material on Twins and Foster Children*, bulletin 47 (New York: SSRC, 1941); Paul Horst et al., *The Prediction of Personal Adjustment: A Survey of Logical Problems and Illustrative Application to Problems of Vocational Selection, School Success, Marriage, and Crime*, bulletin 48 (New York: SSRC, 1941); and Robert Richardson Sears, *Survey of Objective Studies of Psychoanalytic Concepts* (New York: SSRC, 1943).

64. Minutes, PPC, July 29, 1939, pt. 21, October 22–23, 1938 to July 27–28, 1940, SSRCA.

65. Council meeting minutes, September 12–14, 1939, Review of Council Policy, SSRCA. Also "General Notes on the Annual Meeting of the Social Science Research Council, Skytop, Pa., September 11–14, 1939." File, SSRC, 1937–45, CC.

conference created a permanent body in which the ten participating universities cooperated with Washington agencies under the wing of the NBER.[66] The Council meeting fell far short of this endeavor. All the old disagreements came to the surface. As Charles Dollard of the CC pointed out, the discussion confirmed only that "insofar as it reflects interdisciplinary agreement either as to what are acceptable data [or] what are approved methods of gathering and handling them, the term 'social science' has absolutely no meaning."[67] Dollard concluded that the Council ought to spend more on administration, a recommendation that was at the back of the CC grant mentioned earlier. While Committees on the Control of Social Data (1939–45), Dissemination (1939–42), and Research Training (1939–42) were appointed, the Council did not follow through and establish a standing planning committee. Crane asked Dewhurst to prepare a report on research organization and planning. The report was discussed at great length by the PPC, and a consensus emerged around the idea that "research organization" could best be handled by the universities, particularly when "general purpose research" was envisaged.[68] The PPC also attempted to define what was meant by a research field and took preliminary steps toward the provision of guidelines to conduct a review of a field.

Despite the confusion and lack of decision, it was predictable that when Willits began his review of the social sciences he automatically turned to the SSRC. This was in spite of Osborn's acerbic comment made to both Keppel and Fosdick that the Council was not an effective agency for conducting fundamental studies of man.[69] Willits regarded the SSRC's PAC, CSS, and Committees on Employment and on Social Adjustment among the best planning nuclei in the country,[70] which is hardly a surprise given his own involvement in the creation of these very same committees. Willits decided on three major research foci: understanding totalitarian societies, learning how to direct a complex society, and a deeper understanding of people's behavior. Under the second heading Willits asked the PAC to prepare a memorandum on relations between federal, state, and local government. The work of the Council's Committee on Social Adjustment was at the heart of his third area of concern.

66. Council meeting minutes, September 12–14, 1939, appraisal, p. 23, Review of Council Policy, SSRCA.

67. "General Notes on the Annual Meeting of the Social Science Research Council, Skytop, Pa., September 12–14, 1939," p. 1, File, SSRC, 1937–45, CC.

68. Minutes, PPC, March 15, 1940, and April 12, 1940, pt. 21, October 22–23, 1938 to July 27–28, 1940, SSRCA.

69. Referred to in memorandum, Willits to Fosdick, September 16, 1940, p. 6, Folder 5, 910, Program and Policy, 1940–41, RF, 910, 3, 1, RAC.

70. Memorandum, Willits to Fosdick and Walker, August 19, 1940, Folder 5, 910, Program and Policy, 1940–41, RF, 910, 3, 1, RAC.

The SSRC and the War Effort

Inevitably, the war effort overtook both the RF and SSRC's interest in long-range research planning.[71] The magnitude of this effort was overwhelming. Polenberg estimated that between 1940 and 1945 the number of civilians employed by the government rose from 1 million to 3.8 million and expenditures increased dramatically from $9 billion to $98.4 billion.[72] As part of the mobilization, social scientists were brought into the new emergency agencies, like the Office of Price Administration and the War Production Board. One commentator estimated that the number of social scientists working for the federal government doubled from 7,830 in 1938 to approximately 16,000 in 1942. The vast majority of these appointees either did research or served in an advisory role.[73] Yet while there were some points of concentration in particular agencies, social scientists were, for the most part, spread throughout the government service.

In 1939, Stacy May became the director of the Bureau of Research and Statistics, a unit of the Advisory Committee of the Council of National Defense, and proceeded to assemble a group of economists in order to work on estimating war production requirements. This group was later brought under the War Production Board and May along with Simon Kuznets and others became the board's Planning Committee.[74] The SSRC cooperated with the other two national councils to prepare a roster of specialized personnel.[75] With the advent of mobilization at the beginning of 1942, the National Roster of Scientific and Specialized Personnel was overwhelmed with requests for social scientists. To facilitate this process the Civil Service Commission asked the Council to establish an office in Washington. The RF appropriated $25,000 to finance this office with Donald Ramsey Young, University of Pennsylvania, in charge, assisted by Webbink of the SSRC. Young had left the SSRC in July 1940 to return to Pennsylvania and his academic career. He

---

71. This section relies heavily on the accounts of the activities of social scientists during the Second World War provided by Lyons, *Uneasy Partnership*; and Leonard D. White, ed., *Civil Service in Wartime* (Chicago: University of Chicago Press, 1945). Details on the rise of social psychology during this period are contained in Dorwin Cartwright's "Social Psychology in the United States during the Second World War," *Human Relations* 1, no. 2 (November 1947): 333–52. For general accounts of the war and events at home, see Richard Polenberg, *War and Society: The United States, 1941–1945* (1972; Westport: Greenwood Press, 1980); and Bureau of the Budget, *The United States at War* (Washington, D.C.: Government Printing Office, 1946).

72. Polenberg, *War and Society*, p. 240.

73. See John McDiarmid, "The Mobilization of Social Scientists," in White, *Civil Service*, pp. 74–80.

74. Lyons, *Uneasy Partnership*, p. 85.

75. Ibid., p. 103.

made this move because of the uncertainty surrounding the SSRC's funding.[76] Drawing on his experience as the coordinator of the CC study of the American Negro, Young subsequently became the special consultant on interracial relations to the secretary of war.[77] His advice and expertise were used extensively by the Information and Education Division of the Army Research Board in connection with policies and problems of race relations among the armed forces. In 1945, Young took over from Crane as executive director of the SSRC.

The Army Research Board had its beginning in the work of the Joint Army and Navy Committee on Welfare and Recreation. This committee had been created in 1941 with a grant from the CC. Osborn, a former SSRC member and the instigator of the work on social adjustment, was appointed director of the division. Samuel Andrew Stouffer directed the massive research program that the board undertook during the next four years. This program focused on the adjustment of Americans to army life, their reactions to combat, and their expectations as they prepared to demobilize. The team used the relatively new technique, sample survey research, to measure soldiers' attitudes and behaviors. As much as any other work, this coordinated effort brought social psychology to the fore[78] and is currently regarded as a major turning point in the development of modern social policy research.[79] In 1945, the SSRC created the committee "Analysis of Experience of Research Branch, Information and Education Division, Army Service Forces," with Osborn as chair. The research was subsequently published under the supervision of this committee in four volumes by Stouffer (and others) in what has since become a classic social science text, *The American Soldier*.[80] Concern had been raised about race relations in the armed forces. The army's policy of

76. See "General Notes on the Annual Meeting of the Social Science Research Council, Skytop, Pa., September 11–14, 1939," p. 2, File, SSRC, 1937–45, CC, 66.

77. Trustee confidential bulletin, February 1943, "Social Science Serving the War Effort," Folder 4826, 200S, Washington Personnel Office, 1942–45, RF, 1.1, 200, 408, RAC. As noted earlier, at the SSRC Young had played a significant role in coordinating Gunnar Myrdal's massive study of the American Negro, which resulted in the book *An American Dilemma* . The study was funded by the CC.

78. See Cartwright, "Social Psychology."

79. James Coleman, "Sociological Analysis and Social Policy," in Tom Bottomore and Robert A. Nisbet, eds., *A History of Sociological Analysis* (London: Heinemann, 1978), pp. 694–95.

80. Samuel Andrew Stouffer et. al., *The American Soldier*, 4 vols. (Princeton: Princeton University Press, 1949–50). These volumes appeared under the title *Studies in Social Psychology in World War II*: vol. 1, *The American Soldier: Adjustment during Army Life*, by Samuel Andrew Stouffer et al., 1949; vol. 2, *The American Soldier: Combat and Its Aftermath*, by Samuel Andrew Stouffer et al., 1949; vol. 3, *Experiments in Mass Communication*, by Carl I. Hovland, Arthur J. Lumsdaine, and Fred D. Sheffield, 1949; and vol. 4, *Measurement and Prediction*, by Samuel Andrew Stouffer et al., 1950.

segregation was made that much more visible and troublesome to the government as the draft dramatically increased the number of black soldiers. These problems also had to be set against the general background of racial tensions as blacks experienced high unemployment and as they flocked to the cities to try to obtain work. In a repeat of the disastrous events in Chicago twenty-four years earlier, a race riot erupted in Detroit in the summer of 1943.[81] To help ameliorate the problems in the armed forces, the Army Research Board used Young to produce the film *The Negro Soldier*, the Army orientation series, "Why We Fight," and a pamphlet for officers, "Command of Negro Troops."[82] Young also served in an advisory capacity to the Office of War Administration, the State Department, the Department of Justice, the Alien Property Custodian, and the Civil Service Commission. Webbink was called upon as consultant to the War Production Board, in both the labor and statistics divisions.

Both Young and Webbink were intimately involved through the roster in helping to fit social scientists into wartime research units. A head of one emergency unit described this service as "absolutely indispensable."[83] Their advice and recommendations helped fill important posts in offices dealing with international affairs like the Office of Strategic Services and often were the base for the selection of the total staff in certain agencies of the War Manpower Commission. The increase in the number of social scientists involved in government service after the attack on Pearl Harbor was phenomenal. Economists, statisticians, and experts in public administration accounted for the heaviest contributions, but all other social disciplines were involved.[84]

The Applied Psychology Panel was the logical outgrowth of the testing work that had begun during the First World War under Yerkes and the broad testing movement that had become central to industrial psychology and education during the interwar years. The panel focused on the selection and assign-

---

81. See Polenberg, "The Struggle for Equal Rights," in *War and Society*, pp. 99–130. For a more detailed analysis of racial tensions during the war, see Howard Washington Odum, *Race and Rumors of Race* (Chapel Hill: University of North Carolina Press, 1943); and Charles S. Johnson et al., *To Stem This Tide: A Survey of Racial Tension Areas in the United States* (Boston: Pilgrim Press, 1943).

82. For detailed accounts of the operation of the segregation policy, see Richard M. Dalfiume, *Desegregation of the U.S. Armed Forces, 1939–1953* (Columbia: University of Missouri, 1969); and Ulysses Lee, *The Employment of Negro Troops* (Washington, D.C.: Government Printing Office, 1966).

83. Trustee confidential bulletin, February 1943, "Social Science Serving the War Effort," p. 10, Folder 4826, 200S, SSRC—Washington Personnel Office, 1942–45, RF, 1.1, 200, 408, RAC.

84. Paul Webbink, report, "Research in the Social Sciences and the Federal Government, 1944," Folder 4827, 200S, SSRC—Washington Personnel Office, 1944–45, RF, 1.1, 200, 408, RAC. Also Lyons, *Uneasy Partnership*, p. 126.

ment of military personnel.[85] Many social scientists were used in the areas of intelligence gathering, psychological warfare, and propaganda.[86] For example, Lasswell, who had chaired the SSRC's Committee on Pressure Groups and Propaganda in the early 1930s, became the director of the Wartime Communications Research Project. The project was housed at the Library of Congress and specialized in the content analysis of printed enemy propaganda.[87]

While the war had brought social scientists into government in an unprecedented number, the relationship was still tenuous. The NRPB was dissolved in 1943 when the Congress cut off its funding. Roosevelt refused to intervene and thereby allowed the board to disappear. Merriam accounted for the demise of the board by pointing to congressional-executive rivalry, the negative attitudes toward the New Deal that had been simmering since 1933, and the fear that planning would lead to total economic planning and hence socialism.[88] These fears had been fueled by the publication of a pamphlet by Alvin H. Hansen, *After the War—Full Employment* (1942), the pamphlet *Post-War Planning—Full Employment, Security, Building America* (1942), and the controversial report *Security, Work, and Relief Policies* (1942), produced under the direction of Eveline M. Burns. Hansen was a professor of economics at Harvard, and Burns, who had been a student and faculty member at the LSE, was a professor of economics at Columbia. Hansen advanced Keynesian views about the way public debt should be used as an instrument of policy. In the postwar planning pamphlet the NRPB endorsed the position taken by Hansen and went further by including a charter of freedoms and rights. Freedom was translated into the right to "work," "fair pay," "adequate food, clothing, shelter, and medical care," and "security." In a similar vein, the Burns report, which was released in 1943, recommended extensive State intervention through wide-ranging programs in unemployment and medical insurance and welfare and old age assistance. Burns had two years earlier produced a report for the SSRC's CSS, published under the title *British Unemployment Programs, 1920–1938*. Given her association with the LSE and her previous research it was inevitable that her recommendations would be associated with the parallel document that the director of the LSE, Beveridge, produced in Britain. In any event, the NRPB policy documents pro-

85. For an account of the work of the Applied Psychology Panel, see Charles W. Bray, *Psychology and Military Proficiency* (Princeton: Princeton University Press, 1948).

86. See Harry Alpert, "The Growth of Social Research in the United States," in Daniel Lerner, ed., *The Human Meaning of the Social Sciences* (Cleveland: World Publishing Co., 1959), pp. 79–82.

87. See Lyons, *Uneasy Partnership*, p. 114; and Crick, *American Science of Politics*, pp. 179–80.

88. See Merriam, "National Resources Planning Board."

duced a tremendous amount of criticism from Congress and from private business.[89] It should be noted that at the same time that the NRPB was producing its plans for after the war the DSS under Willits had in December 1941 organized a "Postwar Planning Conference" that was far more probusiness and supported the free enterprise system.[90] The SSRC created the Committee on War Studies in 1943 to promote pilot studies on various aspects of social change that were accelerated by war. Finally, in 1943, the NRPB produced two reports by Frank on human resources that seemed to confirm the charges that the board was not only political but also irrelevant to the war effort.[91]

In 1946 when it came to the creation of the most important federal scientific institution, the NSF, the Senate decided to exclude the social sciences from the support specified under the proposed foundation.[92] While there was opposition to the social sciences, whose representatives had become the stereotype of the impractical professor clogging up Washington, the major cause was internal. The SSRC never convinced itself that government support was essential for the growth of science.[93] The old guard that had spent so much time working with government during the interwar years was afraid that social science research would come under government control. It was afraid that university-based research would lose its independence and objectivity and, hence, that fundamental progress would be inhibited. These men were much more comfortable when the network was primarily a coalition between social scientists and philanthropy.

This tension and the deference toward "proper" science came through in October 1945 when Mitchell led a group of SSRC colleagues in the presentation of a document on the federal government and research in the social sciences to the Senate committee hearing testimony on the research bill.[94] The

89. Alvin H. Hansen, *After the War—Full Employment* (Washington, D.C.: Government Printing Office, January 1942); NRPB, *Post-War Planning—Full Employment, Security, Building America* (Washington, D.C., September 1942); and NRPB, *Security, Work, and Relief Policies* (Washington, D.C., 1942). For a detailed account and analysis of these events, see Clawson, *New Deal Planning*, pp. 136–43 and 182–86; and John D. Millet, *The Process of Organization of Government Planning* (New York: Columbia University Press, 1947). Also see Orlans, "Academic Social Scientists," pp. 183–84; and Lyons, *Uneasy Partnership*, pp. 94–97.

90. Folder 87, 910, Program and Policy—Postwar Planning Conference, 1941, RF, 910, 3, 10, RAC.

91. Lawrence K. Frank, "The Wastage of Human Resources" (Washington, D.C.: NRPB, 1942, mimeographed); and Lawrence K. Frank, "Human Conservation—The Story of Our Wasted Resources" (Washington, D.C.: NRPB, 1943, mimeographed).

92. See Lyons, *Uneasy Partnership*, p. 126.

93. Report, "The Federal Government and Research," February 1945, Folder 4827, 200S, SSRC—Washington Personnel Office, 1944–45, RF, 1.1, 200, 408, RAC.

94. "Memorandum of the Social Science Research Council on the Federal Government and Research in the Social Sciences," October 1945, Folder 6, Box 32, Wirth, University of Chicago.

bill was based upon the report by Vannever Bush, *Science: The Endless Frontier* (1945).[95] Bush, a former vice-president of the Massachusetts Institute of Technology and the director of the Office of Scientific Research and Development (OSRD), had been asked by Roosevelt to consider the whole question of postwar government science relations. His report was the result of the work by four groups of scientists who were appointed by the OSRD to consider various aspects of these relations. The committee on research, headed by Bowman, had recommended that a new federal instrumentality be created to run the government side of the relationship. The committee recommended the establishment of a national research foundation to "assist and encourage research in the public interest."[96] Yet as one might expect given the history of the OSRD, the report was heavily biased toward the natural sciences and did not include the social sciences in the recommendations for mandatory support. President Truman endorsed the Bush report but recommended that the social sciences be included. In turn, this position was supported by the American Association for the Advancement of Science.

Mitchell, Gaus, Nourse, Ogburn, and Yerkes all gave evidence before the Senate committee.[97] While there were some differences, it is fair to say that on the whole there was a plaintive quality to their submissions. In a sense these men saw themselves as the protectors of their pure disciplines against the corruption of practical affairs. So while the memorandum discusses all the sciences cooperating to solve social problems, it also states the special problems that social science faced. The memorandum states that "fears have been voiced in some quarters that the social sciences will come to be subjected to government control, and in others that in dealing with disputatious issues it may be difficult to hold clearly in sight the line between fact and opinion." The document continues to claim that "all scientists are necessarily constantly concerned with the maintenance of the freedom of inquiry and the independence of the spirit of research," and that "restraints on objectivity of inquiry by any agency, public or private, tend to debase research into the preparation of apologies and rationalizations for the courses of those under whose dominance research is undertaken," and the research therefore "ceases to be scientific in spirit."[98]

The SSRC through its presentation and the performance of its representatives did much to reinforce the doubts that the politicians had about the lack of

95. Vannever Bush, *Science: The Endless Frontier* (Washington, D.C.: Government Printing Office, 1945).

96. Quoted by Lyons, *Uneasy Partnership*, pp. 127–28.

97. U.S. Congress, Senate, *Science Legislation*, hearings before the Subcommittee on War Mobilization, Committee on Military Affairs, 79th Congress, 1st Sess., 1945, pt. 4.

98. "Memorandum of the Social Science Research Council on the Federal Government and Research in the Social Sciences," October 1945, pp. 6, 7, and 8, Folder 6, Box 32, Wirth, University of Chicago.

scientific advance in the social sciences. When the NSF was finally established in 1950, the legislation incorporated the original Bush proposal that foundation support for the social sciences would be "permissive" but "not mandatory." Yet, while the social sciences as a group of disciplines had stalled on the science/policy divide, individual disciplines did make significant headway. Economics was institutionalized with the enactment of the Employment Act of 1946, which established the Presidential Council of Economic Advisers and the Joint Economic Committee in Congress. Kenneth E. Boulding described this series of events as a "watershed" in the history of the social sciences because it represented "the legitimation of economics as a profession and the establishment of economists as 'Lords spiritual' in the precincts of both the White House and Congress."[99] Nourse became the first chair of the Council of Economic Advisers and carried with him into the office the SSRC's suspicion of advocacy. As Harold Orlans observed, Nourse more than any of his successors tried to remain the detached scholar in what was and continues to be a political job.[100] Similarly, the position of statistics was ensured with the establishment of the Central Statistical Board in 1933 and with the passage of the Federal Report Act in 1942. These two actions put in place a governmentwide statistical system. While the two most scientific areas in the natural science mode had achieved legitimate status as part of the State, the other social science disciplines had been less successful. Of the five disciplines not accounted for, sociology and political science were in the worst position. Psychology and anthropology had status within the scientific community because of their membership in the NRC. The physical psychologists and the physical anthropologists had been used extensively during the war by the OSRD. Further, the psychologists, who had from the beginning of their discipline been closely tied to the physical sciences because of their reliance on experimentalism, were now at the center of the current movement to create a science of society through behaviorism.[101] History had no scientific pretensions and was represented in the American Council of Learned Societies. For John Higham, the SSRC represented a clear break by the scientists from history and the humanities.[102] The two disciplines that were potentially the ones most likely to produce critical studies of governments and of society were the areas that had least claim to scientific status. Worse still from the point of view of the Council, the concept "social science" was almost as

99. Kenneth E. Boulding, *The Impact of the Social Sciences* (New Brunswick: Rutgers University Press, 1966), p. 38.

100. See Orlans, "Academic Social Scientists," pp. 184–89. Also see Nourse, *Economics in the Public Service*; and Edward S. Flash, Jr., *Economic Advice and Presidential Leadership: The Council of Economic Advisers* (New York: Columbia University Press, 1965).

101. Boring, *History of Experimental Psychology*; and Samelson, "Organizing for the Kingdom of Behavior."

102. Higham, "Schism in American Scholarship."

vague in 1946 as it had been in 1923. The boundary that had seemed so strong in 1930 after a decade of expansion was now weak and ill defined.

Conclusion

As they stood in the late 1930s, the relations between the SSRC and the RF were at an impasse. Just about all the resources were being channeled into the programs in social security and public administration. The funds for the regular programs were due to expire in 1940. The optimism that had accompanied the long-term guarantee of funds in the late 1920s was fast disappearing. As all the attention was focused on the relationship between the State, foundations, and social science, so the general program suffered. It was no longer clear why the RF should continue to provide independent funding to the SSRC when the RF could get the job done by attaching social scientists and the resources of institutions like the SSRC to the State. Through the NRPB, the State was undertaking a massive program in social research, which added to the RF's reluctance to make new commitments. Finally, the contradictory messages that came from the SSRC leadership did little to clarify matters.

The Wirth report and the report of the SSRC Committee on Review of Council Policy did nothing to reassure the RF. If anything the accusation that Rockefeller philanthropy had exercised undue control over the Council made the situation more tense.[103] Both Wirth and the review committee were critical of the Council for its lack of independence and its reliance on Rockefeller funding. Wirth was especially critical of the role that Crane had adopted in the relationship between the Council and the RF. With complete independence the Council would, according to these reports, provide the best service to the foundations, to science, and to society. Wirth and the review committee recommended that the Council should seek endowment or long-term funding as the means to guarantee independence. Wirth wanted to take away some of the power exercised by the PPC and the executive director. Wirth and the review committee recommended that the SSRC, as the only national body representing all the social disciplines, should concentrate on the fundamental development of science through planning, cooperation, and integration. The committee was particularly concerned that the SSRC had already missed a unique opportunity to create a science of society and wanted the SSRC to grasp what might be the final chance to fulfill the promise of the early years.

At the same time key officials like Fosdick and Day were calling on the Council to be more independent and to take hold of its national scholarly role.

---

103. While this author has no direct evidence, it is fair to assume that the Rockefeller trustees and officers were particularly sensitive to the problems associated with negative publicity at this time. JDR died in May 1937.

Day, in his new intermediary role as president of Cornell University, was particularly influential in moving the Council toward the promotion, appraisal, and planning of research. In an effort that was reminiscent of the activities of the early Committee on Scientific Methods in the Social Sciences, Day organized the appraisal of what were considered to be outstanding examples of social science research. This activity was perceived as one means of coming to terms with a definition of and a program for fundamental development. But as this chapter demonstrates, the SSRC and the social science community were confused and divided about where the boundary around their disciplines should be drawn. At the base of these divisions were different definitions of science and therefore different perspectives on the best way to achieve fundamental development. These definitions overlapped with the views these social scientists had about autonomy from the State and the foundations. At one end of the continuum, Robert S. Lynd and Wirth hung on to old ideas that favored integration, science, and independence from external direction and control. Merriam, Mitchell, Nourse, Willits, Ogburn, and Day had nothing against doing science on problems determined by external interests but insisted that the division between science and policy be maintained. These men were less and less concerned with overall integration and content to develop integrated fields like public administration and social security that would solve social problems. Crane was always caught in the middle as he tried simultaneously to serve his colleagues and Rockefeller philanthropy. Apart from Lynd, all the leading figures in the matrix of social science that covered the SSRC and Rockefeller philanthropy subscribed to a clear separation between facts and values, between science and policy. Yet in reality, as Lynd was at pains to reveal, the ties between the SSRC, Rockefeller philanthropy, and the State contributed to a blurring of this line. The more social scientists reached for the legitimacy of science through service to the RF and the State, the more they appeared to be drawn away from the original aim of fundamental development through the creation of a science of society.

The same contradictions that plagued the SSRC inevitably were part of the internal debate within the RF. Fosdick was not satisfied with the development of the social sciences, and as he saw it the lack of progress toward "human control." The central question that arose in the RF review was the relationship between the SSRC and the RF. While on the surface both sides agreed that the SSRC should be independent and that science was the only means to solve social problems, it is not clear that the orientation within the RF changed. As the SSRC became primarily a planning organization, the practices that characterized the relationship between the RF and the SSRC during the interwar years continued without alteration. Planning was the central function performed by the Business Research Committee and the Committees on Economic History, Social Adjustment, and, later, War Studies. As war overtook the nation, so the SSRC's program and the RF's program in the social sciences were put on hold. Leading social scientists like Merriam, Frank, Stacy May, Donald Ramsey Young, Webbink, Stouffer, and Lasswell were drawn directly into the war effort or planning for reconstruction. Yet at the end of the war the social sciences as a group of disciplines were excluded from the list of fields that would eventually receive mandatory support under the NSF. This occurred primarily because the definition of the social sciences as sciences lacked clarity and because of the self-doubts that many social scientists still felt about their disciplines. Ironically, the more social scientists stepped across the policy boundary and got involved in planning for a better society, which was the logical extension of RF policy in the 1930s, the more social sciences were viewed with suspicion by the politicians. The unanticipated consequence of doing research for the State was the denial of scientific status by the State.

During the Second World War, the State consolidated the role adopted in the 1930s as the major employer of social scientists and the major funding agency for social research. Rockefeller philanthropy continued to facilitate this relationship. The SSRC was put on hold, and social scientists, it seemed, had indeed lost a unique opportunity to create a science of society. The boundary around this group of disciplines was weaker now than it had been in the early 1920s. Legitimacy and cognitive authority were attached to those disciplines and fields, like economics, statistics, and public administration, that could through their science contribute directly to the maintenance of the social order. The bargain that had been struck between social scientists, the State, and Rockefeller philanthropy deemphasized intellectual and critical functions in favor of technical investigations whose aims were the preservation of the status quo. The by-now-established form of cultural hegemony had as the central element social control through planned State intervention. The new forms of integration in the social sciences under the banners of "behaviorism" and "functionalism" were the logical extension of the work undertaken for the State and Rockefeller philanthropy by the SSRC in the 1920s and 1930s.

The presentations to the Senate committee by the SSRC in 1946 should be regarded as the last hurrah of the old leaders of the social science community. Men like Merriam, Mitchell, and Ogburn were overtaken by younger scholars who had as their leaders Stouffer, Paul L. Lazarsfeld, Lasswell, Parsons, and Kuznets. The exemplar of the new brand of social research was the series of studies that resulted in the publication of *The American Soldier*. It is no accident that a later critic, C. Wright Mills, referred to these studies as an example of "abstracted empiricism" that proved one could do social research that was administratively useful but not concerned with the problems of social science.[104]

---

104. Mills, *The Sociological Imagination*, p. 53.

Part 2

CHAPTER 6

The Impact of the SSRC on the Social Sciences in North America: Changing the Boundaries

When trying to assess the impact of the Council on the social sciences it is essential that these activities be placed in the larger funding context. As noted at the beginning of this book, the Council has to be seen as the central coordinating institution of a policy to increase both the quantity and the quality of social scientific research. Rockefeller philanthropy was the driving force behind these actions. Key universities like Chicago, Columbia, Yale, Harvard, North Carolina at Chapel Hill, Stanford, California at Berkeley, and Pennsylvania as well as research institutes like Brookings and the NBER were chosen as centers of excellence and were developed as prototype research institutions. These institutions received extensive support directly from Rockefeller philanthropy and in turn were supported through the Council when they were appointed to execute research projects. For example, the Seminar on Culture and Personality was set up at Yale by the Council, and Pennsylvania did the work in population redistribution. Suffice it to say that of the more than fifty committees appointed by the Council, twenty-nine were explicitly designed to supervise research. (See table 2, app. 2.) Invariably this meant that academics from the major universities and institutes sat on the committees and that the research benefits accrued to their institutions. Further, as one might expect, postdoctoral fellows tended to be appointed from the universities that housed the leading members of the Council. During the interwar years, 49 percent of the SSRC postdoctoral fellows were graduates of Chicago, Harvard, Columbia, Stanford, Yale, and California at Berkeley. Another 22.5 percent were graduates of Wisconsin, Minnesota, Pennsylvania, Michigan, and Cornell. While a total of thirty-two universities were represented, approximately 70 percent of the fellows came from the eleven universities listed here, which, if one excludes the South, were the leading social science universities in the United States.

Fellowships, Grants-in-Aid, and Conferences

Through fellowships, grants-in-aid, and conferences, the SSRC filled a void and had a major impact on the production of social scientific knowledge and the spread of "scientific" methodological techniques. By the end of the Second World War a whole generation of social scientists occupying responsible academic posts and research positions owed the critical part of their training and their professional development to the SSRC.[1] Between 1923 and 1940 the Council supported 240 Postdoctoral Research Training fellows.[2] (See table 7, app. 2.) This was the first fellowship program instituted by the SSRC and remained the most important and most prestigious. The six founding subjects dominated the awards list. The economists and historians led the list with sixty-three and fifty-three awards respectively. Sociologists and political scientists were next with thirty-four and thirty awards, while psychologists and anthropologists accounted for the bottom positions with twenty-five and seventeen respectively. Included in this group were some of those who became the most famous social scientists in the United States: Blumer, Crane Brinton, Charles Woolsley Cole, John Dollard, John Kenneth Galbraith, Goodrich, Walter L. Dorm, Leo Gershoy, Gosnell, Earl J. Hamilton, Hughes, Kuznets, Lasswell, Charles P. Loomis, Margaret Mead, Neal E. Miller, Redfield, Raymond P. Stearns, Stouffer, Wirth, and Ralph A. Young.

Other fellowship programs were instituted to meet particular needs. Between 1928 and 1933, 108 individuals received fellowships in agricultural economics and rural sociology. Of this total, 86 individuals received support under the heading "agricultural economics" and 22 under the heading "rural sociology." Similarly, between 1930 and 1933, 59 "Southern fellows" were supported in their graduate work. Finally, in 1935–36 the Council began awarding two types of predoctoral fellowships: Predoctoral Field Fellowships in the Social Sciences and Predoctoral Fellowships for Graduate Study in the Social Sciences. Between 1935 and 1940, 111 predoctoral students were supported in their studies.

In summary, between 1925 and 1940 a total of 519 fellows were awarded one or more of the fellowships listed here. By far the most-favored discipline was economics in both its pure academic form (113) and in applied agricultural form (89). Of the other founding disciplines sociology came second with a total of 80 fellows (58 pure academic and 22 rural), history third at 75, and political science fourth at 53. Psychology and anthropology lagged behind with 33 and 26 respectively. Over 90 percent of those fellows were men, and many were destined for important careers in the social sciences. Indeed, the Council during the late 1920s adopted the role of continuing sponsor of those that were chosen to receive a fellowship. As a 1929 report by the fellowship

---

1. See Wirth, "Report," p. 93, SSRCA.

2. It should be noted that the name of these fellowships was changed in 1935 from Research Fellowships to Research Training Fellowships. See Joseph B. Casagrande and Elbridge Sibley, "Fellows of the Social Science Research Council, 1925–1951: Some Statistics," *ITEMS* (SSRC) 6, no. 2 (June 1952): 13–17.

secretary makes clear, the best way to safeguard the "investment" was "to keep close check on these past Fellows during the first few years following the termination of their fellowships with a view to aiding them to secure positions where the opportunities for research are favourable."[3] While there is no obvious way of measuring the success of this policy, it is reasonable to assume that the sponsorship from high-status university departments, well-known research supervisors, and the Council must have invariably led to excellent career opportunities. Some ex post facto measures provide indirect evidence. In 1951, 75 percent of the postdoctoral fellows (1925–40) who were employed occupied academic positions. (See table 8, app. 2.) This figure is supported by the comparable 73 percent figure that emerged from the Council's own analysis in 1952 of the occupational status of all the ex-fellows up to that year.[4] These men and women were spread across North America in fifty-six universities. While most universities only had one ex-fellow, the established centers of excellence at Chicago, Pennsylvania, Columbia, California at Berkeley, Stanford, Yale, and three large research universities, Michigan, Illinois, and Cornell, each had six or more ex-fellows on staff. The group included three presidents (Amherst, Stanford, and Rutgers) as well as thirty-five senior administrators.[5]

While it is always a matter of conjecture to ask what would have happened without the SSRC fellowships, it is clear that they did have a substantial impact. The existing facilities for the provision of research training prior to the Council fellowship scheme were severely limited. With the introduction of the fellowship scheme the Council was able to exert direct influence upon the quality of social research. Those that showed the most promise were chosen and sponsored. As early as 1937, Wirth was able to conclude that the Council fellows displayed "a greater catholicity, sophistication and realism" than their contemporaries and had "a more thorough mastery of the technical research techniques" than their predecessors.[6]

The grants-in-aid program was designed to help individual scholars complete research projects and in some cases to help publish the resulting manuscript.[7] The support went to mature scholars who were completing well-advanced personal investigations. Further, the Committee on Grants-in-Aid

---

3. Van Sickle (fellowship secretary), "Report to the Committee on Research Fellowships," 1929, p. 6, Folder 708, SSRC—Fellowships, 1928–30, LSRM, Series 3, 67, RAC.

4. See Casagrande and Sibley, "Fellows," p. 17, table 8.

5. Vice-presidents, provosts, deans, heads, and/or directors.

6. Wirth, "Report," p. 94, SSRCA.

7. It should be noted that this policy was only in effect for five years, between 1929 and 1934. During these years the Committee on Grants-in-Aid set aside 20 percent of its funds for publication. "The Objectives and Administration of the Social Science Research Council Program of Grants-in-Aid of Research," in Wirth, "Report," app. 6, p. 11, SSRCA.

adopted a policy of not making grants to individuals working in institutions that already had adequate research funding. In parallel with the Southern Fellowship program, the committee began in 1931 to award Southern Grants-in-Aid. Between 1926 and 1940 the Council awarded 589 grants-in-aid.[8] There can be little doubt that the program was successful. According to the survey that the Committee on Grants-in-Aid conducted in 1936, 95 percent of the cases reported a substantial benefit.[9] Of this total 25 percent reported that the work would never have been completed without the grant. The other 75 percent reported that if the work had been finished it would have happened only at an excessive cost to the individuals and their families and that the work would have been less complete and less meritorious. The extensive list of grantee publications that appears in the *Decennial Report* is adequate testimony of the success of this program. Among the disciplines, the historians had by far the best chance of obtaining a grant, which is not surprising given the nature of historiographic projects. The economists and political scientists were next in line when it came to success rates.[10] Finally, it should be noted that the Council was attempting to put its monitoring policy into effect. Between 1926 and 1940, twenty-five ex-postdoctoral fellows had been awarded grants-in-aid. This group included Loomis, Mead, Harold Deutsch, Hughes, Kuznets, and Howard P. Becker.

If fellowships and grants-in-aid were designed to help those at the beginning or the middle of their careers, the conferences were for the most part the preserve of senior scholars. By the end of the interwar years the summer retreat to Hanover and the meetings at Skytop Lodge had become institutions. For the select few who were invited, the conferences seemed to have created an esprit de corps,[11] which helped to confirm and legitimate the social status of those within the social science community. For that small group that controlled the Council, the conferences allowed a limited degree of sponsored mobility for the group's protégés. In this sense the social interaction was as much about controlling the direction of the disciplines, that is, maintaining the current boundaries and the established network, as it was about breaking them down.

The coordinating function was given structural form with the creation of the two regional committees in the South and on the Pacific Coast, and with the Council's Committee on Local University Research Organizations. The

---

8. These figures were compiled from SSRC annual reports; Wirth, "Report," app. 6, SSRCA; and the Furniss report extracts contained in "Excerpts from National Councils, DR 502, Trustees meeting, December 11, 1935," Folder 27, 910, Program and Policy—Appraisal Committee (SSRC) Reports, 1935–38, RF, 910, 3, 2, RAC.

9. Wirth, "Report," app. 6, pp. 6–7, SSRCA.

10. Ibid., annex E, pp. 25–26.

11. Ibid., p. 100.

last-mentioned committee held conferences to which it invited representatives of the university research councils that had been created in the university centers of excellence with Rockefeller money. Yet these attempts at coordination and at consolidating the gains in research did not, on the face of it, meet with much success. There was little evidence of increased cooperation between these institutions, and the Council was not sought out for leadership. On the other hand, the regional policies did achieve some success. From 1930 the Council made attempts to positively discriminate in favor of the South both with regard to fellowships and grants-in-aid and by directing research grants through the Southern Regional Committee. Inevitably, Odum and the University of North Carolina, Chapel Hill, were the two key points of contact. There was not the same level of affirmative action with respect to the Pacific region, but the West had not been discriminated against in the same way as the South during the 1920s.

Finally, there is some evidence that the postdoctoral fellowships program encouraged the provision of university fellowships.[12] It is certainly the case that the grants-in-aid committee policy supporting scholars in the least well-off institutions did result in a widespread distribution of funds. While it was hoped that this money would serve to stimulate funds, one key commentator, Ruml, was quite critical of the program. As he looked back on the program in 1937, he was convinced that the program ought to be abolished because it had become merely a way of giving handouts to individuals and had also discouraged the universities from making any provisions.[13]

Relations with Government

The foregoing account demonstrates that the Council had continuous and, over the period under study, increasingly close relations with government. Looking back it seems inevitable that social scientists should have been drawn into a closer and tighter relation with government. The subject matter with which social scientists concern themselves and the aspirations of social scientists for themselves and their disciplines were one part of the equation. As the world moved into depression so it was predictable that the foundations and the State should turn to social science as a means for solving the enormous social problems facing capitalist society. That the Council was chosen as the conduit through which both the federal government and Rockefeller philanthropy funded research had to do with both the purifying effect of utilizing the Council as an impartial intermediary, as well as the fact that this was the only national organization in the social sciences. Yet there was a great deal of

---

12. Ibid., p. 94.
13. Ruml, notes by Wirth, Folder 1, Box 32, Wirth, University of Chicago.

tension within the Council surrounding the question of the appropriate role for social scientists in making public policy. As Wirth observed, the general position of the Council was "to distinguish between giving advice on technical questions and especially on research problems and procedures on the one hand, and giving advice on government and public policy on the other hand."[14] Yet for all this the boundary between giving research advice and becoming adjuncts to, or cogs within, the policy-making process was difficult to maintain. The onset of the depression meant that social scientists were faced with the question about "the propriety and responsibility of social scientists in relation to policy forming bodies and activities."[15] The conflict among members was between those who regarded social scientists as the best qualified to solve society's social problems versus those who were worried that the progress of these disciplines would be damaged if science was used for purposes for which it was ill suited. For this latter group, the provision of practical service to external institutions not only was a sellout but also directed effort away from fundamental development of these disciplines.

During the interwar period, the Council moved more and more in the direction of providing technical service to the State. Research problems were defined externally, and the research agendas were determined by the responses of Rockefeller philanthropy and the State to the social crises of the period. Rockefeller philanthropy built bridges between the government and the academy and in a real sense bonded social scientists to government purposes. The opportunities that were created were unprecedented. The Hoover commissions in the 1920s culminated in the RST report. The establishment of the Central Statistical Board confirmed the importance that was now attached to the collection and utilization of social statistics. In New Deal Washington the Council provided advice on technical and scientific matters to various presidential committees and the NRPB. Merriam and Ruml were placed at the very center of the governmental stage. With the creation of the Commissions of Inquiry, PAC, and CSS the Council became part of the policy-making process. These initiatives clearly represented cooperative efforts between the foundations and the government with the Council as the purifying agency.[16] The Council moved into the position of standing between donors, the government, and the public. Paid by the foundations the Council became the servant of the State. The depression forced a new interdependence between the public and private sectors. Society needed technicians who could take on social problems in a pragmatic manner. As the Council complied with these demands so it deemphasized theoretical issues and the process of theorizing. Inevitably, this

---

14. Wirth, "Report," p. 131, SSRCA.
15. Ibid., p. 103.
16. Ibid., p. 108.

meant that the further the Council moved in the direction of practical, applied contract research it invested less and less effort in doing fundamental scientific research. Pure research and scientific advance were put on hold. At the point in 1946 where it would have been possible to institutionalize the relationship between the social sciences and government, the process broke down. The social sciences as a block of disciplines was rejected; instead, the discipline of economics, which was regarded as the most scientifically developed, became the standard-bearer.

Social Research

The Council had an enormous impact on changing the status of social research both within the academy and in the public mind. As noted in the last section, while the Council paid lip service to the need for pure research and to a limited extent encouraged such work, it was for the most part pushing social scientists into purposive and applied research. Prior to the creation of the SSRC it is fair to say that research was isolated, specific, and for the most part humanistic. The discipline associations placed little emphasis on research in their programs, and it was only at a few major universities like Chicago and Columbia that there were any significant social science research groupings. As Wirth observed, each social science discipline contained individuals "who were striving to create a body of theory based upon observations of the actual life of society, but they were a relatively small minority."[17] Given this starting point there can be little doubt that the SSRC not only substantially increased the amount of social research conducted in the United States but also pushed and pulled researchers in an empirical direction. The Council was the only recognized national body in the social sciences and took upon itself the responsibilities of leadership. Through the support of individuals and the research committees the Council acted as a stimulus for research. Specifically, the Council took upon itself the function of facilitating and coordinating research across the country and across discipline boundaries. It was certainly the intention after the RST report that the Council would become in Wirth's words "an instrumentality for social planning on a high level."[18] The major objective of the Council had, by 1933, become research planning. The Council focused its attention, and, necessarily, the national social research effort, on integrated fields of study like social security and public administration. The cooperation and coordination of discipline specialists on research topics, and upon a unified social science approach that had characterized efforts in the 1920s, were replaced with the emphasis on integrating disciplines into new

---

17. Ibid., p. 134.
18. Ibid., p. 116.

research/knowledge fields. The difficulties of establishing one perspective on social research, which meant a common universe of discourse, had proved unsurmountable. The existing discipline boundaries were far less permeable than had been expected by both foundation officers and social scientists. The work of the Committee on Scientific Methods in the Social Sciences and the difficulties that Rice faced editing the casebook were testaments to these difficulties.[19] At the heart of the attempts to integrate and hence break down the existing boundaries was the perception of what it meant to be scientific. Science failed to unify the social disciplines and then served as a means to separate them into a hierarchy of more clearly defined units.

Boundary Work

The story of the SSRC is a dramatic case of what has been referred to throughout this study as "boundary work" (fig. 1, app. 1). The creation of a boundary around the social sciences was a continuing dialectical process involving, on the philanthropic side, the family, the trustees, and the officers of Rockefeller philanthropy and, on the social science side, social scientists working within the structures of research institute, university, career, and profession. This process was contained within the broader societal relations of cultural hegemony and ideological and class conflict. Agency and structure were brought together as social scientists; the State and Rockefeller philanthropy participated in the process of mutual legitimation. To understand the history of the SSRC it is necessary to have a synthetic view of the relation between Rockefeller philanthropy and the Council.

The key question is about control and therefore the distribution of power in the social science network. During the interwar years Rockefeller philanthropy exerted substantial and, at times, complete control over the Council. As Crane, executive director of the SSRC, observed in 1935: "The Council will never realize its full potentialities as long as it receives funds so predominantly from one source. The Council has been so dependent on this one source [Rockefeller philanthropy] that the Council has been sometimes supposed to be one of its agencies." Further, as Crane pointed out, "in its financing" the Council "has since been the tail of a kite [to Rockefeller philanthropy], though when organized, the Council hoped for funds which might be used in its own discretion."[20] Similarly, in his SSRC-commissioned report, Wirth made numerous references to philanthropic control. In the section, "To Foundations,"

---

19. Rice, *Methods in Social Science*.

20. This statement (my inserts) was included in a confidential memorandum that Crane sent to Keppel, president of the CC in the summer of 1935. "Confidential Memorandum for Personal Use of Dr. Keppel from Robert T. Crane," 1935 (probably July), File, SSRC, 1932–36, CC.

Wirth noted that because the Council had never had an endowment and had been dependent on foundation funds "it [the Council] has obviously not been a completely free agent." Wirth went on to classify Council action into five categories:

(1) Those in which the Council took the initiative and was successful in obtaining funds from foundations (grants-in-aid program).
(2) Those in which the Council's and foundation's interests in the project were identical or converged (fellowship program).
(3) Those in which the foundation was the initiator and the Council found itself in a position to undertake the work (emergency program).
(4) Those in which the Council appears to be more of a "tail" to the foundation "kite" (public administration projects).
(5) A few instances in which the Council was merely the fiscal agent of the foundation for the carrying on of projects that the foundation found it inexpedient to carry on directly or which the Council could more conveniently manage (Social Trends Inquiry).

Wirth made the point that when direct control was exercised by the foundations it was difficult to pinpoint since "in most instances the Council at least was able to rationalize its activities so as to make them acceptable to itself." Wirth concluded that Rockefeller philanthropy saw the necessity of distancing itself from the research it was funding because "the foundations discovered that they could ill afford to be the direct sponsors of projects which might make them targets of public criticism and which would consequently diminish the value of the work done." The foundation needed a front organization that would serve to coordinate social science activities and to stimulate the development of this group of disciplines. As Wirth observed:

The ultimate aim of the foundations in supporting the Social Science Research Council seems to have been to aid an agency which would undertake the responsibility for viewing the needs and possibilities of the Social Science field as a whole on a broad scale, and to stimulate a strong institutional drive in the universities and research centers which would ultimately result in permanent, sustained and continuing support on an adequate scale for research from sources other than the foundations themselves.[21]

While one must accept the idealist thread running through Rockefeller actions

21. Wirth, "Report," pp. 122–24, SSRCA.

with respect to the Council, it is clear that Wirth underestimated the control that was exercised. The quantity and diversity of evidence in support of extensive control are overwhelming.

The relation between Rockefeller philanthropy and the SSRC is examined under four headings: finance, policy and organization, program, and social science network.

Finance

American philanthropy appropriated approximately $6.25 million to the SSRC between 1924 and 1940. (See table 3, app. 2.) The four major purposes were fellowships (26.30 percent), special projects and enterprises (23.86 percent), general projects (15.61 percent), and general administration (15.20 percent). Of the total appropriations Rockefeller philanthropy and the family were responsible for providing 92.58 percent. (See table 4, app. 2.) The Council spent approximately $5.5 million during the same period. This was a truly staggering sum when one considers that prior to these grants there had been a dearth of support for social research. Even by today's standards using a factor of twelve to convert to current dollars the expenditure of $66 million over fifteen years primarily on research and training is a respectable sum. Rockefeller sources were responsible for 93.56 percent of the total amount disbursed. Other contributions came from the CC, the Russell Sage Foundation, and the Rosenwald Fund. (See table 5, app. 2.) It should be pointed out that the tables do not include the $560,000 that the RF appropriated to fund the RST study.

The largest and most significant influx of funds came in 1927. In that year, the LSRM appropriated $2 million, which guaranteed the operation of the Council to the end of the 1930s. This was a turning point in the history of the social sciences in the United States. For the first time in the combined history of these disciplines the future looked bright and full of hope. The leaders of the SSRC and the social science community were optimistic that they could create a true science of society. After the incorporation of the memorial, the RF continued to be the dominant source of funds throughout the 1930s and 1940s. Not until 1950–51 did the total spent from RF sources drop below the combined total from other sources.

Policy and Organization

The Council was the central cog of a Rockefeller policy that was aimed at integrating social science disciplines. Externally the SSRC linked interdisciplinary research councils that had been created in those universities that the LSRM chose as centers of excellence. The most important university council was the one at Chicago. The SSRC and the University of Chicago council emerged simultaneously and were both chaired by Merriam and received their funds from the LSRM. The stamp of Chicago remained on the SSRC throughout the period. Other centers at Columbia, North Carolina at Chapel Hill, Harvard, Yale, Virginia, Texas at Austin, and Stanford were linked into this scheme. Rockefeller philanthropy had a regional policy that was given form within the SSRC in 1929 with the creation of two regional committees. The Southern Regional Committee emerged in part because of this policy but also in reaction to the dominance of men from Chicago and the Northeast in the affairs of the Council. The Pacific Coast Regional Committee represented a convergence of Rockefeller policy and the efforts of an SSRC insider, Hall, the president of Oregon State University.

Internally, the SSRC ran its business through interdisciplinary committees. By far the most powerful committee and the most significant organizational unit was the PPC. At Ruml's suggestion, the PPC was created to fulfill two functions: first, to keep Rockefeller interest in the SSRC as secret as possible and, second, to allow Rockefeller philanthropy to maintain control over the Council. As Wirth observed:

> the creation of this committee is in part a response to the dependence of the Council upon support from foundations. It was generally felt, in the early days of the Council, that the foundations would not be disposed to turn over to a loose body composed of shifting representatives of different societies over the selection of which the foundations had no control, the large sums of money that they were prepared to give.

For Rockefeller philanthropy to achieve its objectives, it was essential that a new structure be put in place that as Wirth noted preserved the "forms of democracy without some of its substance."[22] The six-member PPC was chosen by the Executive Committee on the basis of research ability and experience. Members did not have to hold Council membership and the twenty-one-member Council was effectively bypassed. The PPC became the "selected, responsible and more continuous nucleus of the Council."[23]

Throughout the period the PPC included non-Council members who exerted significant influence. The list of those who at the time of their appointment to the PPC were non-Council members includes Gay (1925–28), Moulton (1925–30, chair 1926–27), Wilson (1927–28, chair 1928–31, ex officio 1926–27), Bott (1929–33), Lindsay Rogers (1929–38), Nourse (1930–39, chair 1932–39, ex officio 1939–45), Ruml (1931–35), Kendrick (1932–35),

---

22. Wirth, Draft Report, p. 44, Folder 1, Box 32, Wirth, University of Chicago.
23. Wirth, "Report," p. 44, SSRCA.

and Willits (1935–39). Through to 1935 hardly a meeting went by without one or more officers of Rockefeller philanthropy in attendance. Further, key Rockefeller insiders, like Ford (ex officio member 1933–39) and Willits, attended PPC meetings on a regular basis during the latter half of the 1930s. Control was facilitated when in 1931 the Council was enlarged from twenty-one to thirty members in order to include members-at-large. This made the larger body that much more unwieldy and allowed nonelected members entry to the Council or the return of elected members at a later date.[24] Shelby M. Harrison, Russell Sage Foundation, maintained membership either as a representative of ASS or as a member-at-large for twenty-three years, between 1924 and 1948. Finally, in the early 1930s power was concentrated in the New York office with the creation of two full-time positions: the office of president in 1929–30 and, in September 1932, the new office of executive director. This latter position was occupied continuously by Crane from 1932 to 1945. Crane was a founding representative member from APSA, 1923–30. A great deal of power was concentrated in this position. As Wirth observed:

> The executive director is not merely the chief staff officer but is also the active manager of the business of the Council, carries on the liaison with the foundations who are the principal donors of Council's funds, represents the Council with the foundations, often acts as confidential advisor to them, and carries on the day-to-day business of administration. He makes the decisions on the current problems of policy where the general framework of that policy is already laid down by Council action; he represents the Council before other organizations and the general public.

While it was clear that the PPC was Crane's advisory committee, he had to preserve the impression of democracy. As Wirth noted, Crane was "expected to lead without appearing to dominate."[25]

The PPC in conjunction with a few full-time officers effectively ran the SSRC. All policy decisions were made by this body. Further, every key decision was taken with the leadership of a Rockefeller officer. The major policy shifts within the SSRC followed precisely the shifts within Rockefeller philanthropy. In 1929 the SSRC adopted research guidelines covering re-

---

24. For example, between 1923 and 1939 the following members were appointed in this way: Woodworth (APA member, 1925–28, member-at-large, 1929–30), Bowman (member-at-large, 1931–39), Mitchell (AEA member, 1936, ASTA, 1927–31, member-at-large, 1934–39), Mark Arthur May (member, APA, 1931–33 and 1937–39, member-at-large, 1934–35), Shelby M. Harrison (member, ASS, 1924–37, member-at-large, 1938–39), Osborn (member-at-large, 1938–39), and Day (member, ASTA, 1924–31, member-at-large, 1938–39).

25. Wirth, Draft Report, p. 11, Folder 1, Box 32, Wirth, University of Chicago.

search organization, research personnel, research materials, research methods, dissemination, facilities of research, and the Council's public image. The move was led by Ruml and Day and was part of the rationalization of Rockefeller interests as the memorial was merged into the RF. In the early 1930s, the Council moved to adopt fields of concentration and gave recognition to the immediacy of important public and social problems. In recognition of the social emergency engendered by the depression, the Council from 1934 to 1935 organized and coordinated the Rockefeller programs in public administration and social security. Finally, in the late 1930s with war approaching, the Council moved away from direct government service to an emphasis on research planning. Each shift can be traced directly to the same policy changes in either the LSRM or the RF.

Program

All the committees were advisory to the PPC except for the four standing Committees on Investment, Fellowships (Research Training), and Grants-in-Aid and the Executive Committee. During the interwar years the PPC approved sixty such committees. (See table 2, app. 2.) The rest of the program was concerned primarily with conferences, fellowships, and grants-in-aid. It is fair to say that the direct influence of Rockefeller philanthropy can be documented for approximately 90 percent of the program. This is clear even when one examines the utilization of the large block grants like the $750,000 twelve-year grant provided for projects in 1927 by the LSRM. As noted, the control of the Council was exercised internally.

From the start the research focus was on social problems. In line with Rockefeller policy and specific family interests, committees were established on migration, the Eighteenth Amendment, crime, interracial relations, and industrial relations. Fundamental scientific work and problem solving were combined. The RST investigation marked a turning point in the history of the SSRC as these social scientists moved toward more practical, applied research. As this investigation proceeded in the early 1930s, the Council began to concentrate its research efforts through the Committees on Industry and Trade, Personality and Culture, International Relations, and Economic Security and PAC. The movement away from fundamental science and toward application increased in pace. For the last half of the decade, the SSRC was essentially doing research for the RF on behalf of the State. There was a clear shift to practical, social welfare type activities done under contract. Rockefeller philanthropy set the precedent when as part of its Emergency Relief Program $100,000 was provided for a study of government statistics and information services. From this study and the continuing efforts of Rockefeller officers emerged the Central Statistical Board. The SSRC had meantime created the Comittee on Social Statistics, which acted in an advisory capacity to the board. Other examples followed, like the Commissions of Inquiry, endorsed by President Roosevelt, and, most important, the CSS and PAC. The last two committees acted as coordinating agencies on behalf of Rocke-feller philanthropy and the State.

The programs in public administration and social security were one in the eyes of government and Rockefeller philanthropy. These men and women believed that social progress and, by 1933, the survival of the social and economic orders in the United States depended on massive State intervention in the economy and in the provision of welfare. This type of intervention could only work, it was argued, if the functions of government were fulfilled efficiently. It followed that much of the research undertaken under these SSRC programs aimed at producing data that would improve the working of ad-ministrative structures. In the early years of these programs, attempts were made to explain economic change so that ways and means could be developed for ensuring individuals against the cyclical crises. A close relationship developed between leading members of the SSRC; key Rockefeller trustees, officers, and insiders; and the federal government. Woods, Ruml, Merriam, and Mitchell were in close contact with the president's office from the late 1920s. This involvement reached its peak with CAM and the continuing activities of the NRPB.

The rest of the program can be divided into three parts: conferences, fellowships, and grants-in-aid. The degree of control exercised by Rockefeller philanthropy decreases as one moves across these categories. The annual conferences and meetings were orchestrated by Rockefeller officers. The clear intent was to further the major policy objectives of the LSRM and RF con-cerning integration, science, and practicality, and to draw a national boundary around these disciplines. The conferences were a means for spreading the message beyond the chosen universities and the academic insiders to the disciplines. The conferences were also a tangible national symbol of progress in the social sciences and thus served as a means of legitimating these disci-plines.

Rockefeller officers exerted the least direct influence over the fellowship and grants-in-aid programs. Yet Ruml was active in establishing criteria for the main fellowship program. The LSRM approached the Council with the idea and tended to see the program as its own. Rather than run the program as the LSRM did for the rest of the world, Ruml felt it was politic to have the Council be the administrator. Later on, Day pressed for the creation of the critical Committee on Social Science Personnel in 1930. But the main fellow-ship scheme and various subsidiary ones must be set at the side of the SSRC's larger research program and, more specifically, Rockefeller promotion of particular research centers. Rockefeller interests overlapped as fellowships were provided to individuals doing research in a field chosen and developed by the SSRC and a Rockefeller foundation, in a university that was designated as a Rockefeller center of excellence.[26] Finally, the grants-in-aid program only accounted for 4 percent of the total expenditure by the SSRC. While Rockefeller officers did not particularly encourage this option and Ruml was convinced the grants were a waste,[27] the general focus of the work funded under this program was contained within Rockefeller policies.

A Social Science Network

During the interwar years an incestuous relationship developed between Rockefeller philanthropy and the Council. There was continuous movement of personnel between the Council and Rockefeller foundations. Among those on the list were Ruml, Merriam, Day, Willits, Stacy May, Ford, and Van Sickle. It has already been noted how Rockefeller officers and insiders dominated the PPC and hence the affairs of the Council. It is also the case that Council membership remained remarkably stable. Between 1923 and 1939, thirty-one members served five or more years. (See table 6, app. 2.) The longest-serving member was Merriam, who represented the APSA continuously throughout the period. Other important figures were Shelby M. Harrison, Ogburn, Schlesinger, Ford, Mitchell, Day, Crane, and Wilson. All of these men except Crane had close institutional and research ties with Rockefeller philanthropy.

Rockefeller philanthropy used the SSRC as a conduit through which it could influence not only the development of the social sciences but also the way in which society in the United States tackled its major social problems. The organization and structure of the Council made it possible for the Rockefeller group to grapple with the most controversial issues without any public responsibility. A central component of the process of mutual legitimation was that the Council be seen as an independent, objective body. The tension between control and responsibility showed itself most in negotiations between the Council and Rockefeller philanthropy, where one side quite predictably asked for direction, a statement of preference, while the other side complained about the Council's lack of independence and its misperception of the role of philanthropy. The contradictions that were at the heart of the modern concept of philanthropy and were contained in the operation and practices of Rockefeller philanthropy were played out in the relation between Rockefeller

---

26. For an account of the way in which all these activities were tied together, see Fisher, "Role of Philanthropic Foundations."

27. See the comments Ruml made to Wirth. Ruml, handwritten notes by Wirth, 1937, p. 2, Folder 1, Box 32, Wirth, University of Chicago.

foundations and the Council. Foundation officers did want the Council to obtain support from other funding agencies. They sincerely wanted the Council to be an independent, objective, scientific body. Yet while these officers worked toward these goals at both the levels of appearance and reality, they simultaneously exerted enormous influence over the policies and operations of the Council. As previous chapters show, the outcome had more to do with public appearance than with reality.

The stage was set with regard to the issue of independence in a memorandum that Outhwaite sent to Ruml in March 1926. He used the funding request from the SSRC for support of human migration research as a springboard to discuss how the method of financing would reflect the real and perceived autonomy of the SSRC. Outhwaite was clear that the Council had to be handled in a careful and thoughtful manner:

> the way in which we [the LSRM] handle the present request might do a good deal to strengthen or weaken the Council's position as a national deliberative body in the social science field . . . if by our attitude and action, we showed that we respected the Council's judgement and regarded it as perhaps not final but at least authoritative, if we made it an agency that within the limits of its recommendation could use some discretion in the allocation of monies, we should, of course, be increasing its duties, but I believe also be making a commensurate addition to its usefulness to ourselves and to social science generally.

Outhwaite felt that such an approach would change the behavior of the Council. The provision of limited autonomy, he believed, would encourage the Council to "receive and disburse funds and perhaps to take a directive interest in the enterprises which it sponsors or initiates."[28] The internal contradiction contained in Outhwaite's suggestion is one that continued to be played out in the relationship between the foundation and the Council.

As noted earlier, foundation officers constantly pushed the Council to be more independent. This was done both for appearance's sake and also because these men and women believed it would lead to better scientific work and more influence for the social science disciplines. The pressures exerted by Rockefeller officers took different forms depending on the objective. One objective was to make the Council less financially dependent. Ruml maintained this objective throughout the interwar years. In 1927, he complained that the memorial's relationship with the SSRC was unsatisfactory because the Council seemed incapable of developing other sources of funding.[29] This

---

28. Memorandum, Outhwaite to Ruml, March 6, 1926, Folder 711, SSRC—Human Migration, 1926–27, LSRM, Series 3, 67, RAC. My insert.

29. Ruml, August 24, 1927, staff meeting, p. 15, Staff Meetings of the Laura Spelman Rockefeller Memorial, August 24–27, 1927, Hanover, N.H., LSRM, Series 2, 3, RAC.

same concern was echoed in the 1926–27 LSRM "Report of the Executive Committee and Director," in which it was stated the SSRC should be pushed to get alternate sources of funds. For as concluded in the report, the Council was "in a real sense the Memorial's creation" and would not have existed without the sustained financial assistance of the memorial.[30] This discussion was prompted by the application from the SSRC for a large infusion of funds and the concern about whether or not to provide an endowment.

If anything, by the late 1930s, Ruml's position was stronger. He was clear that the Council had to be put in a position of independence from the foundations if it was going to function effectively.[31] Similarly, Day was conscious of the overwhelming dependence of the Council on Rockefeller funds, so much so that he felt forced to resign as an ASTA Council member and, later, in 1932, refused SSRC President Wilson's invitation to become a member-at-large. Day's reticence here links to a second objective concerning public appearances. Day stressed that he did not want to cause embarrassment either to the Council, to himself as a Rockefeller officer, or to both. As Wilson observed: "Day himself is very anxious that the Council should not appear to be just a Rockefeller baby."[32] This concern was a constant theme in discussions between Rockefeller philanthropy and the Council. In the 1926–27 report referred to earlier, the memorial asked the question whether or not there was "a danger that the Council may come to be regarded as a little more than an agency of the Memorial." To which came the self-conscious reply in the report: "The Memorial has not undertaken to shape the plans of the organization; these have been evolved by the Council's own members. Moreover the Memorial has carefully avoided the exercise of any undue influence."[33]

It is significant that Ruml would say this so clearly to his colleagues and trustees when in practice Rockefeller officers interfered all the time. An example is the long memorandum from Frank to Crane sent in July 1927. The document is a candid commentary on the purpose and functioning of the SSRC, at the end of which Frank asked that Crane not quote him "in view of our [LSRM] relation to the Council."[34] It was clear that the Council provided an essential service to Rockefeller philanthropy. As the 1926–27 report concludes: "through the Council the Memorial is able to promote lines of work which clearly need to be done but which could not possibly be undertaken

---

30. "Report of the Executive Committee and Director, 1926–27," November 22, 1927, pp. 33–34, Folder 29, Dockets, November 1927, LSRM, Series 1, 4, RAC.

31. Ruml, handwritten notes by Wirth, 1937, p. 2, Folder 1, Box 32, Wirth, University of Chicago.

32. Wilson to Keppel, March 16, 1932, File, SSRC, 1932–36, CC.

33. "Report of the Executive Committee and Director, 1926–27," November 22, 1927, pp. 32–33, Folder 29, Dockets, November 1927, LSRM, Series 1, 4, RAC.

34. Letter/memorandum, Frank to Crane, July 13, 1927, Folder 684, SSRC, 1927, LSRM, Series 3, 64, RAC. My insert.

wisely by the Memorial itself."[35] For this service to be provided effectively the Council had to behave in a discrete manner.

The third objective for the foundation officers was to have the Council demonstrate its independence in the negotiations between itself and philanthropy. Nowhere is this made more clear than in Day's response in 1936 to Wilson, who had referred to possible antagonism if the RF should "operate in the field of international relations" as it had in the field of international health. Day lashed back by pointing out that it was the Council that operates not the RF and as an internal aside said: "It is difficult to get over to the Council the idea that we'd *like* them to develop independently."[36] From the earliest days Rockefeller officers had felt somewhat uncomfortable about responding to requests for the funding of specific projects. Rather than be seen to discriminate between projects and then be open to the charge of censorship, the officers wanted the SSRC to be seen to take control of research funding. The Council would then best serve Rockefeller philanthropy in the role of a competent and representative body of advisers.[37] A couple of examples illustrate the tension. One is the correspondence between Ogburn and Day during the late 1920s concerning grants to Adler, at the University of Chicago. Of concern was a conditional part of the grant that Ogburn was trying to get the RF to release. In the end, Day made it explicit that the Council must communicate formally with the RF and, hence, make the boundary clear between the two institutions.[38] A second example is a negotiation conducted by the CSS in 1935. Donald Ramsey Young, on behalf of the SSRC, related to Van Sickle that the CSS wanted to farm out a particular problem that the committee believed to be important: "but potentially embarrassing to them." As Young put it, the Council felt the CSS needed permission from the RF to go ahead. Van Sickle was adamant that the committee should only bring large projects that were beyond the committee's finances to the RF's attention.[39] In effect, social scientists were being encouraged to display independence even though all the actors knew where the power was housed in these resources exchanges. Just as it was necessary for the State to appear to be

---

35. "Report of the Executive Committee and Director, 1926–27," November 22, 1927, p. 33, Folder 29, Dockets, November 1927, LSRM, Series 1, 4, RAC.

36. Excerpts of letter, Wilson to Day, September 28, 1936 (with inserts for Day and Walker), Folder 4767, 200S, SSRC—International Relations, 1932–36, RF, 200, 1.1, 403, RAC.

37. "Report of the Executive Committee and Director, 1926–27," November 22, 1927, pp. 37 and 33, Folder 29, Dockets, November 1927, LSRM, Series 1, 4, RAC.

38. See the correspondence between Ogburn and Day, 1929, Folder 716, SSRC—Project Budgets, 1929–30, LSRM, Series 3, 68, RAC.

39. Interview, Van Sickle with Young, December 3, 1935, Folder 4713, 200s, SSRC—Economic Security, 1934–35, RF, 1.1, 200, 397, RAC.

acting in the interests of all, so social scientists had to pretend they were autonomous.

As one might expect, there was confusion among the ranks of social scientists. The anonymous article referred to earlier, "The Fat Boys," provides some insight into the exaggerated respect that social scientists were willing to bestow on foundation officials. And, when one considers how little money had been available to these disciplines prior to the entry of the memorial, it is not surprising that social scientists took great care not to offend the golden goose. At the same time, many social scientists were as concerned about independence as the foundation officers. By the late 1920s Robert S. Lynd, as secretary of the SSRC, was adamant that the Council ought not to be publicly associated with Rockefeller philanthropy.[40] Similarly, in 1934, Beard came to the defense of Crane and remonstrated with the members of the Council who felt they were just rubber stamps to Crane and the foundations. In a statement about the importance of separation, Beard observed: "Foundations must justify to the public their use of funds. In matters intellectual there are no objective criteria for satisfying the public."[41] By the mid-1930s, Crane had become terribly concerned about maintaining the appearance of independence and the need to break the Rockefeller tie. His meticulous editing of Wirth's manuscripts and the limited circulation of the report was more than an exercise in self-protection. Similarly, the memorandums to the RF's committee and to Keppel at the CC illustrate his desire to create a new, independent working relationship.

For Crane, the need for independence was an essential step in legitimizing the social sciences. Scientific objectivity and the pursuit of knowledge for its own sake were the building blocks of the emerging boundary that the Council was creating around these disciplines. The details of his position, and indeed the position of a number of Council members, were explicated in a confidential interview with Keppel at the CC and a memorandum that followed. Crane stated categorically that the Council in its financing had been the "tail of a kite" that was Rockefeller philanthropy. Further, he believed that this dependency on one source of funding left the impression for the public that the SSRC was an agency of Rockefeller philanthropy, a situation that prevented the Council from realizing its potential. As far as he was concerned, money had been made available for "grandstand play" research, which often appeared to be nonscientific and, invariably, was intended to have immediate social impact. According to Crane: "It was time that we got down

---

40. Lynd to Day, September 26, 1928, Folder 685, SSRC, 1928–31, LSRM, Series 3, 64, RAC.

41. Beard to Crane, September 25, 1934. Collected by Wirth, Folder 1, Box 32, Wirth, University of Chicago.

to basic, less spectacular work out of which real advance comes."[42] With independence the Council could take the lead in making sure that the social sciences advanced as scientific disciplines. Crane wanted the social sciences to lose the taint of external and presentist biases.

The issue of independence was a central part of the boundary work being conducted by the power brokers on both sides of the philanthropy–social science relationship. Inevitably, the same tensions underlaid the discussions about relations between the social sciences and government. As contract research became the norm for the Council, questions were increasingly raised about what was the most appropriate relationship. The problematic nature of this relationship is illustrated by a report to the National Resources Committee in 1937, "Relations of Government to Scientific Research," prepared by Charles H. Judd (University of Chicago and member-at-large of the Council). In this report Judd, who was himself an insider at the Council, noted that the SSRC was both concerned about and in some ways hostile to the idea of cooperating with government in matters involving research. As noted earlier, the PPC considered this to be a misrepresentation growing out of the distinction that it had made between giving advice on alternative policies that were dependent upon social objectives versus the use of basic research to provide advice that did not involve a subjective choice of goals.[43] The PPC wanted to cooperate fully with the government as long as its service was within its sphere of scientific competence. The SSRC consolidated this position in the report that the Council produced in 1945 under the heading "The Federal Government and Research," which was then presented to the NSF Senate hearings. The Council emphasized "the great importance of maintaining the social scientists' complete independence with respect to many delicate problems of government policy and action." The Council wanted national research to be organized in such a way so that the work and the research would be accountable to the public. Yet independence, decentralization, and diversity of funding had to be maintained and achieved. As concluded in the Report:

> Research will yield its optimum positive benefits only if the independence of research is aggressively maintained. If the freedom of research which is peculiarly essential in a democratic society is to be preserved, any tendency toward centralized control, whether governmental or private, over all the work within any given field must be vigorously combat-

---

42. "Confidential Memorandum for Personal Use of Dr. Keppel from Robert T. Crane," 1935 (probably July), and "Memorandum of Interview, SSRC, July 16, 1935: Keppel with Dr. R. T. Crane," File, SSRC, 1932–36, CC.

43. Minutes, PPC, September 13, 1937, pt. 20, January 16, 1937–September 14, 1937, SSRCA.

ted. It is therefore of the greatest importance that a diversity of sources of support for research be maintained and fostered.[44]

It is ironic that the perceived lack of independence from Rockefeller philanthropy should have led the Council to take such a strong position with regard to government funding. The proposed NSF offered a legitimate place among the sciences to the social disciplines and a major alternate source of funding from philanthropy. Perhaps the danger of losing everything loomed too large. The old tension between "the human agency of the social problem . . . and the quiet respectability of objective science" was beneath the stance taken by these social scientists.[45] In any event, the exclusion of the social sciences was a terrible blow to these disciplines. The destiny of the Council as perceived by Rockefeller philanthropy and social scientists like Merriam was blocked by reactions to the very power relations that they had fostered.

Science and Integration

The events described focus upon the constantly recurring policy theme that linked integration to scientism. There was substantial agreement among social scientists and the officers representing large-scale philanthropy that the time was ripe for converting the social disciplines into sciences in the natural science mode. Further, they subscribed in some practical sense to the idea that one could not be scientific unless one approached a problem in an integrated manner. Therefore, to be scientific meant a cooperative, multidisciplinary approach. Social scientists like Merriam and Mitchell along with key foundation officers like Ruml and Day were strong proponents of this idea. Alongside the efforts of these individuals there was widespread support for cooperation and interrelation in the social science literature of the 1920s. Mitchell, as a leader of this movement, was also clear about the importance of the LSRM's program and specifically the SSRC as elements in this trend.[46]

One could reasonably argue that this trend was a residual element of progressivism and the ideas that tied together the precursor of the Council, namely, the ASSA. Ruml and Merriam saw an essential link between studying "real" problems and doing so collaboratively. The SSRC took on the mantle of

---

44. "The Federal Government and Research," minutes, PPC, April 14, 1945, app. 1, pp. 221 and 224, pt. 23, September 14, 1942 to July 28–29, 1945, SSRCA.

45. For a discussion of how this tension related to the history of the social sciences in the early part of this century, see the analysis of Albion W. Small's career by Ernest Becker, "The Tragic Paradox of Albion Small and American Social Science," in *The Lost Science of Man* (New York: George Braziller, 1971), p. 6.

46. Mitchell to Fosdick, January 18, 1927, Correspondence: Raymond B. Fosdick, WCMC, Columbia University.

integration in an attempt to combat and reverse the continuing trend toward specialization. Contained in these efforts was an optimism that clearly did emerge out of the progressive era. Nowhere was this optimism more clearly expressed than in the book by Ogburn and Goldenweiser, *The Social Sciences and Their Interrelations* (1927). In their introductory essay these two authors described how the social sciences would "constitute the contribution of the twentieth century to human thought and power. Civilization nurtured and strengthened by the natural and exact sciences must henceforth look for its preservation and enhancement to the sciences of society."[47]

The Council was the leading edge of the attempt to break down the boundaries between the social disciplines. The Council was the centerpiece of the discourse coalition that was formed between social scientists and philanthropy. This was the case at the general levels of policy both within Rockefeller philanthropy and within the Council but also was present in the specific policies that governed the Council's program, namely, fellowships, grants-in-aid, conferences, and research committees. The shift toward interdisciplinary programs in social security and public administration was the logical extension of the early efforts. Throughout the period under study the language of justification speaks of "coordination," "cooperation," "cross-fertilization," and "integration." Such efforts were deemed to be simultaneously more scientific and more realistic in that the work would be more likely to lead to solutions to the pressing social problems that faced society in the United States.

From the Council's inception in the early 1920s, Merriam talked about the Council as a means for "taking up in greater detail the question of scientific methods in the social sciences" and for planning some large research projects in which "cooperative effort may be able to advance the boundary lines of knowledge."[48] For Merriam, the Council was a means for bringing social scientists from different disciplines together in order to avoid duplication, foster cooperation, and stimulate research in fields not covered by parochial interests. The effort was always linked to the development of scientific methods and, significantly, the development of scientific social control.[49] For Merriam, it was impossible to separate integration from the study of social problems. He wanted the SSRC to focus on certain major problems that by definition involved more than one discipline. These views converged perfectly with the policy being developed by Ruml at the LSRM. The policy focused on

---

47. Ogburn and Goldenweiser, *Social Sciences*, p. 9.

48. Merriam to Ruml, June 5, 1923, in "Confidential Report to Colonel Woods on Activities of Seven Organizations Assisted by the Laura Spelman Rockefeller Memorial," Folder 678, Social Science—Pamphlet and Report, LSRM, Series 3, 63, RAC.

49. Merriam is quoted in the report of the Executive Committee and Director, 1926–27, p. 27, Folder 29, Dockets, November 1927, LSRM, Series 1, 4, RAC.

correlating existing work in order to further cooperative relations and joint research between universities and between disciplines.[50] As Day observed later, the LSRM in the mid-1920s sought further "collaboration between various academic departments within the university, since the basis of departmental divisions was traditional and essentially artificial" and "a united attack upon social phenomena was needed to yield significant data." The memorial sought through agencies like the Council to "bring about a new synthesis of the various disciplines looking toward a new and more fruitful division of labour."[51]

Even though the RF deemphasized the general policy of collaboration in the university research centers during the early 1930s, the policy toward the SSRC, and the Council's view of itself, remained remarkably constant. Bringing together social scientists who were working in separate disciplined compartments continued as the major objective of Council policy for Merriam and others. In 1934, Ruml's SSRC Committee on the Improvement of Research Organization came up with ten criteria, two of which dealt with this theme. Numbers seven and eight, respectively, posited the facilitation of collaboration in research organizations and the encouragement of teaching institutions to ignore departmental lines and use all fields to solve social problems.[52] The RF in 1935 still regarded its support of the Council as important in "stimulating cooperative research,"[53] and in 1937, the Council stated in its own appraisal that the dominant and controlling purpose of the Council was "intellectual leadership in the facilitation and coordination of research in the social sciences." While in the same report the Council recognized its lack of success in achieving synthesis, it reaffirmed cross-fertilization of ideas and cooperation between social science disciplines as the central component in its drive to promote research. The focus on cultivating scientifically the no-man's-land dividing these fields of research was, as before, tied to the internal unity of the social problem approach.[54] During the 1930s, a shift occurred in policy and program away from general attempts to break down boundaries toward an emphasis on integration within particular research fields. This latter form of integration would, it was expected, occur as a result of proper coordination.

50. "Correlating the Existing Work in the Social Sciences," in "Memorial Policy in Social Science: Extracts from Various Memoranda and Dockets," February 16, 1924, Folder 677, Social Sciences—Policy, LSRM, Series 3, 63, RAC.

51. "The Rockefeller Foundation Agenda for Special Meeting, April 11, 1933," Folder 168, 900, Program and Policy—Reports, PRO-23, PRO-24, 1933, RF, 900, 3, 23, RAC.

52. "Report of the Committee on the Improvement of Research Organization," minutes, PPC, March 17, 1934, app. 1, p. 29, pt. 19, October 22, 1933–November 7, 1936, SSRC.

53. "Resolution—Institutional Support, April 10, 1935," Folder 1, 910, Program and Policy, 1928, RF, 910, 3, 1, RAC.

54. Report of the Committee on Review of Council Policy, app. 15, p. 1, Review of Council Policy, SSRCA.

As a general guide to the program the Council adopted what might be called the "two-discipline" perspective. As the label implies, this meant that the Council was meant to look with favor on those applications for fellowships or grants-in-aid or research grants that involved more than one discipline. The initial fellowship committee established policy guidelines that remained intact for the period under study. With the encouragement of Ruml it was decided that there should be no disciplinary quotas and that merit ought to be the major criterion.[55] No effort was made to follow departmental lines of demarcation, and further, because some of the research problems were on the borderland between social sciences or belonged to two or more of these disciplines, the committee hoped that its work would "contribute toward a more intimate cooperation of all the sciences represented in the Council in solving problems of human behaviors."[56] In other words, the policy was favorable toward cooperative work but was not prescriptive. This policy was made explicit in 1935 when, in conjunction with changing the postdoctoral fellowships to emphasize training rather than research, preference was given to candidates with doctorates in one field who wanted to study in an adjacent field. In a similar way, it was assumed that the grants-in-aid program would encourage cooperative work. This view was made explicit in 1929 when the Council stated that, in part, preference would be given to proposals that promised results that would be useful in two or more disciplines.[57]

While there was some hesitation in the implementation of the policy for fellowships and for grants-in-aid, this certainly was not the case with the conferences. From the beginning, the aim was to accelerate the "tendency toward the breaking down of department categories" in the social sciences.[58] For Merriam the conferences would create the "conditions under which new contacts, new insights, new integrations, new valuations may be gained; and new ways opened in the direction of social advance."[59] This was to be accomplished first by bringing the leading members of the various disciplines together both academically and socially. Further, the policy became part of the formal agenda of the conferences on a number of occasions and was the explicit purpose of the subsidiary meetings of the university research coun-

---

55. Ruml to Merriam, October 27, 1924, Folder 706, SSRC—Fellowships, 1924–25, LSRM, Series 3, 65, RAC.

56. "Annual Report of the SSRC Fellowship Committee," p. 7. Attached to the letter, Merriam to Ruml, April 6, 1925, Folder 706, SSRC—Fellowships, 1924–25, LSRM, Series 3, 65, RAC.

57. Wirth, "Report," p. 98, SSRCA.

58. "Summer Conference for Social Scientists, March 18, 1926," p. 4, Folder 19, Dockets, March–April 1926, LSRM, Series 1, 1, RAC.

59. Merriam, report of SSRC to LSRM, December 27, 1926, p. 19, Folder 687, SSRC—Reports, LSRM, Series 3, 64, RAC.

cils.[60] Yet by far, the most important initiative was in the area of research, for in this area the convergence between science and integration was most explicit.

For both social scientists and foundation officers connected with the Council, the route toward legitimacy for the social sciences was clear. The Council's primary purpose was to establish, and further, multidisciplinary, social problem–oriented, scientific research. Mitchell talked about the benefits of the cross-fertilization[61] of ideas and of bringing methods and techniques of different disciplines together in order to get a better purchase on social problems.[62] This approach was for Mitchell the essence of the scientific method. Similarly, Merriam made clear that one could not adequately investigate social problems that went beyond the boundaries of departmental subjects from only one point of view. He was confident that the new patterns of research would bring disciplines together and thereby break down the discipline/specialist boundaries within universities.[63] In 1929 the Council formalized its intention under the objective of the facilitation of research by adopting the rule that projects ought to involve the cooperation of two or more disciplines.[64] As noted earlier, this effort was made through research advisory committees during the first decade of the Council's life but then shifted to direct action aimed at integrating social problem fields like social security and public administration. The shift here was away from university-based, independent, and potentially fundamental research toward government-based, externally directed work with little potential for developing the social science disciplines. In preparing the ground for the creation of these committees, Day described what he regarded as the significant feature of these fields. For Day these fields "cut athwart recognized disciplines" and represented "areas of possible interest in scientific research having to do with certain striking developments in our social system and emergence of fairly definite problems."[65] The major goal was the integration of these fields in order to solve the technical problems faced by the State as it tried to make the New Deal work.

---

60. "Report to the SSRC of a Committee of Representatives of University Research Councils, Hanover, August 26, 27, 28, 1929," minutes, PPC, November 16, 1919, app. 4, p. 44, pt. 9, November 16, 1919–April 3, 1930, SSRCA.

61. Proposal/letter, Mitchell to Ruml, October 28, 1927, Folder 4676, 200S, SSRC—Administrative Budget, 1927–32, RF, 1.1, 200, 395, RAC. Also Merriam, minutes, PPC, August 20, 1929, p. 122, pt. 8, August 19–30, 1929, Hanover Conference, 1929, SSRCA.

62. Conference, 1926, p. 470, Folders 696–97, SSRC—Conference Report, 1926, LSRM, Series 3, 66, RAC.

63. Report, SSRC Conference, 1927, pp. 1–2, Folders 699 and 700, SSRC—Conference Report, 1927, LSRM, Series, 66, RAC.

64. Wirth, "Report," p. 88, SSRCA.

65. "Staff Conference, Friday, October 3, 1930," pp. 2–3, Folder 2, 910, Program and Policy, 1929–32, RF, 3, 910, 1, RAC.

Throughout the period the language of justification for breaking down the boundaries invariably involved references to science. Science was synonymous with realism. Good science, whether focused on social or natural phenomena, was empirical. Statements had to be based on contact with, observation and measurement of, the external "real" world. Because the "real social problems" were not compartmentalized into sociology, political science, or economics, it followed quite logically that to do good science one had to utilize all relevant perspectives. Methodologically, social scientists, like natural scientists, had, in Day's words, to develop a scientific habit of mind that involved "an objective, dispassionate treatment and interpretation of dependable observations."[66] Yet despite all the optimism and the tremendous amount of effort expended, the results were meager. The Council had, by the Second World War, moved the social science disciplines a relatively short distance along the road to integration.

While the overwhelming weight of evidence is negative, there were some commentators who gave the Council high marks for its efforts to break down disciplinary boundaries. Perhaps as a means for maintaining the enthusiasm of the Canadian social scientists who were attempting to set up their own committee, Mitchell, at a meeting in Ottawa, made it clear that in his view the United States SSRC had made a real contribution toward reducing departmentalization of the social sciences within the universities.[67] Similarly, while Wirth was terribly critical of the Council's performance, he did find space to be complimentary. He noted that the Council had "exercised a timely influence in breaking down the obstructions arising out of the strict delimitation of the social science disciplines. It leveled some of the academic fences or at least made it more easy and more respectable to carry on conversation over the fences." Further, Wirth felt that the Council had served to decrease "disciplinary isolation" and had been a "wholesome influence" through attempts to coordinate research on particular problems.[68] Yet, as indicated earlier, these judgments must be set within Wirth's more general negative evaluation of the Council. He felt that the talk about cooperation and interdisciplinary research had turned out to be a "delusion." As far as he was concerned the actual interdisciplinary cooperation was negligible and tended to be used as a slogan by social scientists in order to obtain support.[69] While

---

66. "A Brief Summary of the Conference of Trustees and Officers, October 1930," pp. 14–15, Folder 166, Program and Policy—Reports, PRO-15, PRO-22, 1926–30, RF, 900, 22, RAC.

67. Minutes of the CSSRC, 1940–44, report of meeting of Social Science Research Committee, November 6, 1938, SSFC, Public Archive of Canada, Ottawa. Also, letter, John Robbins (future secretary/treasurer of the CSSRC) to Charles Dollard (assistant to the president of the CC for grants-in-aid and overseas visits), November 8, 1938, File, CSSRC, 1938–45, CC.

68. Wirth, "Report," pp. 139–40, SSRCA.

69. Ibid., p. 145.

Wirth credited the Council with some limited influence in coordinating research, he was sure that any integrative influence upon research was negligible.[70] Rather than cross-fertilization Wirth reported that some regarded the Council's activities as a contribution to "cross-sterilization,"[71] a label that seems at least unkind if not inaccurate from this distance. Wirth noted that the two-discipline perspective had, for all intents and purposes, not been implemented with regard to fellowships, grants-in-aid, or research funding.[72] These comments were vaguely reminiscent of Robert S. Lynd's warnings in 1928 about the two-discipline rule, when he said that the Council should guard against the situation where the attacking disciplines simply unlimber their respective guns without any attempt to integrate their activities.[73] The most that could be said about the impact of the Council was that it had brought people together and thereby broadened their outlook beyond the narrow compartments of discipline. It was Wirth's hope that these contacts might "ultimately contribute to the emergence of a more systematic and integrated view of social science."[74]

The most damning judgment came from Charles Dollard, assistant to the president at the CC, who, after attending the annual meeting of the Council in September 1939, observed that "insofar as it [the Council] reflects interdisciplinary agreement either as to what are acceptable data [or] what are approved methods of gathering and handling them, the term 'social science' has absolutely no meaning."[75] There was plenty of evidence to support this conclusion. At the 1938 meetings, many of the participants were critical of the whole idea of cross-fertilization. On the one hand, the psychologists complained about exploitation, while, on the other hand, the economists charged that their territory was being raided. Slichter, the economist, added his voice to these criticisms by noting the failure of the experiment at Harvard to introduce an interdepartmental degree combining political science and economics. According to Slichter, students were being discouraged from taking the degree because graduates, it had been found, were not well grounded in either discipline.[76] Similar dissatisfaction had been voiced by the political scientists in the late 1920s who, according to Merriam and Ogburn, felt that

70. Ibid., p. 151.

71. Ibid., p. 146.

72. Ibid., pp. 88, 94, and 98.

73. "Confidential Memorandum by R. S. Lynd, August 15, 1928," minutes, PPC, app. 3, p. 3, pt. 5, SSRCA.

74. Wirth, "Report," p. 141, SSRCA.

75. Charles Dollard, "Report on Annual Meeting of the SSRC," September 11–14, 1939, File, SSRC, 1937–45, CC.

76. "Annual Meeting, SSRC, Buck Hill Falls, Pa.," September 13–15, 1938, File, SSRC, 1937–45, CC.

they were being discriminated against. Merriam noted that political scientists were not submitting projects because they felt the Council's policy of concentrating on borderline research damaged their chances of success. Mitchell reported that the economists simply did not understand the orientation of the Council.[77] The protection of discipline boundaries became more prevalent over the interwar period as the disciplines themselves grew stronger within universities and with the growth of the discipline associations. The PPC concluded in 1939 that it was generally agreed in the Council that the constituent societies "had little knowledge of and apparently little interest in the work of the Council."[78] What had been achieved was not a move toward "obscuring departmental lines" as claimed in one report,[79] but rather the Council had established a liaison among the various social sciences.[80]

The liaison extended beyond the social sciences to cut across the boundary between the academy and the world of affairs. Indeed, the liaison between the academy, foundations, and government around social problems might be regarded as the Council's major achievement.[81] Yet the gap between the natural sciences and the social sciences remained almost as large as ever. This was contrary to Merriam's early hopes of increasing the cooperation between the two blocks of disciplines through the overlapping NRC/SSRC committee and by inviting the APA and AAA, who were already members of the NRC, to join the SSRC.[82] Rather than serving as a bond between the two councils, the anthropologists and the psychologists grew increasingly uncomfortable with their bifurcated position between the NRC and SSRC. Both groups felt that they were not getting their fair share of SSRC research funds.[83] The anthropologists had expressed their unhappiness about the fellowship program in 1929. They wanted fellowships to be open to predoctoral candidates so that they could be used to support anthropological fieldwork, an activity that the

---

77. Minutes, PPC, January 26–27, 1929, pt. 6, SSRCA.

78. Report of the Committee on Review of Council Policy, app. 15, p. 22, Review of Council Policy, SSRCA.

79. "Report to the SSRC of a Committee of Representatives of University Research Councils, Hanover, August 26, 27, 28, 1929," minutes, PPC, November 16, 1929, app. 4, p. 44, pt. 9, November 16, 1929–April 3, 1930, SSRCA.

80. Tugwell, "Preliminary Report—Possibilities of Research—Columbia University," p. 21, Folder 2, 910, Program and Policy, 1929–32, RF, 3, 910, 1, RAC.

81. See Furniss report extracts, contained in "Excerpts from National Councils, DR 502," trustees meeting, December 11, 1935, Folder 27, 910, Program and Policy—Appraisal Committee (SSRC) Reports, 1935–38, RF, 910, 3, 2, RAC.

82. Merriam, report of SSRC to LSRM, December 27, 1926, Folder 687, SSRC—Reports, LSRM, Series 3, 64, RAC.

83. Letter/memorandum, Robert S. Lynd to Day, September 21, 1928, Folder 685, SSRC, 1928–31, LSRM, Series 3, 64, RAC.

anthropologists regarded as somewhat unusual to their discipline.[84] The problems associated with the relative importance of disciplines was never dealt
with even though a clear hierarchy existed. Neither the reasons for ordering or
the relations between the disciplines were ever discussed to the point that a
realistic policy could emerge. The focus was on the social sciences as a whole
so that the criteria for inclusion, and, therefore, the definition of the boundary
separating social sciences from other disciplines, were never made explicit.
These factors all contributed in some degree to the lack of integration at the
level of ideas, methods, and structures. Wirth, who made a strong case for
integration in his report,[85] concluded that in essence the Council had tried to
move too quickly without the benefit of some fundamental knowledge. As the
committee that reviewed his report concluded: "The realization that all the
social sciences have a common problem in social behaviour will remain a
rather empty concept until we learn much more than we know now about the
way in which economic, political and social activities interact."[86] In other
words, rather than doing research in the field of "human engineering" the
Council ought to have concentrated on the goal of fundamental, and necessarily theoretical, advance for the social sciences.

84. Van Sickle, "Report of the Committee on Research Fellowships," 1929, p. 2, Folder
708, SSRC—Fellowships, 1928–30, LSRM, Series 3, 65, RAC.

85. Wirth, "Report," p. 153, SSRCA.

86. Report of the Committee on Review of Council Policy, app. 15, p. 4, Review of
Council Policy, SSRCA.

CHAPTER 7

Conclusion

The foregoing account of the history of the SSRC during the interwar years provides substantial evidence to support the contention that the Council was the most important institutional element in the history of the social sciences during that period. The Council was a bold experiment. It was the first council of its kind anywhere in the world and was used as a model for the creation of similar councils, first in Canada and then later in other, mainly commonwealth, countries. The Council was both a symbol and an indicator of the major changes that occurred in the social sciences during the 1920s and 1930s. The intent was to create a new social science paradigm that would incorporate the separate disciplines into an integrated, social problem–oriented whole. These men and women wanted to create a supradiscipline that would cut across the barriers between idealism and realism, between pure and applied approaches, and between those parts of each discipline that were scientific in a natural science mode. As we have seen, the results were simultaneously more and less than was expected, depending on where one stood in the early years. What is clear from this account is that one cannot understand the history of the social sciences, or for that matter the development of any knowledge unit, without actively placing events in their social and necessarily structural context. The boundary work model is an attempt to outline what Foucault called at one level the "grid of specification" and, at another level, the relation power/knowledge. As one would expect, social scientists and the disciplines that housed them reacted to and were part of the dramatic societal changes during the 1920s and 1930s. In this way, the story of the Council is central to our understanding of the emergence of the "Welfare State" and, therefore, the means by which social order has been maintained in democratic capitalist societies since that time.

The 1920s can be regarded as the boom years when in the words of one commentator "the world was the parish of every research agency and social studies were regarded as sciences."[1] Mitchell labeled the 1920s as the "conscious decade" for the social sciences, when the general public became aware

---

1. Memorandum, Robert M. Lester (secretary, CC) to Keppel, July 26, 1932, File, SSRC, 1932–36. CC.

of the importance of some social disciplines and social scientists became conscious of the need to work together.[2] By the end of the Second World War the boom was over. The social sciences had been molded to fit in with changes in the relation between the private and public sectors. From the cockpit of crisis in the late 1920s, and through the 1930s, we saw the emergence of the modern welfare capitalist State. Through the SSRC, Rockefeller philanthropy played a critical role in changing the public/private relation. The service conception of social research, housed in the progressive social problem orientation was supported in the 1920s by people like Ruml, Merriam, Woods, Fosdick, Mitchell, Ogburn, and Day. Through this alliance of interests these men were able to place the resources, the prestige, and, necessarily, the power of Rockefeller philanthropy behind these efforts. By the early 1930s a new alliance between the trustees of Rockefeller philanthropy and the State pressed for a more practical orientation. The shift that occurred was away from basic research and fundamental development of the social sciences, toward the practical social welfare activities that later characterized postwar federal contract research. It was a shift from pure and purposive research toward explicitly applied research. Rather than independent critics of government or foundations, social scientists had become scientific servants of the State. There can be little doubt that by the beginning of the Second World War the social sciences had become more applied than anyone imagined possible in the early 1920s. Yet significantly, the optimism of the early years had been overtaken by a tentativeness that made external audiences suspicious. Society and government were skeptical of the social sciences, and social scientists were concerned about the lack of progress toward scientific respectability for their disciplines.[3]

Different and competing definitions of science were built into the basic structure of the Council. In the early years, science as a concept and an ideal was the central aspect of the ideological convergence that emerged between Rockefeller philanthropy and the Council. Science meant objective, empirical study that led to practical improvements in social affairs. The form of cultural hegemony was changing. That part of the ideology that emphasized social control linked scientific social research to the major social problems that faced society in the United States. The new science of society offered theoretical, methodological, and practical advance. The SSRC was also a key element in the resource strategies of academics, foundation officers, and trustees.[4] Social

---

2. See Heaton, *Scholar in Action*, p. 206. Also see the comments by Mark Arthur May in Wirth, *Eleven Twenty-six*, p. 130.

3. Ibid.

4. See Silva and Slaughter, "Modernizing Managers and Dependent Intellectuals," in *Serving Power*, pp. 69–97.

scientists like Merriam and Mitchell saw in the Council the prospect of unprecedented support for their disciplines at the national level. The Council was a means of creating new patterns of authority in the social sciences within the academy and in national affairs. Foundation officers and trustees like Ruml and Fosdick saw the Council as a means for the production of legitimate knowledge by an independent body.

The 1920s were a time of tremendous optimism. The massive infusion of funds from Rockefeller philanthropy effectively guaranteed the future of the Council to the end of the 1930s. In 1929, the appointment of the RTC seemed to place a permanent seal of approval on the social sciences. Yet by 1930 there were already warning signals that science would not serve as the catalyst to break down boundaries between disciplines. Science as an ideal set of practices to be attained did as much to divide and demarcate the social disciplines as bring them together. The solution was to favor purposive scientific work, which allowed for disinterestedness and objectivity but clearly underplayed the push for theoretical development. The pressure from Rockefeller philanthropy on social scientists was for more concentrated research on specific danger zones that threatened society. In this way, social scientists moved to the ideological center, as they understood the limits of behavior that would be tolerated by resource holders. Social reform opportunities were identified, and services to State bureaucracies were pursued. The problem for social scientists was how to serve power respectably so that they simultaneously avoided political controversy and increased their academic reputations. The problem was solved by Rockefeller philanthropy. Social scientists used Rockefeller resources to provide assistance to the State. They were not the paid servants of either capitalists or politicians and their efforts had the hallmark of public and, therefore, disinterested service.

As the economic and social orders collapsed, so the bargain struck between Rockefeller philanthropy and the social scientists increasingly involved the State. The balance shifted toward the practical, technocratic side of the efforts to increase social control. The social control ideology was gradually refined to include the concepts "planning" and "intelligence." In the process of mutual legitimation, social scientists were much more willing than before to put aside fundamental, theoretical development in favor of practical, applied, purposive science. Planning became the central element of the emerging form of cultural hegemony. *Methods in Social Science: A Case Book* and the RST report were key indicators of the rise of empiricism and how much the social sciences had come to rely on technique when making scientific claims.

The alliance that emerged in the 1930s between the State, Rockefeller philanthropy, and social scientists involved a dramatic shift within the SSRC from fundamental development to an almost exclusive emphasis on practical service. The transformation saw the gradual refinement of the discourse on social control to include the concepts of social intelligence and planning. The depression and the crisis of the State were met with a new relationship between the public and private sectors. The form of cultural hegemony that became dominant in this period made State intervention and State capitalism the means for controlling social problems. Planning and intelligence had become the central components in the ideology of social control. The goal was to prevent the collapse of liberal democratic capitalism. Through the SSRC, social scientists sought to strengthen the boundary around their disciplines by entering public life as experts and by adapting themselves to the strictures of contract research. The political and economic challenges had to be met with objective social planning that utilized social intelligence. Social scientific knowledge was promoted because of its ability to legitimate planning and control. As it involved the SSRC, this process of mutual legitimation was funded, guided, and to some extent controlled by Rockefeller philanthropy.

The centerpiece of the Council's efforts became the painstaking work in the two fields of concentration: public administration and social security. Through this work and their participation in the NRPB and the CAM, social scientists became adjuncts to the State. The level of involvement in public affairs was unprecedented. Social scientists were used to build the infrastructure of the State. The production of social scientific knowledge was part of the technical rationalization of capitalism. As the State became the major tool for maintaining social control, social scientists shifted their attention away from fundamental development of their disciplines. Social control ideology moved from means to ends, from an emphasis on pure science to an emphasis on applied policy. The SSRC led the movement away from fundamental science to concrete studies of practical concern.

As the goal of a science of society receded so it became increasingly difficult to interrelate or coordinate disciplines. Integration increasingly occurred under the fields of concentration, and the disciplines became more concerned with their own development rather than some larger commitment to the social sciences. The shift from fundamental, theoretically grounded research toward more practical, technical approaches was accompanied by the retreat of social scientists behind the boundaries of their own disciplines. The pressing need was to increase the cognitive authority of their individual disciplines by simultaneously raising the claim that knowledge within their territories was both scientific and practical. The signal of this retreat came during the work of the Committee on Scientific Methods in the Social Sciences, whose members could not agree on a definition of either "method" or "scientific practice." Little headway was made in cutting across the boundaries that separated the social disciplines. As the ties that bound social scientists to the State became stronger, the disciplines of statistics, economics, psychology, and (through public administration) political science were pushed to the forefront of the process of mutual legitimation. The disciplines of sociology, anthropology, history, and academic political science were left behind. The contrast was particularly noticeable and significant for sociology. Sociologists more than any other group had sought to create a science of society and had failed. While many of the leading social scientists welcomed the alliance with the State, others were skeptical and worried about the trend precisely because it inhibited the development of the social sciences in a fundamental way.

By the end of the decade, the relations between the Council and Rockefeller philanthropy were at an impasse. The guaranteed funding was coming to an end, and it was no longer clear why the RF should provide independent funding when it could get the job done by attaching social scientists and institutions like the SSRC to the State. The Council criticized itself and was criticized by Rockefeller philanthropy for straying away from the goal of fundamental development, for not fulfilling its role as national leader, and for its lack of independence.

While the RF was proud of the job that the Council had done,[5] and while it was generally agreed that the Council had influenced the social sciences in the right direction, namely, in a more empirical, realistic, and scientific direction,[6] there was a feeling of disappointment and dissatisfaction about the lack of progress. The questions that were raised by Robert S. Lynd, Crane, and increasingly Day were echoed by Wirth in 1937 who observed that "no seriously consistent thought has been given to the establishment of and clarification of social science." He continued: "The difficulty may well be that we do not as yet have even the beginnings of a systematic social science."[7] Until there was a clear conception of the leading problems of the social sciences, it was, according to Wirth, like collecting pebbles on a beach. Wirth criticized the Council for not performing to its capacity the "function of furnishing intellectual leadership to American social science." As he put it, the Council had not "perceivably aided in providing for social science a more tenable and fruitful theoretical base and has not exerted its potential influence in making empirical research bear directly upon pivotal theoretical issues in social science."[8] In a similar vein, Crane had been increasingly uneasy since the mid-1930s about the neglect of fundamental work.[9]

---

5. John Robbins (future secretary/treasurer of the CSSRC to Harold A. Innes (professor of political economy, University of Toronto, and future member of the executive of the CSSRC), February 2, 1939, File, Harold A. Innes, 1940–53, SSFC, MG 28 1 81, vol. 14, Public Archive of Canada.

6. Wirth, "Report," pp. 139–41, SSRCA.

7. Ibid., p. 80.

8. Ibid., p. 150.

9. As early as 1935 Crane was warning that the Council should stay clear of nonscientific work. "Confidential Memorandum for Personal Use of Dr. Keppel from Robert T. Crane," 1935 (probably July), File, SSRC, 1937–45, CC.

In response to the critique the Council concentrated its attention on the planning function and sought endowments. Yet social scientists were confused and divided among themselves about where the boundary around their disciplines should be drawn. The old tension between advocacy (reformism) and objectivity (scientism) was still present. This tension was displayed in the different definitions of science employed by social scientists and the different perspectives on the best way to achieve fundamental development. The divisions were exacerbated as social scientists through their work for the State were faced with choices between science and policy. The more social scientists reached for the legitimacy of science through service to the RF and the State, the more they appeared to be drawn away from the original aim of fundamental development through the creation of a science of society.

As war overtook the nation, so the SSRC's program and the RF's program in the social sciences were put on hold. The State consolidated its role as the major employer of social scientists and the major funding agency for social research. The SSRC, it appeared, had missed a unique opportunity to establish a science of society. The boundary around this group of disciplines was weaker now than it had been in the early 1920s. Legitimacy and cognitive authority were attached to those disciplines and fields like economics, statistics, and public administration that would through their science contribute directly to the maintenance of the social order. The bargain that had been struck between social scientists, the State, and Rockefeller philanthropy deemphasized intellectual and critical functions in favor of technical investigations whose aims were the preservation of the status quo. By now, the established form of cultural hegemony had as the central element social control through planned State intervention.

By the end of the Second World War, fundamental development had been channeled into the "kingdom of behaviorism," and the stage was set for the rise of the behavioral sciences and the policy sciences.[10] These forms of integration and coordination picked up on the elements of the bargain that the SSRC had helped to create during the interwar years. This bargain emphasized technique rather than theory and practicality rather than utopian thinking and deemphasized the critical, advocacy function of the social sciences in favor of neutral science and objectivity. The science of society had been replaced with what C. Wright Mills later called "abstracted empiricism." The void of fundamental development was filled by the inclusive and inherently conservative theory, structural functionalism.

By 1946, the idea of a fundamental social science had changed. The ball,

---

10. See the section on behaviorism in Somit and Tannenhaus, *Development of American Political Science*, pp. 173–94; and the section on policy sciences in Crick, *American Science of Politics*, pp. 177–80.

as Latour (1987) would have it in his rugby game metaphor, had been picked up by other players who had modified it and changed its shape. Success depended on the extent social scientists coupled their fate with philanthropy and the State. Yet this success meant that the very idea of a social science was transformed. The exchanges served to translate fundamental development into new forms of integration. Fundamental social science incorporated new forms of integration under the banner of structural functionalism and behaviorism. The Department of Social Relations at Harvard University under the leadership of Parsons was the epitome of the new approach.

The history of the social sciences during the interwar years was marked by an overwhelming emphasis on social control. The alliance between the State, philanthropy, and social scientists that emerged during these years was based on commitments to practicality, efficiency, and planning. Within the ideology of social control the shift was from means to ends. The ends in this case were the preservation of the social and economic orders in the United States and, therefore, the protection of the interests of the ruling class. Advocacy itself was not removed from the enterprise but was simply channeled in the "right" direction. The leading social scientists searched for ways to increase social control as a means for enhancing the inevitable progress toward the ideal of democracy. The intellectual residue of the social evolutionary perspective was the belief that the political and economic system in the United States was on the right track and simply needed to be helped along.

A public battle occurred in the late 1930s and the 1940s between the senior leaders in the social sciences, as represented by Mitchell, and a younger, more critical group, as represented by Robert S. Lynd. It was a battle between the arch-empiricists and the pure social scientists. For Lynd, the failure of the SSRC to reorient the social sciences toward interdisciplinary work was "due to the inability of social scientists, trained to work within the grooves of the present disciplines, to grasp imaginatively the possibilities inherent in working closely with scientists trained in other disciplines."[11] Mark Arthur May observed that the attempts to create interdisciplinary forms of research by the SSRC had met with great resistance. He recalled attending meetings where cross-fertilization had been translated into cross-sterilization. In May's view, academic culture rewarded rugged individualism, so inevitably social scientists talked more about integration than they tried to put it into practice.[12] Similarly in 1943, Luther L. and Jessie S. Bernard lamented that the "social science movement," as they called it, had been swamped by the then current emphasis on instrumentalism.[13] But the blame was not just lo-

---

11. Lynd, *Knowledge for What?* p. 169.
12. Wirth, *Eleven Twenty-Six*, p. 133.
13. Bernard and Bernard, *Origins of American Sociology*.

cated with social scientists or even academic culture. The failure was also caused by the intervention of Rockefeller philanthropy and the State. While it appeared that social scientists had missed an opportunity, the promise always contained contradictions and may well have simply been an illusion. As social scientists sought legitimacy through science, they became more specialized, more abstract, more technical, and increasingly tied to external agendas.

The main accomplishment of the Council had been the improvement of research competence,[14] not fundamental progress. In an interview a few months before he retired as executive director of the SSRC, Crane evaluated the Council's progress. According to Joseph C. Devereux, president of the CC, Crane "felt a great deal of the bad results and bad stimulation had occurred in the social sciences" because there had been an "emphasis upon results of a practical nature that had subtracted from attention to research."[15] Finally, the most poignant evaluation came from Ruml in 1951. In response to a complaint from Merriam about the degree of departmentalization at the University of Chicago, Ruml reflected on the history of the social sciences over the last thirty years and concluded that little progress had been made. As a reason for this lack of development, Ruml was inclined to think that "the boys were more interested in getting the money than they were in the development of their subject matter on a fundamental basis." Ruml concluded that there must be something fundamentally wrong with the universities as settings for social research.[16] That the original architects of the Council should be so disillusioned by developments is sad testimony to the reverses that had occurred since the heady days of the mid-1920s.

The central questions still remain unanswered: Given the tremendous input of resources into the social sciences why was the Council not more successful in achieving its major objectives concerning fundamental scientific advance? Why was the boundary that separated the social sciences from other knowledge as unclear in 1945 as it had been in 1920? Why did the trend toward departmentalization and specialization continue despite the explicit attempts by the Council to break down the boundaries between the social science disciplines? Finally, we must ask about the implications of the story of the Council for our understanding of the limits and possibilities of the relation between social scientists and the society in which they live. The formation of a new bargain between social scientists and those in power during the 1930s should provide insight into the exchange limits between power/knowledge.

---

14. R. G. Trotter (professor of history, Queen's University and future chairman of the CSSRC) to Robbins, April 30, 1941, File, R. G. Trotter, 1940–51, SSFC, vol. 22, Public Archive of Canada.

15. Interview, Devereux (president of the CC) with Crane, July 2, 1945, File, SSRC, 1937–45, CC.

16. Ruml to Merriam, July 13, 1951, Folder 11, Series 1, Box 3, Ruml, University of Chicago.

There can be little doubt that the interwar years in the United States were a time when a concerted campaign was mounted to break down the boundaries between the social science disciplines. At no time since have so many human and financial resources been mobilized to support such an effort. What was attempted was no less than a revolution—the creation of a new social science paradigm. With such lofty aims it is not surprising that the results fell some-what short. What is surprising, given the size of the effort, is that so little was achieved in this direction. The explanation is on the face of it quite simple yet in reality is extremely complex. The boundary work model provides a guide toward such an explanation.

Within the social science network the three most important groups of boundary workers were the Rockefeller trustees and officers, government officials and politicians, and the social scientists. These individuals were housed in the structures of philanthropy, State, professional associations, and the academy. The creation of a new boundary around the social sciences was symbolized by the new Council and represented an alliance between individ-uals and structural interests as well as a convergence at the ideological level. It is suggested that the alliance between philanthropy and social science was set within an emergent form of cultural hegemony. The central notion was that knowledge would solve social problems and thereby increase social control. The knowledge had to be scientific. The most scientific knowledge was that which emerged from integrated studies on "real" problems conducted in a natural scientific manner. Science, practicality, and realism were merged. Leading social scientists, and especially the most prominent empiricists, agreed with the trustees and officers of Rockefeller philanthropy that the way forward along the road to a more efficient and controlled democracy was through the production of social scientific knowledge. In this way, the class and status interests of the participants in both structures were served. Further, politicians like Hoover and other government officials were increasingly turn-ing to the social scientists for help with social and economic problems. Still it must be said that the early work of the Council favored what is described in this study as "pure" and "purposive" research. Indeed it is fair to say that the conception of integrated research around which the alliance was formed col-lapsed these two categories into one.

The history of the Council involved simultaneously the attempt to break down the boundaries between disciplines and the attempt to create a new boundary around the social sciences. It is clear that these objectives were not met. The boundary work relations increasingly involved struggles to create scientific boundaries around single disciplines rather than a group discipline boundary. A good part of the explanation is housed within the long-term structural trend toward an increasing division of labor and, within knowledge systems, the corollary of increasing fragmentation and specialization. Be-cause the story of the Council is about an effort to obstruct the long-term trend, it also lays bare some of the internal contradictions of power/knowledge that are based on the conflicting interests of those involved.

Another part of the explanation must reside with Rockefeller philanthropy. Rockefeller foundations, as represented by the trustees and officials, exerted substantial control over the Council. Rockefeller support was the excessively dominant factor in the history of the SSRC. It follows therefore that the change in Rockefeller policy in the early 1930s that we can describe broadly as a significant shift toward more practical, explicitly applied research was reflected in the Council's activities. In addition, the allied shift from discipline integration, toward field integration, was part of this impact. As we have seen, the Council moved steadily at first and then dramatically away from fundamental scientific approaches and away from discipline integration as goals. Yet the broader explanation must involve a consideration of changes at the level of cultural hegemony and ideology as well as the interplay between the various class interests that were involved.

The control of the ruling class over the production of social science knowledge was exercised indirectly through Rockefeller philanthropy and through the State. These foundations served society and the ruling class simultaneously by funding research that would maintain, restore, and reaffirm the social order. Philanthropy was not a concerned but a disinterested bystander. Rockefeller philanthropy served a whole array of interests, not least of which were the interests of the family, the trustees, and the officers. As noted in the body of this work, the Rockefeller foundations had clearly defined policy objectives that were based on an ideology of sophisticated conservatism. The watchwords of this ideology were "efficiency," "control," and "planning." During the interwar years these ideas were central to the cultural hegemonic equilibrium. By the early 1930s, the balance had been weighed in favor of these ideas, as both the State, and institutions like the foundations, tried to grapple with societal crises. The ideology moved from a position of emergence to one of dominance. Social planning based on social intelligence became the organizing principle of Roosevelt's New Deal. All efforts had to be applied to the pressing problems that threatened the structural basis of social order in society in the United States. Integration as an aim was not lost but was dislodged from the ideal of fundamental scientific development of the social sciences. The individual disciplines were described as having already achieved scientific status so that their potential was now ready to be utilized in the posited fields of inquiry, namely, social security and public administration. Practical applicability was elevated to the center of the equilibrium as the best means for achieving social control. Rockefeller philanthropy facilitated the State's need for more and more technocratic help.

Central to the analysis is the process of mutual legitimation that was beneath the bargain struck between social scientists, Rockefeller philanthropy, and the State. The boundary work links these individuals and structures into cultural hegemony and the legitimation function that each State serves. This "moving equilibrium" had by the early 1930s tilted firmly in the direction of the interests served by Rockefeller philanthropy and the State. The government used social scientists for its own ends. For as Orlans observed, "Social scientists are recruited by governmental and private agencies not just to provide useful information and analysis, but to defend the interests of the agency against attacks by rival experts."[17] In the process of mutual legitimation, the State and the interests it represents are dominant. The major force then and now is the general legitimation function that States serve in order to protect their own actions and policies.

To maintain the social order it was necessary to harness social scientific knowledge both to justify the new role of the State and to incorporate the new experts into the operation of deficit financing and State welfare. While there is no evidence of conspiracy, it was clearly in the interests of the ruling class to move the social science disciplines away from studies that might be critical of the structure of capitalist society. The attempts to integrate during the 1920s were implicitly dangerous because this research was much more likely to produce fundamentally critical results and conclusions. The fact that sociology and political science, potentially the most critical disciplines, remained the weakest at the end of the period provides some indirect evidence to support this view. If the objective had been the search for a solution to social problems, then the objective of integration ought to have remained a high priority or, at a minimum, particular attention ought to have been given to promoting sociology and political science as disciplined sciences. Instead, Rockefeller philanthropy used the SSRC to push social scientists away from fundamental development of social science toward applied research.

The process of trying to create a strong boundary around the social sciences was fraught with contradictions that can be seen to have their base in the class locations of the participants. Broadly speaking, the foundation trustees, politicians, and bureaucrats directly represented the ruling class in their emphasis on practical social control. The trustees pushed policies that over the interwar period meant more specialization and increasingly the concentration of resources on research that dealt with immediate problems. It is through the actions of the trustees that we can get glimpses of the relation between the economic mode and the cultural mode of production. As noted earlier, while the influence is indirect because class interest works through the State and philanthropy, it is nonetheless powerful. The foundation officers and

---

17. Orlans, "Academic Social Scientists," p. 172.

the academic social scientists were much less predictable. Both groups displayed behavior that reflected their contradictory class locations. The officers, who for the most part had extensive training in the social sciences, were committed to fundamental research that would advance the social science disciplines. They wanted to increase the autonomy and objectivity of the social science disciplines by doing pure scientific research. At the same time their concerns were tempered by their pragmatism. The focus on social problems incorporated part of the reformism that was at the heart of the social science tradition and pushed them toward purposive research. The pure/purposive approaches were collapsed into the objective of integrated, social problem–oriented research, which for the trustees presented the most scientific approach.

The conflicts between the trustees and officers were about the tension involved in trying to accommodate objectives that at base were contradictory—that is, between science and practicality, idealism and realism, and pure and applied research. The consensus in the 1920s represented the alliance where all interests were served and, indeed, all the objectives could be simultaneously pursued. By the 1930s, the shift away from discipline integration was a symbol of the triumph of "practicality," "realism," and "application." The officers implemented the policies and, for the most part, agreed with the trend. Yet throughout the 1930s, Ruml and Day attempted to hold onto their original conception of the best form of development for the social sciences.

To understand the roles adopted by academic social scientists it is necessary to focus on the relations between foundation officials and the leading members of the SSRC. As noted, their actions were set within the institutional frameworks that housed them, namely, professional and research associations, research institutes, universities, and the foundations. Just as the foundation officials were increasingly caught in a dilemma, so it was with the academic social scientists. For these academic social scientists it was an easy task in the 1920s to form alliances with the Rockefeller officials along the lines of integrated social science. Interests at both the levels of hegemony and class converged. The objectives of all the institutions were consistent as they either formulated the policies or helped implement them in the research institutes and universities. Further, while the discipline associations were not receiving support from Rockefeller philanthropy, professional interests were being served in general by the press toward science. Throughout the interwar years there remained substantial agreement about the need to develop social studies into social sciences. Science, as a concept and as an ideal, was the central aspect of the ideological convergence that emerged between the foundations and the social scientists. Science meant objective, empirical, integrated studies that furthered the fundamental development of social science and also led to practical improvement in social affairs. As with the foundations, the consensus among social scientists visibly broke down in the early 1930s although there were plenty of indications that all was not well during the 1920s.

There is certainly testimony to support the verdict that many social scientists were more interested in furthering their own careers, institutions, and disciplines rather than the development of integrated social science. While for some this merely represented a selfish interest, for the most part these reactions seem to have been reasonable strategies given the long-term structural trends toward division and professionalization. These strategies went beyond the promotion of individual status and seemed to be the best means for promoting young disciplines along the pure scientific route so that this knowledge would become more legitimate and more authoritative. The structural context enveloped individuals in what Foucault called a "grid of specification," which involved career, university department, professional associations, and the publishing industry. The grid pushed inevitably in the direction of specialization. Further, as Wirth pointed out, it was dangerous for young scholars to take the two-discipline rule seriously because their careers were likely to suffer.[18] This was exacerbated by the relative youth of the disciplines concerned. Necessarily, theoretical and practical difficulties arise when attempts are made to develop borderlines between disciplines that are themselves struggling to demarcate their own territory. These disciplines had low cognitive authority and lacked legitimate status and, hence, either the strength or the specificity that would allow individuals to reach beyond the boundaries.

The contradictory class positions of social scientists became increasingly visible as social scientists divided into what Robert S. Lynd labeled as the "scholars" and the "technicians."[19] Involved here were different views about the best ways to further the social science disciplines. The contradictory class positions of social scientists meant that they simultaneously represented the interests of those who ruled, those who were ruled, and themselves as knowledge producers. In the 1920s, with the attempts to create a new boundary around the social sciences we can observe both the bourgeois and the proletarian sides of their class location. The ideological convergence between the elements of the dominant ideology that were the emergent form of cultural hegemony and the ideas and interests of these social scientists both inside and outside Rockefeller philanthropy were responsible for the creation of the Council, and the efforts for the rest of the decade aimed at strengthening the boundary. By the early 1930s, the effort to integrate collapsed as social scientists in response to external changes began to polarize around the two

---

18. Wirth, "Report," p. 94, SSRCA.
19. Lynd, *Knowledge for What?* p. 1.

parts of the bourgeois class location that were represented by the purists and the applied technocrats.

Professionalism cut across these two definitions as did the general orientation toward a more scientific approach. Drawn into the equation was that part of the proletarian location that resulted in an emphasis on more separation between disciplines and, therefore, more specialization and fragmentation within the institutions that housed them. What was lost or at least de-emphasized were those elements of the bourgeois and proletarian sides that emphasized integration, that resulted in purposive research, and that had the potential for bringing about radical change. The residuals of progressivism were pushed out of the new alliance at the levels of ideology and class. The new pragmatism meant that research should be applied, that social scientists should become the technical servants of power, and that, as servants, they should produce disciplined knowledge that would increase social control and thereby maintain the status quo. There was a perceptible drift toward conservatism—an undertow to all the boundary work that pushed participants away from integration and toward a disciplined scientific orientation. This orientation was increasingly tied to applied tasks and separated from the production of knowledge that might be critical of capitalism. The capacity of social scientists to do critical work was undermined in this process. Interdisciplinary work had the most potential for challenging the status quo and disrupting the social order. While the danger signals were apparent to all, there was no conspiracy; rather it was an almost inevitable convergence of interests that were housed in ideologies, class positions, and changes in the social structure.

Against this background the strategy that appealed to many social scientists involved in the Council was to accept the support for their disciplines without actually embracing the integrative science policies. A substantial gap existed between SSRC policy and the actions of Council members. Wirth documented extensively the lack of effort in this regard or, as he put it, the "sins of omission." The relation between the Council and the constituent professional societies was remote.[20] Only on rare occasions were problems of constituent associations discussed, and there is no evidence that these considerations were aimed at the long-term objectives. Similarly, the division of labor between the various disciplines, or for that matter the possibilities for interaction between them, was never really discussed.[21] The Council did not establish what interests it or its disciplines had in common. No persistent effort was made to identify the major problems facing social science, precisely because the Council did not recognize the prior objective of developing

---

20. Wirth, "Report," p. 169, SSRCA.
21. Ibid., p. 85.

a "systematic social theory."[22] Social scientists had not developed a common theoretical base and had great difficulty agreeing on common practices, even though with the exception of history all these disciplines pursued the ideal of science. Little or no understanding of the relationship between social theory and social research emerged from their deliberations. While the subject matter of the social sciences created difficulties and peculiar problems, and therefore was an obstacle, one would have expected a more sustained effort. The obvious questions that were prior to the Roman Numerals were asked only intermittently, especially by Day and Ruml, but they were never really answered.

The lack of clarification was brought to a head in the 1930s as the Council was challenged by the State and Rockefeller philanthropy to come to terms with its own practices, particularly what was meant by "science." The polarization, referred to earlier, was in part a result of the lack of clarity about the boundary around the social sciences and specifically that part of the boundary that separated science from nonscience. The polarization of social scientists was based on contrasting definitions of science and necessarily images of what constituted scientific behavior. While the definitions of practices remained vague and usually involved the attempt to weld the techniques of the natural sciences to social studies, there were clear divisions within the general perspective. The divisions were based upon the degree to which individuals adhered to the goals of objectivity, discipline status, integration, theory building, and independence. While both Lynd and Wirth divided the Council and social scientists into two groups, it seems appropriate to expand this classification. Wirth described two opposing groups, each wanting to make the social disciplines more scientific: on the one hand, those who sought to develop those fundamental ideas and practices that would tie the social sciences together and, on the other hand, those who saw this search as a metaphysical exercise that would go nowhere and who believed that scientific methods would develop as social researchers collected the needed data.[23] There are clear similarities between these two groups and Lynd's fundamental scholars and his technical "picks and shovelers." These two groups can be broken down into six subgroups. (See table 9, app. 2.)

The "Disciplined Fundamentalists" went along with the efforts to integrate but were clear in their own minds that fundamental development of the social sciences would come from within disciplines. Second, the "Progressive Fundamentalists" created and led the Council and believed that fundamental development of the social sciences could best be achieved by collapsing the boundaries between pure and purposive research and between the social disci-

---

22. Ibid., pp. 150 and 145.
23. Ibid., p. 82.

plines. This group corresponds to both Lynd's and Wirth's fundamental categories.

A third group, the "Disciplined Decision Oriented," corresponds to Wirth's opposing group, who were firmly in favor of doing disciplined work on the pressing social problems. Groups two and three believed that scientific advance would come from studying the pressing social problems. For all three groups of scholars the applied approach was not scientific because they felt that social scientists who did this work gave up their independence and necessarily their objectivity. Similarly, these social scientists also regarded a technical approach as being less scientific because of the disregard for theory. Group four, the "Disciplined Methodologists" were the forerunners of what C. Wright Mills called the "Abstracted Empiricists," that is, social scientists who saw the best possible opportunity for advance in disciplined, methodological endeavors. Groups five and six, the "Disciplined Pick and Shovelers" and the "Pragmatic Empiricists," correspond to Lynd's opposing category. The difference is a combination of their perception of the need to maintain independence from external direction and the attachment to their discipline. Both groups believed it was possible to maintain a scientific approach whether the work was purposive or applied. But there was not an explicit commitment to advancing their own disciplines or the group of disciplines. As we have seen, the history of the Council was marked by a continuous movement and some dramatic shifts in the direction of pragmatic empiricism.

In fighting a rearguard action at the end of the 1930s and through the early 1940s, groups one and two, the Disciplined Fundamentalists and the Progressive Fundamentalists, contributed to the decline of Council. While these men were coming to terms with the new social context, they were still out of touch. The plea in Wirth's report for scientific pragmatism represented the views of Lynd and Crane, as well as the older leaders, Merriam, Mitchell, and Day. As Wirth noted, no rule stated that social scientists should stop when the results of their work held promise of some potential social value; indeed to accept that science had an instrumental function led to the opposite conclusion.[24] Yet these men felt that the Council and social scientists must stay within the realm of science and thereby maintain a strict separation between science and policy.[25] As Wirth concluded: "There is no reason for the Council to avoid problems of current social significance providing it confines its work on these problems to the scope becoming a scientific body." This meant that the Council should not engage in propaganda and should not put itself in the position of being a service organization to any external interest. As with many of the leading social scientists, Wirth was clear that potentially the social

---

24. Ibid., pp. 3, 103, and 154.
25. Ibid., p. 159.

sciences had much to offer society as long as the knowledge produced was scientific.[26] In this way, independence by the end of the 1930s became both a central criterion for judgment by social scientists and a central objective. The scholars were determined to create and maintain their independence from both philanthropy and the State, while the technicians wanted to be part of the policy-making process.

The opportunity to create the sort of fundamental change that these men desired had passed. They had missed what, with hindsight, must be regarded as a unique opportunity. After a decade of explicitly purposive and applied work it was difficult to turn the clock back. These men were out of touch with the changes that they themselves had unwittingly brought about. Ironically, the Council now came under criticism from men like Osborn for not being scientific enough. In 1940 Osborn described the Council as being far more historical and philosophical in its outlook than other social scientific organizations in which he participated. Osborn categorically stated that the Council was not an effective agency through which to initiate fundamental studies of "man" or "man's adjustment in modern society."[27] Both Osborn and Charles Dollard (CC) charged the Council with being unrepresentative, first, because the membership was heavily weighted geographically in favor of the Northeast and Chicago and, second, because a high proportion of these men were sixty-five years old or more.[28] Time had passed these men by, yet they still spoke for the social sciences as a whole. As they approached the "threshold of scienticity," these leaders of the Council were unwilling to embrace the technical part of the pure approach to their disciplines and still wanted to hold onto some of the progressive assumptions. This indecision was the external indicator of the contradictions that were housed in their class positions and in the nature of social scientific knowledge.

By emphasizing the need for independence because of the controversial nature of the questions that social scientists asked, and because these disciplines were young and still on the road to becoming sciences, these men undermined their own case for legitimacy. The expression of these fears increased the doubts that others harbored concerning the scientific legitimacy and cognitive authority that the social disciplines possessed. The lack of scientific credentials was used against the social scientists. Only the economists were able to achieve the external legitimacy and the internal cognitive authority necessary to take them beyond the threshold that makes a "disci-

---

26. Ibid., pp. 161 and 154.

27. These comments are referred to in memorandum, Willits to Fosdick, September 16, 1940, Folder 5, 910, Program and Policy, 1940–41, RF, 910, 3, 1, RAC.

28. "Charles Dollard and Annual Meeting of Social Science Research Council, Buck Hill Falls, Pa.," September 13–15, 1938; and letter, Osborn to Keppel, September 16, 1938, File, SSRC, 1937–45, CC.

plined scientific" boundary. By bringing together the scholarly and the technical aspects the economists were the most successful in establishing a strong boundary.

Disciplined science is both a relation and an ideal type. Legitimacy and cognitive authority are maximized the more a knowledge unit conforms to the ideal that is disciplined science. The sides of this relation reach from discipline into legitimation, power, and cultural hegemony and from science into cognitive authority, knowledge, and boundary work. (See fig. 1, app. 1.) An emergent form of cultural hegemony, the striving to maximize a disciplined scientific approach, and the class interests of capitalists, politicians and government officials, foundation officials, and economists all converged to produce this boundary. Professional economists increasingly conformed to the negative bourgeois side of their contradictory class positions, which meant that in the process of doing boundary work they conformed to and propagated elements of the dominant ideology.

The convergence around an integrated approach had turned out to be delusory as the structural forces of ideology, division of labor, profession, and class combined to push toward disciplined practicality. Nowhere was this more obvious than in the social science departments of the major research universities, which had experienced substantial growth in the 1930s. One commentator calculates that between 1929 and 1939 the number of faculty in the research universities increased by 45 percent.[29] If anything, one might argue that the Council's emphasis on integration seemed to impede the development of individual disciplines and therefore was an obstacle to fundamental development in the social sciences.

By the end of the 1930s, a new bargain had been struck between social scientists and society in the United States. The bargain was weighted heavily in favor of the interests of the most powerful segments in society and was coordinated by the State and Rockefeller philanthropy. In return for skilled service and policy research, a new generation of social scientists received status, mobility, and financial reward. Legitimacy was traded for service. Society recognized the utility of skills that promised to contribute to better administration, to more amiable foreign relations, and to a more stable and efficient economy. The enormous power of Rockefeller philanthropy was used to fix the new definition of social scientists as technicians. The new corps would provide the expertise and the knowledge necessary to make the new relation between the public and the private sectors work. The push was away from fundamental development toward applied research. Problems were chosen externally. Social scientists brought to their tasks not only the skills

---

29. Roger L. Geiger, *To Advance Knowledge: The Growth of American Research Universities, 1900–1940* (New York: Oxford University Press, 1986).

associated with their disciplines but also they brought the legitimacy of academic science. Through the Council, social scientists subordinated their interests to those of external elites. Yet it was a bargain that necessarily involved reciprocity. Perceived scientific legitimacy was as important to Rockefeller philanthropy and the State as it was for the social scientists. It is ironic that the outcomes were even more extreme than men like Ruml, Day, Merriam, and Mitchell wanted. Fundamental development of the social sciences was simply overwhelmed by the response of those in power to the pressing needs of society. Changes in the basic structure of society were mediated through the third sector, namely, Rockefeller philanthropy, in order to produce a more specialized, technocratic response on the part of social scientists.

Part of the problem for many of the Council was their naïveté with regard to the relation between themselves and society. In line with academic tradition, these social scientists regarded themselves and their work in the universities as autonomous, independent structures that ought to receive unencumbered support that would allow them to conduct pure or purposive research. For these men, social science had no debt to pay to society or, more precisely, had no contracts to fulfill with external agents. To become involved in the policy-making process directly was improper, irresponsible, and likely to inhibit progress in their disciplines. Yet it became increasingly obvious that the relation between social scientists and society was an exchange relation. Throughout the history of the Council, social scientists were expected to produce knowledge that contributed to the maintenance of the social order. The agents were Rockefeller philanthropy, and they collected the debts that social scientists accumulated. This is not to argue that social scientists were any different from other academics with regard to the sort of relation they established, only that the contract was likely to be more open to scrutiny than, say, the work of physical scientists. Instead, one might argue that because social scientists study social processes of which they are a part, there is a greater need to reconcile the interests of society with the interests of social science.[30] One inescapable conclusion is that social scientists and the social science disciplines are extremely sensitive to changes in the wider society.

As other authors have suggested,[31] social science moves in tandem with the structural changes in the economy so that in times of economic expansion we would expect not only growth but a preponderance of pure/purposive research. The bargain involves a minimum amount of surveillance and direction from external sources and can move in critical, even radical, directions. In times of economic recession or depression, we would expect a growth in

30. Wirth also makes this argument, Wirth, "Report," p. 139, SSRCA.
31. Rush, Christensen, and Malcolmson, "Lament for a Notion." Also see Alchon, *Invisible Hand*; and Critchlow, *Brookings Institution*.

applied research and the concomitant increase in external control. This plausible explanation certainly accounts for the contrast in the Council's history between the 1920s and the 1930s. But there was more to it than simply a knee-jerk response on the part of social scientists to these external forces.

The resistance exhibited by some social scientists speaks to the complicated nature of these social relations. Many social scientists opposed the integration route either openly or quietly because they regarded the policy as a utopian exercise. And indeed, the evidence suggests that integration in its weakest form of cross-fertilization has the potential of debilitating the progress of the fields involved toward legitimate discipline status. Logically this would be particularly the case when disciplines are young and trying to mark out their distinct territory. The internal contradiction here is that as those boundaries get stronger so we would expect that it becomes more difficult to cross them. Of particular interest would be attempts to provide bridges between established disciplines within blocks of disciplines and between such blocks. One early attempt to provide a serviceable bridge, as Yerkes put it,[32] between the natural and social sciences, was the promotion of social biology.[33] In any event, this is an open question and one worth pursuing in future research.

Clearly, another implication of this work is that the State institutions that were developed in the post–Second World War era like the NSF and the National Institute of Education were modeled on the foundations and took over the primary role of agents for the ruling class. Just as the foundations presented themselves as doing work for the good of humanity, so the NSF took it the next step and described itself as doing work for the good of society. If one accepts this characterization, and it is an empirical question, then we would expect that the research funding provided by such bodies would fit the exchange relation model used to describe the Council's activities. Rather than a transfer, the funding relationship is reciprocal. The reciprocity involves balancing the long- and short-term interests of those in power with the interests of social scientists. Foundations, and now the State, play mediating roles between the powerful and the academics. The contradictions involved in these relationships are incorporated into the structure of philanthropy and the State and necessarily the bargains that are struck. The question of interest is to explore how the bargain has changed and how the form of the exchange relationship has altered with the direct participation of the State.

The peculiarly sensitive position of social scientists appears not only to

---

32. Yerkes to Merriam, January 29, 1925, p. 3, Folder 827, Yale University Institute of Psychology, 1922–26, LSRM, Series 3, 79, RAC.

33. For an account of the development of social biology at the LSE, see Fisher, "Impact of American Foundations," pp. 429–75.

push toward more extreme responses on their part but places them at a disadvantage in the wider society. They come under suspicion from all parts of the political spectrum whenever they get involved in either purposive or applied research. The political left regards their actions as confirmation that social scientists are merely servants for the ruling class, willing to use their science in the service of those in power. The political right is equally critical, tending to see such action as confirmation that these studies are not objective or important and merely the work of biased radicals who favor the sort of State intervention that was typified by the New Deal.

Finally, while structures are people and nothing is predetermined, this study does suggest rather depressing conclusions when one asks the question about the limits of the roles that social scientists can adopt in a liberal, democratic, capitalist society. Is it possible for a social scientist to reach a position of leadership in his or her discipline and to become famous in the society at large without compromising in the direction of the interests of the ruling class? To what extent can social scientists become Gramsci's radical organic intellectuals? Further, is it likely that a knowledge unit will achieve the legitimacy that has been bestowed on economics, psychology, and anthropology in the last forty years unless these disciplines take on the role of servants to the interests of that small minority in society who exercise economic power? This study would suggest that the answer to all these questions is likely to be no although the answers will always be mixed and involve the potential for the production of knowledge that is fundamentally critical of the social order. This line of questioning leads specifically to studies of boundary work in social fields that have taken the role of critic seriously. Such studies might well increase our understanding of the delicate balance that is at the heart of the relation between social scientific knowledge and the structures of power in contemporary society.

The tension between the social problem and the scientific problem is at the heart of what it means to be an intellectual in modern society. In *The Last Intellectuals: American Culture in the Age of Academe* Russell Jacoby described the modern intellectual as one who is captured by department, field, discipline, or profession at the expense of public culture. Academic culture has made intellectuals invisible as they got lost in the universities. For Jacoby, "The full weight of academization hit the generation born after 1940" because "they grew up in a world where non-university intellectuals hardly existed." As academic culture took over, public culture lost its critics—those who were most concerned with social reform. "When academic freedom succumbs to professionalization," according to Jacoby, "it becomes purely academic."[34]

34. Russell Jacoby, *The Last Intellectuals: American Culture in the Age of Academe* (New York: Noonday Press, Farrar, Straus and Giroux, 1987), pp. 17 and 130.

The history of the SSRC illustrates how the stage was set for the loss of freedom, not just to profession and discipline but also in the process of providing service to the State and the ruling class. For the most part, social scientists had by the mid-1940s opted for uncritical, applied academic science. This is not to argue that social scientists had stopped being advocates. To think of the problem as one involving a choice between advocacy and objectivity oversimplifies the decisions made by social scientists. Advocacy remained as an option throughout the interwar period. What changed significantly was what social scientists could advocate and who they could legitimately represent. To be scientific increasingly meant that social scientists could only advocate the ideology that served the interests of the State and the ruling class. Rockefeller philanthropy was the social force that facilitated this form of mutual legitimation.

Fundamental development of a social problem–oriented science of society that could serve the public was put on hold. The critical element in the process of boundary work would have been to demarcate the social sciences from the natural sciences. This was never achieved. It was never really clear what distinguished the social scientific mode from the natural scientific mode. In this sense, the social sciences as a group of disciplines never really became scientific. These disciplines took up a position somewhere on the boundary between science and nonscience and have remained in that position ever since.

Appendixes

Appendix 1

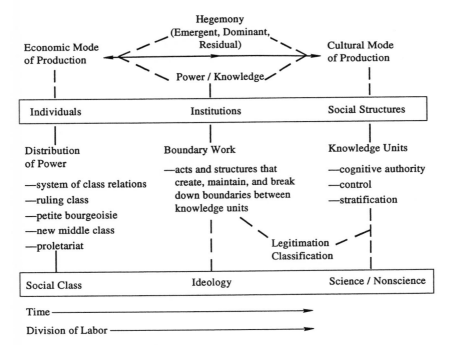

Fig. 1. Boundary work: the production and reproduction of cultural hegemony

Appendix 2

TABLE 1. Appropriations to the Council Showing Years Covered by Donors, Classified by Major Purposes, 1924 to 1939–40

	Amount	Granting Period in Years	1924	1925	1926–27	1927–28	1928–29	1929–30	1930–31	1931–32	1932–33	1933–34	1934–35	1935–36	1936–37	1937–38	1938–39	1939–40
Committees																		
I. Committee on International News and Communication	$1,291	2.50	x	x	x													
I. Committee on International Relations	1,209	2.50		x	x	x												
I. Committee on Scientific Problems of Human Migration	2,500	2.50	x	x	x													
Total	5,000																	
Special projects and planning																		
I. Mechanization of industry	15,500	1.50	x	x														
I. Mechanization of industry	15,500	3.50		x	x	x	x											
I. Statistical study of great migrations	14,500	3.50		x	x	x	x											
III. Study of operation of 18th Amendment	16,000	2.00			x	x												
II. Research planning in field of international relations	31,250	7.50							x	x	x	x	x	x	x			
V. Study of national interest	25,000	2.00									x	x						

X.	Inquiry into and promotion of effective corporate and organization among colleges in the South	5,000	1.00				x		
X.	Ditto	5,000	1.00			x			
XI.	Research planning in industry and trade	3,000	4.00		x	x	x	x	
XII.	Study of social, economic, political, and educational conditions in the southern United States	45,000	3.00		x	x	x	x	
II.	Study of Tennessee River Valley and adjacent sections	10,000	0.75			x			
II.	Planning and study of unemployment reserves and relief	100,000	1.50			x	x		
II.	Place of a controlled national economy in an international system	5,000	1.50			x	x		
II.	Study of population redistribution	60,000	1.00			x	x		
II.	Study of retail prices	78,000	2.00			x	x	x
II.	Study of retail prices	1,500	0.50			x			
XIII.	Inquiry on public service personnel	67,500	1.50			x	x		
II.	Statistics on payroll administration	1,230	0.50			x			

(continued)

TABLE 1—*Continued*

	Amount	Granting Period in Years	1924	1925	1926–27	1927–28	1928–29	1929–30	1930–31	1931–32	1932–33	1933–34	1934–35	1935–36	1936–37	1937–38	1938–39	1939–40
II. Research in public administration	15,000	1.00																
II. Operating staff in public administration	150,000	5.00												x				
II. Research planning in field of economic security	225,000	3.00												x	x	x	x	x
II. Administrative problems in social security	80,000	1.00												x	x	x		
II. Study of administrative development of TVA	20,000	2.50												x	x			
II. Regional studies of labor market in relation to unemployment compensation	15,500	0.50												x	x	x		
II. Study of administration of grants-in-aid in England	3,000	1.00													x			
II. Unemployment relief policies and practices in the state of New Jersey	15,000	1.00														x		
II. Projects, conferences, etc., in field of public service administration	15,000	1.00														x		
II. Research planning in field of social security	60,000	2.00													x	x	x	x

Item	Amount	Rate			
II. Study and appraisal of work of agencies engaged in municipal or governmental research	18,000	1.50	x		
II. Survey on programs and training in public administration	17,500	1.00	x		
II. Survey and appraisal of council-manager form of local government	28,000	1.50	x	x	
II. Study of state unemployment compensation administration	30,000	1.50	x	x	
II. Study of mobility of labor and unemployment	12,000	2.00	x	x	
II. Projects, conferences, etc., in field of social security	15,000	1.00		x	
II. Projects, conferences, etc., in field of public administration	15,000	1.00	x		
II. Study of state unemployment compensation administration	20,000	1.00		x	
II. Study of state unemployment compensation administration	12,500	1.00			x
II. Projects, conferences, etc., in field of social security	15,000	1.00			x

(continued)

TABLE 1—*Continued*

	Amount	Granting Period in Years	1924	1925	1926–27	1927–28	1928–29	1929–30	1930–31	1931–32	1932–33	1933–34	1934–35	1935–36	1936–37	1937–38	1938–39	1939–40
II. Projects, conferences, etc., in field of public administration	15,000	1.00																x
II. Research planning in field of social security to 1940	60,000 (10,000)	2.00																x
II. Research planning in field of public administration to 1940	60,000 (10,000)	2.00																x
Total	1,205,480																	
Summer conferences																	
I. Summer conference	555	1.00		x														
I. Summer conference	17,000	1.00			x													
I. Summer conference	25,000	1.00				x												
I. Summer conference	15,000	1.00					x											
I. Summer conference	15,000	1.00						x										
II. Summer conference	15,000	1.00							x									
II. Summer conference	12,500	1.00								x								
Total	100,055																	
Postdoctoral fellowships																	
I. Postdoctoral fellowships	49,000	1.00		x														
I. Postdoctoral fellowships	57,000	1.00			x													

I. Postdoctoral fellowships	66,300	1.00				x								
I. Postdoctoral fellowships	80,000	1.00			x									
I. Postdoctoral fellowships	90,000	1.00		x										
II. Postdoctoral fellowships	180,000	2.00		x	x									
II. Postdoctoral fellowships	180,000	2.00					x	x						
II. Postdoctoral fellowships	90,000	1.00							x					
II. Postdoctoral fellowships	75,000	1.00								x				
II. Postdoctoral fellowships	50,000	1.00									x			
II. Postdoctoral fellowships	50,000	1.00										x		
II. Postdoctoral fellowships to 1940	150,000 (100,000)	3.00											x	x
Total	**1,067,300**													

Council general administration

IV. Council general administration	3,000	1.00	x				
I. Council general administration	25,000	5.50	x	x	x	x	x
IV. Council general administration	1,500	0.50	x				
IV. Council general administration	5,000	1.00	x				

(continued)

TABLE 1—*Continued*

	Amount	Granting Period in Years	1924	1925	1926–27	1927–28	1928–29	1929–30	1930–31	1931–32	1932–33	1933–34	1934–35	1935–36	1936–37	1937–38	1938–39	1939–40
IV. Council general administration	5,000	1.00			x													
IV. Council general administration	10,000	1.00					x											
IV. Council general administration	5,000	1.00						x										
IV. Council general administration	5,000	1.00							x									
IV. Council general administration	5,000	1.00								x								
IV. Council general administration	2,500	0.50									x							
IV. Council general administration	2,500	1.00										x						
IV. Council general administration	2,500	1.00											x					
IV. Council general administration	3,750	1.00												x				
IV. Council general administration	3,750	1.00													x			
IV. Council general administration	5,000	1.00														x		
IV. Council general administration	5,000	1.00															x	
IV. Council general administration	5,000	1.00																x
V. Council general administration	25,000	5.00			x	x	x	x	x									

Item	Amount	
V. Council general administration	25,000	5.00
V. Council general administration	15,000	2.00
V. Council general administration	75,000	3.00
V. Council general administration	75,000	3.00
VII. Council general administration	50,000	5.00
I. Council general administration	550,000	12.00
II. Council general administration	80,000	2.00
VI. Council general administration	5,000	1.00
Total	**949,500**	
Agricultural fellowships		
I. Agricultural fellowships	150,000	5.00
Southern fellowships		
IX. Southern fellowships	50,000	5.00
Southern grants-in-aid		
IX. Grants-in-aid	15,000	3.50
IX. Grants-in-aid	10,000	4.00
IX. Grants-in-aid to 1940	15,000	4.00
	(7,500)	
Total	**32,500**	

(continued)

TABLE 1—Continued

	Amount	Granting Period in Years	1924	1925	1926–27	1927–28	1928–29	1929–30	1930–31	1931–32	1932–33	1933–34	1934–35	1935–36	1936–37	1937–38	1938–39	1939–40
Conference and planning fund																		
II. Conference and planning fund	250,000	6.00									x	x	x	x	x			
II. Conference and planning fund to 1940	150,000 (115,000)	4.00														x	x	x
Total	365,000																	
Council grants-in-aid																		
II. Council grants-in-aid	105,000	4.00									x	x	x	x				
II. Council grants-in-aid	25,000	1.00												x				
II. Council grants-in-aid	25,000	1.00													x			
II. Council grants-in-aid	75,000	3.00														x	x	x
Total	230,000																	
Special project budgets																		
I. Special project budget	50,000	4.00			x	x	x	x										
I. Special project budget	85,000	3.00			x	x	x											
I. Special project budget	42,500	1.50				x	x											
I. Special project budget	19,500	1.00			x													
Total	197,000																	
General project budget																		
I. General project budget	750,000	5.00					x	x	x	x	x							

II. General project budget	225,000	6.00		x	x	x	x	x	x						
Total	975,000														
Miscellaneous															
I. Social science abstracts	500,000	8.00	x	x	x	x	x	x	x						
II. Special instruction in agricultural and rural sociology	40,000	6.00		x		x		x							
IX. Conference on Operation of a Family Day Care Center	1,000	0.50				x									
VIII. Conference on Relation of Psychiatry to Social Science	1,500	0.50		x											
Total	542,500														
Predoctoral fellowships															
XII. Predoctoral fellowships	100,000	2.00					x								
XII. Predoctoral fellowships	100,000	2.00					x	x							
XII. Predoctoral fellowships	100,000	2.00						x	x						
II. Predoctoral fellowships	75,000	3.00							x	x	x	x			
Total	375,000														

Notes: I—LSRM
II—RF
III—John D. Rockefeller, Jr.
IV—Russell Sage Foundation
V—CC
VI—CF
VII—Julius Rosenwald, Jr.
VIII—Revell McCallum
IX—Julius Rosenwald Fund
X—Carnegie Fund, Advancement of Teaching
XI—Falk Foundation
XII—GEB
XIII—SF

Source: This table was compiled from the records of the SSRC and the CC and the material at the RAC. The figures in parentheses are the amounts appropriated to the end of 1939/40.

TABLE 2. SSRC Committees, 1923–40

Committees	1923–24	1924–25	1925–26	1926–27	1927–28	1928–29	1929–30	1930–31	1931–32	1932–33	1933–34	1934–35	1935–36	1936–37	1937–38	1938–39	1939–40
Scientific Methods in the Social Sciences (1923–29)	x	x	x	x	x	x											
Annual Publication of an Index and Digest of State Session Laws (1923–27)	x	x	x	x													
Executive (1925–)			x	x	x	x	x	x	x	x	x	x	x	x	x	x	x
International News and Communications (1924–27)		x	x	x													
Research Fellowships in Social Science (1924–33)		x	x	x	x	x	x	x	x	x							
Population: Scientific Aspects of Human Migration (1924–27)		x	x	x													
Population (1927–29)					x	x											
Joint Population with NRC (1929–30)							x										
Population Review (1931–32)									x								
Population Redistribution (1934–37)												x	x	x			
Migration (1936–38)														x	x		
Problems and Policy (1925–)			x	x	x	x	x	x	x	x	x	x	x	x	x	x	x
Social Science Abstracts (1925–27)			x	x													
Eighteenth Amendment (1925–28)			x	x	x												
Interracial Relations (1925–30)			x	x	x	x	x										
Crime (1925–28, 1929–32)			x	x	x		x	x	x								
Special Commission Review—Institute of																	

Program											
Criminology and Criminal Justice (1932–33)		X									
Agriculture—Social and Economic:											
Agriculture–Social and Economic Research (1925–42)		X	X		X	X	X	X	X	X	X
Fellowships in Agricultural Economics and Rural Sociology (1928–33)						X			X	X	X
Corporate Relations (1926–30)		X	X	X		X	X	X	X	X	X
Cultural Areas (1926–28)		X	X	X							
Industrial Relations (1926–30)		X	X	X		X	X	X	X	X	X
International Relations (1926–38)		X	X	X		X	X	X	X	X	X
Pioneer Belts (1926–28)		X	X	X		X	X	X	X	X	X
Grants-in-Aid (1926–); standing committee from 1928		X	X			X	X	X	X	X	X
Problems of Philanthropic Financing (1927–29)		X	X	X		X	X	X	X	X	X
Investments (1928–)			X	X		X	X	X	X	X	X
Technical Committee on Attitudes and Public Opinion (1928–30)		X	X	X		X	X	X	X	X	X
Business Research (1928–31)				X	X	X	X	X			
Family (1928–32)				X	X	X	X				
Public Administration (1928–45)		X	X	X		X	X	X	X	X	X
Social Statistics											
Social Statistics (1929–36)		X	X	X	X	X	X	X	X	X	X
Utilization of Social Data (1929–31) merged into statistics				X	X	X					

(continued)

TABLE 2—*Continued*

Committees	1923-24	1924-25	1925-26	1926-27	1927-28	1928-29	1929-30	1930-31	1931-32	1932-33	1933-34	1934-35	1935-36	1936-37	1937-38	1938-39	1939-40
Government Statistics and Information Services, joint ASTA (1933-37)											x	x	x	x			
Materials for Research (1929-40)							x	x	x	x	x	x	x	x	x	x	x
Pacific Coast Regional (1929-46)							x	x	x	x	x	x	x	x	x	x	x
Southern Regional (1929-47)							x	x	x	x	x	x	x	x	x	x	x
Southern Fellowships (1929-33)							x	x	x	x							
Scientific Publications (1929-32)							x	x	x								
Chicago World Fair (1930-33)								x	x	x							
Personality and Culture (1930-34)								x	x	x	x						
Seminar on Culture and Personality (1930-34)								x	x	x	x						
Social Science Personnel (1930-33), fellowship committee merged								x	x	x							
Industry and Trade (1931-45)									x	x							
Incorporated Business Research, Corporate Relations, and Industrial Relations											x	x	x	x	x	x	x
Consumption and Leisure (1931-32)									x								
Pressure Groups and Propaganda (1931-34)									x	x	x						
Special Research in Aspects of Social Medicine (1933-34)											x						

Committee (year)	1	2	3	4	5	6	7
Commissions of Inquiry on Public Problems (1933–37)							
Public Relations (1933–35)	×			×			
Government Research in Social Science (1934–35)	×						
Government Research (1938–39)							
National Planning and Social Science (1934)						×	
National Academy of Social Science (1934–35)							
Improvement of Research Organization (1934–35)		×					
Freedom of Inquiry (1935–38)		×					
Social Security (1935–43)			×				×
University Social Science Research Organizations (1935–46)			×		×		
Social Aspects of the Depression (1936–38)			×	×			×
Review of Grants-in-Aid (1936–37)				×			
Review of Council Policy (1937–38)				×			
Appraisal of Research (1937–46)							
Guide for Study of Local History (1938–45)				×	×	×	×
Control of Social Data (1939–45)					×		×
Dissemination (1939–42)							×
Research Training (1939–42)							×
Survey of Research by Business (1939–40)							×

TABLE 3. Total Appropriations by Purposes, 1924 to 1939–40

Category	Amount	Percentage
General administration	$949,500	15.20
Conference and planning	465,055	7.44
General projects	975,000	15.61
Fellowships	1,642,300	26.30
Grants-in-aid	262,500	4.20
Special project and enterprises	1,407,480	22.86
Miscellaneous (including $500,000 for abstracts)	542,500	8.39
Totals	6,244,335	100.00

TABLE 4. Appropriations by Donors, 1924 to 1939–40

Donors	Amount	Percentage
LSRM	$2,577,355	41.27
RF	2,780,980	44.54
GEB	345,000	5.53
CC	235,000	3.76
Julius Rosenwald Fund	83,500	1.34
Russell Sage Foundation	69,500	1.11
SF	67,500	1.08
Julius Rosenwald, Jr.	50,000	0.80
John D. Rockfeller, Jr.	16,000	0.26
Carnegie Fund, Advancement of Teaching	10,000	0.16
CF	5,000	0.08
Falk Foundation	3,000	0.05
Revell McCallum	1,500	0.02
Total	6,244,335 .	100.00
Total Rockefeller sources	5,786,835	92.58

TABLE 5. SSRC Disbursements, 1924–40, by Source of Funds

	LSRM and RF	Russell Sage	CC	Julius Rosenwald Fund	GEB	SF	Other Sources	Total
1924	9,801	—	—	—	—	—	—	9,801
1925	46,436	2,659	—	—	—	—	—	49,095
1926	43,021	1,530	—	—	—	—	4,479	49,030
1926–27	138,365	1,305	1,924	—	—	—	15,450	157,044
1927–28	224,521	6,027	5,405	—	—	—	3,896	239,849
1928–29	368,485	6,580	3,889	—	—	—	5,990	384,944
1929–30	413,680	6,499	5,006	2,098	—	—	12,146	439,429
1930–31	422,615	5,781	8,004	22,491	—	—	14,111	473,042
1931–32	366,379	5,460	8,632	18,819	8,632	—	16,620	424,542
1932–33	422,844	3,825	14,895	—	26,684	—	13,196	481,444
1933–34	379,593	2,616	14,759	—	7,507	20,911	7,292	432,678
1934–35	274,366	2,896	9,003	—	15,393	46,589	3,763	352,010
1935–36	320,135	2,787	9,226	—	57,164	—	2,105	391,417
1936–37	421,471	2,775	14,528	1,743	51,421	—	—	491,938
1937–38	344,204	3,464	17,671	3,714	60,567	—	—	429,620
1938–39	300,633	3,985	20,135	2,717	14,463	—	—	341,933
1939–40	276,388	3,475	17,849	3,334	351	—	—	301,397
Total	4,772,937	61,664	150,966	54,916	242,182	67,500	99,048	5,449,213
Percentage	87.59	1.13	2.77	1.01	4.44	001.24	1.82	100.00

TABLE 6. Council Membership by Years of Service, Representation, and Institution, 1923–39/40

Individual	Number of Years on Council	Association(s) Represented	Institution/ University	Senior Offices Held
Charles E. Merriam	17	APSA	Chicago	Chairman 1923–27
William Fielding Ogburn	16	ASS	Chicago	Chairman, 1933–36 Vice-chairman, 1930
Guy S. Ford	15	AHA	Minnesota, Minneapolis	Chairman, 1936–39 Vice-chairman, 1933–36
Shelby M. Harrison	15	ASS and M.A.L.	Russell Sage Foundation	
Arthur M. Schlesinger, Jr.	15	AHA	Harvard	Chairman, 1930–33 Vice-chairman, 1927–32
Wesley C. Mitchell	13	AEA, ASTA, and M.A.L.	Columbia	Chairman, 1927–29 Vice-chairman, 1926 Treasurer, 1930–31
Isaiah Bowman	9	M.A.L.	American Geo- graphical Society	Treasurer, 1931–32
Charles H. Judd	9	M.A.L.	Chicago	
Edmund E. Day	8	ASTA and M.A.L.	Michigan	Treasurer, 1924–26
John Dickinson	8	M.A.L.	Pennsylvania	
Arnold B. Hall	8	APSA	Oregon	
Ralph Linton	8	AAA	Wisconsin, Madison	
Robert T. Crane	7	APSA	Michigan	Secretary, 1927–29 Permanent secretary, 1931–32 Executive director, 1932–40
Edwin B. Wilson	7	ASTA	Harvard	President, 1927–31 Chairman, 1939–42
Mark Arthur May	6	APA and M.A.L.	Yale	
Edward Sapir	6	AAA	Yale	

TABLE 6—*Continued*

Individual	Number of Years on Council	Association(s) Represented	Institution/ University	Senior Offices Held
Alfred M. Tozzer	6	AAA	Harvard	Secretary, 1933
George E. Barnett	5	AEA	Johns Hopkins	
William A. Berridge	5	ASTA	Metropolitan Life Insurance	
Harry A. Millis	5	AEA	Chicago	
Adolf Meyer	5	M.A.L.	Johns Hopkins	
Roy F. Nichols	5	AHA	Pennsylvania	
A. T. Poffenberger	5	APA	Minnesota, Minneapolis	
Robert Redfield	5	AAA	Chicago	
Horace Secrist	5	AEA	Northwestern	
William Anderson	4	APSA		
Francis Stuart Chapin	4	ASS	Minnesota, Minneapolis	
Fay-Cooper Cole	4	AAA	Chicago	
Carlton J. H. Hayes	4	AHA		
Lindsay Rogers	4	APSA		
W. I. Thomas	4	ASS	New York City	
Robert Sessions Woodworth	4	APA and M.A.L.	Columbia	President, 1931–32 Treasurer, 1927–30

TABLE 7. SSRC Postdoctoral Research Fellowships and Research Training by Year and Discipline

Year	Economics	History	Sociology	Political Science	Psychology	Anthropology	Other[a]	Total
1925–26	4	2	4	2	1	—	2	15
1926–27	4	1	1	3	2	—	1	12
1927–28	8	6	—	1	—	1	—	16
1928–29	4	4	1	3	2	2	2	18
1929–30	3	4	3	3	2	1	3	19
1930–31	7	11	1	4	5	1	3	32
1931–32	6	2	8	3	1	1	1	22
1932–33	11	7	1	2	3	5	2	31

1933–34	3	1	6	2	1	—	1	14
1934–35	5	3	2	—	2	1	1	14
1935–36	3	4	1	—	3	—	—	11
1936–37	—	5	3	2	1	—	2	13
1937–38	3	1	2	1	1	1	—	9
1938–39	—	1	—	2	—	1	—	4
1939–40	2	1	1	2	1	3	—	10
Total	63	53	34	30	25	17	18	240
Percentage	26.25	22.08	14.17	12.50	10.42	7.08	7.50	

Note: The program began under the heading "Research Fellowships."

[a] The "Other" category included the following disciplines and fields: philosophy, statistics, English, education, geography, and international relations.

TABLE 8. Occupation of Postdoctoral Fellows (1925–40) in 1951

	Number	Percentage of Total	Percentage of Those Employed
Total	240	100	—
Number employed	226	—	100
Academic	169	70	75
U.S. government	27	11	12
Other social science disciplines	18	8	8
All other occupations	12	5	5
Deceased	6	3	—
Unknown	8	3	—

Source: Calculated from the data contained in SSRC, *Fellows of the Social Science Research Council, 1925–1951* (New York, 1951).

TABLE 9. A Typology of Social Science Roles

Definitions of Social Scientists	Conceptions of Scientific Research		
	Pure	Purposive	Applied
Scholars	1 Disciplined Fundamental	2 Progressive Fundamental	3 Disciplined Decision Oriented	
Technicians	4 Disciplined Methodologists		5 Disciplined "Pick and Shovel"	6 Pragmatic Empiricists

Selected Bibliography

Manuscript Collections

Angell, James Rowland. Presidential Papers. Yale University, New Haven.

Burgess, Ernest W. Papers. University of Chicago, Chicago.

Carnegie Corporation. Files. Carnegie Corporation, New York.

Columbia University. Central Files, President's Office. Columbia University, New York.

Commonwealth Fund. Papers. Commonwealth Fund, New York.

Division of Social Science. Files. University of Chicago Collections, Chicago.

Institute of Human Relations. Yale University, New Haven.

Laura Spelman Rockefeller Memorial. Rockefeller Philanthropy Collections, Rockefeller Archive Center, Tarrytown, N.Y.

Merriam, Charles E. Papers. University of Chicago, Chicago.

Mitchell, Wesley C. Papers. Columbia University, New York.

Odum, Howard W. Papers. Southern Historical Collection, University of North Carolina, Chapel Hill.

Ogburn, William Fielding. Papers. University of Chicago, Chicago.

Redfield, Robert. Papers. University of Chicago, Chicago.

Rockefeller Family Archive. Rockefeller Center, New York.

Rockefeller Foundation. Rockefeller Philanthropy Collections. Rockefeller Archive Center, Tarrytown, N.Y.

Ruml, Beardsley. Papers. Department of Special Collections. University of Chicago, Chicago.

Russell Sage Foundation. Files. Russell Sage Foundation, New York.

Social Science Federation of Canada. Papers. Public Archive of Canada, Ottawa.

Social Science Research Committee. University of Chicago Collections, Chicago.

Social Science Research Council. Files. Social Science Research Council, New York.

Spelman Fund. Rockefeller Philanthropy Collections, Rockefeller Archive Center, Tarrytown, N.Y.

University of Chicago. President's Papers. University of Chicago Collections, Chicago.

University of Texas. President's Office Records. University of Texas, Austin.

Wilbur, Ray Lyman. Presidential Papers, Stanford University Archives. Palo Alto, Calif.

Willits, Joseph Henry. Papers (1). University of Pennsylvania, Philadelphia; Rocke-
    feller Archive Center, Tarrytown, N.Y.
Wirth, Louis. Papers. University of Chicago, Chicago.
Yale University. Records of the Provost. Yale University, New Haven.

Interviews

Havinghurst, Robert J. Interview with author. Vancouver, British Columbia, July 19,
    1979.
Johnson, Guy Benton and Johnson, Guion Griffis. Interview with author. Chapel Hill,
    June 24, 1982.

Books, Dissertations, and Articles

Abrams, Philip. *Historical Sociology*. Bath: Open Books, 1982.
Adamson, Walter L. *Hegemony and Revolution: A Study of Antonio Gramsci's Politi-
    cal and Cultural Theory*. Berkeley and Los Angeles: University of California
    Press, 1980.
Alchon, Guy. *The Invisible Hand of Planning: Capitalism, Social Science, and the
    State in the 1920s*. Princeton: Princeton University Press, 1985.
Allport, Gordon Willard. *The Use of Personal Documents in Psychological Science*.
    Bulletin 49. New York: Social Science Research Council, 1942.
Alpert, Harry. "The Growth of Social Research in the United States." In Daniel
    Lerner, ed., *The Human Meaning of the Social Sciences*. Cleveland: World Pub-
    lishing Co., 1959.
Altmeyer, Arthur J. *The Formative Years of Social Security*. Madison: University of
    Wisconsin Press, 1966.
American Political Science Association. "Meeting." 1921. *American Political Science
    Review* 16 (1922): 111–15.
———. "Meeting." 1922. *American Political Science Review* 17 (1923): 108–13.
———. "Committee on Political Research, Report." *American Political Science Re-
    view* 18 (1924): 574–600.
———. "Report of the Committee on Policy." *American Political Science Review* 24
    (1930): 1–199.
Andrews, F. Emerson. *Philanthropic Foundations*. New York: Russell Sage Founda-
    tion, 1956.
Angell, James Rowland. "Autobiography of James Rowland Angell." In C. Mur-
    chison, ed., *A History of Psychology in Autobiography*. New York: Russell and
    Russell, 1961.
Anyon, J. "Social Class and School Knowledge." *Curriculum Inquiry* 11 (1981): 3–
    42.
Apple, Michael W. *Ideology and Curriculum*. London: Routledge and Kegan Paul,
    1979.
———. *Cultural and Economic Reproduction in Education*. Boston: Routledge and
    Kegan Paul, 1982.

Apple, Michael W., and Weis, Lois, eds. *Ideology and Practice in Schooling*. Philadelphia: Temple University Press, 1983.

―――. "Ideology and Schooling." *Education and Society* 3 (1985): 45–63.

Arnove, Robert F., ed. *Philanthropy and Cultural Imperialism: The Foundations at Home and Abroad*. Bloomington: Indiana University Press, 1982.

Aronowitz, Stanley. *Science as Power: Discourse and Ideology in Modern Society*. Minneapolis: University of Minnesota Press, 1988.

Aronowitz, Stanley, and Giroux, Henry A. *Education under Siege*. South Hadley, Mass.: Bergin and Garvey Publishers, 1985.

Ashmore, Malcolm. *The Reflexive Thesis: Wrighting Sociology of Scientific Knowledge*. Chicago: University of Chicago Press, 1989.

Atkinson, Raymond Cumings. *The Federal Role in Unemployment Compensation Administration*. Committee on Social Security. Washington, D.C.: Social Science Research Council, 1941.

Atkinson, Raymond Cumings, et al. *The Administration of Public Employment Offices in the United States*. Studies in Administration, vol. 5. Chicago: Public Administration Service, 1939.

Atkinson, Raymond Cumings; Odencrantz, L.; and Deming, B. *Public Employment in the United States*. New York: Social Science Research Council, 1938.

Auerbach, Lewis E. "Scientists in the New Deal." *Minerva* 3 (1965): 457–82.

Banks, Olive. "The Sociology of Education, 1952–1982." *British Journal of Educational Studies* 30 (1982): 18–31.

Barber, Bernard. *Science and the Social Order*. New York: Collier Books, 1962.

Baritz, Loren. *The Servants of Power: A History of the Use of Social Science in American Industry*. Middleton: Wesleyan University Press, 1960.

Barnes, Barry. *T. S. Kuhn and Social Science*. New York: Columbia University Press, 1982.

Barnes, Harry Elmer. *History and Social Intelligence*. New York: Knopf, 1926.

―――. *The History and Prospects of the Social Sciences*. New York: Knopf, 1925.

Barnes, Harry Elmer; Becker, Howard; and Becker, Frances Bennet, eds. *Contemporary Social Theory*. New York: D. Appleton-Century Co., 1940.

Barrett, Michael, et al., eds. *Ideology and Cultural Reproduction*. New York: St. Martin's Press, 1979.

Bates, Thomas R. "Gramsci and the Theory of Hegemony." *Journal of the History of Ideas* 36 (April–July 1975): 351–66.

Beard, Charles A. "Limitations to the Application of Social Science Implied in Recent Social Trends." *Social Forces* 11 (May 1933): 505–10.

―――. *The Open Door at Home: A Trial Philosophy of National Interest*. New York: Macmillan, 1934.

―――. *America Faces the Future*. 1932. Freeport: Books for Libraries, 1969.

Becker, Ernest. *The Lost Science of Man*. New York: George Braziller, 1971.

Ben-David, Joseph. *Fundamental Research and the Universities*. Paris: OECD, 1968.

―――. *The Scientist's Role in Society: A Comparative Study*. Englewood Cliffs: Prentice Hall, 1971.

"Benefactions to Universities: British and American." *Nature* 115 (1925): 629–31.

Benjamin, Gerald, ed. *Private Philanthropy and Public Elementary and Secondary Education*. Proceedings of the Rockefeller Archive Center Conference, June 8, 1979. Tarrytown, N.Y.: Rockefeller Archive Center, 1979.

Bennett, Tony; Martin, Graham; Mercer, Colin; and Woollacott, Janet, eds. *Culture, Ideology, and Social Process: A Reader*. London: Open University Press, 1981.

Berger, P. L., and Luckman, T. *The Social Construction of Reality*. New York: Doubleday and Co., 1966.

Berle, Adolf A., Jr., and Means, Gardiner C. *The Modern Corporation and Private Property*. New York: Macmillan, 1933.

Berman, Edward H. "Foundations, United States: Foreign Policy and African Education, 1945–1975." *Harvard Educational Review* 49, no. 2 (May 1979): 145–79 plus responses.

———. *The Influence of the Carnegie, Ford, and Rockefeller Foundations in American Foreign Policy: Ideology and Philanthropy*. Albany: State University of New York Press, 1984.

Bernard, Luther L. "The Social Sciences as Discipline: The United States." In *Encyclopedia of the Social Sciences*. 1933. New York: Macmillan, 1937.

———, ed. *The Fields and Methods of Sociology*. New York: Farrar and Rinehart, 1934.

Bernard, Luther L., and Bernard, Jessie S. "Century of Progress in the Social Sciences." *Social Forces* 11 (May 1933): 488–505.

———. *Sociology and the Study of International Relations*. New Series, Social and Philosophic Sciences, vol. 4. St. Louis: Washington University Studies, 1934.

———. *Origins of American Sociology: The Social Science Movement in the United States*. New York: Thomas Y. Crowell, 1943.

Bernstein, Basil. *Towards a Theory of Educational Transmissions*. Vol. 3 of *Class, Codes, and Control*. Rev. ed. London: Routledge and Kegan Paul, 1977.

———. "Codes, Modalities, and the Process of Cultural Reproduction: A Model." In Michael W. Apple, ed., *Cultural and Economic Reproduction in Education*. Boston: Routledge and Kegan Paul, 1982.

———. *The Structuring of Pedagogic Discourse*. Vol. 4 of *Class, Codes, and Control*. London: Routledge, 1990.

Bernstein, Richard. *Praxis and Action*. Philadelphia: University of Pennsylvania Press, 1971.

Black, John D., ed. *Scope and Method of Research in Agricultural Economics and Rural Sociology*. Advisory Committee on Social and Economic Research in Agriculture. New York: Social Science Research Council, 1930.

Bledstein, Burton. *The Culture of Professionalism: The Middle Class and the Development of Higher Education in America*. New York: W. W. Norton, 1976.

Bloor, David. *Knowledge of Social Imagery*. London: Routledge and Kegan Paul, 1976.

Blumer, Herbert. *An Appraisal of Thomas and Znaniecki's "The Polish Peasant in Europe and America."* Bulletin 44. New York: Social Science Research Council, 1939.

Bocock, Robert. *Hegemony*. London: Tavistock Publications, 1986.

Boggs, Carl. *Gramsci's Marxism*. London: Pluto Press, 1976.

————. *The Two Revolutions: Antonio Gramsci and the Dilemmas of Western Marxism.* Boston: Southend Press, 1984.

Bohme, G., and Stehr, N., eds. *The Knowledge Society.* Dordrecht: D. Reidel, 1986.

Boring, Edwin G. *A History of Experimental Psychology.* 1929. New York: Appleton-Century-Crofts, 1950.

————, ed. *Psychology for the Armed Services.* Washington, D.C.: Infantry Journal, 1945.

Bottomore, Tom, and Nisbet, Robert A., eds. *A History of Sociological Analysis.* London: Heinemann Educational Books, 1978.

Boulding, Kenneth E. *The Impact of the Social Sciences.* New Brunswick: Rutgers University Press, 1966.

Boulding, Kenneth E., and Senesh, L., eds. *The Optimum Utilization of Knowledge: Making Knowledge Serve Human Betterment.* Boulder: Westview Press, 1983.

Bourdieu, Pierre. "Intellectual Field and the Creative Project." *Social Science Information* 8, no. 2 (1969): 89–119.

————. *Distinction: A Social Critique of Taste.* Cambridge: Harvard University Press, 1984.

————. *Homo Academicus.* Trans. Peter Collier. Stanford: Stanford University Press, 1988.

Bourdieu, Pierre, and Passeron, J. C. *Reproduction in Education and Society.* London: Sage, 1977.

————. *The Inheritors: French Students and Their Relation to Culture.* Trans. Richard Nice. Chicago: University of Chicago Press, 1979.

Bowles, S., and Gintis, Herbert. *Schooling in Capitalist America: Educational Reform and the Contradictions of Economic Life.* New York: Basic Books, 1976.

Bowman, Isaiah. "The Scientific Study of Settlement." *Geographical Review* 16 (October 1926): 647–53.

Bray, Charles W. *Psychology and Military Proficiency.* Princeton: Princeton University Press, 1948.

Brazil, Wayne. "Howard Odum: The Building Years, 1884–1930." Ph.D. diss., Harvard University, 1975.

Bremner, Robert H. *American Philanthropy.* Chicago: University of Chicago Press, 1960.

Brick, Howard. *Daniel Bell and the Decline of Intellectual Radicalism: Social Theory and Political Reconciliation in the 1940s.* Madison: University of Wisconsin Press, 1986.

Brigham, Carl C. *Examining Fellowship Applications.* Social Science Research Council. Princeton: Princeton University Press, 1935.

Brown, Richard E. *Rockefeller Medicine Man: Medicine and Capitalism in America.* Berkeley and Los Angeles: University of California Press, 1979.

Buck, Paul, ed. *The Social Sciences at Harvard: From Inculcation to the Open Mind.* Cambridge: Harvard University Press, 1965.

Bulmer, Martin. "The Early Institutional Establishment of Social Science Research: The Local Community Research Committee at the University of Chicago, 1923–30." *Minerva* 18 (1980): 51–110.

————. *The Chicago School of Sociology: Institutionalization, Diversity, and the Rise of Sociological Research.* Chicago: University of Chicago Press, 1985.

Bulmer, Martin, and Bulmer, Joan. "Philanthropy and Social Science in the 1920's: Beardsley Ruml and the Laura Spelman Rockefeller Memorial, 1922–29." *Minerva* 19 (1981 [appeared in 1983]): 347–407.

Burawoy, M., and Skocpol, Theda, eds. *Marxist Inquiries: Studies of Labor, Class, and States.* Supplement to the *American Journal of Sociology* 88. Chicago: University of Chicago Press, 1982.

Bureau of the Budget. *The United States at War.* Washington, D.C.: Government Printing Office, 1946.

Burgess, Ernest W. "George Edgar Vincent, 1864–1941." *American Journal of Sociology* 46 (1941): 887.

Burke, P. "Historical Sociology: A Review Essay." *American Journal of Sociology* 90 (1985): 905–8.

Burner, David. *Herbert Hoover: A Public Life.* New York: Knopf, 1979.

Burns, Arthur F. *Wesley Mitchell and the National Bureau.* Twenty-ninth Annual Report of the National Bureau of Economic Research. New York: National Bureau of Economic Research, 1949.

————, ed. *Wesley Clair Mitchell, The Economic Scientist.* New York: National Bureau of Economic Research, 1952.

Burns, Eveline M. *British Unemployment Programs, 1920–1938.* Committee on Social Security. Washington, D.C.: Social Science Research Council, 1941.

Bush, Vannever. *Science: The Endless Frontier.* Washington, D.C.: Government Printing Office, 1945.

Bye, Raymond T. *An Appraisal of Frederick C. Mills' "The Behaviour of Prices."* Bulletin 45. New York: Social Science Research Council, 1940.

Callon, Michael; Law, John; and Rip, Arie, eds. *Mapping the Dynamics of Science and Technology.* London: Macmillan, 1986.

Carnoy, Martin. *The State and Political Theory.* Princeton: Princeton University Press, 1984.

Carnoy, Martin, and Levin, Henry M. *Schooling and Work in the Democratic State.* Stanford: Stanford University Press, 1985.

Cartwright, Dorwin. "Social Psychology in the United States during the Second World War." *Human Relations* 1, no. 2 (November 1947): 333–52.

Casagrande, Joseph B., and Elbridge, Sibley. "Fellows of the Social Science Research Council, 1925–1951: Some Statistics." *ITEMS* (Social Science Research Council) 6, no. 2 (June 1952): 13–17.

Catlin, G. E. G. *The Science and Method of Politics.* New York: Knopf, 1927.

Chamov, John. *Work Relief Experience in the United States.* Committee on Social Security. Washington, D.C.: Social Science Reasearch Council, 1943.

Chapin, Francis Stuart. *Field Work and Social Research.* New York: Century Co., 1920.

————. "The Present State of the Profession." *American Journal of Sociology* 39 (1934): 506–8.

Chapin, Francis Stuart, and Queen, Stuart A. *Research Memorandum on Social Work in the Depression.* Committee on Social Aspects of the Depression, bulletin 39. New York: Social Science Research Council, 1937.

Cheit, Earl F., and Lobman, Theo E., eds. *Foundations and Higher Education Grant Making from Golden Years through Steady State*. Berkeley: Carnegie Council on Policy Studies, 1979.

Cheyney, E. P. *The History of the University of Pennsylvania: 1740–1940*. Philadelphia: University of Pennsylvania Press, 1940.

Chicago Commission on Race Relations. *The Negro in Chicago: A Study of Race Relations and a Race Riot in 1919*. Chicago: University of Chicago Press, 1922.

Chubin, Daryl E. *Sociology of Sciences: An Annotated Bibliography on the Invisible College, 1972–1981*. New York: Garland Publishing, 1983.

Church, Robert L. "Economists as Experts: The Rise of an Academic Profession in the United States." In Lawrence Stone, ed., *The University in Society*. Princeton: Princeton University Press, 1974.

Cicourel, Aaron V. *Method and Measurement in Sociology*. New York: Free Press, 1964.

Clark, John Maurice. *Strategic Factors in Business Cycles*. New York: National Bureau of Economic Research, 1934.

Clark, Terry N. "The Stages of Scientific Institutionalization." *International Social Sciences Journal* 24 (1972): 658–71.

Clawson, Marion. *New Deal Planning: The National Resources Planning Board*. Baltimore: Johns Hopkins University Press, 1981.

Coats, Alfred W. "The First Two Decades of the American Economic Association." *American Economic Review* 51 (September 1961): 624–37.

Coben, Stanley. "Foundation Officials and Fellowships: Innovation in the Patronage of Science." *Minerva* 14 (1976): 225–40.

———. "American Foundations as Patrons of Science: The Commitment to Individual Research." In Nathan Reingold, ed., *The Sciences in the American Context: New Perspectives*. Washington, D.C.: Smithsonian Institution Press, 1979.

Cohen, I. B., ed. *The Sciences and the Social Sciences*. New York: Norton, Norton and Co., 1985.

Cohen, Ira J. *Structuration Theory: Anthony Giddens and the Constitution of Social Life*. New York: St. Martin's Press, 1989.

Coleman, James. "Sociological Analysis and Social Policy." In Tom Bottomore and Robert A. Nisbet, eds., *A History of Sociological Analysis*. London: Heinemann Educational Books, 1978.

Collins, Randall. *Sociology since Midcentury: Essays in Theory Accumulations*. New York: Academic Press, 1981.

Collins, Selwyn De Witt, and Tibbits, Clark. *Research Memorandum on Social Aspects of Health in the Depression*. Committee on Social Aspects of the Depression, bulletin 36. New York: Social Science Research Council, 1937.

Connery, Robert C. *The Men's Clothing Code under N.R.A.* Studies in Administration, vol. 4. Chicago: Public Administration Service, 1938.

Cook, Paul B. *Academicians in Government from Roosevelt to Roosevelt*. New York: Garland Publishing, 1981.

Coser, Lewis M. *Men of Ideas*. New York: Free Press, 1965.

———. "American Trends." In Tom Bottomore and Robert A. Nisbet, eds., *A History of Sociological Analysis*. London: Heinemann Educational Books, 1978.

Cozzens, Susan E., and Gieryn, Thomas F. "Introduction: Putting Science back in

Society." In Susan E. Cozzens and Thomas F. Gieryn., eds. *Theories of Science in Society*. Bloomington: Indiana University Press, 1990.

———., eds. *Theories of Science in Society*. Bloomington: Indiana University Press, 1990.

Cravens, Hamilton C. "The Abandonment of Evolutionary Social Theory in America: The Impact of Academic Professionalization upon American Sociological Theory, 1890–1920." *American Studies* 12, no. 2 (1971): 5–20.

———. *The Triumph of Evolution: American Scientists and the Heredity-Environment Controversy, 1900–1940*. Philadelphia: University of Pennsylvania Press, 1978.

Craver, Earline. "Patronage and the Directions of Research in Economics: The Rockefeller Foundation in Europe, 1924–1938." *Minerva* 24 (1986): 205–22.

Crawford, Elizabeth T. "The Sociology of the Social Sciences: An International Bibliography." *Social Science Information* 9, no. 1 (1970): 79–93; 9, no. 4 (1970): 137–49; 10, no. 2 (1971): 121–34; 10, no. 5 (1971): 73–84; 11, no. 1 (1972): 99–112; 12, no. 2 (1973): 113–22; 12, no. 6 (1973): 93–102; 13, no. 3 (1974): 215–23; 14, no. 1 (1975): 169–90.

———. "The Sociology of the Social Sciences: A Trend Report and Bibliography." *Current Sociology* 19 (1971): 1–97.

Crick, Bernard. *The American Science of Politics: Its Origins and Conditions*. London: Routledge and Kegan Paul, 1959.

Critchlow, Donald T. *The Brookings Institution, 1916–1952: Expertise and the Public Interest in a Democratic Society*. DeKalb: Northern Illinois University Press, 1985.

Cross, Stephen J., and Albury, William R. "Walter B. Cannon, L. J. Henderson, and the Organic Analogy." *OSIRIS*, 2d ser., 3 (1987): 165–92.

Curti, Merle E. *American Scholarship in the Twentieth Century*. Cambridge: Harvard University Press, 1953.

———. *American Philanthropy Abroad: A History*. New Brunswick: Rutgers University Press, 1963.

Curti, Merle E., and Nash, Roderick. *Philanthropy in the Shaping of American Higher Education*. New Brunswick: Rutgers University Press, 1965.

Curtis, J. E., and Petras, J. W., eds. *The Sociology of Knowledge: A Reader*. London: Duckworth, 1970.

Dale, Roger. *The State and Educational Policy*. Philadelphia: Open University Press, 1989.

Dalfiume, Richard M. *Desegregation of the U.S. Armed Forces, 1939–1953*. Columbia: University of Missouri, 1969.

Devine, J. E. *Films as an Aid in Training Public Employees*. New York: Social Science Research Council, 1937.

Dibble, Vernon L. *The Legacy of Albion Small*. Chicago: University of Chicago Press, 1975.

Diner, S. J. *A City and Its Universities: Public Policy in Chicago, 1892–1919*. Chapel Hill: University of North Carolina Press, 1980.

Dittberner, Job L. *The End of Ideology and American Social Thought, 1930–1960*. Ann Arbor: UMI Research Press, 1979.

Dorfman, Joseph. *The Economic Mind in American Civilization.* 5 vols. New York: Viking, 1949.

Douglas, Jack. *The Impact of Sociology: Readings in the Social Sciences.* New York: Appleton-Century-Crofts, 1970.

————, ed. *Understanding Everyday Life.* Chicago: Aldine Publishing Co., 1970.

Duncan, Otis Dudley. *William F. Ogburn on Culture and Social Change.* Chicago: University of Chicago Press, 1964.

Dupree, A. Hunter. *Science in the Federal Government.* Cambridge: Harvard University Press, Belknap Press, 1959.

————. *Science in the Federal Government: A History of Policies and Activities to 1940.* New York: Harper, 1964.

Eakins, David W. "The Development of Corporal Liberal Policy Research in the United States, 1865–1965." Ph.D. diss., University of Wisconsin, 1966.

Easton, David. "Harold Lasswell: Policy Scientist." *Journal of Politics* 12 (August 1950): 450–77.

Easton, Lloyd D., and Guddat, Kurt H., eds. *Writings of the Young Marx on Philosophy and Society.* New York: Anchor Books, Doubleday and Co., 1967.

Education Policies Commission. *Research Memorandum on Education in the Depression.* Committee on Social Aspects of the Depression, bulletin 28. New York: Social Science Research Council, 1937.

Elias, Norbert. "Sociology of Knowledge: New Perspectives." *Sociology* 5, no. 2 (1971): 149–68; 5, no. 3 (1971): 355–70.

————. "Theory of Science and History: Comments on a Recent Discussion." *Economy and Society* 1 (1972): 117–34.

Ellul, Jacques. *The Technological Society.* New York: Knopf, 1964.

"Endowments in International Education." *Nature* 112 (1923): 220–21.

Epstein, Ralph. *Industrial Profits in the United States.* New York: National Bureau of Economic Research, 1934.

Faris, Robert E. L. *Chicago Sociology, 1920–1932.* San Francisco: Chandler Publishing Co., 1967.

"The Fat Boys." *New Republic*, February 2, 1927, pp. 500–501.

Feis, Herbert. *Research/Activities of the League of Nations.* Old Lime, Conn.: Old Lime Press, 1929.

Femia, Joseph V. *Gramsci's Political Thought: Hegemony, Consciousness, and the Revolutionary Process.* Oxford: Clarendon Press, 1987.

Fine, William F. "Progressive Evolutionism and American Sociology, 1890–1920." Ph.D. diss., University of Iowa, 1976.

Fisher, Donald. "The Impact of American Foundations on the Development of British University Education, 1900–1939." Ph.D. diss., University of California, Berkeley, 1977.

————. "The Rockefeller Foundation and the Development of Scientific Medicine in Great Britain." *Minerva* 16 (1978): 20–41.

————. "American Philanthropy and the Social Sciences in Great Britain, 1919–1939: The Reproduction of a Conservative Ideology." *Sociological Review* 28, no. 2 (1980): 277–315.

———. "The Role of Philanthropic Foundations in the Reproduction and Production of Hegemony: Rockefeller Foundations and the Social Sciences." *Sociology* 17, no. 2 (1983): 206–33.

———. "Philanthropic Foundations and the Social Sciences: A Response to Martin Bulmer." *Sociology* 18, no. 4 (1984): 580–87.

———. "The Scientific Appeal of Functionalism: Rockefeller Philanthropy and the Rise of Social Anthropology." *Anthropology Today* 2, no. 1 (February 1986): 5–8.

———. "Boundary Work: Toward a Model of the Relation Power/Knowledge." *Knowledge* 10, no. 2 (1988): 156–76.

———. "Boundary Work and Science: The Relation between Power and Knowledge." In Susan E. Cozzens and Thomas F. Gieryn, eds., *Theories of Science in Society*. Bloomington: Indiana University Press, 1990.

———. *The Social Sciences in Canada: Fifty Years of National Activity by the Social Science Federation of Canada*. Waterloo: Wilfrid Laurier University Press, 1991.

Fisher, Donald, and Gilgoff, Betty. "The Crisis in B. C. Public Education: The State and the Public Interest." In Terry Wotherspoon, ed., *The Political Economy of Canadian Schooling*. Toronto: Methuen, 1987.

Flash, Edward S., Jr. *Economic Advice and Presidential Leadership: The Council of Economic Advisers*. New York: Columbia University Press, 1965.

Fleming, Donald, and Bailyn, Bernard, eds. *The Intellectual Migration: Europe and America, 1930–1960*. Cambridge: Harvard University Press, 1969.

Fosdick, Raymond B. *The Old Savage in the New Civilization*. Garden City: Doubleday, Doran, and Co., 1928.

———. *The Story of the Rockefeller Foundation*. New York: Harper and Bros., 1952.

———. *Chronicle of a Generation: An Autobiography*. New York: Harper and Bros., 1958.

Foucault, Michel. *The Archeology of Knowledge*. Trans. A. M. Sheridan Smith. New York: Pantheon, Random House, 1972.

———. *Discipline and Punish*. New York: Vintage Books, 1979.

———. *Power/Knowledge: Selected Interviews and Other Writings, 1972–1977*. Ed. Colin Gordon. Brighton, Sussex: Harvester Press, 1980.

Francis, E. K. "American Sociology at the Crossroads." *Review of Politics* 12 (April 1950): 247–54.

———. "History of the Social Sciences: Some Reflections on the Re-integration of Social Science." *Review of Politics* 13 (July 1951): 354–74.

Frank, Lawrence K. "The Emancipation of Economics." *American Economic Review* 14 (March 1924): 37–38.

———. "The Wastage of Human Resources." Washington, D.C.: National Resources Planning Board, 1942. Mimeographed.

———. "Humane Conservation—The Story of Our Wasted Resources." Washington, D.C.: National Resources Planning Board, 1943. Mimeographed.

Frase, R. *Administration of Unemployment Insurance and Public Employment Service in Germany*. Committee on Social Security. New York: Social Science Research Council, 1938.

Frazier, Franklin E. *The Negro Family in Chicago*. Chicago: University of Chicago Press, 1932.

Freiberg, J. W., ed. *Critical Sociology*. New York: Irvington, 1979.

Furner, Mary O. *Advocacy and Objectivity: A Crisis in the Professionalization of American Social Science, 1865–1905*. Lexington: University Press of Kentucky, 1975.

Gaus, John M. "Social Science Research Council's Committee on Public Administration." *American Political Science Review* 29 (October 1935): 876–78.

Gaus, John M.; White, Leonard D.; and Dimock, Marshall E. *The Frontiers of Public Administration*. Chicago: University of Chicago Press, 1936.

Gaus, John M., and Wolcott, Leon. *Public Administration and the United States Department of Agriculture*. Studies in Administration, vol. 10. Chicago: Public Administration Service, 1940.

Geddes, P. "Proposed Co-Ordination of the Social Sciences." *Sociological Review* (London) 16 (January 1924): 54–65.

Gee, Wilson, ed. *Research in the Social Sciences: Its Fundamental Methods and Objectives*. New York: Macmillan, 1929.

———. *Social Science Research Organizations in American Universities and Colleges*. New York: D. Appleton-Century Co., 1934.

Geiger, Roger L. *To Advance Knowledge: The Growth of American Research Universities, 1900–1940*. New York: Oxford University Press, 1986.

Gettys, Luella C. *The Administration of Canadian Conditional Grants*. Studies in Administration, vol. 3. Chicago: Public Administration Service, 1938.

Giddens, Anthony. "Classical Social Theory and the Origins of Modern Sociology." *American Journal of Sociology* 81 (1976): 703–29.

———. *Control Problems in Social Theory: Action, Structure, and Contradiction in Social Analysis*. London: Macmillan, 1979.

Gieryn, Thomas F. "Boundary Work and the Demarcation of Science from Non-Science: Strains and Interests in Professional Ideologies of Scientists." *American Sociological Review* 48 (1983): 781–95.

Gieryn, Thomas F., and Figert, Anne E. "Ingredients for a Theory of Science in Society: O-Rings, Ice-Water, C-Clamp, Richard Feynman, and the Press." In Susan E. Cozzens and Thomas F. Gieryn, eds., *Theories of Science in Society*. Bloomington: Indiana University Press, 1990.

Gilbert, James. *Designing the Industrial State: The Intellectual Pursuit of Collectivism in America, 1880–1940*. Chicago: University of Chicago Press, 1972.

Gillespie, Richard P. "Manufacturing Knowledge: A History of the Hawthorne Experiments." Ph.D. diss., University of Pennsylvania, 1985.

Glenn, John M.; Brandt, Lilian; and Andrews, F. Emerson. *Russell Sage Foundation 1907–1946*. 2 vols. New York: Russell Sage Foundation, 1947.

Gold, David A.; Lo, Clarence Y. H.; and Wright, Erik Olin. "Recent Developments in Marxist Theories of the Capitalist State," pt 1. *Monthly Review*, October 1975, pp. 29–43.

———. "Recent Developments in Marxist Theories of the Capitalist State," pt 2. *Monthly Review*, November 1975, pp. 36–51.

Goldenweiser, Alexander. *History, Psychology, and Culture*. New York: Knopf, 1933.

———. "Future of the Social Sciences." *Sociology and Social Research* 19 (March 1935): 341–48.

Goldenweiser, E. G. "Research and Policy [Economics]." *American Statistical Association Journal* 39 (March 1944): 1–9.

Goodrich, Carter, et al. *Migrative and Economic Opportunity: The Report of the Study of Population Redistribution*. Philadelphia: University of Pennsylvania Press, 1936.

Goodson, I. F. *School Subjects and Curriculum Change*. London: Croom Helm, 1983.

———. *Social Histories of the Secondary Curriculum*. London: Falmer Press, 1985.

Gottschalk, Louis Reichental; Kluckhohm, Clyde; and Angell, Robert. "The Use of Personal Documents in History, Anthropology, and Sociology." Committee on Appraisal of Research, bulletin 53. New York: Social Science Research Council, 1945.

Gould, Stephen J. *The Mismeasure of Man*. New York: W. W. Norton, 1981.

Gouldner, Alvin W. *The Coming Crisis of Western Sociology*. New York: Avon Books, 1971.

———. *The Dialectic of Ideology and Technology: The Origins, Grammar, and Future of Ideology*. New York: Seabury Press, 1976.

———. *The Future of Intellectuals and the Rise of the New Class*. New York: Seabury Press, 1979.

Graham, George A. *Education for Public Administration*. New York: Social Science Research Council, 1941.

Gramsci, Antonio. *Letters from Prison*. Ed. and trans. Lynne Lawner. London: Cape, 1975.

———. *Selections from the Prison Notebooks*. Ed. and trans. Q. Hoare and G. Nowell-Smith. London: Lawrence and Wishart, 1971.

———. *Selections from Political Writings, 1910–1920*. Ed. and trans. Q. Hoare. London: Lawrence and Wishart, 1977.

———. *Selections from Political Writings, 1921–1926*. Ed. and trans. Q. Hoare. London: Lawrence and Wishart, 1978.

Grant, Margaret. *Preliminary Report on the Status of Industrial Pension Plans*. Committee on Social Security. Washington, D.C.: Social Science Research Council, 1936.

Greenstein, F. I., and Polsby, N., eds. *The Handbook of Political Science*. Vol. 1. Reading: Addison-Wesley, 1975.

Grossman, David M. "American Foundations and the Support of Economic Research, 1913–29." *Minerva* 20 (1982): 59–82.

Groves, E. R., and Ogburn, William Fielding. *American Marriage and Family Relationships*. New York: Henry Holt and Co., 1928.

Gruber, Carol Singer. *Mars and Minerva: World War I and the Uses of Higher Learning in America*. Baton Rouge: Louisiana State University Press, 1975.

Gutting, Gary, ed. *Paradigms and Revolutions*. London: University of Notre Dame Press, 1980.

Habermas, Jurgen. *Knowledge and Human Interests*. Boston: Beacon Press, 1971.

———. *Legitimation Crisis*. Boston: Beacon Press, 1975.

Hagendijk, Rob. "Structuration Theory, Constructivism, and Scientific Change." In Susan E. Cozzens and Thomas F. Gieryn, eds., *Theories of Science in Society*. Bloomington: Indiana University Press, 1990.

Hamilton, Peter. *Knowledge and Social Structure: An Introduction to the Classical Argument in the Sociology of Knowledge*. London: Routledge and Kegan Paul, 1974.

Hammersley, Martyn, and Atkinson, Paul. *Ethnography: Principles in Practice*. London: Tavistock Publishers, 1983.

Hansen, Alvin H. *After the War—Full Employment*. Washington, D.C.: Government Printing Office, January 1942.

Hansen, Donald A., and Johnson, V. A. "Educational Services." In M. E. Olsen and M. Micklin, eds., *Handbook of Applied Sociology*. New York: Praeger, 1981.

Haraway, Donna. "Animal Sociology and a Natural Economy of the Body Politic." *Signs* 4 (1978–79): 21–60.

Harris, Marvin. *The Rise of Anthropological Theory*. New York: Thomas Y. Crowell, 1968.

Harrison, Shelby M. *Social Conditions in an American City*. New York: Russell Sage Foundation, 1920.

Harrison, Shelby M., and Andrews, F. Emerson. *American Foundations for Social Welfare*. New York: Russell Sage Foundation, 1946.

Harvey, Charles E. "Robert S. Lynd, John D. Rockefeller, Jr., and Middletown." *Indiana Magazine of History* 79 (December 1983): 330–54.

Haskell, Thomas L. *The Emergence of Professional Social Science: The American Social Science Association and the Nineteenth Century Crisis of Authority*. Urbana: University of Illinois Press, 1977.

Hauser, P. M. "Are the Social Sciences Ready? Social Research Possible under the Aegis of a National Science Foundation." *American Sociological Review* 11 (August 1946): 379–84.

Hawley, Ellis W. *The Great War and the Search for a Modern Order, 1917–1933*. New York: St. Martin's Press, 1979.

Heaton, Herbert. *A Scholar in Action: Edwin F. Gay*. Cambridge: Harvard University Press, 1952.

Herskovitz, Melville J. *Acculturation: The Study of Culture Contact*. New York: J. J. Augustin, 1938.

———. *Franz Boas*. New York: Scribner, 1953.

Herteler, J. O. "The Sources and Methods of Historical Sociology." In Luther L. Bernard, ed., *The Fields and Methods of Sociology*. New York: Farrar and Rinehart, 1934.

Heyl, Barbara S. "The Harvard 'Pareto' Circle." *Journal of the History of the Behavioural Sciences* 4 (1968): 316–34.

Heyl, John D., and Heyl, Barbara S. "The Sumner-Porter Controversy at Yale: Pre-Paradigmatic Sociology and Institutional Crisis." *Sociological Inquiry* 46 (1976): 41–49.

Higham, John. "The Schism in American Scholarship." *American Historical Review* 72 (October 1966): 1–21.

Higham, John; Krieger, Leonard; and Gilbert, Felix. *History: The Development of Historical Studies in the United States*. Englewood Cliffs: Prentice Hall, 1965.

Hinkle, Roscoe C. *Founding Theory of American Sociology, 1881–1915*. London: Routledge and Kegan Paul, 1980.

Hinkle, Roscoe C., and Hinkle, Gisella J. *The Development of Modern Sociology*. New York: Random House, 1965.

Hoffman, John. *The Gramscian Challenge: Coercion and Consent in Marxist Political Theory*. Oxford: Basil Blackwell, 1984.

Hofstadter, Richard. *The Age of Reform*. New York: Knopf, 1955.

———. *Social Darwinism in American Thought*. Boston: Beacon Press, 1955.

Hogan, Michael J. *Informal Entente: The Private Structure of Co-operation in Anglo-American Economic Diplomacy, 1918–1928*. Columbia: University of Missouri Press, 1977.

Holzner, Bukart. *Reality Construction in Society*. Cambridge, Mass.: Schenken, 1968.

Holzner, Bukart, and Marx, John H. *Knowledge Application: The Knowledge System in Society*. Boston: Allyn and Bacon, 1979.

Homan, Paul T. "Economics in the War Period." *American Economic Review* 37 (December 1946): 855–71.

Hoover, Herbert. *The Memoirs of Herbert Hoover: The Cabinet and the Presidency, 1920–1933*. New York: Macmillan, 1952.

Horowitz, Irving Louis. *C. Wright Mills: An American Utopian*. New York: Free Press, 1983.

———, ed. *The Use and Abuse of Social Science*. New Brunswick: Transaction Books, 1971.

Horst, Paul, et al. *The Prediction of Personal Adjustment: A Survey of Logical Problems and Illustrative Application to Problems of Vocational Selection, School Success, Marriage, and Crime*. Committee on Social Adjustment, bulletin 48. New York: Social Science Research Council, 1941.

House, Floyd N. *The Range of Social Theory: A Survey of the Development, Literature, Tendencies, and Fundamental Problems of the Social Sciences*. New York: Henry Holt and Co., 1929.

———. *The Development of Sociology*. New York: McGraw-Hill, 1936.

Hovland, Carl I., et al. *Experiments in Mass Communication*. Vol. 3, *Studies in Social Psychology in World War II*. Princeton: Princeton University Press, 1949.

Howe, Barbara. "The Emergence of the Philanthropic Foundation as an American Social Institution, 1900–1920." Ph.D. diss., Cornell University, 1976.

Huber, Franz. *Changes in Employment Practices Resulting from the Operation of the Social Security Program*. Committee on Social Security. Washington, D.C.: Social Science Research Council, 1940.

Jacoby, Russell. *The Last Intellectuals: American Culture in the Age of Academe*. New York: Noonday Press, Farrar, Straus and Giroux, 1987.

Janowitz, Morris. *The Last Half-Century: Societal Changes and Politics in America*. Chicago: University of Chicago Press, 1978.

Jay, Martin. "The Frankfurt School in Exile." *Perspectives in American History* 6 (1972): 339–85.

———. *The Dialectical Imagination: A History of the Frankfurt School and the Institute of Social Research, 1923–1950*. Boston: Little, Brown and Co., 1973.

Jencks, Christopher, and Riesman, David. *The Academic Revolution*. Phoenix ed. Chicago: University of Chicago Press, 1977.

Jerome, Harry. *Migration and Business Cycles*. New York: National Bureau of Economic Research, 1926.

Jessop, Bob. *Theories of the State*. New York: New York University Press, 1983.

Joerg, W. L. G., ed. *Pioneer Settlement: Cooperative Studies by Twenty-Six Authors*. New York: American Geographical Society, 1932.

Johnson, Alvin S. *Pioneers' Progress: An Autobiography*. New York: Viking, 1952.

Johnson, Charles S. *The Negro in American Civilization*. New York: Henry Holt, 1930.

————. *Patterns of Negro Segregation*. London: V. Gollancz, 1944.

Johnson, Charles S., et al. *To Stem This Tide: A Survey of Racial Tension Areas in the United States*. Boston: Pilgrim Press, 1943.

Johnson, Guy Benton, and Johnson, Guion Griffis. *Research in Service to Society: The First Fifty Years of the Institute for Research in Social Science of the University of North Carolina*. Chapel Hill: University of North Carolina Press, 1980.

Joll, James. *Gramsci*. London: Fontana, 1977.

Jones, Alan H. *Philanthropic Foundations and the University of Michigan, 1922–1965*. Ann Arbor: University of Michigan School of Education, 1972.

Karabel, J. "The Sociology of Education: Perils and Possibilities." *American Sociologist* 14 (1979): 85–91.

Karabel, J., and Halsey, A. H., eds. *Power and Ideology in Education*. New York: Oxford University Press, 1977.

Kargon, Robert, and Hodes, Elizabeth. "Karl Compton, Isaiah Bowman, and the Politics of Science in the Great Depression." *ISIS* 76 (1985): 301–18.

Karl, Barry D. *Executive Reorganization and Reform in the New Deal*. Cambridge: Harvard University Press, 1963.

————. "The Power of Intellect and the Politics of Ideas." *Daedalus* 86 (1968): 1002–35.

————. "Presidential Planning and Social Science Research: Mr. Hoover's Experts." *Perspectives in American History* 3 (1969): 347–409.

————. *Charles E. Merriam and the Study of Politics*. Chicago: University of Chicago Press, 1974.

————. "Philanthropy, Policy Planning, and the Bureaucratization of the Democratic Ideal." *Daedalus* 105 (1976): 129–49.

————. "The Citizen and the Scholar: Ships that Crash in the Night." In William H. Kruskal, ed., *The Social Sciences: Their Nature and Uses*. Chicago: University of Chicago Press, 1982.

————. *The Uneasy State: The United States from 1915–1945*. Chicago: University of Chicago Press, 1983.

Karl, Barry D., and Katz, Stanley N. "The American Private Philanthropic Foundation and the Public Sphere, 1890–1930." *Minerva* 19 (1981): 236–70.

Keddie, N. "Classroom Knowledge." In M. F. D. Young, ed., *Knowledge and Control*. London: Collier-Macmillan, 1971.

Keppel, Frederick P. "Responsibility of Endowments in the Promotion of Knowledge." *American Philosophical Society Proceedings* 77, no. 4 (1937): 591–603.

Kerr, Clark. *Migration to the Seattle Labor Market Area*. Committee on Social Security. Washington, D.C.: Social Science Research Council, 1942.

Key, V. O., Jr. *The Administration of Federal Grants to States*. Studies in Administration, vol. 1. Chicago: Public Administration Service, 1937.

Kiger, Joseph C. "The Four Councils." *Educational Record* 39 (1958): 367–73.

———. *American Learned Societies*. Washington: Public Affairs Press, 1963.

———. "Foundation Support of Educational Innovation by Learned Societies, Councils, and Institutes." In Matthew B. Miles, ed., *Innovations in Education*. New York: Teachers College Press, 1964.

Kinchcloe, Samuel Clarence. *Research Memorandum on Religion in the Depression*. Committee on Social Aspects of the Depression, bulletin 33. New York: Social Science Research Council, 1937.

Kirkendall, Richard S. *Social Scientists and Farm Politics in the Age of Roosevelt*. Columbia: University of Missouri, 1966.

Knorr, Karin D.; Krohn, R.; and Whitley, R., eds. *The Social Process of Scientific Investigation*. Dordrecht: D. Reidel, 1981.

Knorr-Cetina, Karin. *The Manufacture of Knowledge: An Essay on the Constructivist and Contextual Nature of Science*. Oxford: Pergamon, 1981.

Knorr-Cetina, Karin, and Mulkay, Michael. *Science Observed: Perspectives on the Social Studies of Science*. London: Sage, 1983.

Kohler, Robert E. "The Management of Science: The Experience of Warren Weaver and the Rockefeller Foundation Programme in Molecular Biology." *Minerva* 14 (1976): 275–306.

———. "A Policy for the Advancement of Science: The Rockefeller Foundation, 1924–29." *Minerva* 16 (1978): 480–515.

———. "Science and Philanthropy: Wickliffe Rose and the International Education Board." *Minerva* 23 (1985): 75–95.

———. "Science, Foundations, and American Universities in the 1920s." *OSIRIS* 2d ser., 3 (1987): 135–64.

Kohlstedt, Sally Gregory. *The Formation of the American Scientific Community*. Urbana: University of Illinois Press, 1976.

Kolko, Gabriel. *The Triumph of Conservatism: A Reinterpretation of American History*. New York: Free Press, 1967.

Koontz, L. K. "Social Sciences in the National Science Foundation." *Pacific Historical Review* 15 (March 1945): 1–30.

Kroeber, A. L.; Canning, J. B.; Terman, L. M.; and Ogburn, William Fielding. *How Far Are Forces Controllable?* San Francisco: Social Science Research Council of the Pacific Coast, 1933.

Kruskal, William H., ed. *The Social Sciences: Their Nature and Uses*. Chicago: University of Chicago Press, 1982.

Kuhlman, Augustus Frederick. "Social Science Research Council: Its Origin and Objectives." *Social Forces* 6 (June 1928): 583–88.

———. "Social Science Research Council and the Preservation of Source Materials." *Library Quarterly* 3 (July 1933): 229–47.

———. *Committee on Survey of Research on Crime and Criminal Justice*. Social Science Research Council. New York: H. W. Wilson Co., 1929.

Kuhn, Thomas S. *The Structure of Scientific Revolutions*. 1962. Enl. ed. Chicago: University of Chicago Press, 1970.

————. *The Essential Tension*. Chicago: University of Chicago Press, 1977.

Kuklick, Henrika. "A 'Scientific Revolution': Sociological Theory in the United States, 1930–1945." *Sociological Inquiry* 43 (1973): 3–22.

————. "The Organization of Social Science in the United States." *American Quarterly* 28 (1976): 124–41.

————. "Boundary Maintenance in American Sociology: Limitations to Academic 'Professionalization'." *Journal of the History of the Behavioural Sciences* 16 (1980): 201–19.

————. "Restructuring the Past: Towards an Appreciation of the Social Context of Social Science." *Sociology Quarterly* 21 (1980): 5–21.

Kulp, Clarence Arthur. *Social Insurance Coordination; An Analysis of German and British Organization*. Committee on Social Security. Washington D.C.: Social Science Research Council, 1938.

Kurtz, Lester R. *Evaluating Chicago Sociology*. Chicago: University of Chicago Press, 1984.

Lagemann, Ellen Condliffe. *Private Power for the Public Good: A History of the Carnegie Foundation for the Advancement of Teaching*. Middletown: Wesleyan University Press, 1983.

————. "A Philanthropic Foundation at Work: Gunnar Myrdal's *American Dilemma* and the Carnegie Corporation." *Minerva* 25 (1987): 441–70.

————. *The Politics of Knowledge: The Carnegie Corporation, Philanthropy, and Public Policy*. Middletown: Wesleyan University Press, 1989.

Landis, Paul H. *Loss of Rural Manpower to War Industry through Migration*. Committee on Social Security. Washington, D.C.: Social Science Research Council, 1943.

Landsdale, Robert T., et al. *The Administration of Old Age Assistance*. Studies in Administration, vol. 6. Chicago: Public Administration Service, 1939.

Lane, F. C. "Social Sciences and the Humanities." *American Philosophical Society Proceedings* 92, no. 5 (1948): 356–62.

Lasch, Christopher. *The New Radicalism in America, 1889–1963: The Intellectual as a Social Type*. New York: Knopf, 1965.

————. *The Agony of the American Left*. New York: Knopf, 1967.

Laski, Harold J. *The Dangers of Obedience and Other Essays*. London: Harper and Bros., 1930.

Lasswell, Harold D. *Propaganda Techniques in the World War*. 1930. New York: Knopf, 1927.

————. *World Politics and Personal Insecurity*. Chicago: University of Chicago Press, 1934.

————. *Propaganda and Promotional Activities*. Minneapolis: University of Minnesota Press, 1935.

————. *The Analysis of Political Behavior: An Empirical Approach*. New York: Oxford University Press, 1948.

————. *Politics: Who Gets What, When, How*. New York: P. Smith, 1950.

————. *Psychopathology and Politics*. New York: Viking, 1960.

————. "The Cross-Disciplinary Manifold: The Chicago Prototype." In Albert Lepawsky and Edward Beulring, eds., *Search for World Order*. New York: Appleton-Century-Crofts, 1971.

Lasswell, Harold D.; Casey, Ralph D.; and Smith, Bruce Lannes. *Propaganda and Promotional Activities: An Annotated Bibliography*. Minneapolis: University of Minnesota Press, 1935.

Lasswell, Harold D., and Kaplan, Abraham. *Power and Society: A Framework for Political Enquiry*. New Haven: Yale University Press, 1950.

Lasswell, Harold D., and Lerner, Daniel, eds. *The Policy Sciences: Recent Developments in Scope and Method*. Stanford: Stanford University Press, 1951.

Latour, Bruno. *Science in Action: How to Follow Scientists and Engineers through Society*. Cambridge: Harvard University Press, 1987

Latour Bruno, and Woolgar, Steve. *Laboratory Life: The Construction of Scientific Facts*. 2d ed. 1979. Princeton: Princeton University Press, 1986.

Lazarsfeld, Paul L. "The Sociology of Empirical Social Research." *American Sociological Review* 27 (1962): 757–67.

Lazarsfeld, Paul L., and Thielens, Roger, Jr. *The Academic Mind: Social Scientists in Times of Crisis*. Glencoe: Free Press, 1958.

Lear, Linda J. *Harold L. Ickes: The Aggressive Progressive, 1874–1933*. New York: Garland Publishing, 1981.

Lee, Ulysses. *The Employment of Negro Troops*. Washington, D.C.: Government Printing Office, 1966.

Lengermann, Patricia M. "The Founding of the American Sociological Review: The Anatomy of a Rebellion." *American Sociological Review* 44 (1979): 185–98.

Lerner, Daniel, ed. *The Human Meaning of the Social Sciences*. Cleveland: Meridian Books, World Publishing Co., 1959.

Lewis, David J., and Smith, Richard L. *American Sociology and Pragmatism: Mead, Chicago Sociology, and Symbolic Intervention*. Chicago: University of Chicago Press, 1980.

Lieberman, Jethro. *The Tyranny of the Experts: How Professionals Are Closing the Open Society*. New York: Walker, 1970.

Lindblom, Charles, and Cohen, David K. *Usable Knowledge: Social Science and Social Problem Solving*. New Haven: Yale University Press, 1979.

Lindeman, Edward C. *Wealth and Culture: A Study of 100 Foundations and Community Trusts and Their Operation during the Decade, 1921–1930*. New York: Harcourt, Brace and Co., 1936.

Lomax, Elizabeth. "The Laura Spelman Rockefeller Memorial: Some of Its Contributions to Early Research in Child Development." *Journal of the History of the Behavioural Sciences* 13 (1977): 283–93.

Lukacs, George. *History of Class Consciousness*. Cambridge: MIT Press, 1971.

Lundberg, George A., ed. *Trends in American Sociology*. New York: Harper and Bros., 1929.

Lynch, Frederick. "Social Theory and the Progressive Era." *Theory and Society* 4 (Summer 1977): 195–210.

Lynd, Robert S. *Knowledge for What? The Place of Social Science in American Culture*. Princeton: Princeton University Press, 1939.

Lynd, Robert S., and Lynd, Helen M. *Middletown*. New York: Harcourt Brace, 1929.

———. *Middletown in Transition*. New York: Harcourt Brace, 1937.

Lyons, Eugene. *Herbert Hoover: A Biography*. Garden City: Doubleday and Co., 1964.

Lyons, Gene Martin. *The Uneasy Partnership: Social Science and the Federal Government in the Twentieth Century*. New York: Russell Sage Foundation, 1969.

Lyons, Gene Martin, and Morton, Louis. *Schools for Strategy: Education and Research in National Security Affairs*. New York: Praeger, 1965.

McCall, G. J., and Weber, G. H., eds. *Social Sciences and Public Policy: The Roles of Academic Disciplines in Policy Analysis*. London: Associated Faculty Press, 1984.

McCarthy, K. D. "American Cultural Philanthropy: Past, Present, and Future." *Annals of the American Academy of Political and Social Sciences* 471 (January 1984): 13–26.

McCormick, T. C. "Development of Cooperative Social Research in Leading Northern Universities; and Its Status in Colleges and Universities of the Southwest." *Southwest Social Sciences Quarterly* 13 (March 1933): 368–71.

McCune, Robert Paul. "Origins and Development of the National Science Foundation and Its Division of Social Sciences, 1945–61." Ed.D. diss., Ball State University, 1971.

McDiarmid, John. "The Mobilization of Social Scientists." In Leonard D. White, ed., *Civil Service in Wartime*. Chicago: University of Chicago Press, 1945.

McEntire, Davis, ed. *Pacific Coast, 1944–1950*. Pacific Coast Committee on Social Statistics. Berkeley: Social Science Research Council, 1952.

MacIver, Robert M. "Intellectual Cooperation in the Social Sciences." *American Philosophical Society Proceedings* 90, no. 4 (1946): 309–13.

———. *As a Tale That is Told*. Chicago: University of Chicago Press, 1968.

Maclup, Fritz. *The Production and Distribution of Knowledge in the United States*. Princeton: Princeton University Press, 1962.

MacNeil, Douglas Harrison. *Seven Years of Unemployment Relief in New Jersey, 1930–1936*. Committee on Social Security. Washington, D.C.: Social Science Research Council, 1938.

Macrae, Duncan, Jr. *The Social Function of Social Science*. New Haven: Yale University Press, 1976.

Madge, John. *The Origins of Scientific Sociology*. New York: Free Press, 1962.

Magat, Richard. *The Ford Foundation at Work: Philanthropic Choices, Methods, and Styles*. New York: Plenum Publishing Corporation, 1979.

Mandelbaum, Maurice. *The Problem of Historical Knowledge*. New York: Liveright Publishing Corporation, 1938.

Mangold, G. B. "Sociologists and the Public." *Sociology and Social Research* 22 (March 1938): 303–11.

Manicas, Peter T. *The Death of the State*. New York: Putnams, 1974.

———. *A History and Philosophy of the Social Sciences*. Oxford: Basil Blackwell, 1987.

Mannheim, Karl. "Review." Stuart A. Rice, ed., *Methods in Social Science* 38 (September 1932): 273–82.

———. *Ideology and Utopia: An Introduction to the Sociology of Knowledge*. Trans.

Louis Wirth and Edward Shils. New York: Harvest Books, Harcourt, Brace and World, 1936.

Marks, Russel. "Legitimating Industrial Capitalism." In Robert F. Arnove, ed. *Philanthropy and Cultural Imperialism: The Foundations at Home and Abroad.* Bloomington: Indiana University Press, 1982.

Martin, Wilfred B. W. "Neglected Aspects in the Sociology of Education in Canada." *Canadian Journal of Education* 3, no. 4 (1978): 18–30.

Martindale, Don. *The Nature and Types of Sociological Theory.* Cambridge: Houghton Mifflin Co., 1960.

Marx, Karl. *The Economic and Philosophic Manuscripts of 1844.* Ed. Dirk J. Struik, trans. Martin Milligan. New York: International Publishers, 1964.

———. "The German Ideology Extracts." In Lloyd D. Easton and Kurt H. Guddat, eds., *Writings of the Young Marx on Philosophy and Society.* New York: Anchor Books, Doubleday and Co., 1967.

———. *The Grundrisse.* Ed. and trans. David McLellan. New York: Harper and Row, 1971.

———. *The German Ideology.* London: Lawrence and Wishart, 1974.

Matscheck, Walter. *The Administration of Unemployment Compensation in Wisconsin and New Hampshire.* Mimeograph 52. Chicago: Public Administration Service, 1936.

———. *The Administration of Unemployment Compensation Benefits in Wisconsin.* Chicago: Public Administration Service, 1937.

———. *Administration and Unemployment Insurance and Public Employment Service in Great Britain.* Committee on Social Security. New York: Social Science Research Council, 1938.

Matscheck, Walter, and Atkinson, Raymond Cumings. *Problems and Procedures of Unemployment Compensation in the States.* Chicago: Public Administration Service, 1939.

Matthews, Fred H. *Quest for an American Sociology: Robert E. Park and the Chicago School.* Montreal: McGill-Queens University Press, 1977.

May, Dean L. *From New Deal to New Economics: The Liberal Response to the Recession.* New York: Garland Publishing, 1981.

May, Mark Arthur. "A Retrospective View of the Institute of Human Relations at Yale." *Behavior Science Notes* 6 (1971): 141–72.

May, Mark Arthur, and Doob, Leonard W. *Competition and Cooperation.* Bulletin 25. New York: Social Science Research Council, 1937.

Merriam, Charles E. "The Present State of the Study of Politics." *American Political Science Review* 15 (1921): 173–85.

———. "Some of the Vital Problems of Political Research." *American Political Science Review* 16 (1922): 315–21.

———. *New Aspects of Politics.* Chicago: University of Chicago Press, 1925.

———. *The Role of Politics in Social Change.* New York: New York University Press, 1936.

———. "The National Resources Planning Board." *Public Administration Review,* Winter 1941, pp. 116–21.

———. "The Education of Charles Merriam." In Leonard D. White, ed., *The Future of Government in the United States*. Chicago: University of Chicago Press, 1942.

———. "The National Resources Planning Board: A Chapter in American Planning Experience." *American Political Science Review* 38 (1944): 1075–88.

Merriam, Charles E., and Gosnell, Harold F. *Non-Voting: Causes and Methods of Control*. Chicago: University of Chicago Press, 1924.

Merriam, John C., and Weaver, W. "Most Important Methods of Promoting Research as Seen by Research Foundations and Institutions." *American Philosophical Society Proceedings* 77, no. 4 (1937): 605–10.

Miles, Matthew B., ed. *Innovations in Education*. New York: Teachers College Press, 1964.

Miller, Robert Moats. *Harry Emersen Fosdick: Preacher, Pastor, Prophet*. New York: Oxford University Press, 1985.

Millet, John D. *The Works Progress Administration in New York City*. Studies in Administration, vol. 2. Chicago: Public Administration Service, 1938.

———. *The Process of Organization of Government Planning*. New York: Columbia University Press, 1947.

Milliband, Ralph A. *The State in Capitalist Society*. New York: Basic Books, 1969.

Mills, C. Wright. *The Sociological Imagination*. London: Oxford University Press, 1959.

Mills, Frederick C. *Economic Tendencies in the United States: Aspects of Pre-War and Post-War Changes*. New York: National Bureau of Economic Research, 1932.

Mitchell, Lucy Sprague. *Two Lives: The Story of Wesley Clair Mitchell and Myself*. New York: Simon and Schuster, 1953.

Mitchell, Wesley C. "Third Annual Report of the Chairman." In *Third Annual Report of the Social Science Research Council, 1926–27*. New York: Social Science Research Council, 1927.

———. "Research in the Social Sciences." In Leonard D. White, ed., *The New Social Science*. Chicago: University of Chicago Press, 1930.

———. "The National Bureau's First Quarter Century." In *Twenty-Fifth Annual Report*. New York: National Bureau of Economic Research, 1945.

———. *The Backward Art of Spending Money and Other Essays*. 1937. New York: Augustus M. Kelley, 1950.

Moley, Raymond. *The First New Deal*. New York: Harcourt, Brace, and World, 1966.

Morawaski, J. G. "Organizing Knowledge and Behaviour at Yale's Institute of Human Relations." *ISIS* 77 (1986): 219–42.

Mosher, Frederick C. *Democracy and the Public Service*. New York: Oxford University Press, 1968.

Moulton, Harold G. "Co-operation in Social Science Research." In Leonard D. White, ed., *The New Social Science*. Chicago: University of Chicago Press, 1930.

———. *Income and Economic Progress*. Washington, D.C.: Brookings Institution, 1935.

———. *The Formation of Capital*. Washington, D.C.: Brookings Institution, 1936.

Moulton, Harold G.; Leven, Maurice; and Warburton, Clark. *America's Capacity to Consume*. Washington, D.C.: Brookings Institution, 1934.

Mowrer, Ernest. *Family Disorganization*. Chicago: University of Chicago Press, 1927.

Mulkay, Michael. *Science and the Sociology of Knowledge*. London: George Allen and Unwin, 1979.

———. *The Word and the World: Explorations in the Form of Sociological Analysis*. London: George Allen and Unwin, 1985.

Mullins, Nicholas. *Theories and Theory Groups in Contemporary American Sociology*. New York: Harper and Row, 1973.

Murchison, C., ed. *A History of Psychology in Autobiography*. New York: Russell and Russell, 1961.

Murdoch, G. P. "Cross-Cultural Survey by the Institute of Human Relations, Yale University." *American Sociological Review* 5 (1940): 361–70.

Myrdal, Gunnar. *An American Dilemma: The Negro Problem and Modern Democracy*. New York: Harper and Bros., 1944.

National Bureau of Economic Research. *Business Cycles and Unemployment*. New York, 1923.

———. *Seasonal Operations of the Construction Industries: The Facts and The Remedies*. New York, 1924.

National Planning Board. *Final Report, 1933–1934*. Washington, D.C.: Government Printing Office, 1934.

National Resources Committee. *Relation of the Federal Government to Research*. Vol. 1 of *Research—A National Resource*. Washington, D.C., 1938.

———. *Industrial Research*. Vol. 2 of *Research—A National Resource*. Washington, D.C., 1940.

———. *Business Research*. Vol. 3 of *Research—A National Resource*. Washington, D.C., 1941.

National Resources Planning Board. *Post-War Planning—Full Employment, Security, Building America*. Washington, D.C., September 1942.

———. *Security, Work, and Relief Policies*. Washington, D.C., 1942.

Neilsen, Waldemar. *The Big Foundations*. New York: Columbia University Press, 1972.

Neuberger, Otto. *Administration of Short-Term Benefits in Germany*. Committee on Social Security. Washington, D.C.: Social Science Research Council, 1938.

Nichols, Roy F. "History and the Social Science Research Council." *American Historical Review* 50 (April 1945): 491–99.

———. "History of the Science of Society: The Problem of Synthesis." In *Social Sciences at Mid-Century*. Minneapolis: University of Minnesota Press, 1952.

Nisbet, Robert A. *The Quest for Community*. New York: Oxford University Press, 1953.

Noble, David N. *The Progressive Mind, 1890–1917*. Chicago: Rand McNally, 1970.

———. *America by Design: Science, Technology, and the Rise of Corporate Capitalism*. New York: Knopf, 1977.

Nourse, Edwin, G. *Agricultural Economics*. Chicago: University of Chicago Press, 1916.

———. *American Agriculture and the European Market*. New York: McGraw-Hill, 1924.

————. *Price Making in a Democracy*. Washington, D.C.: Brookings Institution, 1944.

————. *Economics in the Public Service*. New York: Harcourt Brace, 1953.

Nourse, Edwin G., et al. *America's Capacity to Produce*. Washington, D.C.: Brookings Institution, 1934.

Nourse, Edwin G., and Drury, Horace B. *Industrial Price Policies and Economic Progress*. Washington, D.C.: Brookings Institution, 1938.

Oberschall, Anthony, ed. *The Establishment of Empirical Sociology*. New York: Harper and Row, 1972.

Odum, Howard Washington. "Notes on Recent Trends in the Application of the Social Sciences." *Social Forces* 11 (May 1933): 477–88.

————. *American Regionalism: A Cultural-Historical Approach to National Integration*. New York: Henry Holt, 1938.

————. *Race and Rumors of Race*. Chapel Hill: University of North Carolina Press, 1943.

————. *American Sociology: The Study of Sociology in the United States through 1950*. New York: Longman, 1951.

————. *Southern Regions of the United States*. Chapel Hill: University of North Carolina Press, 1936; New York: Agathon Press, 1969.

Ogburn, William Fielding. *Social Change with Respect to Culture and Original Nature*. New York: B. W. Heubsch, 1922.

Ogburn, William Fielding, and Goldenweiser, Alexander, eds. *The Social Sciences and Their Interrelations*. Boston: Houghton and Mifflin Co., 1927.

Ogg, F. A. *Research in the Humanistic and Social Sciences*. New York: Century, 1928.

————. *Research in the Humanities and Social Sciences*. Twentieth Century Co. N.p., 1934.

Oleson, Alexander, and Voss, John, eds. *The Organization of Knowledge in Modern America, 1860–1920*. Baltimore: Johns Hopkins University Press, 1979.

Olsen, M. E., and Micklin, M., eds. *Handbook of Applied Sociology*. New York: Praeger, 1981.

Oppenheimer, Franz. "History and Sociology." In William Fielding Ogburn and Alexander Goldenweiser, eds., *The Social Sciences and Their Interrelations*. Boston: Houghton Mifflin Co., 1927.

"The Organization of Science." *Nature* 140 (1937): 521–23.

Orlans, Harold. "Social Science Research Policies in the United States." *Minerva* 9 (1971): 7–31.

————. "The Advocacy of Social Science in Europe and America." *Minerva* 14 (1976): 6–32.

————. "Academic Social Scientists and the Presidency: From Wilson to Nixon." *Minerva* 24 (1986): 172–204.

Panunzio, C. "Social Science and Societal Planning." *Sociology and Social Research* 19 (March 1935): 324–34.

Parascandola, John. "Organismic and Holistic Concepts in the Thought of L. J. Henderson." *Journal of the History of Biology* 4 (1971): 63–113.

Park, Robert E., and Burgess, Ernest W. *Introduction to the Science of Sociology* (1921). 2d ed. Chicago: University of Chicago Press, 1924.

Parsons, Talcott. *The Structure of Social Action*. New York: McGraw-Hill, 1937.
———. "Sociology, 1941–1946." *American Journal of Sociology* 53 (1947): 245–57.
———. "On Building Social System Theory: A Personal History." *Daedalus* 99 (1970): 826–81.
Peterson, Peter J. *Foundations, Private Giving, and Public Policy*. Chicago: University of Chicago Press, 1972.
Polenberg, Richard. *Reorganizing Roosevelt's Government, 1936–1939: The Controversy over Executive Reorganization*. Cambridge: Harvard University Press, 1966.
———. *War and Society: The United States, 1941–1945*. Westport: Greenwood Press, 1980.
Popper, Karl R. *The Logic of Scientific Discovery*. New York: Harper and Row, 1965.
Poulantzas, Nicos. *Classes in Contemporary Capitalism*. London: New Left Books, 1975.
———. "The Political Crisis and the Crisis of the State." In J. W. Freiberg, ed., *Critical Sociology*. New York: Irvington, 1979.
President's Committee on Administrative Management. *Report of the Committee, with Studies of Administrative Management in the Federal Government*. Washington, D.C.: Government Printing Office, 1937.
Pressman, Jack D. "Uncertain Promise: Psychosurgery and the Development of Scientific Psychiatry, 1935–1955." Ph.D. diss., University of Pennsylvania, 1986.
Price, Don K. *Government and Science*. New York: New York University Press, 1954.
Rabinow, Paul. *The Foucault Reader*. New York: Pantheon, 1985.
Ravetz, Jerome R. *Scientific Knowledge and Its Social Problems*. New York: Oxford University Press, 1971.
Ray, Donald P., ed. *Trends in Social Science*. New York: Philosophical Library, 1961.
Recent Economic Changes in the United States. Report of the Committee on Recent Economic Changes of the President's Conference on Unemployment. New York: McGraw-Hill, 1929.
Recent Social Trends in the United States. Report of the President's Research Committee on Social Trends, 2 vols. New York: McGraw-Hill, 1933.
Reckless, Walter C. *The Etiology of Delinquent and Criminal Behavior: Planning Report for Research*. New York: Social Science Research Council, 1943.
Redfield, Robert. "Anthropology: A Natural Science?" *Social Forces* 4 (June 1926): 715–21.
Reed, James. "Robert M. Yerkes and the Mental Testing Movement." In Michael M. Sokal, ed. *Psychological Testing and American Society, 1890–1930*. New Brunswick: Rutgers University Press, 1990.
Reeves, Thomas C., ed. *Foundations under Fire*. Ithaca: Cornell University Press, 1970.
Reingold, Nathan, ed. *The Sciences in the American Context: New Perspectives*. Washington, D.C.: Smithsonion Institution Press, 1979.
"Research in the Modern State." *Nature* 127 (1931): 559–61.
Rex, J. A. "The Spread of the Pathology of Natural Science to the Social Sciences." *Social Review Monogram* 16 (1970): 143–62.

Rice, Stuart A. *Quantitative Methods in Politics*. New York: Knopf, 1928.

————, ed. *Methods in Social Science: A Case Book*. Chicago: University of Chicago Press, 1931.

Rice, Stuart A., and Green, M. "Interlocking Memberships of Social Science Societies." *American Statistical Association Journal* 24 (September 1929): 303–6.

Richardson, John G., ed. *Handbook of Theory and Research for the Sociology of Education*. Westport: Greenwood Press, 1987.

Richardson, Theresa R. *The Century of the Child: The Mental Hygiene Movement and Social Policy in the United States and Canada*. Albany: State University of New York Press, 1989.

Rogow, Arnold A., ed. *Politics, Personality, and Social Science in the Twentieth Century: Essays in Honor of Harold D. Lasswell*. Chicago: University of Chicago Press, 1969.

Ross, Dorothy. *G. Stanley Hall: The Psychologist as Prophet*. Chicago: University of Chicago Press, 1972.

————. "The Development of the Social Sciences." In Alexander Oleson and John Voss, eds., *The Organization of Knowledge in Modern America, 1860–1920*. Baltimore: Johns Hopkins University Press, 1976.

Rucker, Darnell. *The Chicago Pragmatists*. Minneapolis: University of Minnesota Press, 1969.

Ruml, Beardsley. "Recent Trends in Social Science." In Leonard D. White, ed., *The New Social Science*. Chicago: University of Chicago Press, 1930.

Rush, G. B.; Christensen, E.; and Malcomson, J. "Lament for a Notion: The Development of Social Science in Canada." *Canadian Review of Sociology and Anthropology* 18, no. 4 (1981): 519–44.

Russell Sage Foundation. *Effective Use of Social Science Research in the Federal Services*. New York, 1950.

"Russell Sage Foundation." *Social Service Review* 23 (June 1949): 247–48.

Russett, Cynthia E. *The Concept of Equilibrium in American Social Thought*. New Haven: Yale University Press, 1966.

Rutkoff, Peter M., and Scott, William B. *New School: A History of the New School for Social Research*. New York: Free Press, 1986.

Salzman, Jack, ed. *Philanthropy and American Society: Selected Papers*. American Cultural Studies. New York: Columbia University, 1987.

Samelson, Franz. "Putting Psychology on the Map: Ideology and Intelligence Testing." In A. R. Buss, ed., *Psychology in a Social Context*. New York: Irvington, 1979.

————. "Organizing for the Kingdom of Behavior: Academic Battles and Organizational Policies in the Twenties." *Journal of the History of the Behavioural Sciences* 21 (1985), 33–47.

Sanderson, Ezra Dwight. *Research Memorandum on Rural Life in the Depression*. Committee on Social Aspects of the Depression, bulletin 34. New York: Social Science Research Council, 1937.

Satariano, William A. "Immigration and the Popularization of the Social Sciences, 1920–1930." *Journal of the History of the Behavioural Sciences* 15 (1979): 310–20.

Saunders, Charles B., Jr. *The Brookings Institution: A Fifty Year History*. Washington, D.C.: Brookings Institution, 1966.

Schlesinger, Arthur M., Jr. *The Crisis of the Old Order*. Boston: Houghton Mifflin Co., 1957.

―――. *The Coming of the New Deal*. Boston: Houghton Mifflin Co., 1959.

Schlossman, Stephen C. "Philanthropy and the Gospel of Child Development." *History of Education Quarterly* 21 (Fall 1981): 273–99.

Schulman, Jay; Brown, Carol; and Kahn, Roger. "Report on the Russell Sage Foundation." *Insurgent Sociologist* 11 (Summer 1972): 2–34.

Schwendinger, Herman, and Schwendinger, Julia R. *The Sociologists of the Chair: A Radical Analysis of the Formative Years of North American Sociology (1883–1922)*. New York: Basic Books, 1974.

Sears, Robert Richardson. *Survey of Objective Studies of Psychoanalytic Concepts*. Report prepared for the Committee on Social Adjustment. New York: Social Science Research Council, 1943.

Seligman, Edwin R. A., and Johnson, Alvin S., eds. *Encyclopedia of the Social Sciences*. 15 vols. New York: Macmillan, 1930–35.

Sellin, Johan Thorsten. *Research Memorandum on Crime in the Depression*. Committee on Social Aspects of the Depression, bulletin 27. New York: Social Science Research Council, 1937.

―――. *Culture, Conflict, and Crime*. Subcommittee on Delinquency of the Committee on Personality and Culture, bulletin 41. New York: Social Science Research Council, 1938.

Seybold, Peter James. "The Development of American Political Sociology—A Case Study of the Ford Foundation's Role in the Production of Knowledge." Ph.D. diss., State University of New York, 1978.

Shannon, Fred Albert. *An Appraisal of Walter Prescott Webb's "The Great Plains: A Study in Institutions and Environment."* Panel discussion and commentary, bulletin 46. New York: Social Science Research Council, 1940.

Sharp, R., and Green, A. *Education and Social Control*. London: Routledge and Kegan Paul, 1975.

Shaw, Clifford R. *The Jack-Roller: A Delinquent Boy's Own Story*. Chicago: University of Chicago Press, 1930.

―――. *The Natural History of a Delinquent Career*. Chicago: University of Chicago Press, 1931.

Shaw, Clifford R., and McKay, Henry D. *Social Factors in Juvenile Delinquency*. National Commission on Law Observance and Enforcement, Report on the Causes of Crime, vol. 2. Washington, D.C.: Government Printing Office, 1931.

Sherif, M., and Sherif, C., eds. *Interdisciplinary Relationships in the Social Sciences*. Chicago: Aldine Publishing Co., 1969.

Shils, Edward. "Tradition, Ecology, and Institution in the History of Sociology." *Daedalus* 99 (1970): 760–825.

―――. *The Calling of Sociology and Other Essays on the Pursuit of Learning*. Chicago: University of Chicago Press, 1980.

Shore, Marlene. *The Science of Social Redemption: McGill, the Chicago School, and the Origins of Social Research in Canada*. Toronto: University of Toronto Press, 1987.

Shotwell, James T. *Intelligence and Politics*. New York: Century Co., 1921.

Shoup, Laurence H., and Minter, William. *Imperial Brains Trust: The Council on Foreign Relations and United States Foreign Policy*. New York: Monthly Review Press, 1977.

Sibley, Elbridge. *Support for Independent Scholarship and Research*. New York: Social Science Research Council, 1951.

———. *The Education of Sociologists in the United States*. New York: Russell Sage Foundation, 1963.

———. *Social Science Research Council: The First Fifty Years*. New York: Social Science Research Council, 1974.

Silva, Edward T., and Slaughter, Sheila A. *Serving Power: The Making of the Academic Social Science Expert*. Westport: Greenwood Press, 1984.

Simey, T. S. *Social Science and Social Purpose*. London: Constable and Co., 1968.

Simon, Roger. *Gramsci's Political Thought*. London: Lawrence and Wishart, 1982.

Skocpol, Theda. "Political Responses to Capitalist Crisis: Neo-Marxist Theories of the State and the Case of the New Deal." *Politics and Society* 10 (1980): 155–99.

Small, Albion W. "A Decade of Sociology." *American Journal of Sociology* 11 (1906): 1–10.

———. "Relation of Sociology to Other Sciences." *American Journal of Sociology* 12 (1907): 11–31.

———. *The Meaning of Social Science*. Chicago: University of Chicago Press, 1910.

———. "Fifty Years of Sociology in the United States." *American Journal of Sociology* 21 (1916): 721–864.

———. *Origins of Sociology*. Chicago: University of Chicago Press, 1924.

Smith, Dennis. *The Chicago School: A Liberal Critique of Capitalism*. New York: St. Martin's Press, 1988.

Smith, Laurence D. *Behaviorism and Logical Positivism: A Reassessment of the Alliance*. Stanford: Stanford University Press, 1986.

Smith, Thomas V., and White, Leonard D., eds. *Chicago: An Experiment in Social Science Research*. Chicago: University of Chicago Press, 1929.

Social Science Research Center, ed. *Social Sciences at Mid-Century*. Minneapolis: University of Minnesota Press, 1952.

Social Science Research Conference of the Pacific Coast. Proceedings and Minutes. San Francisco, 1930–46.

Social Science Research Council. *Annual Report*. Chicago, 1924–26. New York, 1927–.

———. *Social Science Abstracts*. No. 1. Menasha, Wis., 1929.

———. *Annual Report of the Chairman of the Pacific Coast Regional Committee of the Social Science Research Council*. San Francisco, 1930–46.

———. *Agenda for the 4th Regular Meeting, and for the Meeting of the Executive Committee of the Social Science Research Conference of the Pacific Coast*. San Francisco, 1931.

———. *Decennial Report, 1923–1933*. New York, 1934.

———. *Program of Research in International Relations, "Survey of the Economic, Social, and Political Relations of Canada and the United States." Outline of Plan*. New York, 1934.

————. *Survey of the Economic, Social, and Political Relations of Canada and the United States: Outline of Plan*. New York, 1934.

————. *Fellows of the Social Science Research Council, 1925–1939*. New York, 1939.

————. *ITEMS* (Social Science Research Council), 1, no. 1 (March 1947).

————. *The Recruitment, Selection, and Training of Social Scientists*. New York, 1948.

————. *Fellows of the Social Science Research Council, 1925–1951*. New York, 1951.

————. American Geographical Society of New York. *Pioneer Settlement: Cooperative Studies by Twenty-six Authors*. New York: American Geographical Society, 1932.

————. Committee on Government Statistics and Information Services. New York: American Statistical Association and the Social Science Research Council, 1937.

————. Committee on Organization for Research. *A Directory of Social Science Research Organizations in Universities and Colleges*. New York, 1950.

————. Committee on Social Security. *Pamphlet Series*. Nos. 1–9, 1940–41. Washington, D.C., 1940.

————. *Projects and Source Materials in Social Statistics, Pacific Coast*. Subcommittee on Social Statistics. Berkeley: University of California, 1944.

Social Science Research Council. United States National Resources Committee. *Science Committee*. Washington, D.C.: Government Printing Office, 1938–41.

Sokal, Michael M., ed. *Psychological Testing and American Society, 1890–1930*. 1987. New Brunswick: Rutgers University Press, 1990.

Somit, Albert, and Tannenhaus, Joseph. *The Development of American Political Science: From Burgess to Behaviourism*. 1967. New York: Irvington, 1982.

————, eds. *American Political Science: A Profile of a Discipline*. New York: Atherton Press, 1964.

Spicer, Edward H. "The Use of Social Scientists by the War Relocation Authority." *Applied Anthropology* 5, no. 2 (Spring 1946): 16–36.

Stanfield, John H. *Philanthropy and Jim Crow in American Social Science*. Westport: Greenwood Press, 1985.

Sterner, Richard M. E. *The Negro's Share: A Study of Income, Consumption, Housing, and Public Assistance*. New York: Harper and Bros., 1943.

Stewart, Bryce M., and Givens, Meredith B. *Unemployment Reserves and Relief*. New York: Social Science Research Council, 1934.

Stocking, George W., Jr. *The Shaping of American Anthropology, 1883–1911: A Franz Boas Reader*. New York: Basic Books, 1974.

————. "Philanthropoids and Vanishing Cultures: Rockefeller Funding and the End of the Museum Era in Anglo-American Anthropology." In George W. Stocking, ed., *Objects and Others: Essays on Museums and Material Culture*. Madison: University of Wisconsin Press, 1985.

Stone, Harold A.; Price, Don K.; and Stone, Katharine. *City Manager Government in the United States*. New York: Social Science Research Council, 1940.

————. *City Manager Government in Nine Cities*. New York: Social Science Research Council, 1940.

———. *City Manager Government in Seven Cities*. New York: Social Science Research Council, 1940.

Stone, Lawrence, ed. *The University in Society*. Princeton: Princeton University Press, 1974.

Storr, Richard J. *The Beginnings of Graduate Education in America*. Chicago: University of Chicago Press, 1953.

Stouffer, Samuel Andrew, et al. *The American Soldier*. 4 vols. Princeton: Princeton University Press, 1949.

Stouffer, Samuel Andrew, and Lazarsfeld, Paul L. *Research Memorandum on the Family in the Depression*. Committee on Social Aspects of the Depression, bulletin 29. New York: Social Science Research Council, 1937.

Sumner, William G., and Keller, Albert G. *The Science of Society*. New Haven: Yale University Press, 1927.

Szack, Jerry. *History of Sociological Thought*. Westport: Greenwood Press, 1979.
———. "Reflections on the History of Sociology." *International Social Sciences Journal* 33 (1981): 248–59.

Thomas, Dorothy Swaine. *Research Memorandum on Migration Differentials*. Committee on Migration Differentials. New York: Social Science Research Council, 1938.

Thomas, J., ed. "Chicago School: The Tradition and the Legacy [symposium]." *Urban Life* 11 (January 1983): 387–511.

Thomas, W. I. *The Child in America*. New York: Knopf, 1928.

Thomas, W. I., with the assistance of Robert E. Park and Herbert A. Miller. *Old World Traits Transplanted*. New York: Harper and Row, 1921.

Thomas W. I., and Znaniecki, Florian. *The Polish Peasant in Europe and America*. 2 vols. New York: Knopf, 1927.

Thompson, E. T. "Sociology and Sociological Research in the South." *Social Forces* 23 (March 1945): 356–65.

Thompson, Warren Simpson. *Research Memorandum on Internal Migration in the Depression*. Committee on Social Aspects of the Depression, bulletin 30. New York: Social Science Research Council, 1937.

Thrasher, Frederic. *The Gang: A Study of 1,313 Gangs in Chicago*. Chicago: University of Chicago Press, 1927.

Tobey, Ronald Charles. *The American Ideology of Rational Science, 1919–1930*. Pittsburgh: University of Pittsburgh Press, 1971.

Touraine, Alain. *The Academic System in American Society*. New York: McGraw-Hill, 1974.

Trahair, Richard C. S. *The Humanist Temper: The Life and Work of Elton Mays*. New Brunswick: Transaction Books, 1984.

Trattner, Robert. *From Poor Law to Welfare State*. New York: Free Press, 1974.

Treudley, M. B. "Study of American Philanthropists." *Social Forces* 18 (March 1940): 364–74.

Tugwell, Rexford Guy. *The Battle for Democracy*. New York: Columbia University Press, 1935.
———. *The Democratic Roosevelt: A Biography of Franklin D. Roosevelt*. Garden City: Doubleday and Co., 1957.

———. *The Brains Trust*. New York: Viking, 1968.

———. *Roosevelt's Revolution: The First Year—A Personal Perspective*. New York: Macmillan, 1977.

Tugwell, Rexford Guy, and Hill, Howard C. *Our Economic Society and Its Problems*. New York: Harcourt, Brace and Co., 1934.

Turner, Stephen P. *The Search for a Methodology of the Social Sciences*. Dordrecht: D. Reidel, 1986.

Turner, Stephen P. and Turner, Jonathon H. *The Impossible Science: An Institutional Analysis of American Sociology*. New York: Russell Sage Foundation, 1990.

Twentieth Century Fund. *The Townsend Crusade*. New York: Twentieth Century Fund, 1936.

———. *More Security for Old Age*. New York: Twentieth Century Fund, 1937.

UNESCO. *Main Trends of Research in the Social and Human Sciences Part One: Social Sciences*. Paris: UNESCO, 1970.

United States Congress. Senate. *Science Legislation*. Hearings before the Subcommittee on War Mobilization, Committee on Military Affairs. 79th Congress, 1st sess., 1945. Pt 4.

United States Office of Education. *Public Affairs Pamphlets: An Index to Inexpensive Pamphlets on Social, Economic, Political, and International Affairs*. Revised February 1937. Washington, D.C.: Government Printing Office.

Vaile, Roland Snow. *Research Memorandum on Social Aspects of Consumption in the Depression*. Committee on Social Aspects of the Depression, bulletin 35. New York: Social Science Research Council, 1937.

Vance, Rupert Bayless. *Research Memorandum on Population Redistribution within the United States*, bulletin 42. New York: Social Science Research Council, 1938.

Veysey, Lawrence. *The Emergence of the American University*. Chicago: University of Chicago Press, 1965.

Vincent, George E. "Development of Sociology." *American Journal of Sociology* 1 (1905): 145–60.

Wagner, Peter, and Wittrock, Bjorn. *Social Sciences and Societal Development: The Missing Perspective*. WZB-Papers P87-4. Berlin: Wissenschaftszentrum, 1987.

Walder, P., ed. *Between Labour and Capital*. London: Black Rose Press, 1978.

Waldo, D. "Political Science: Tradition, Discipline, Profession, Science, Enterprise." In F. I. Greenstein and N. Polsby, eds., *The Handbook of Political Science*, vol. 1. Reading: Addison-Wesley, 1975.

Walker, H. M. "Role of the American Statistical Association." *American Statistical Association Journal* 40 (March 1945): 1–10.

Waples, Douglas. *Research Memorandum on Social Aspects of Reading in the Depression*. Committee on Social Aspects of the Depression, bulletin 37. New York: Social Science Research Council, 1937.

Ware, E. E. *The Study of International Relations in the United States*. New York: Social Science Research Council, 1934.

Watson, Bruce, and Tarr, William. *The Social Sciences and American Civilization*. New York: John Wiley and Sons, 1964.

Watson, G. "The Social Construction of Boundaries between Social and Cultural Anthropology in Britain and North America." *Journal of Anthropological Research* 40 (Fall 1984): 351–66.

Watson, Robert Irving. *The History of Psychology and the Behavioural Sciences: A Bibliographic Guide*. New York: Springer Publishers, 1978.

Weaver, Warren, ed. *U.S. Philanthropic Foundations: Their History, Structure, Management, and Record*. New York: Harper and Row, 1967.

Weinstein, James. *The Corporate Ideal and the Liberal State, 1900–1918*. Boston: Beacon Press, 1968.

Wexler, P. *The Sociology of Education: Beyond Equality*. Indianapolis: Bobbs-Merrill Co. 1976.

Whitaker, Ben. *The Philanthropoids: Foundations and Society*. New York: William Morrow and Co., 1974.

White, Clyde R., and White, Mary K. *Research Memorandum on the Social Aspects of Relief Policies in the Depression*. Committee on Social Security and Committee on Social Aspects of the Depression, bulletin 38. New York: Social Science Research Council, 1937.

White, Leonard D. *Introduction to the Study of Public Administration*. New York: Macmillan, 1926.

———. *Civil Service in Wartime*. Chicago: University of Chicago Press, 1945.

———. *The State of the Social Sciences*. Chicago: University of Chicago Press, 1956.

———, ed. *The New Social Science*. Chicago: University of Chicago Press, 1930.

Whitley, R. *The Intellectual and Social Organization of the Sciences*. Oxford: Clarendon Press, 1984.

Whitty, Geoff. *Sociology and School Knowledge: Curriculum Theory, Research, and Politics*. London: Methuen, 1986.

Wiebe, Robert H. *The Search for Order, 1877–1920*. New York: Hill and Wang, 1967.

———. *Segmented Society: An Introduction to the Meaning of American Society*. New York: Oxford University Press, 1975.

Willcox, W. F., ed. *International Migration*. Committee on Scientific Aspects of Human Migration. New York: National Bureau of Economic Research, 1929–31.

Williams, Raymond. "Base and Superstructure in Marxist Cultural Theory." *New Left Review* 83 (1973): 3–16.

———. *Marxism and Literature*. Oxford: Oxford University Press, 1977.

Willis, Paul. *Learning to Labor: How Working Class Kids Get Working Class Jobs*. 1977. New York: Columbia University Press, 1981.

Wilson, Thomas P. "Normative and Interpretative Paradigms in Sociology." In Jack Douglas, ed., *Understanding Everyday Life*. Chicago: Aldine Publishing Co., 1970.

Wirth, Louis. *The Ghetto*. Chicago: University of Chicago Press, 1928.

———. "The Social Sciences." In Merle E. Curti, ed., *American Scholarship in the Twentieth Century*. Cambridge: Harvard University Press, 1953.

———, ed. *Eleven Twenty-Six: A Decade of Social Science Research*. Chicago: University of Chicago Press, 1940. Reprint ed. New York: Arno Press, 1970.

Wissler, Clark. "Developments in Anthropology." In E. C. Hayes, ed., *Recent Developments in the Social Sciences*. Philadelphia: Lippincott, 1927.

Wittrock, Bjorn. *Social Knowledge and Public Policy: Eight Models of Interaction*. P87-1. Berlin: Wissenschaftszentrum, 1987.

Wittrock, Bjorn, and Elzinga, Aanj, eds. *The University Research System: The Public Policies of the Home of Scientists*. Stockholm: Almqvist and Wiksell, 1985.

Wittrock, Bjorn, and Wagner, Peter. "Social Science and State Developments: The Structuration of Discourse in the Social Sciences." Paper presented at the International Sociology Association, History of Sociology Section, Amsterdam, 1989.

Wittrock, Bjorn; Wagner, Peter; and Wollmann, Heinrich. *Social Science and the Modern State: Knowledge, Institutions, and Societal Transformations*. WZB-Papers P87-3. Berlin: Wissenschaftszentrum, 1987.

Woods, Peter. *Inside Schools: Ethnography in Educational Research*. London: Routledge and Kegan Paul, 1986.

Woodworth, Robert Sessions. *Heredity and Environment: A Critical Survey of Recently Published Material on Twins and Foster Children*. Committee on Social Adjustment, bulletin 47. New York: Social Science Research Council, 1941.

Woofter, Thomas J., Jr. *Black Yeomanry: Life on St. Helena Island*. New York: Henry Holt, 1930.

Woolgar, Steve. *Science: The Very Idea*. London: Tavistock Publications, 1988.

————, ed. *Knowledge and Reflexivity: New Frontiers in the Sociology of Knowledge*. London: Sage, 1988.

Wotherspoon, Terry, ed. *The Political Economy of Canadian Schooling*. Toronto: Methuen, 1987.

Woytinsky, Wladimir S. *The Labor Supply in the United States*. Committee on Social Security. Washington, D.C.: Social Science Research Council, 1936.

————. *Labor in the United States: Basic Statistics for Social Security*. Committee on Social Security. Washington, D.C.: Social Science Research Council, 1938.

————. *Three Aspects of Labor Dynamics*. Committee on Social Security. Washington, D.C.: Social Science Research Council, 1942.

————. *Earnings and Social Security in the United States*. Committee on Social Security. Washington, D.C.: Social Science Research Council, 1943.

Wright, Erik Olin. "Intellectuals and the Class Structure of Capitalist Society." In P. Walder, ed., *Between Labour and Capital*. London: Black Rose Press, 1978.

————. *Class, Crisis, and the State*. London: New Left Books, 1978.

Wright, Erik Olin, and Singleman, J. "Proletarianization in the Changing American Class Structure." In M. Burawoy and Theda Skocpol, eds., *Marxist Inquiries: Studies of Labor, Class, and States*. Supplement to the *American Journal of Sociology* 88. Chicago: University of Chicago Press, 1982.

Wright, Quincy. *Research in International Law since the War: A Report to the International Relations Committee of the Social Science Research Council*. Washington, D.C.: Carnegie Endowment for International Peace, 1930.

Yerkes, Robert M., ed. *The New World of Science: Its Development during the War*. New York: Century Co., 1920.

————. "The Work of [the] Committee on Scientific Problems of Human Migration, National Research Council." *Journal of Personnel Research* 3 (1924–25): 189–96.

Young, Donald Ramsey. *Research Memorandum on Minority Peoples in the Depression*. Committee on Social Aspects of the Depression, bulletin 31. New York: Social Science Research Council, 1937.

Young, M. F. D., ed. *Knowledge and Control*. London: Collier-Macmillan, 1971.

Zeitlin, Irving M. *Ideology and the Development of Sociological Theory*. Englewood Cliffs: Prentice Hall, 1968.

Znaniecki, Florian. *Cultural Sciences: Their Origin and Development*. Urbana: University of Illinois Press, 1952.

Index

Abrams, Philip, 1
Academics, between labor and capital,
20. *See also* New middle class
Academic social scientists, 27; and
commitment to pure scientific re-
search, 65; and interests of ruling
class, 65; and mutual legitimation, 8
Academy, represented by Merriam,
Charles E., 27
Adler, Herman, 53, 216; and Behavior
Research Fund, 53; as director of In-
stitute for Juvenile Research, 53
Agricultural Adjustment Administration,
137
Agricultural Relief Act, 129
Alchon, Guy, 8n.22, 12, 97; and tech-
nocratic bargain, 97
Alexander, W. W., 54
Allport, Floyd H., 60
Alsberg, Carl L., and Asian agriculture,
study of, 63
American Anthropological Association
(AAA), 5n.17, 31, 50, 53, 226
American Association for the Advance-
ment of Science, 168, 192; and sup-
port for social sciences, 192
American Council of Learned Societies
(ACLS), 28, 29, 36, 44, 80, 193; and
historians, 28; and model for SSRC,
44; as prospective social science or-
ganization, 36
American Economic Association
(AEA), 5n.17, 28, 31, 79; dissat-
isfaction with organization of social

research, 28; and promotion of eco-
nomics, 79
American Geographical Society, 62
American Historical Association
(AHA), 5n.17, 31, 71, 92
American Political Science Association
(APSA), 5n.17, 27, 28–29, 31, 43,
210, 226; and committee on political
research, 28–29
American Psychological Association
(APA), 5n.17, 31, 50
American Public Welfare Association,
148
American Science Teachers Association,
168
American Social Science Association
(ASSA), 4–5, 27–28, 219. *See also*
Haskell, Thomas L.
American Sociological Society (ASS),
5n.17, 28, 29, 31, 45, 50, 51, 77,
100, 210; and Committee on Stan-
dardization of Research, 29; dissat-
isfaction with organization of social
research, 28; and international news
project, 45
American Soldier, The (four volumes),
188
American Statistical Association
(ASTA), 5n.17, 30, 31, 74, 79, 128;
and Committee on Government Statistics and Information Services, 128;
and promotion of statistics, 79
Amherst College, and fellowships, 201
Anderson, William, 273